JOONAS SILDRE

BETWEEN TWO SOUNDS

ARVO PÄRT'S JOURNEY TO HIS MUSICAL LANGUAGE

TRANSLATED FROM THE ESTONIAN BY ADAM CULLEN

Plough

Published by Plough Publishing House
Walden, New York
Robertsbridge, England
Elsmore, Australia
www.plough.com

First published by Arvo Pärt Centre as *Kahe heli vahel*.
Copyright © 2018 by Joonas Sildre, Copyright © 2018 by Arvo Pärt Centre
Editor: Aile Tooming

English translation by Adam Cullen. Copyright © 2024 by Adam Cullen
Editors of the English translation: Marrit Andrejeva, Nikita Andrejev,
Kristina Kõrver, Mari Laaniste
This translation published with permission.

ISBN: 978-1-63608-134-2
27 26 25 24   1 2 3 4

A catalog record for this book is available from the British Library.
Library of Congress Cataloging-in-Publication Data

Names: Sildre, Joonas, author, illustrator. | Tooming, Aile, editor. |
   Cullen, Adam, 1986- translator.
Title: Between two sounds : Arvo Pärt's journey to his musical language /
   Joonas Sildre ; editor, Aile Tooming ; English translation by Adam
   Cullen.
Other titles: Kahe heli vahel. English
Description: Walden, New York : Plough Publishing House, 2024. |
   Summary:
   "A graphic novel follows the celebrated Estonian composer through the
   upheavals that led to his distinctive style."-- Provided by publisher.
Identifiers: LCCN 2024001827 (print) | LCCN 2024001828 (ebook) | ISBN
   9781636081342 (hardcover) | ISBN 9781636081335 (epub)
Subjects: LCSH: Pärt, Arvo--Comic books, strips, etc. |
   Composers--Estonia--Biography--Comic books, strips, etc. | LCGFT:
   Biographical comics. | Graphic novels.
Classification: LCC ML410.P1755 S5613 2024 (print) | LCC ML410.P1755
   (ebook) | DDC 780.92 [B]--dc23/eng/20240216
LC record available at https://lccn.loc.gov/2024001827
LC ebook record available at https://lccn.loc.gov/2024001828

Printed in the United States of America

FOR ELINA

PROLOGUE

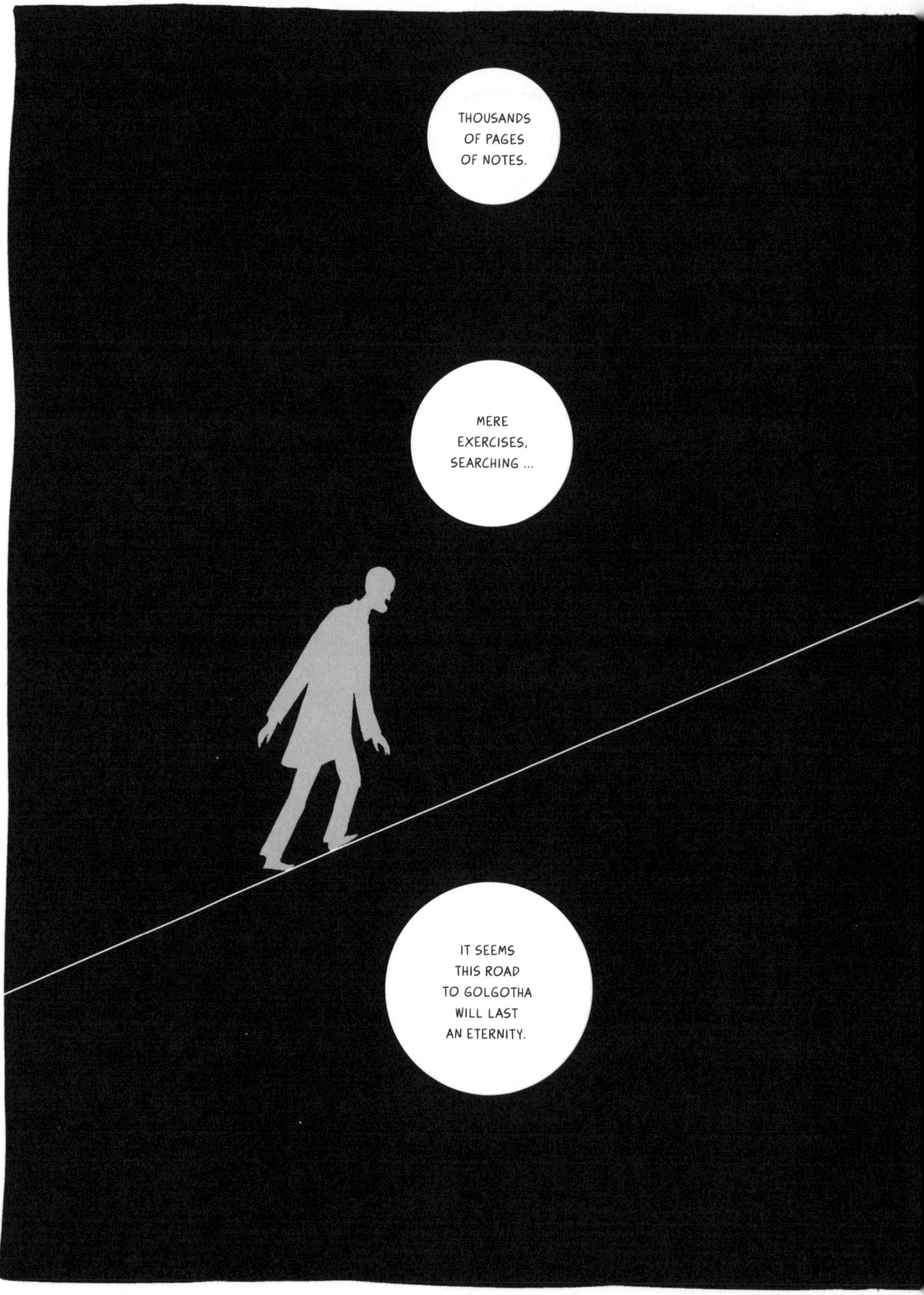
THOUSANDS OF PAGES OF NOTES.
MERE EXERCISES, SEARCHING ...
IT SEEMS THIS ROAD TO GOLGOTHA WILL LAST AN ETERNITY.

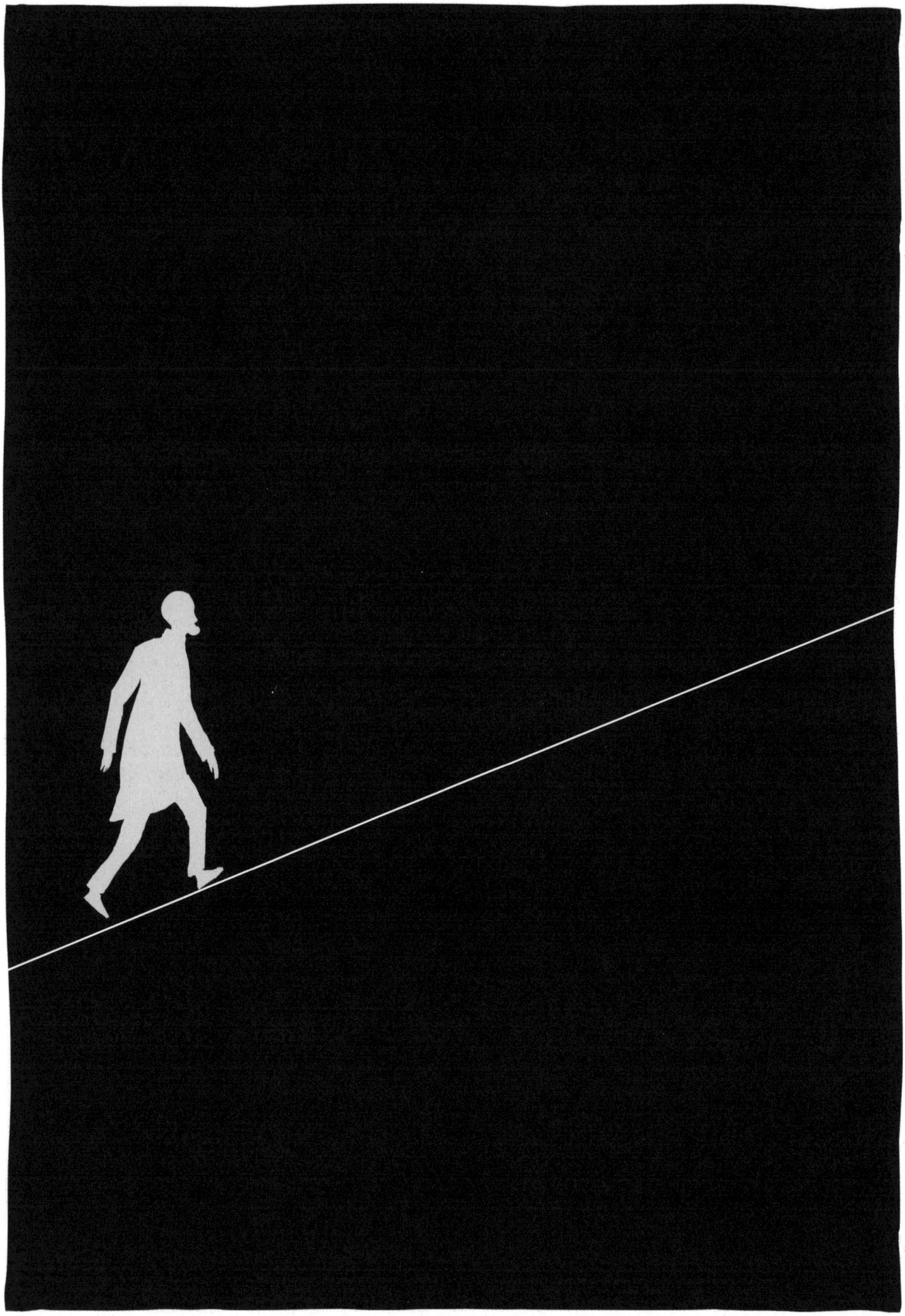

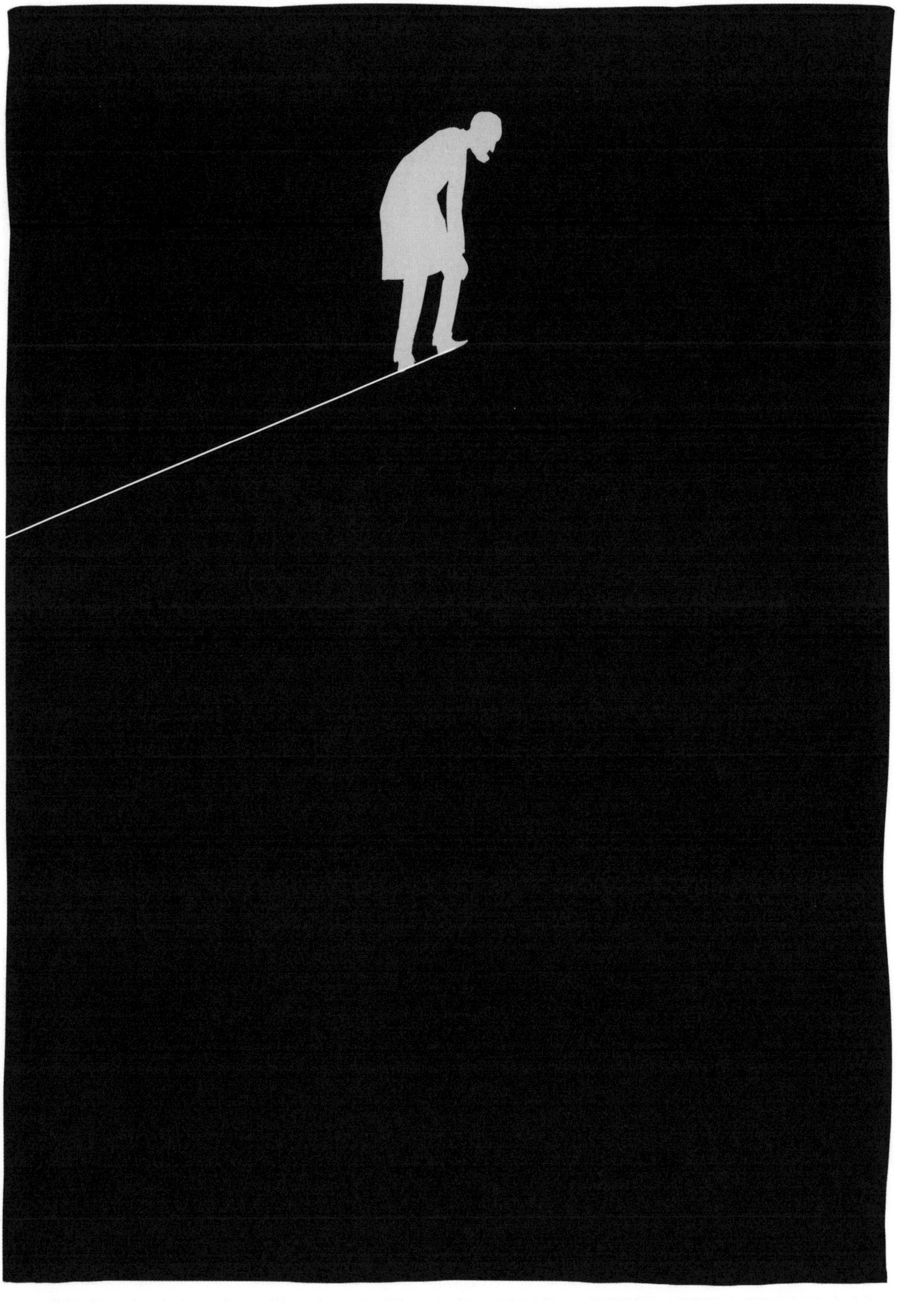

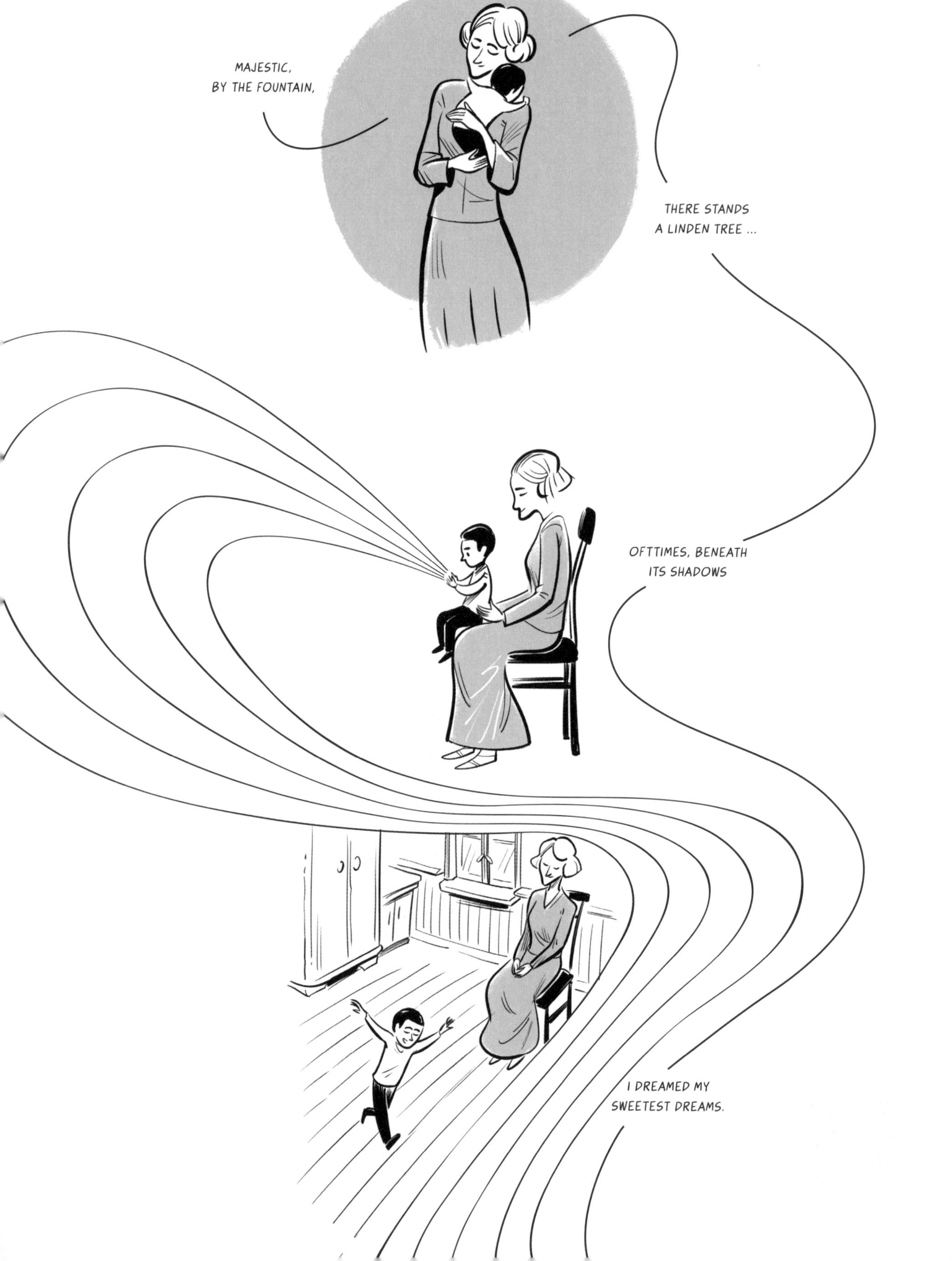
MAJESTIC,
BY THE FOUNTAIN,
THERE STANDS
A LINDEN TREE ...
OFTTIMES, BENEATH
ITS SHADOWS
I DREAMED MY
SWEETEST DREAMS.

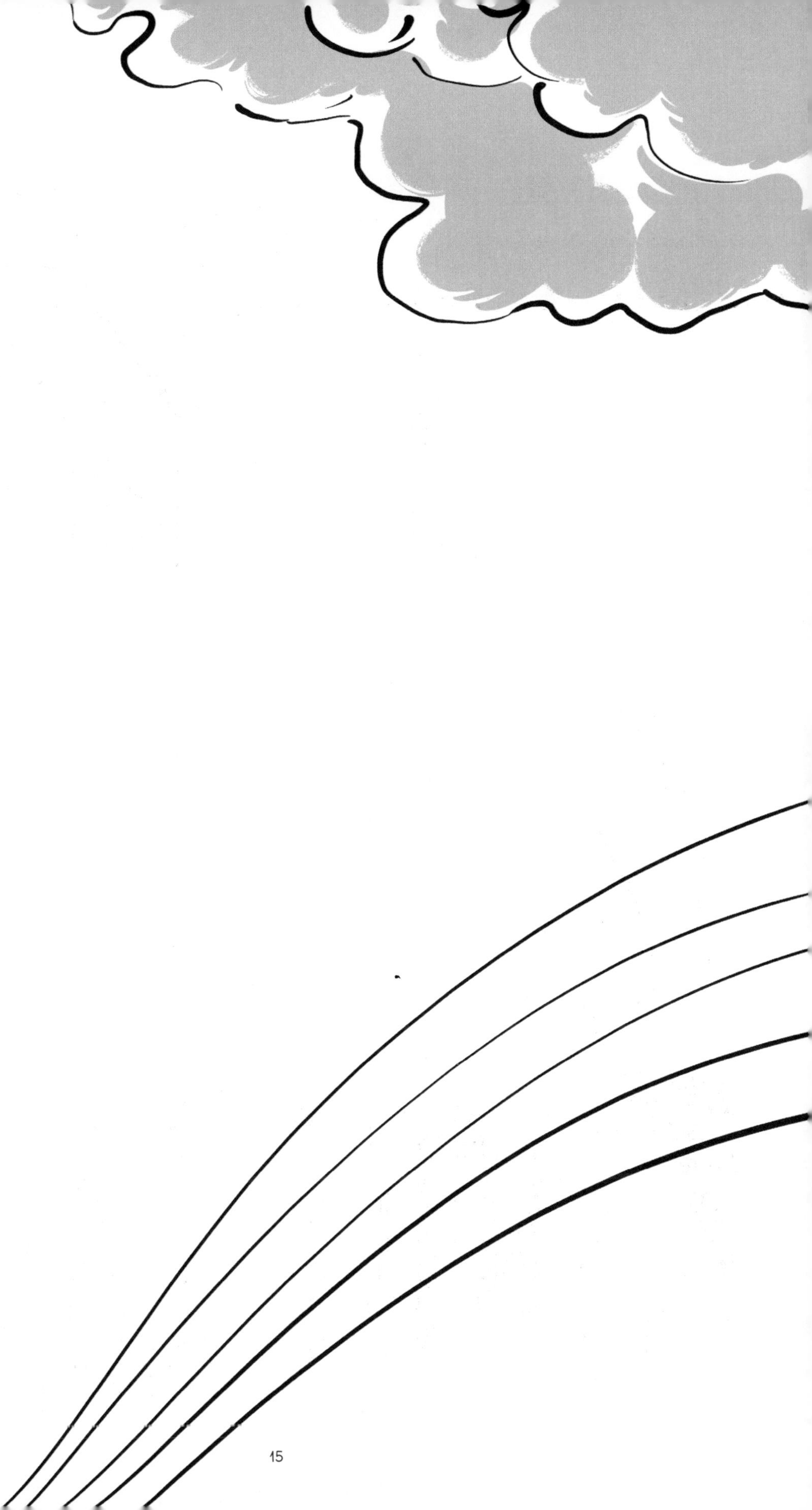

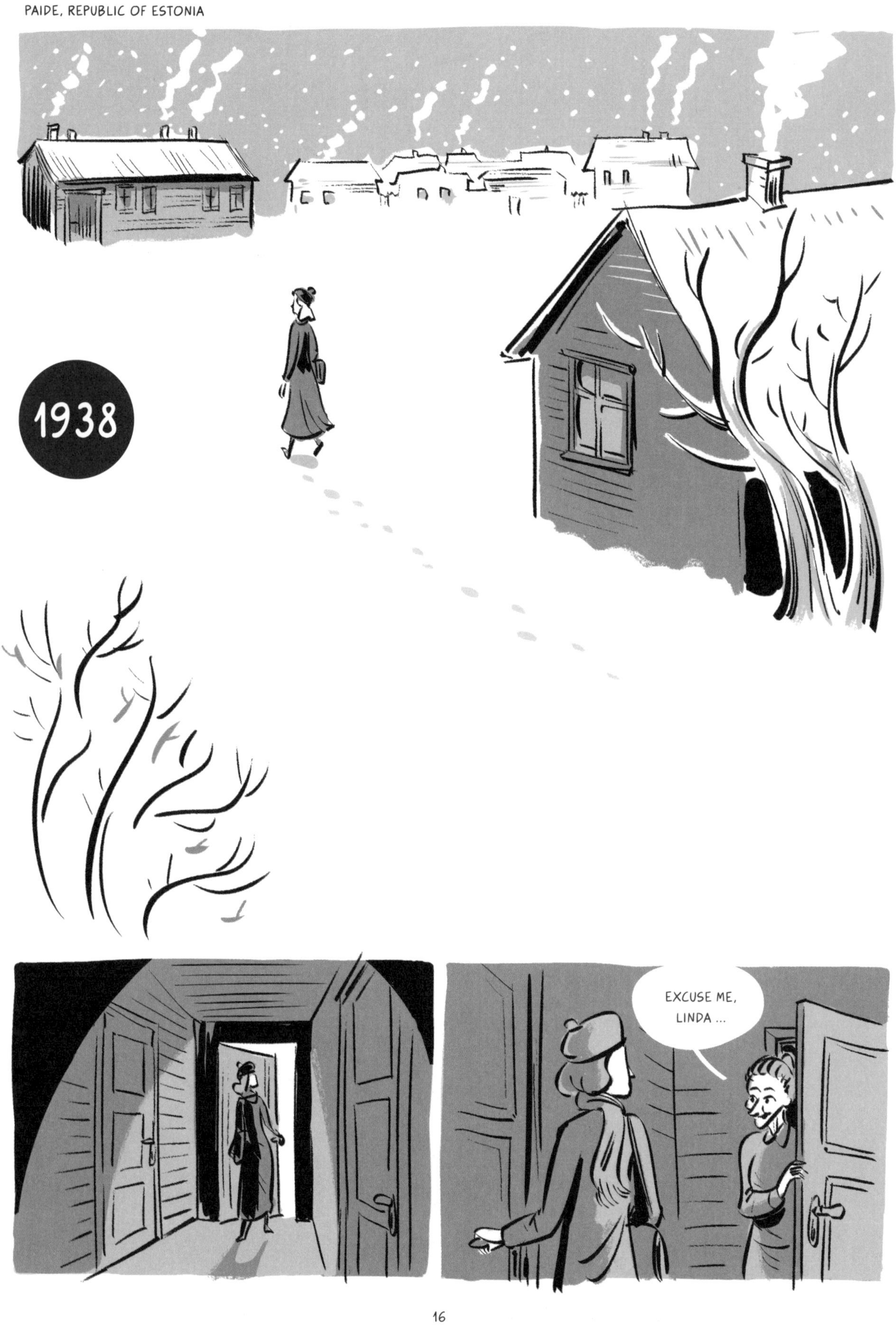
PAIDE, REPUBLIC OF ESTONIA
1938
EXCUSE ME, LINDA ...

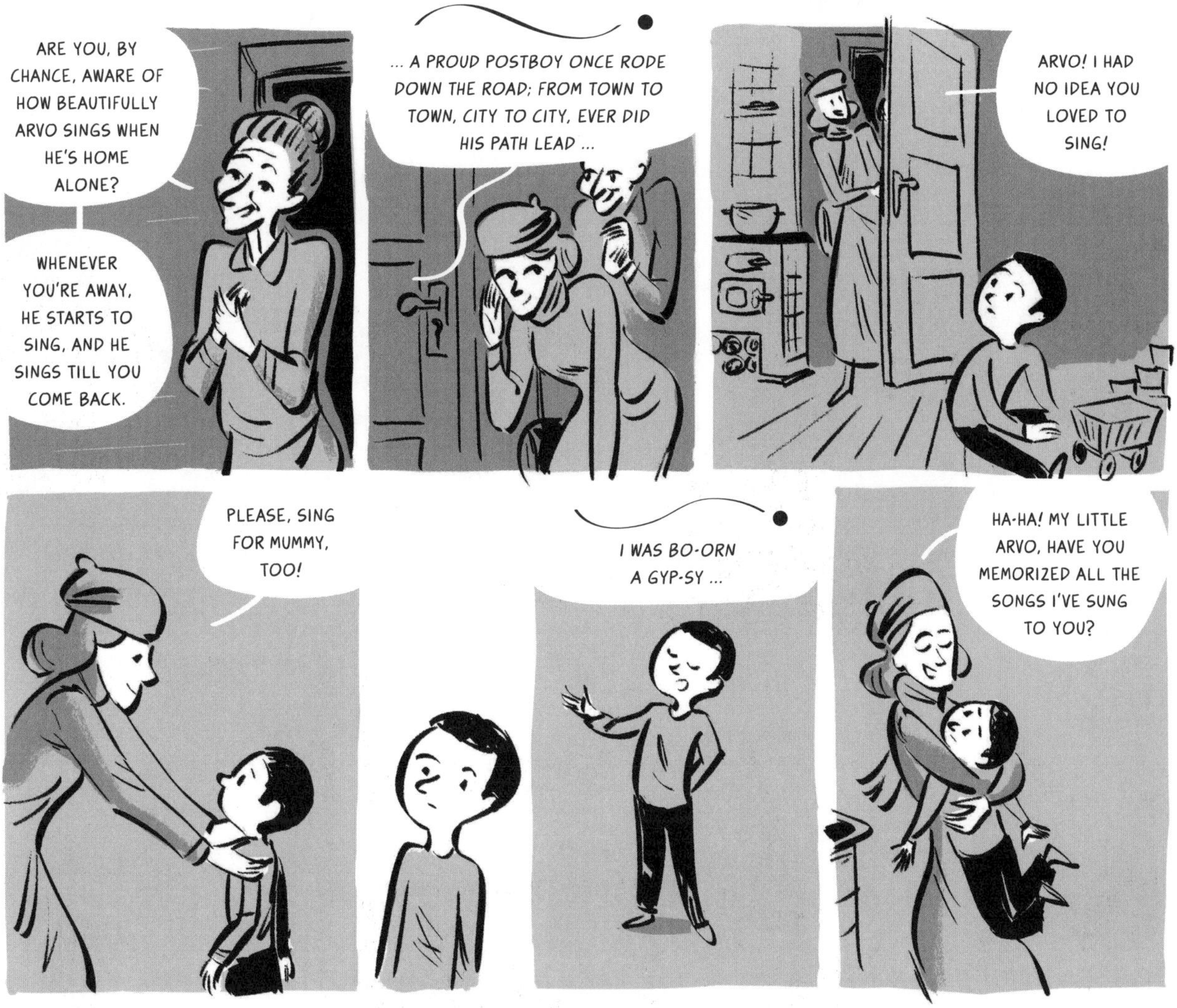
ARE YOU, BY CHANCE, AWARE OF HOW BEAUTIFULLY ARVO SINGS WHEN HE'S HOME ALONE?
WHENEVER YOU'RE AWAY, HE STARTS TO SING, AND HE SINGS TILL YOU COME BACK.
... A PROUD POSTBOY ONCE RODE DOWN THE ROAD; FROM TOWN TO TOWN, CITY TO CITY, EVER DID HIS PATH LEAD ...
ARVO! I HAD NO IDEA YOU LOVED TO SING!
PLEASE, SING FOR MUMMY, TOO!
I WAS BO-ORN A GYP-SY ...
HA-HA! MY LITTLE ARVO, HAVE YOU MEMORIZED ALL THE SONGS I'VE SUNG TO YOU?

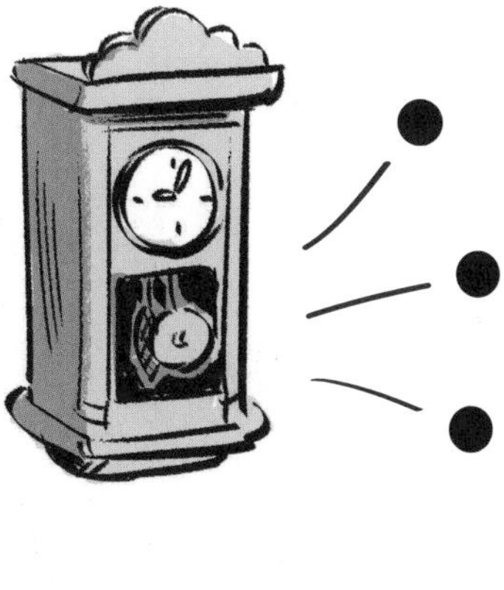

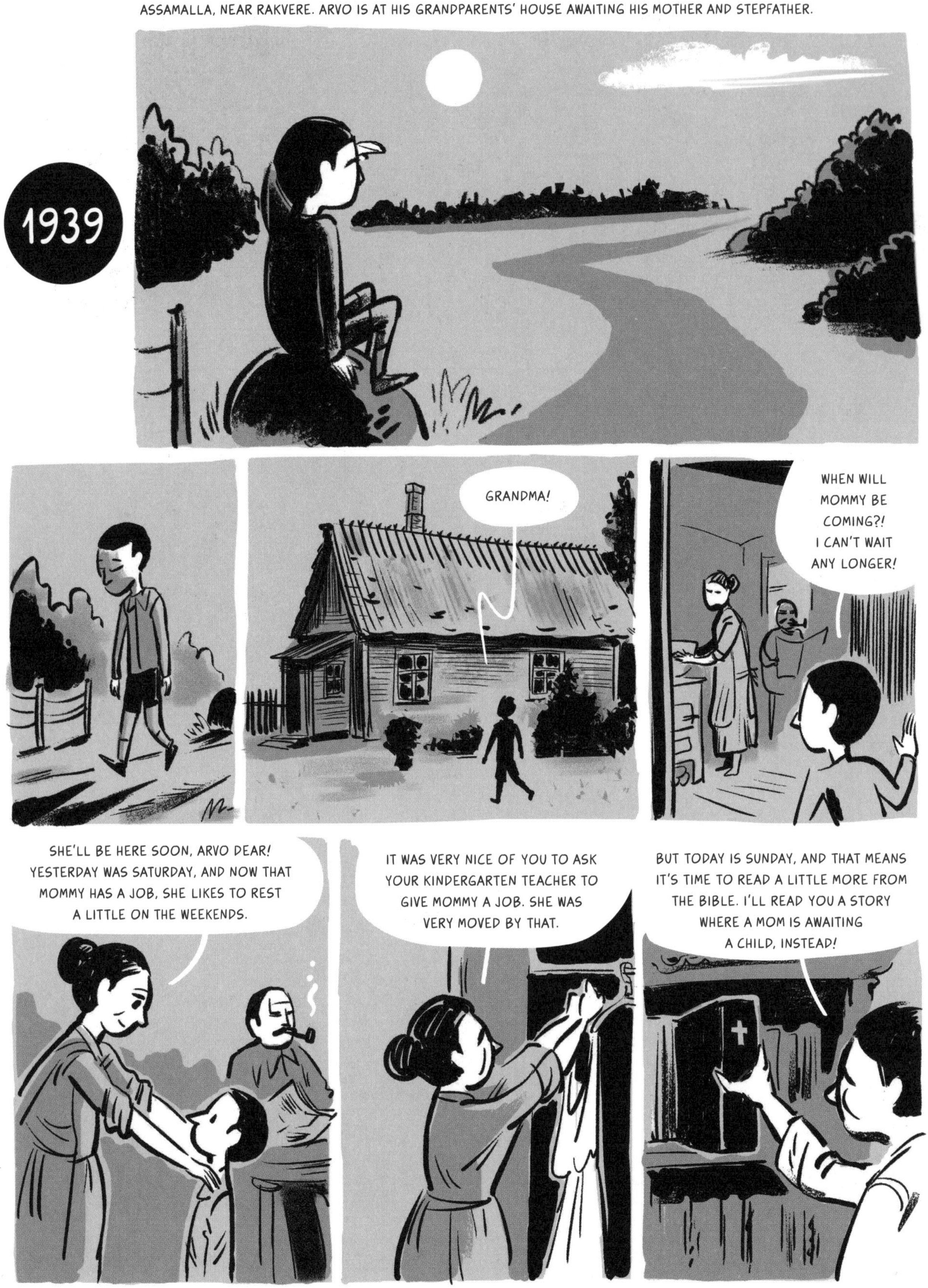
ASSAMALLA, NEAR RAKVERE. ARVO IS AT HIS GRANDPARENTS' HOUSE AWAITING HIS MOTHER AND STEPFATHER.
1939
GRANDMA!
WHEN WILL MOMMY BE COMING?! I CAN'T WAIT ANY LONGER!
SHE'LL BE HERE SOON, ARVO DEAR! YESTERDAY WAS SATURDAY, AND NOW THAT MOMMY HAS A JOB, SHE LIKES TO REST A LITTLE ON THE WEEKENDS.
IT WAS VERY NICE OF YOU TO ASK YOUR KINDERGARTEN TEACHER TO GIVE MOMMY A JOB. SHE WAS VERY MOVED BY THAT.
BUT TODAY IS SUNDAY, AND THAT MEANS IT'S TIME TO READ A LITTLE MORE FROM THE BIBLE. I'LL READ YOU A STORY WHERE A MOM IS AWAITING A CHILD, INSTEAD!

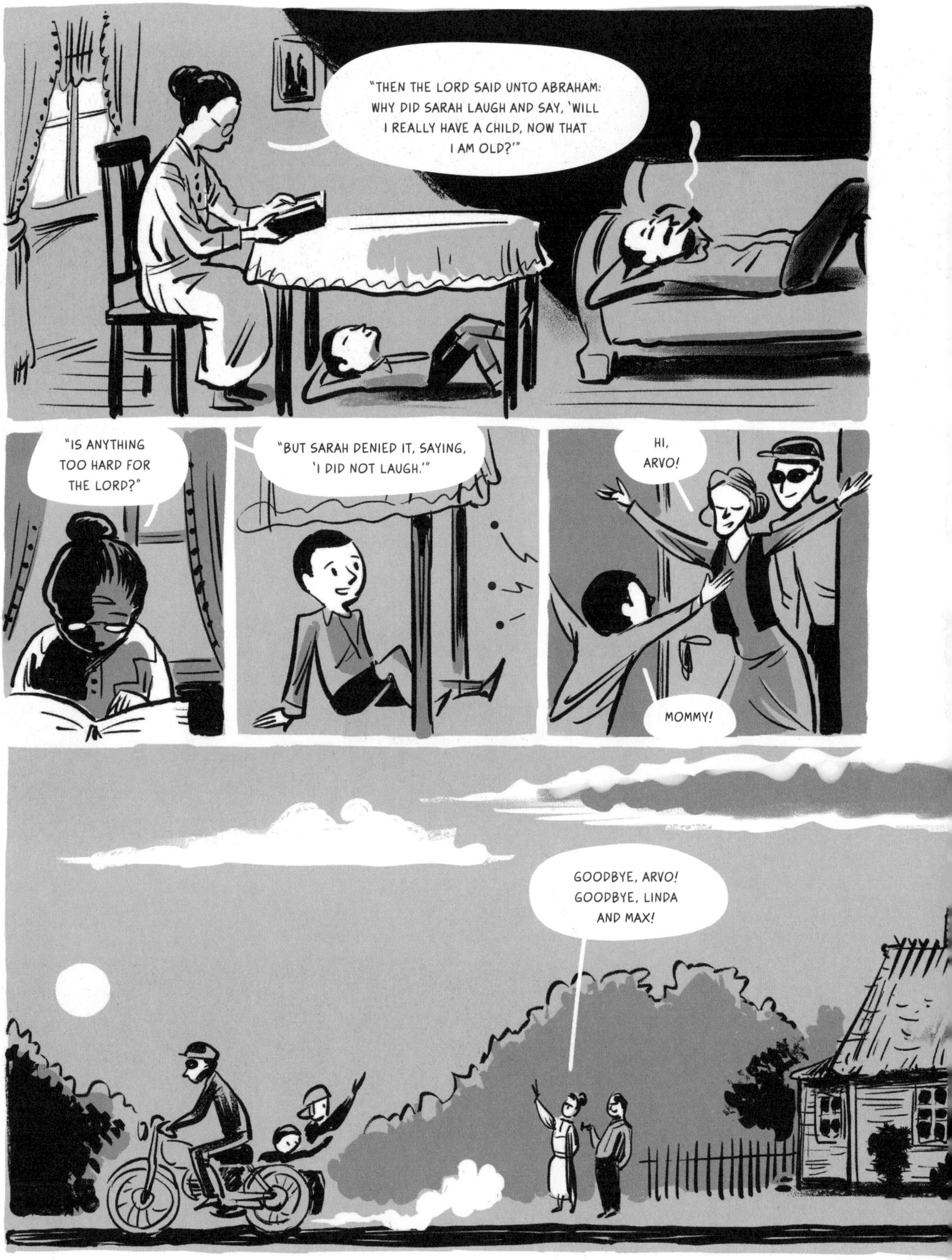
"THEN THE LORD SAID UNTO ABRAHAM: WHY DID SARAH LAUGH AND SAY, 'WILL I REALLY HAVE A CHILD, NOW THAT I AM OLD?'"
"IS ANYTHING TOO HARD FOR THE LORD?"
"BUT SARAH DENIED IT, SAYING, 'I DID NOT LAUGH.'"
HI, ARVO!
MOMMY!
GOODBYE, ARVO! GOODBYE, LINDA AND MAX!

YOU KNOW WHAT, ARVO? WE'RE GOING TO MOVE HERE, INTO YOUR STEPFATHER'S APARTMENT SOON.

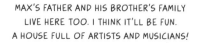

MAX'S FATHER AND HIS BROTHER'S FAMILY LIVE HERE TOO. I THINK IT'LL BE FUN. A HOUSE FULL OF ARTISTS AND MUSICIANS!

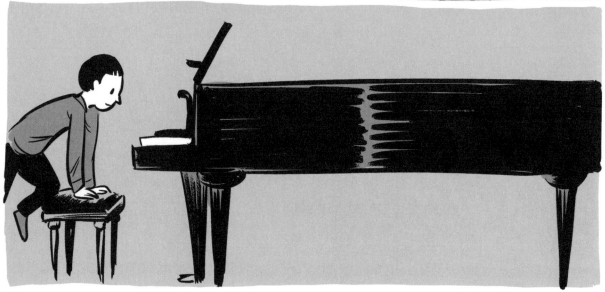

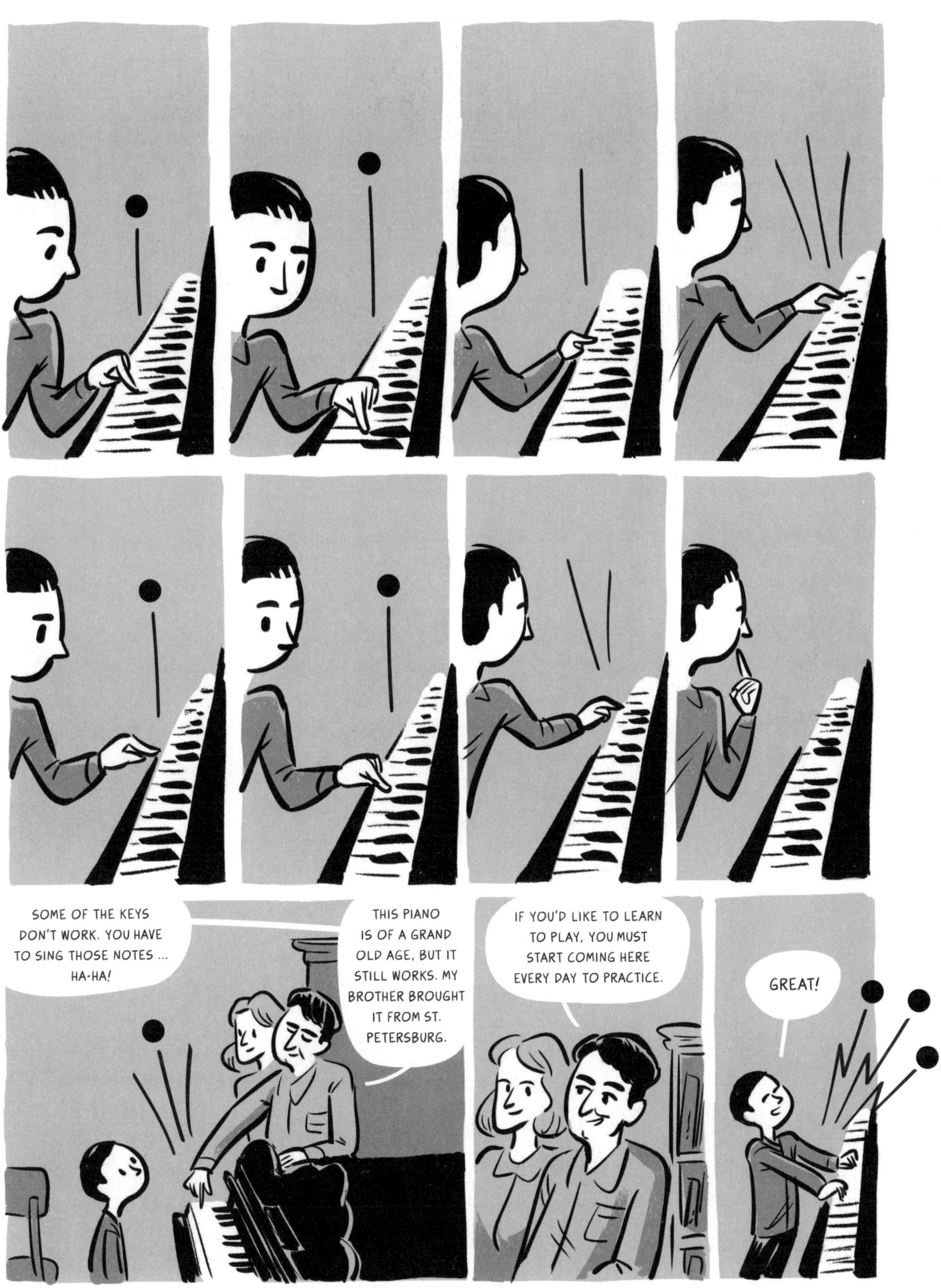
SOME OF THE KEYS DON'T WORK. YOU HAVE TO SING THOSE NOTES ... HA-HA!
THIS PIANO IS OF A GRAND OLD AGE, BUT IT STILL WORKS. MY BROTHER BROUGHT IT FROM ST. PETERSBURG.
IF YOU'D LIKE TO LEARN TO PLAY, YOU MUST START COMING HERE EVERY DAY TO PRACTICE.
GREAT!

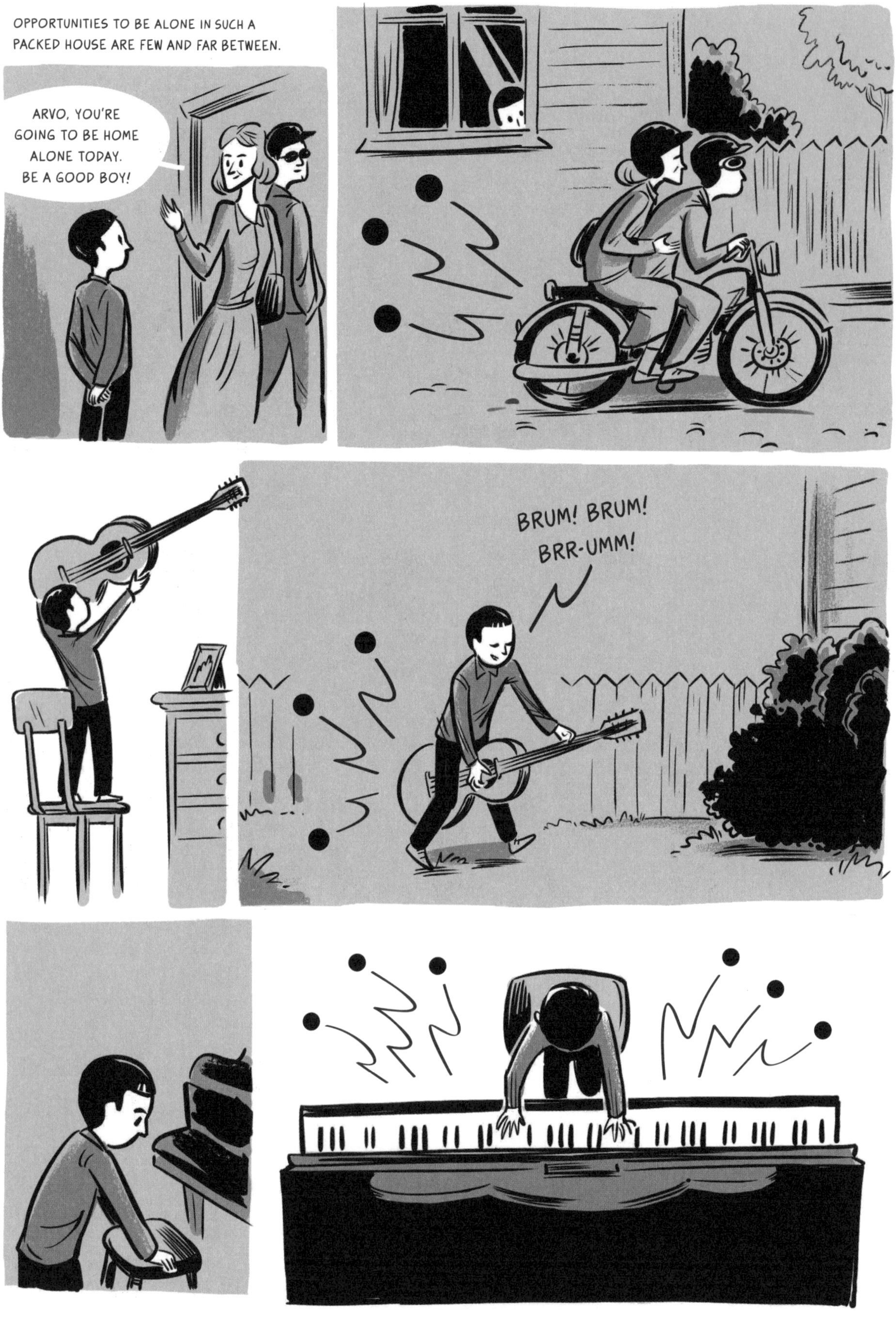
OPPORTUNITIES TO BE ALONE IN SUCH A PACKED HOUSE ARE FEW AND FAR BETWEEN.
ARVO, YOU'RE GOING TO BE HOME ALONE TODAY. BE A GOOD BOY!
BRUM! BRUM! BRR-UMM!

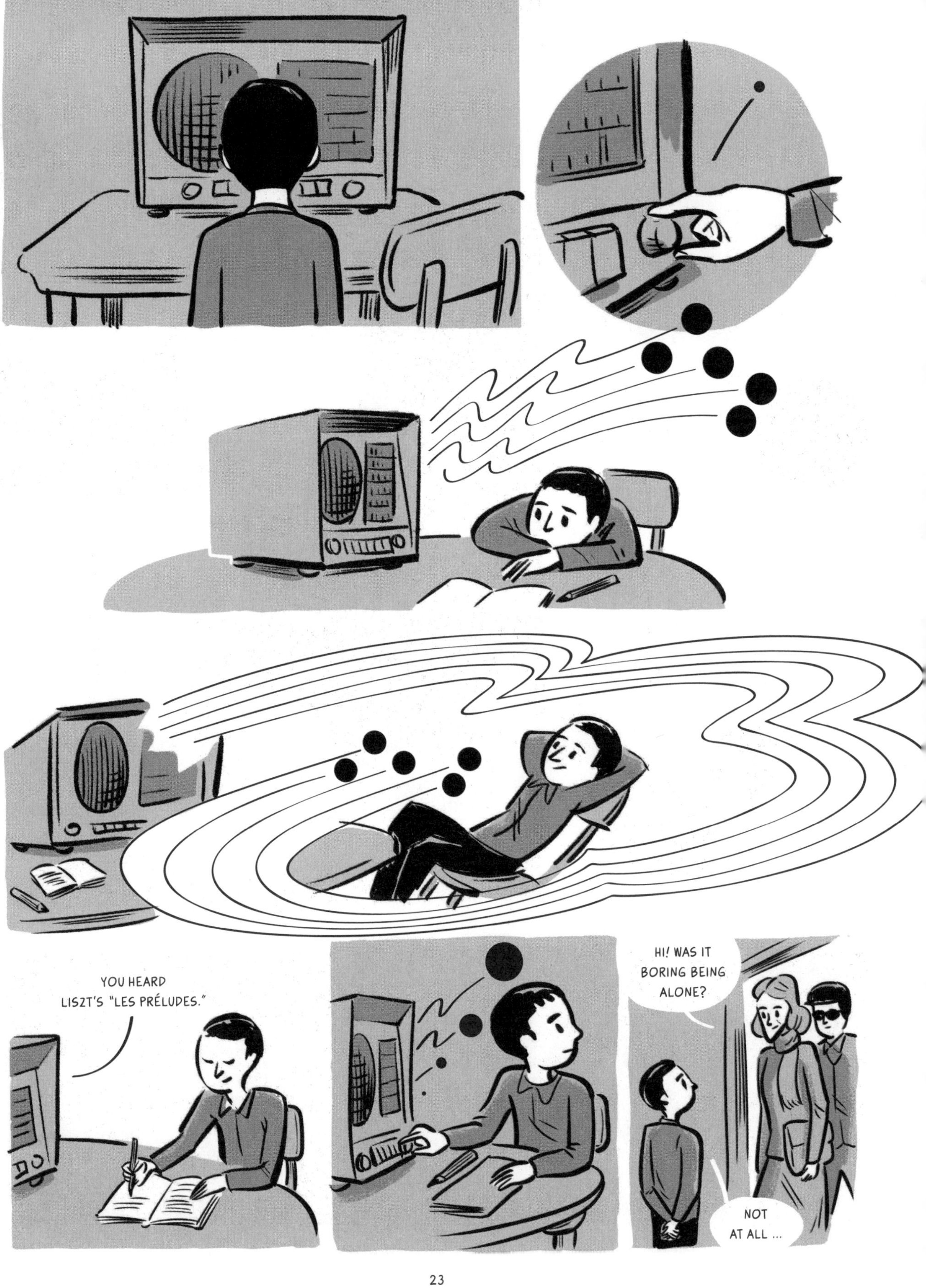
YOU HEARD
LISZT'S "LES PRÉLUDES."
HI! WAS IT
BORING BEING
ALONE?
NOT
AT ALL ...

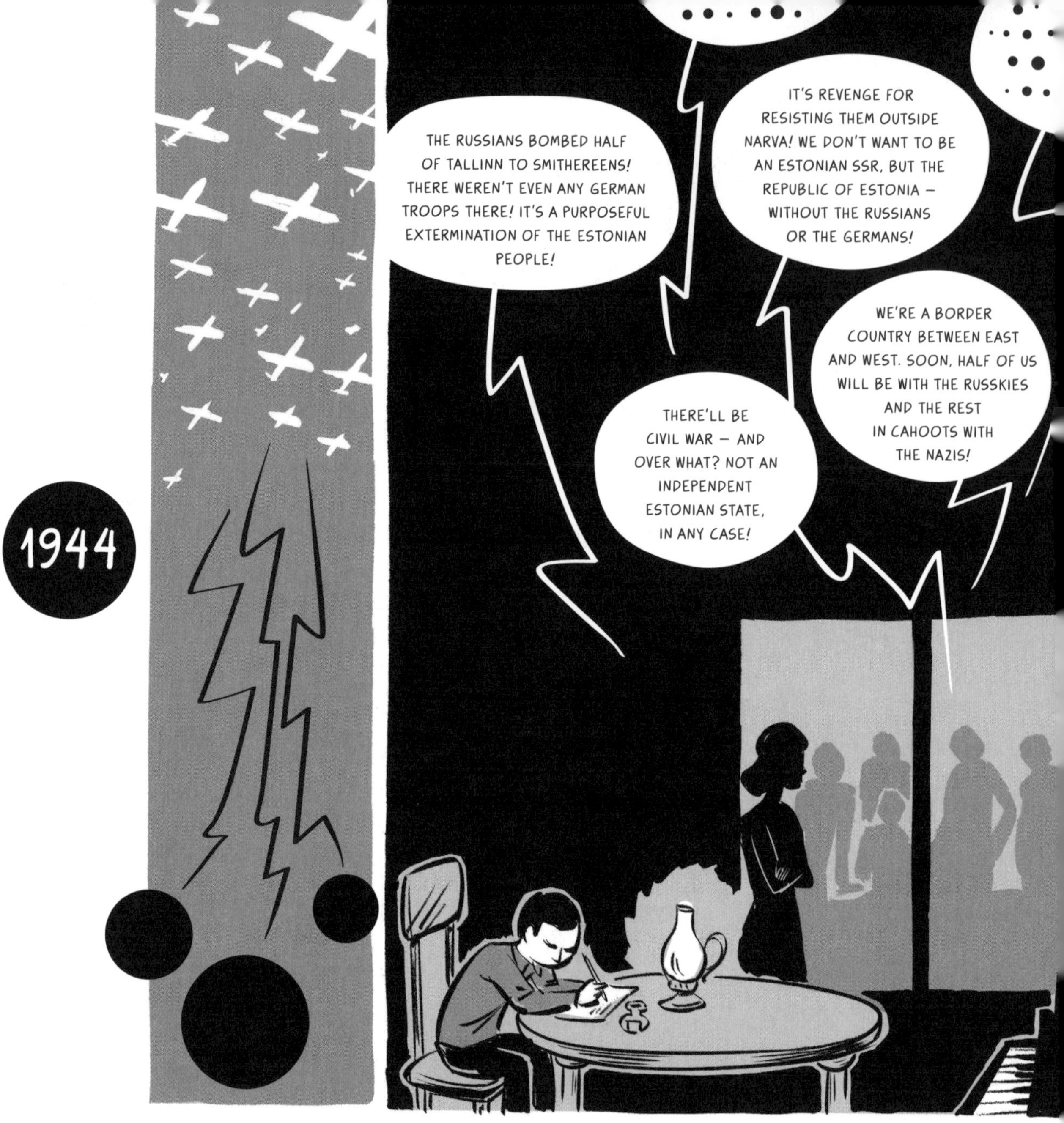
1944
THE RUSSIANS BOMBED HALF OF TALLINN TO SMITHEREENS! THERE WEREN'T EVEN ANY GERMAN TROOPS THERE! IT'S A PURPOSEFUL EXTERMINATION OF THE ESTONIAN PEOPLE!
IT'S REVENGE FOR RESISTING THEM OUTSIDE NARVA! WE DON'T WANT TO BE AN ESTONIAN SSR, BUT THE REPUBLIC OF ESTONIA – WITHOUT THE RUSSIANS OR THE GERMANS!
THERE'LL BE CIVIL WAR – AND OVER WHAT? NOT AN INDEPENDENT ESTONIAN STATE, IN ANY CASE!
WE'RE A BORDER COUNTRY BETWEEN EAST AND WEST. SOON, HALF OF US WILL BE WITH THE RUSSKIES AND THE REST IN CAHOOTS WITH THE NAZIS!

RAKVERE'S MARKET SQUARE. THE CALM BEFORE THE STORM ...

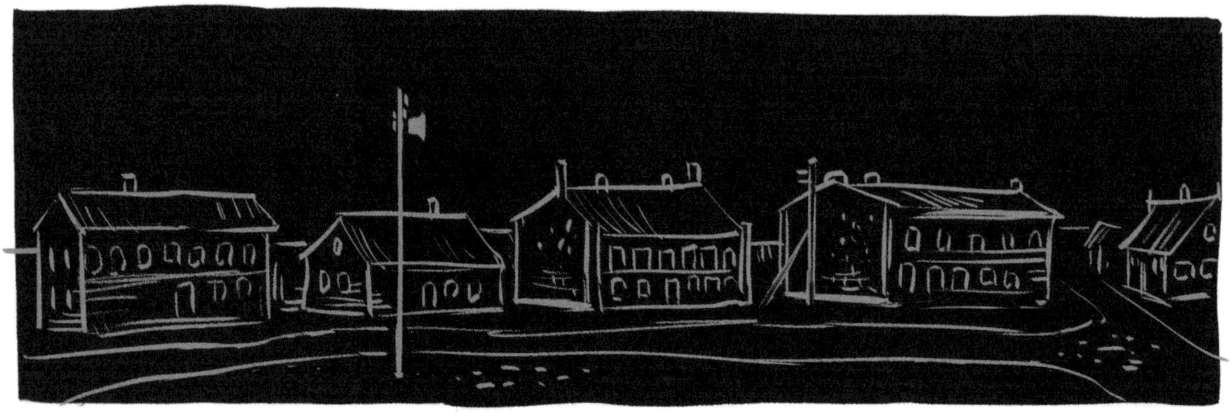

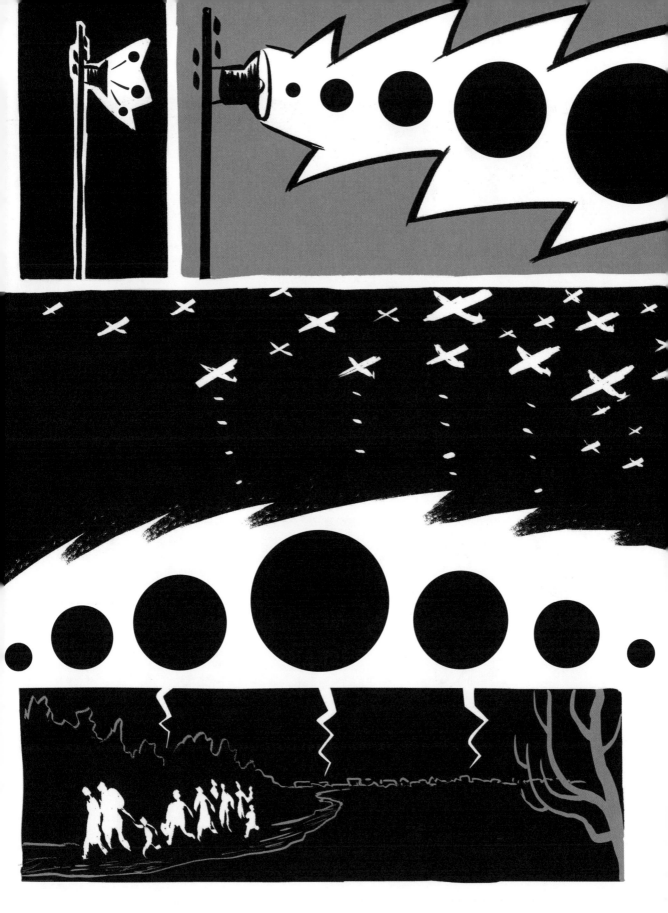

ONE WEEK LATER, BACK IN RAKVERE. THE KUHLBERGS' HOUSE, WHERE ARVO LIVED, WAS UNTOUCHED BY THE BOMBING.

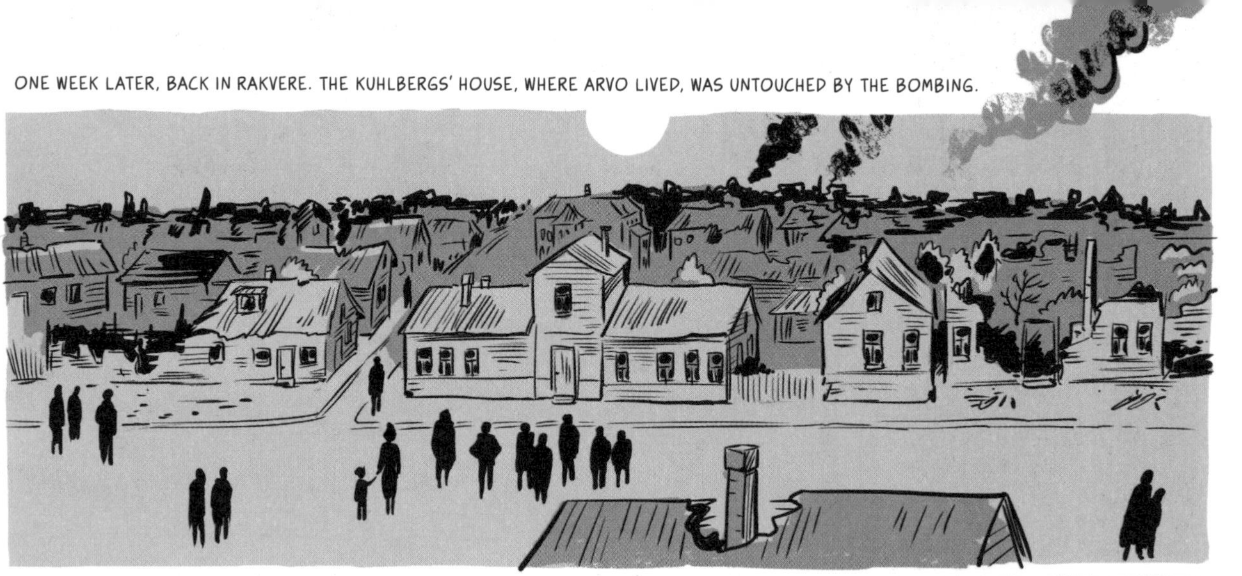

THOUGH RUSSIAN SOLDIERS DID COME A'LOOTING ...

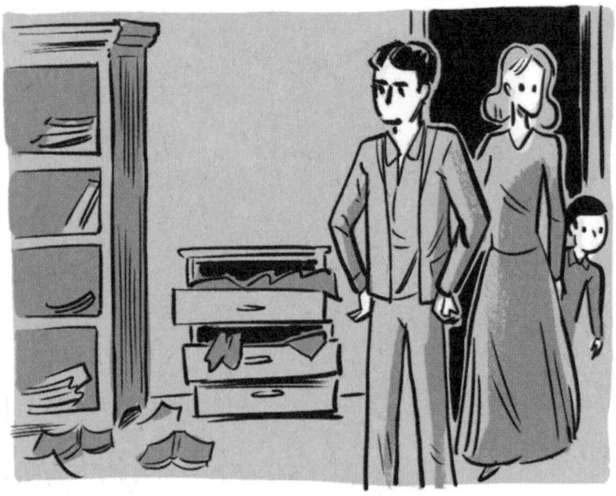

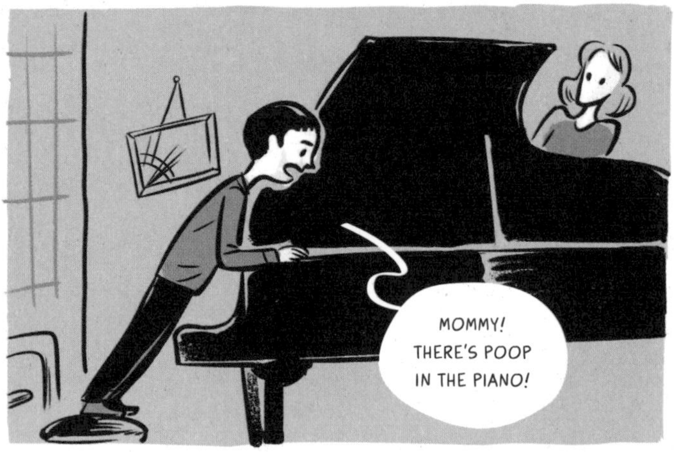
MOMMY! THERE'S POOP IN THE PIANO!

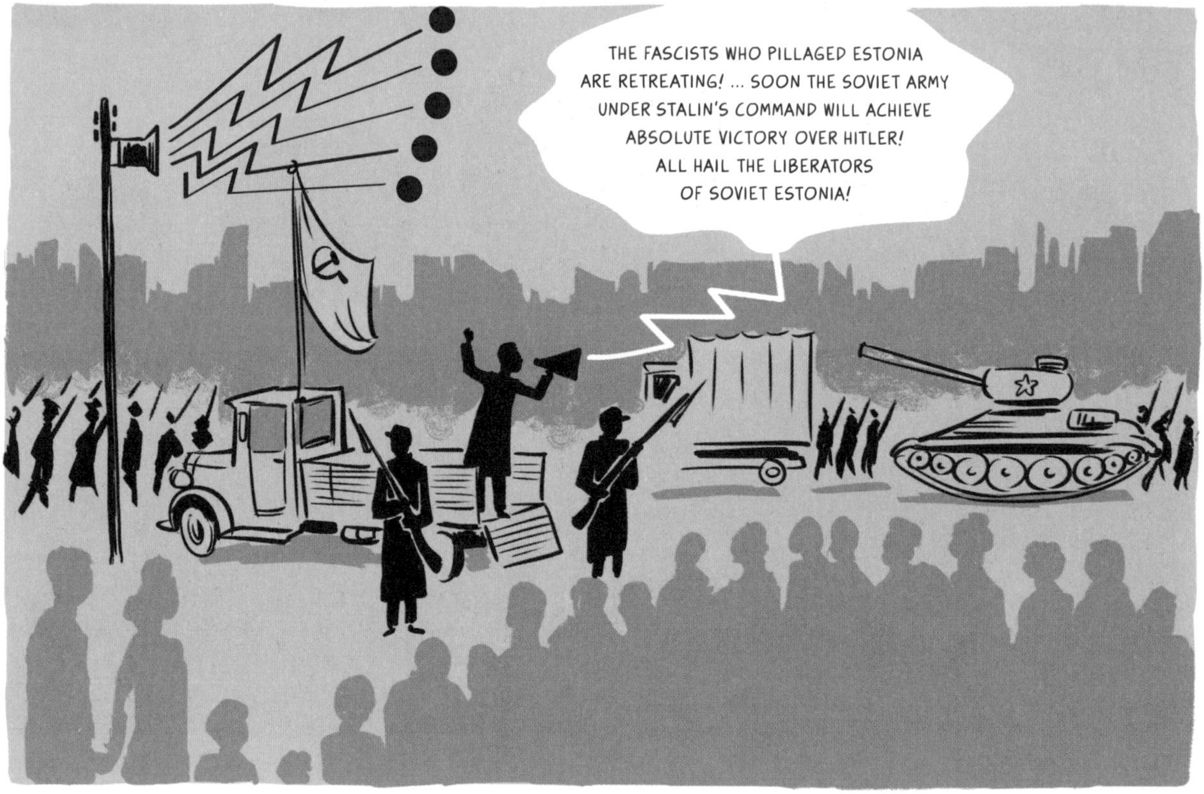
THE FASCISTS WHO PILLAGED ESTONIA ARE RETREATING! ... SOON THE SOVIET ARMY UNDER STALIN'S COMMAND WILL ACHIEVE ABSOLUTE VICTORY OVER HITLER! ALL HAIL THE LIBERATORS OF SOVIET ESTONIA!

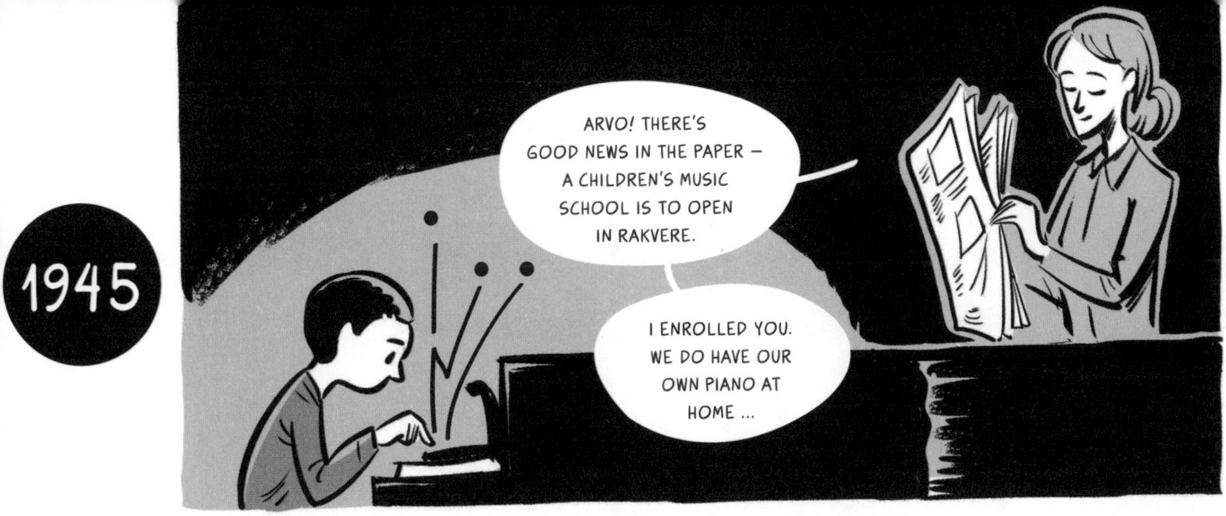
1945
ARVO! THERE'S GOOD NEWS IN THE PAPER – A CHILDREN'S MUSIC SCHOOL IS TO OPEN IN RAKVERE.
I ENROLLED YOU. WE DO HAVE OUR OWN PIANO AT HOME ...

THE SCHOOL, WHICH WAS STARTED BY ENTHUSIASTS, DOESN'T HAVE ITS OWN SPACE YET.

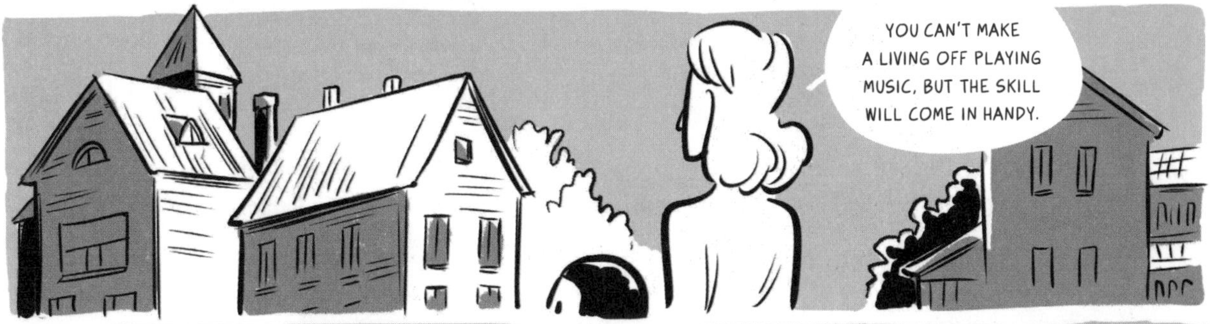
YOU CAN'T MAKE A LIVING OFF PLAYING MUSIC, BUT THE SKILL WILL COME IN HANDY.

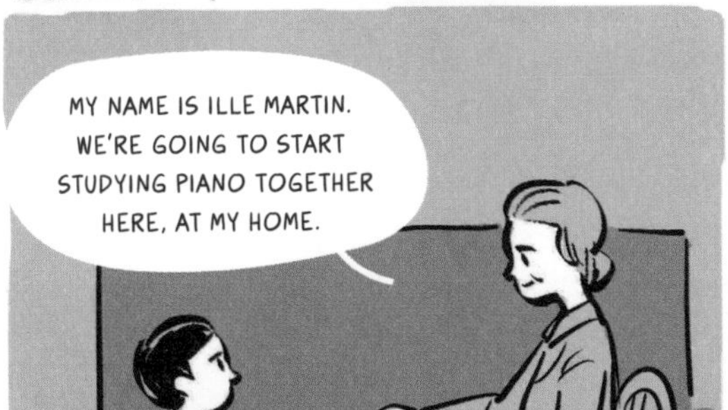
MY NAME IS ILLE MARTIN. WE'RE GOING TO START STUDYING PIANO TOGETHER HERE, AT MY HOME.

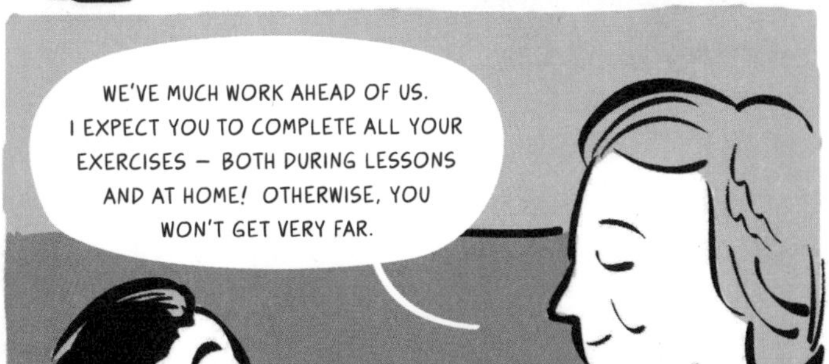
WE'VE MUCH WORK AHEAD OF US. I EXPECT YOU TO COMPLETE ALL YOUR EXERCISES – BOTH DURING LESSONS AND AT HOME! OTHERWISE, YOU WON'T GET VERY FAR.

MISS MARTIN IS AN OLD-FASHIONED WOMAN WHO HAS LITTLE EXPERIENCE WITH CHILDREN.

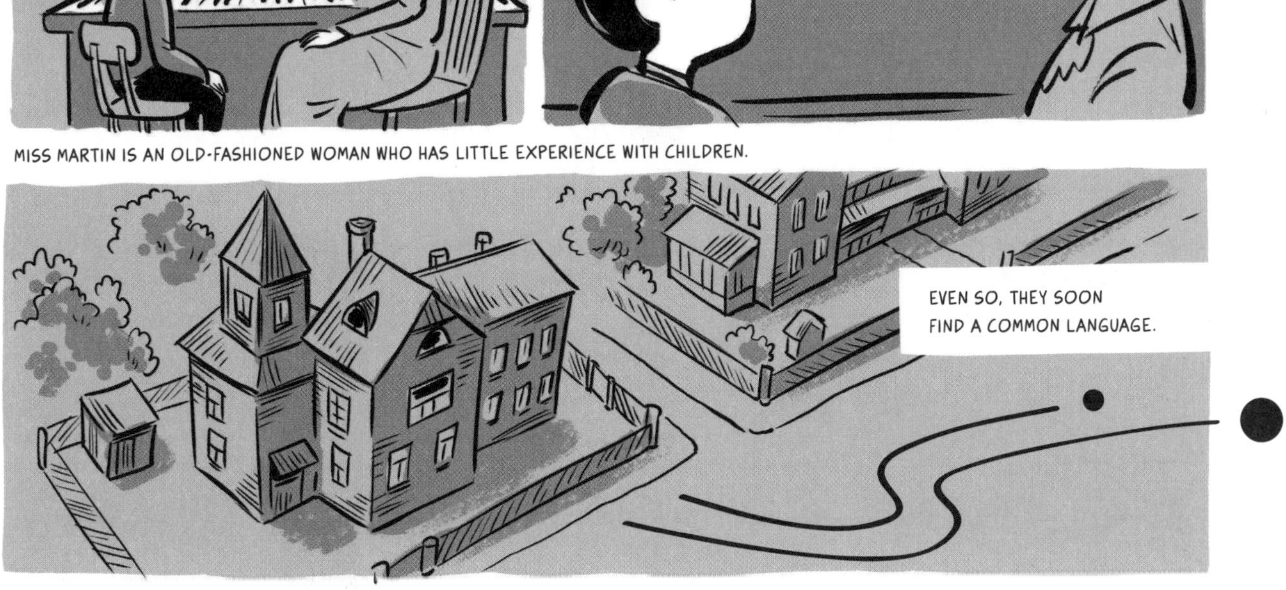
EVEN SO, THEY SOON FIND A COMMON LANGUAGE.

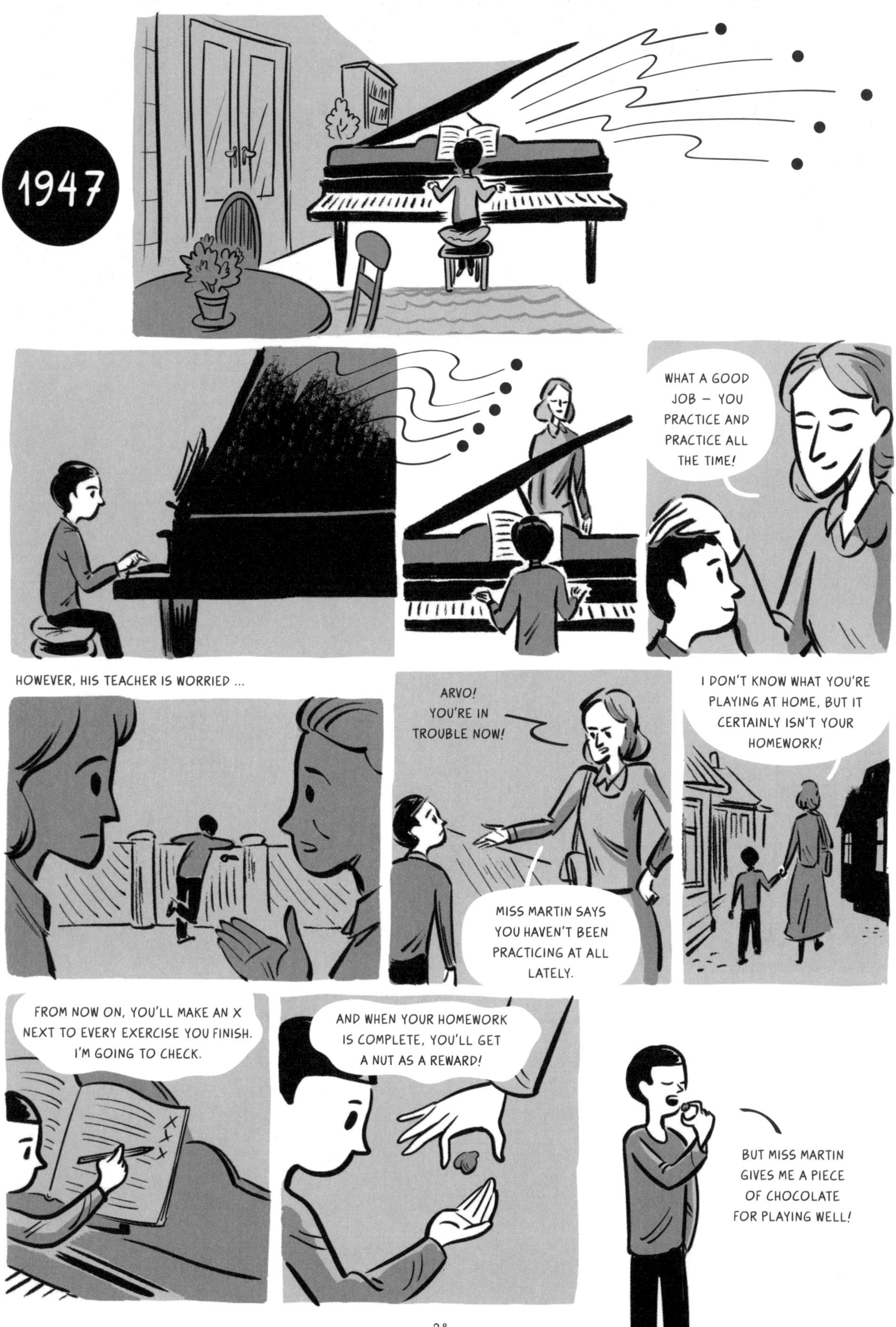
1947
WHAT A GOOD JOB – YOU PRACTICE AND PRACTICE ALL THE TIME!
HOWEVER, HIS TEACHER IS WORRIED ...
ARVO! YOU'RE IN TROUBLE NOW!
MISS MARTIN SAYS YOU HAVEN'T BEEN PRACTICING AT ALL LATELY.
I DON'T KNOW WHAT YOU'RE PLAYING AT HOME, BUT IT CERTAINLY ISN'T YOUR HOMEWORK!
FROM NOW ON, YOU'LL MAKE AN X NEXT TO EVERY EXERCISE YOU FINISH. I'M GOING TO CHECK.
AND WHEN YOUR HOMEWORK IS COMPLETE, YOU'LL GET A NUT AS A REWARD!
BUT MISS MARTIN GIVES ME A PIECE OF CHOCOLATE FOR PLAYING WELL!

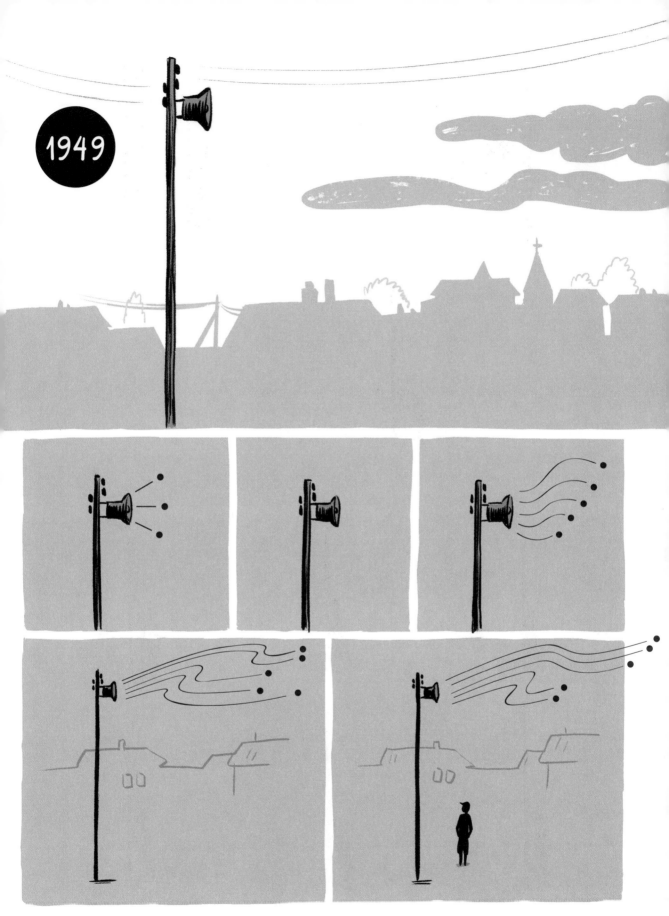

ESTONIAN RADIO IS PLAYED OVER THE LOUDSPEAKER ON RAKVERE'S MARKET SQUARE.

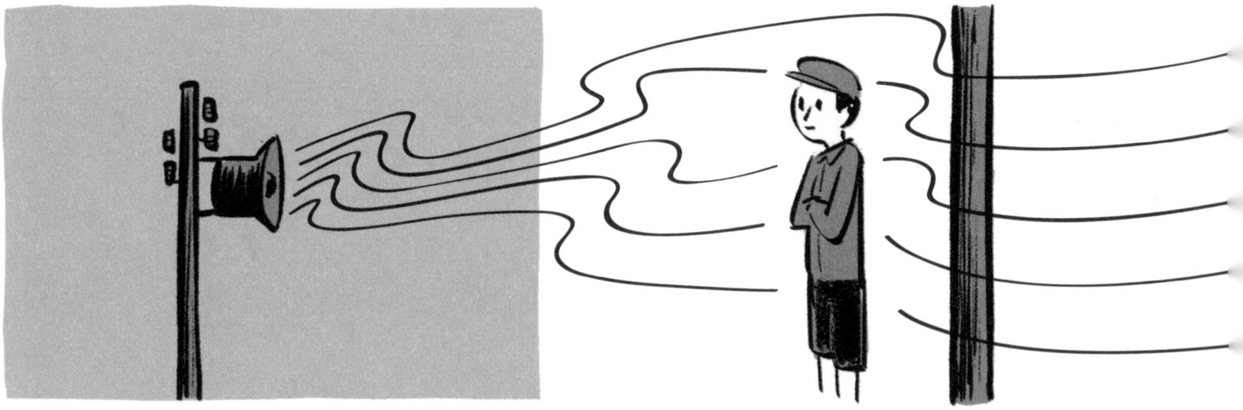

SINCE HE CAN'T ALWAYS LISTEN TO THE RADIO AT HOME, TEENAGE ARVO VISITS THE SPEAKER TO ENJOY SYMPHONY BROADCASTS.

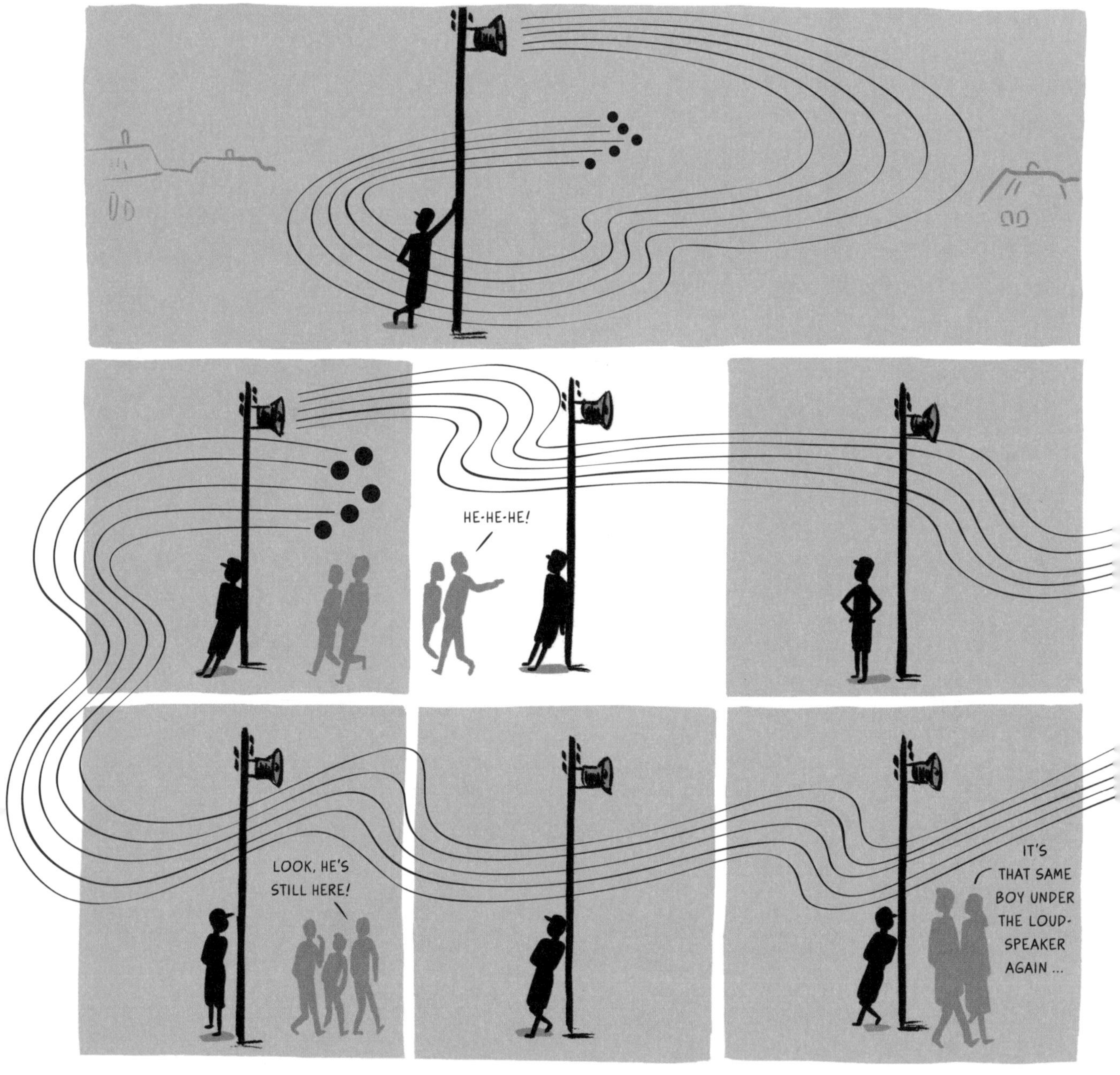
HE-HE-HE!
LOOK, HE'S STILL HERE!
IT'S THAT SAME BOY UNDER THE LOUD-SPEAKER AGAIN ...

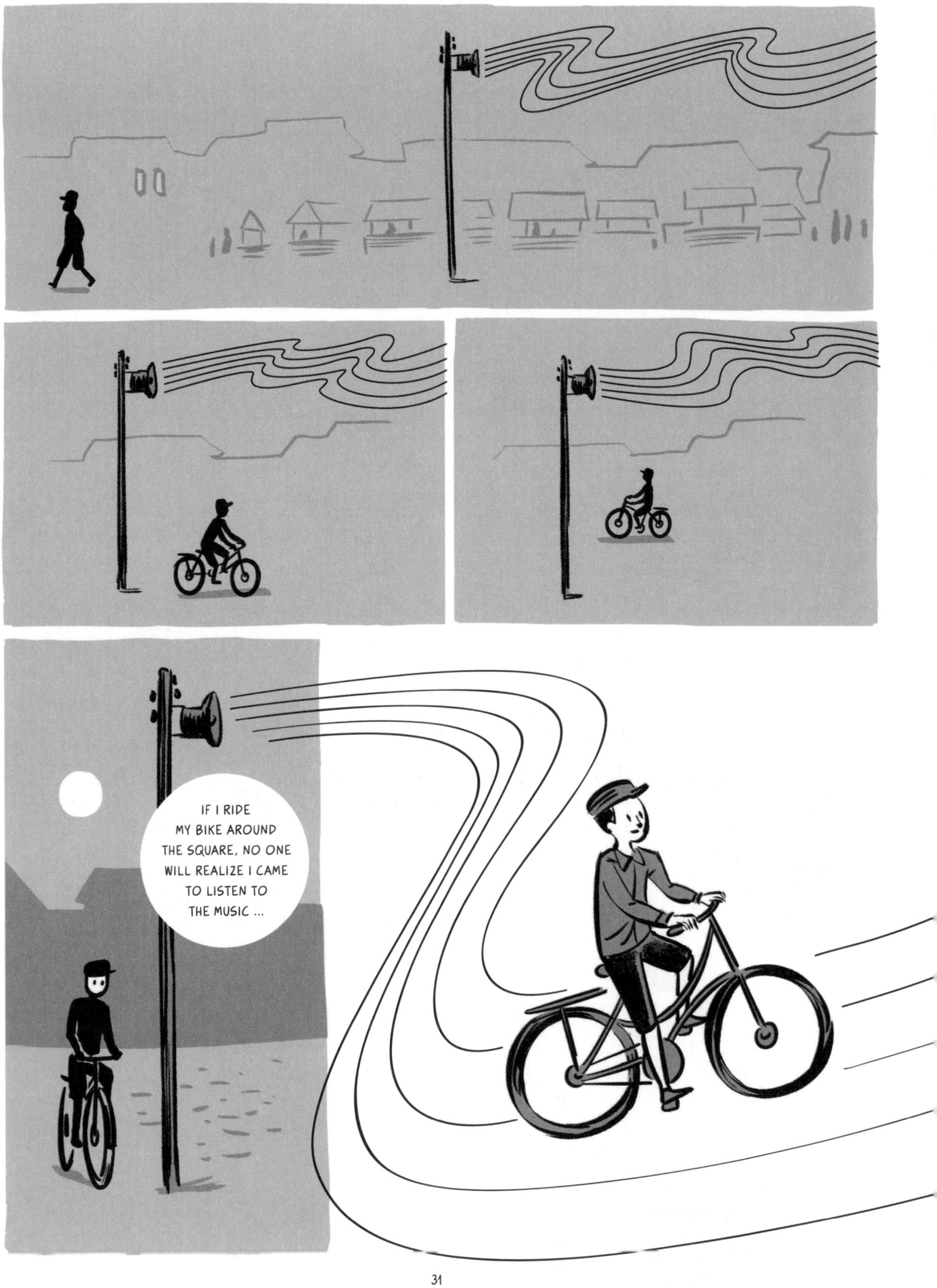
IF I RIDE MY BIKE AROUND THE SQUARE, NO ONE WILL REALIZE I CAME TO LISTEN TO THE MUSIC ...

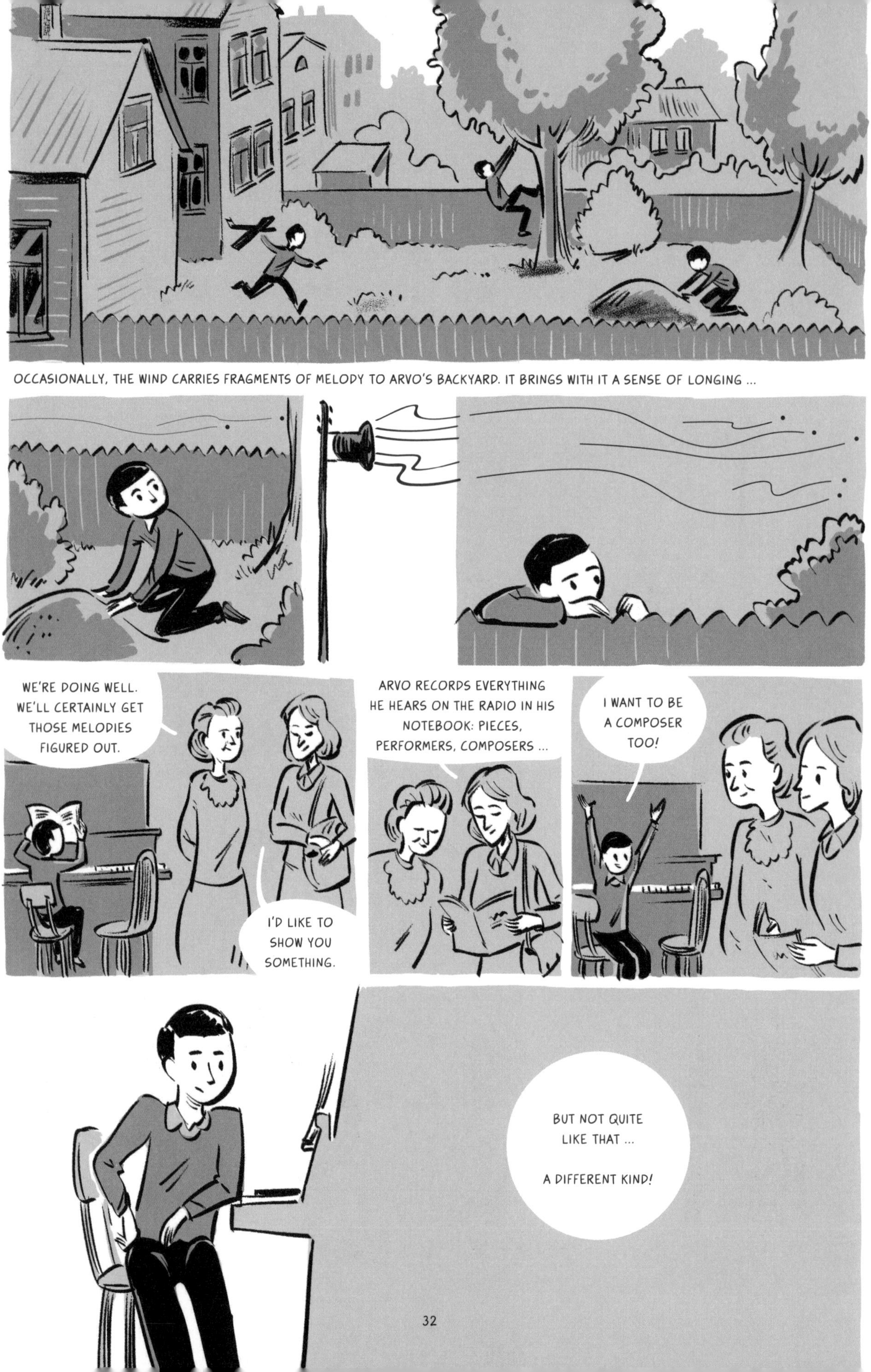
OCCASIONALLY, THE WIND CARRIES FRAGMENTS OF MELODY TO ARVO'S BACKYARD. IT BRINGS WITH IT A SENSE OF LONGING ...
WE'RE DOING WELL. WE'LL CERTAINLY GET THOSE MELODIES FIGURED OUT.
I'D LIKE TO SHOW YOU SOMETHING.
ARVO RECORDS EVERYTHING HE HEARS ON THE RADIO IN HIS NOTEBOOK: PIECES, PERFORMERS, COMPOSERS ...
I WANT TO BE A COMPOSER TOO!
BUT NOT QUITE LIKE THAT ...
A DIFFERENT KIND!

1951

HAVE YOU NOT DONE YOUR HOMEWORK?

OH, I WAS JUST IMPROVISING A LITTLE TO IT ...

WELL, FINE. I'M NOT GOING TO ARGUE ABOUT THAT TODAY.

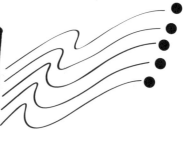

COME AND ACCOMPANY THE SINGERS AT THE MUSIC SCHOOL TOMORROW!

RAKVERE HIGH SCHOOL. ARVO ISN'T THRILLED ABOUT SCHOOLWORK. QUITE THE OPPOSITE ...

ARVO! DO YOU KNOW THE ANSWER?

PSST! WHAT'S THE ANSWER?

THINK FOR YOURSELF!

WE'RE WAITING!

BUT WHAT WAS THE QUESTION?

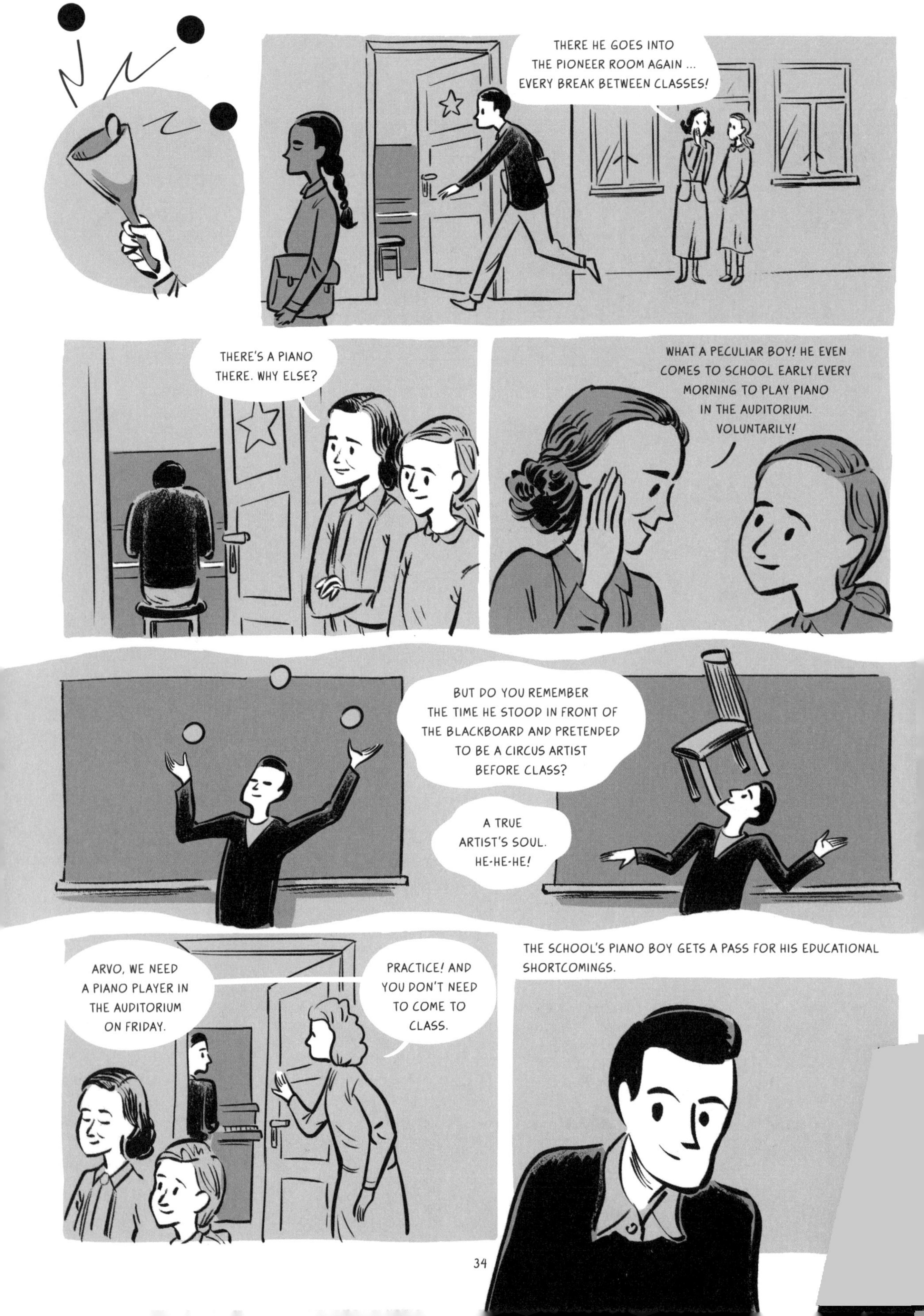
THERE HE GOES INTO THE PIONEER ROOM AGAIN ... EVERY BREAK BETWEEN CLASSES!
THERE'S A PIANO THERE. WHY ELSE?
WHAT A PECULIAR BOY! HE EVEN COMES TO SCHOOL EARLY EVERY MORNING TO PLAY PIANO IN THE AUDITORIUM. VOLUNTARILY!
BUT DO YOU REMEMBER THE TIME HE STOOD IN FRONT OF THE BLACKBOARD AND PRETENDED TO BE A CIRCUS ARTIST BEFORE CLASS?
A TRUE ARTIST'S SOUL. HE-HE-HE!
ARVO, WE NEED A PIANO PLAYER IN THE AUDITORIUM ON FRIDAY.
PRACTICE! AND YOU DON'T NEED TO COME TO CLASS.
THE SCHOOL'S PIANO BOY GETS A PASS FOR HIS EDUCATIONAL SHORTCOMINGS.

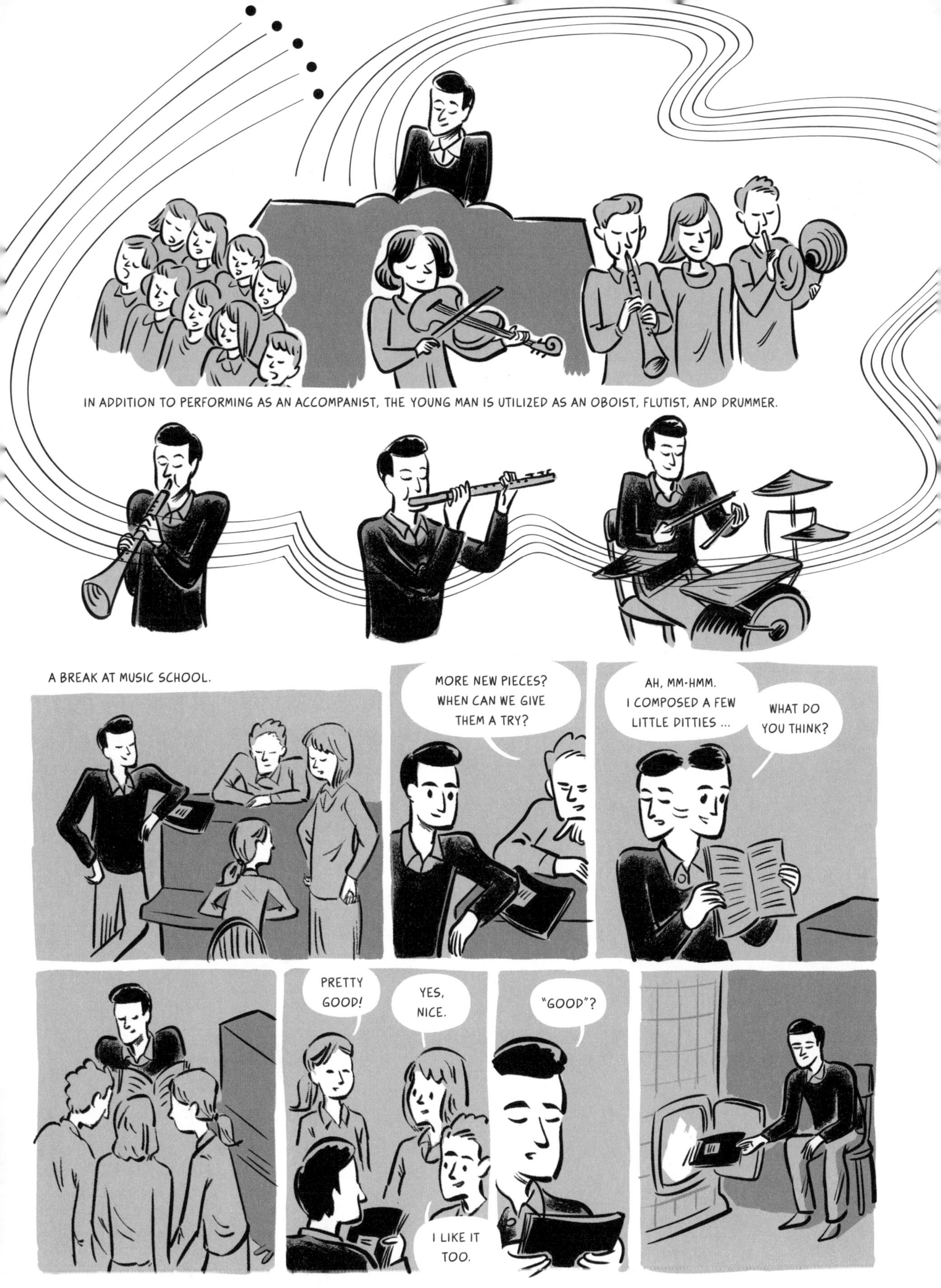
IN ADDITION TO PERFORMING AS AN ACCOMPANIST, THE YOUNG MAN IS UTILIZED AS AN OBOIST, FLUTIST, AND DRUMMER.
A BREAK AT MUSIC SCHOOL.
MORE NEW PIECES? WHEN CAN WE GIVE THEM A TRY?
AH, MM-HMM. I COMPOSED A FEW LITTLE DITTIES ...
WHAT DO YOU THINK?
PRETTY GOOD!
YES, NICE.
I LIKE IT TOO.
"GOOD"?

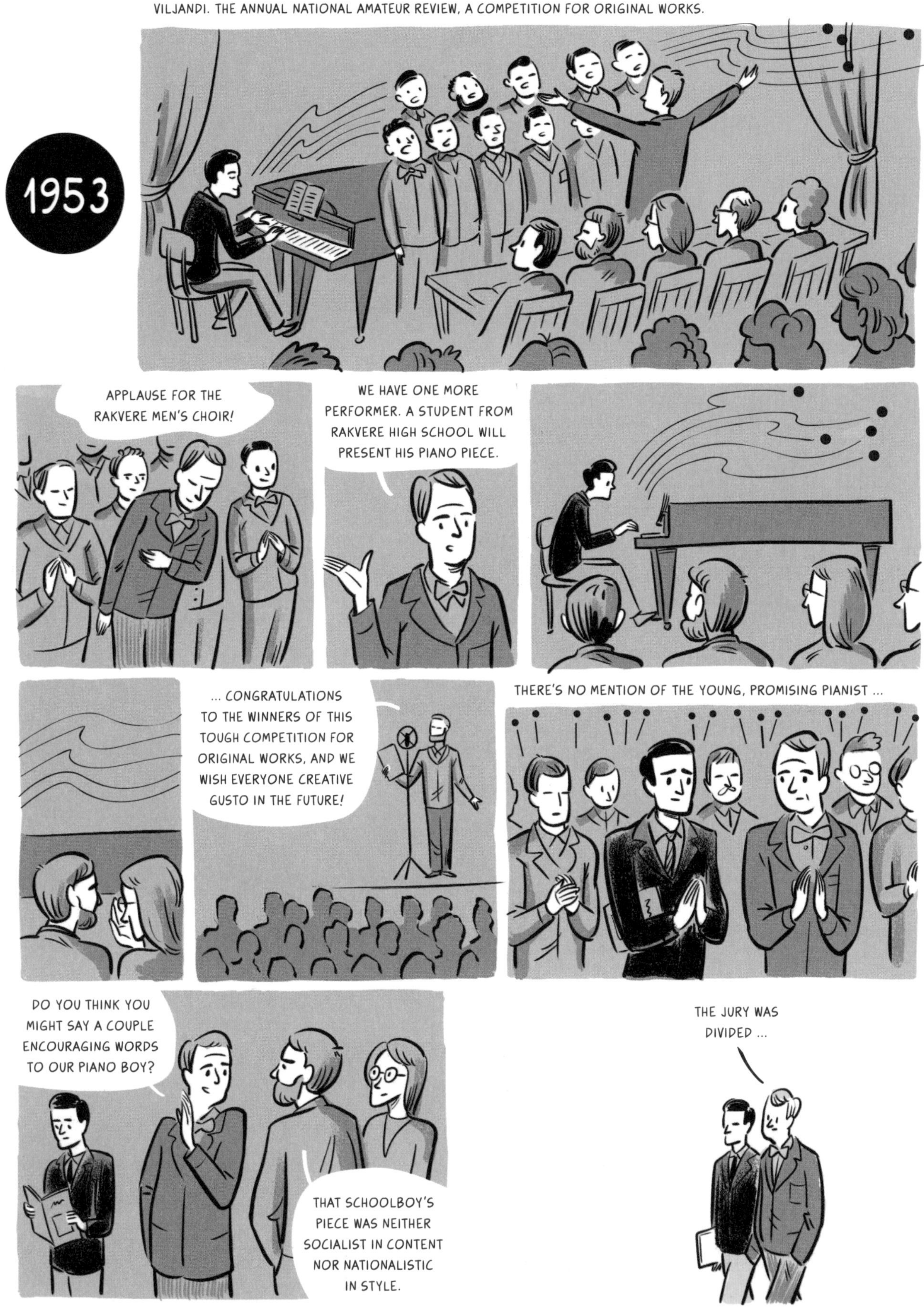
VILJANDI. THE ANNUAL NATIONAL AMATEUR REVIEW, A COMPETITION FOR ORIGINAL WORKS.
1953
APPLAUSE FOR THE RAKVERE MEN'S CHOIR!
WE HAVE ONE MORE PERFORMER. A STUDENT FROM RAKVERE HIGH SCHOOL WILL PRESENT HIS PIANO PIECE.
... CONGRATULATIONS TO THE WINNERS OF THIS TOUGH COMPETITION FOR ORIGINAL WORKS, AND WE WISH EVERYONE CREATIVE GUSTO IN THE FUTURE!
THERE'S NO MENTION OF THE YOUNG, PROMISING PIANIST ...
DO YOU THINK YOU MIGHT SAY A COUPLE ENCOURAGING WORDS TO OUR PIANO BOY?
THAT SCHOOLBOY'S PIECE WAS NEITHER SOCIALIST IN CONTENT NOR NATIONALISTIC IN STYLE.
THE JURY WAS DIVIDED ...

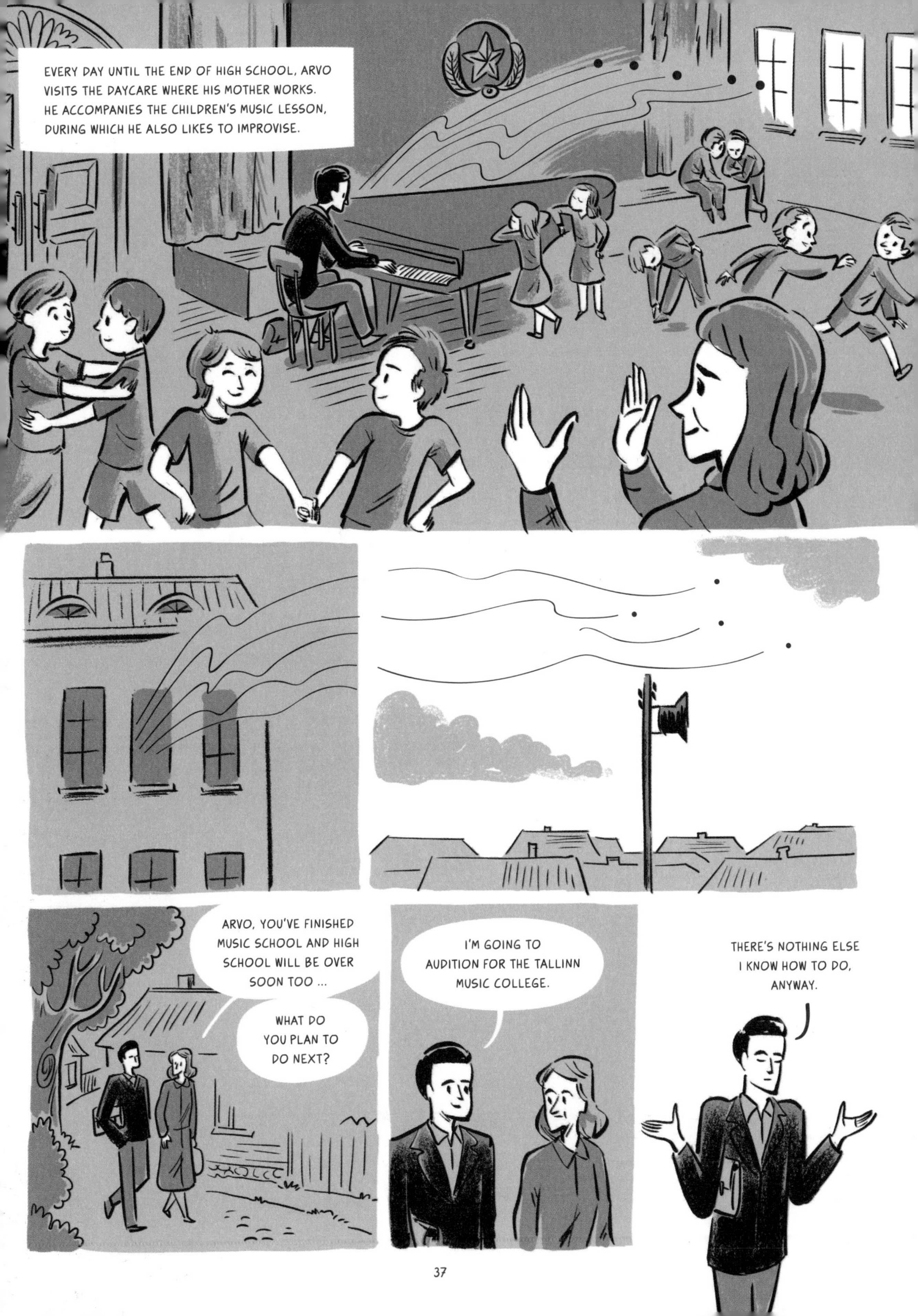
EVERY DAY UNTIL THE END OF HIGH SCHOOL, ARVO VISITS THE DAYCARE WHERE HIS MOTHER WORKS. HE ACCOMPANIES THE CHILDREN'S MUSIC LESSON, DURING WHICH HE ALSO LIKES TO IMPROVISE.
ARVO, YOU'VE FINISHED MUSIC SCHOOL AND HIGH SCHOOL WILL BE OVER SOON TOO ...
WHAT DO YOU PLAN TO DO NEXT?
I'M GOING TO AUDITION FOR THE TALLINN MUSIC COLLEGE.
THERE'S NOTHING ELSE I KNOW HOW TO DO, ANYWAY.

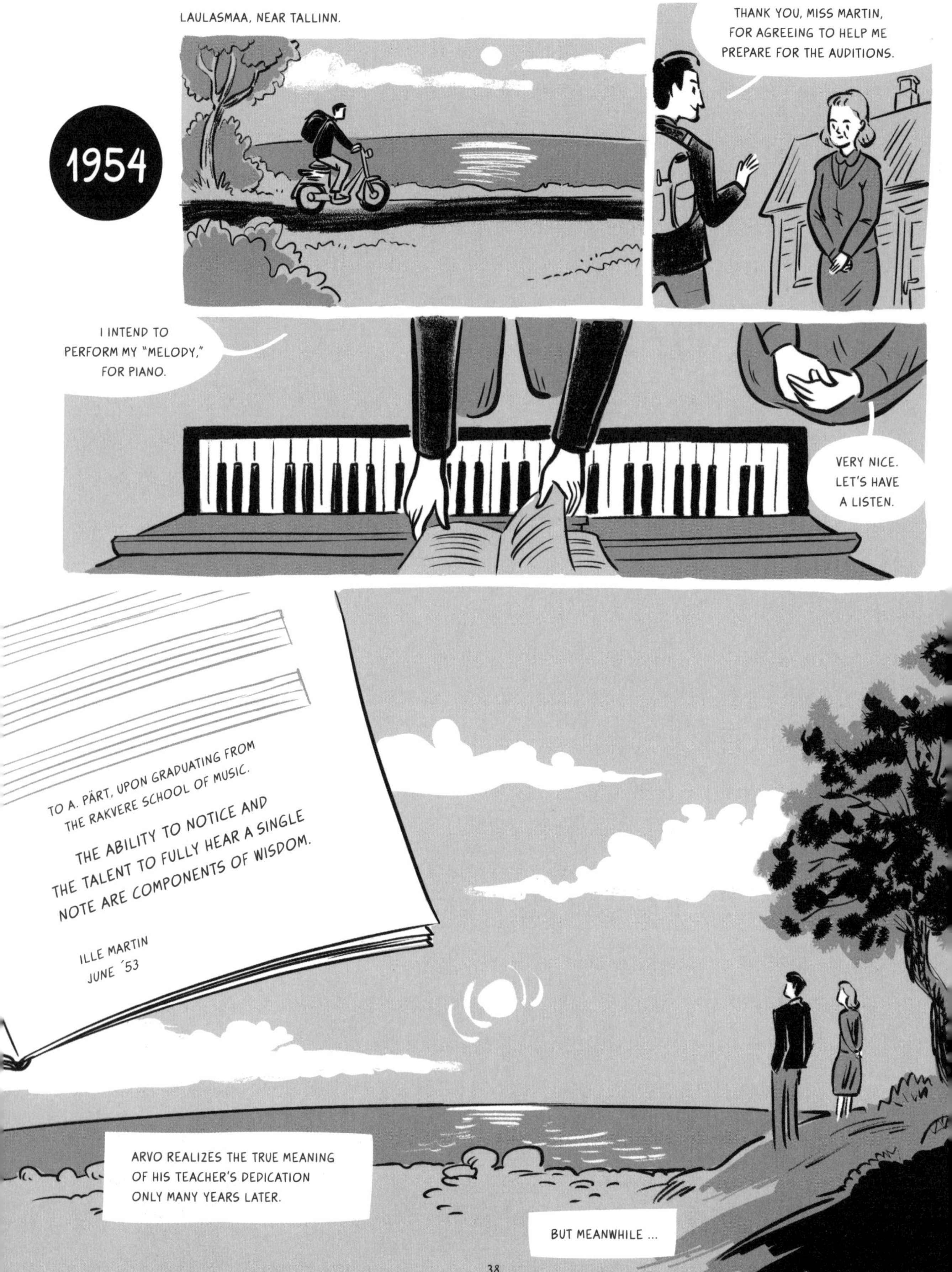
1954
LAULASMAA, NEAR TALLINN.
THANK YOU, MISS MARTIN, FOR AGREEING TO HELP ME PREPARE FOR THE AUDITIONS.
I INTEND TO PERFORM MY "MELODY," FOR PIANO.
VERY NICE. LET'S HAVE A LISTEN.
TO A. PÄRT, UPON GRADUATING FROM THE RAKVERE SCHOOL OF MUSIC.
THE ABILITY TO NOTICE AND THE TALENT TO FULLY HEAR A SINGLE NOTE ARE COMPONENTS OF WISDOM.
ILLE MARTIN
JUNE ´53
ARVO REALIZES THE TRUE MEANING OF HIS TEACHER'S DEDICATION ONLY MANY YEARS LATER.
BUT MEANWHILE ...

CREDO

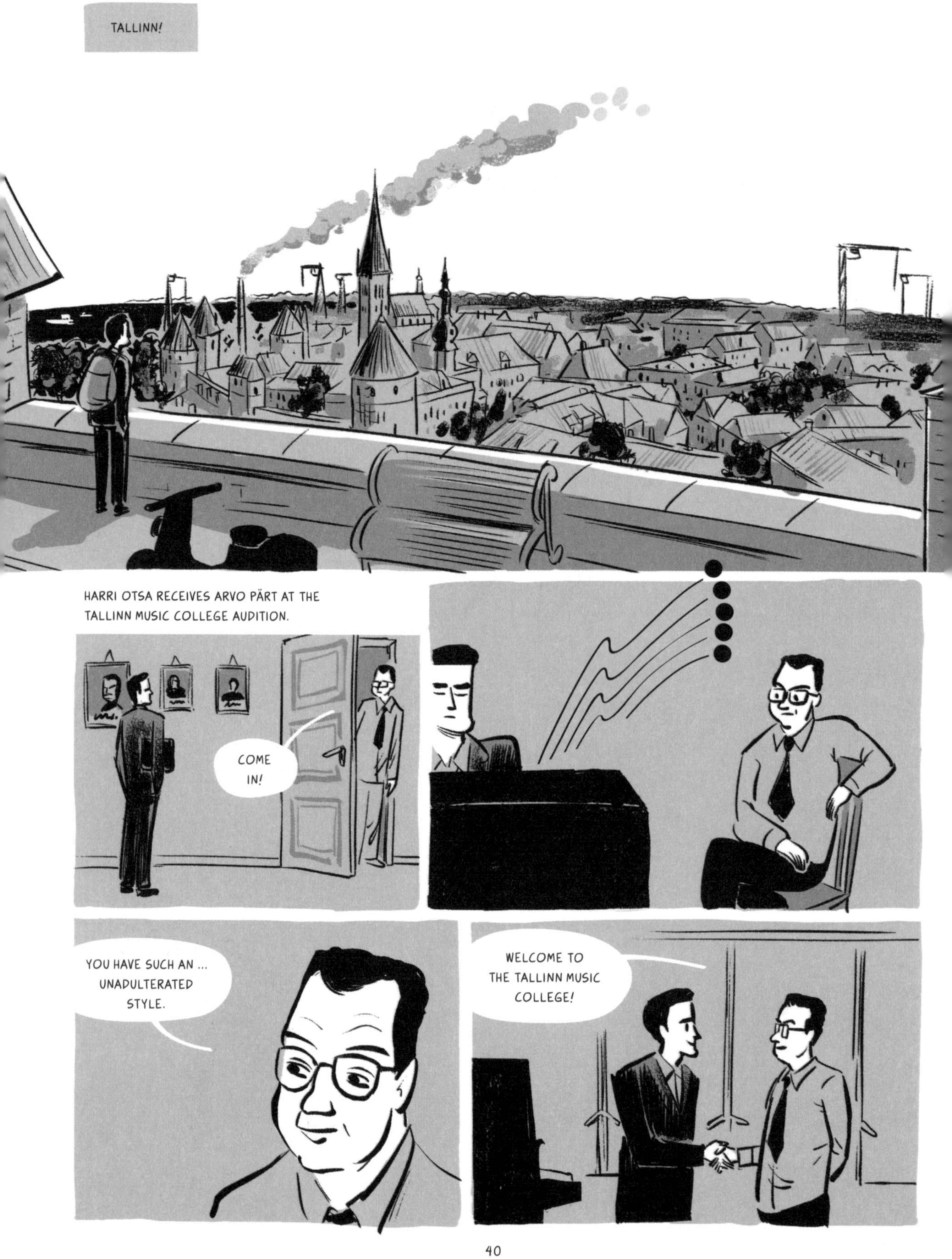
TALLINN!
HARRI OTSA RECEIVES ARVO PÄRT AT THE TALLINN MUSIC COLLEGE AUDITION.
COME IN!
YOU HAVE SUCH AN ... UNADULTERATED STYLE.
WELCOME TO THE TALLINN MUSIC COLLEGE!

AND HIS STUDIES COMMENCE, AT LEAST FOR A WHILE ...

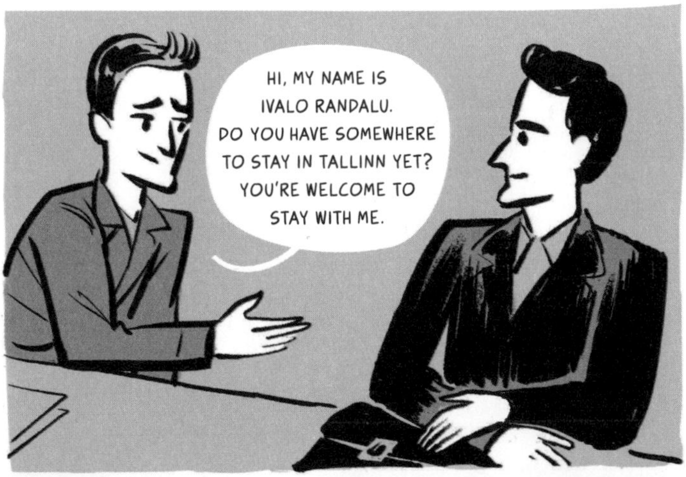
HI, MY NAME IS IVALO RANDALU. DO YOU HAVE SOMEWHERE TO STAY IN TALLINN YET? YOU'RE WELCOME TO STAY WITH ME.

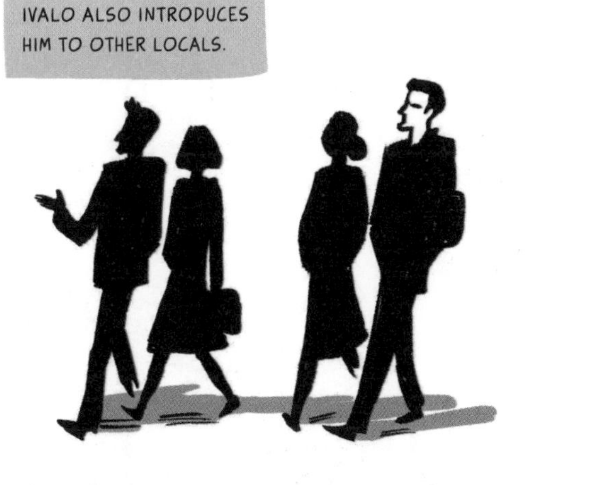
IVALO ALSO INTRODUCES HIM TO OTHER LOCALS.

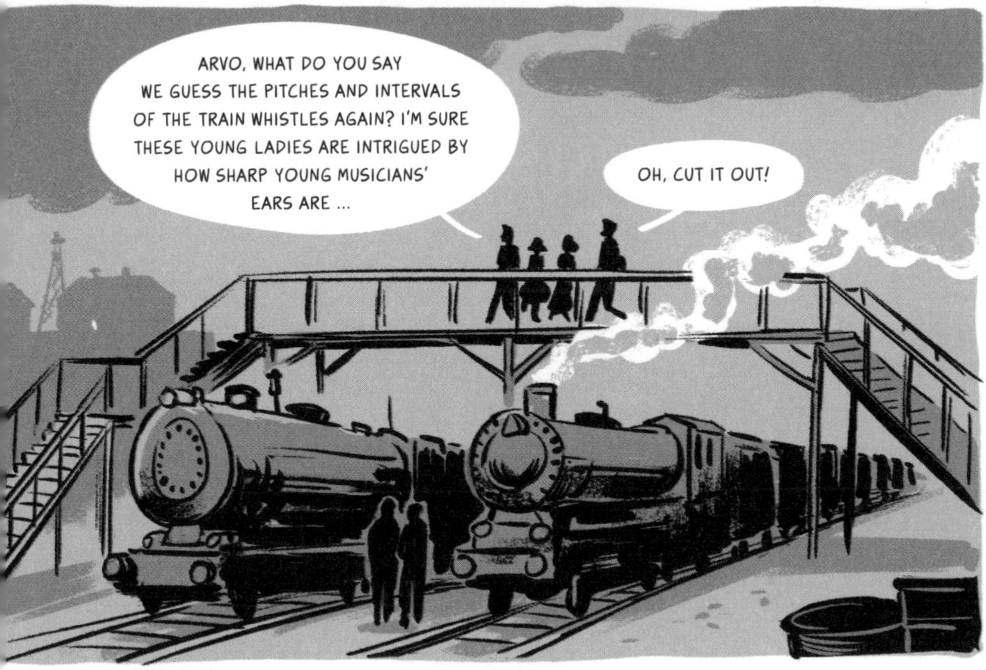
ARVO, WHAT DO YOU SAY WE GUESS THE PITCHES AND INTERVALS OF THE TRAIN WHISTLES AGAIN? I'M SURE THESE YOUNG LADIES ARE INTRIGUED BY HOW SHARP YOUNG MUSICIANS' EARS ARE ...
OH, CUT IT OUT!

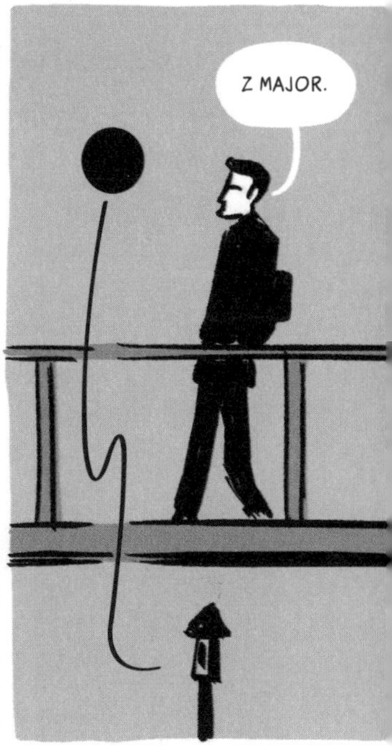
Z MAJOR.

YET MUSIC SCHOOL MUST BE PUT ON HOLD WHEN ARVO IS CALLED UP FOR MILITARY SERVICE.

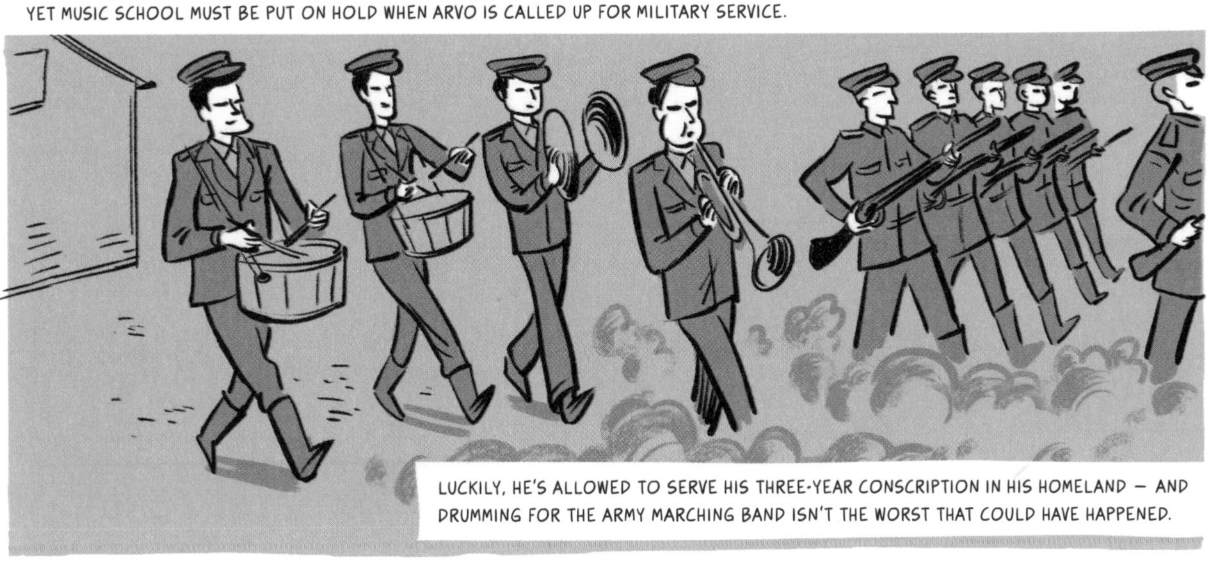
LUCKILY, HE'S ALLOWED TO SERVE HIS THREE-YEAR CONSCRIPTION IN HIS HOMELAND — AND DRUMMING FOR THE ARMY MARCHING BAND ISN'T THE WORST THAT COULD HAVE HAPPENED.

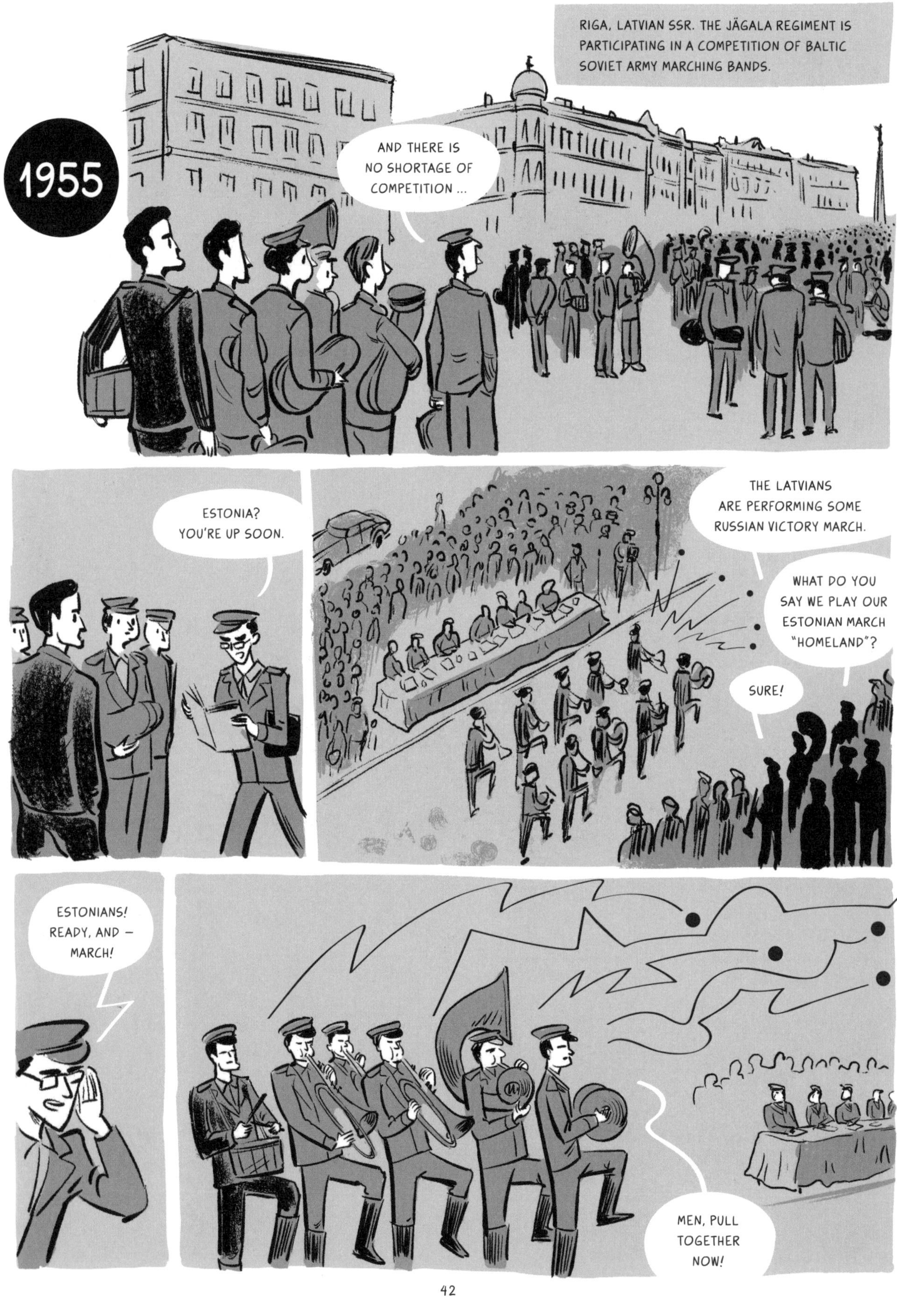
1955
RIGA, LATVIAN SSR. THE JÄGALA REGIMENT IS PARTICIPATING IN A COMPETITION OF BALTIC SOVIET ARMY MARCHING BANDS.
AND THERE IS NO SHORTAGE OF COMPETITION ...
ESTONIA? YOU'RE UP SOON.
THE LATVIANS ARE PERFORMING SOME RUSSIAN VICTORY MARCH.
WHAT DO YOU SAY WE PLAY OUR ESTONIAN MARCH "HOMELAND"?
SURE!
ESTONIANS! READY, AND — MARCH!
MEN, PULL TOGETHER NOW!

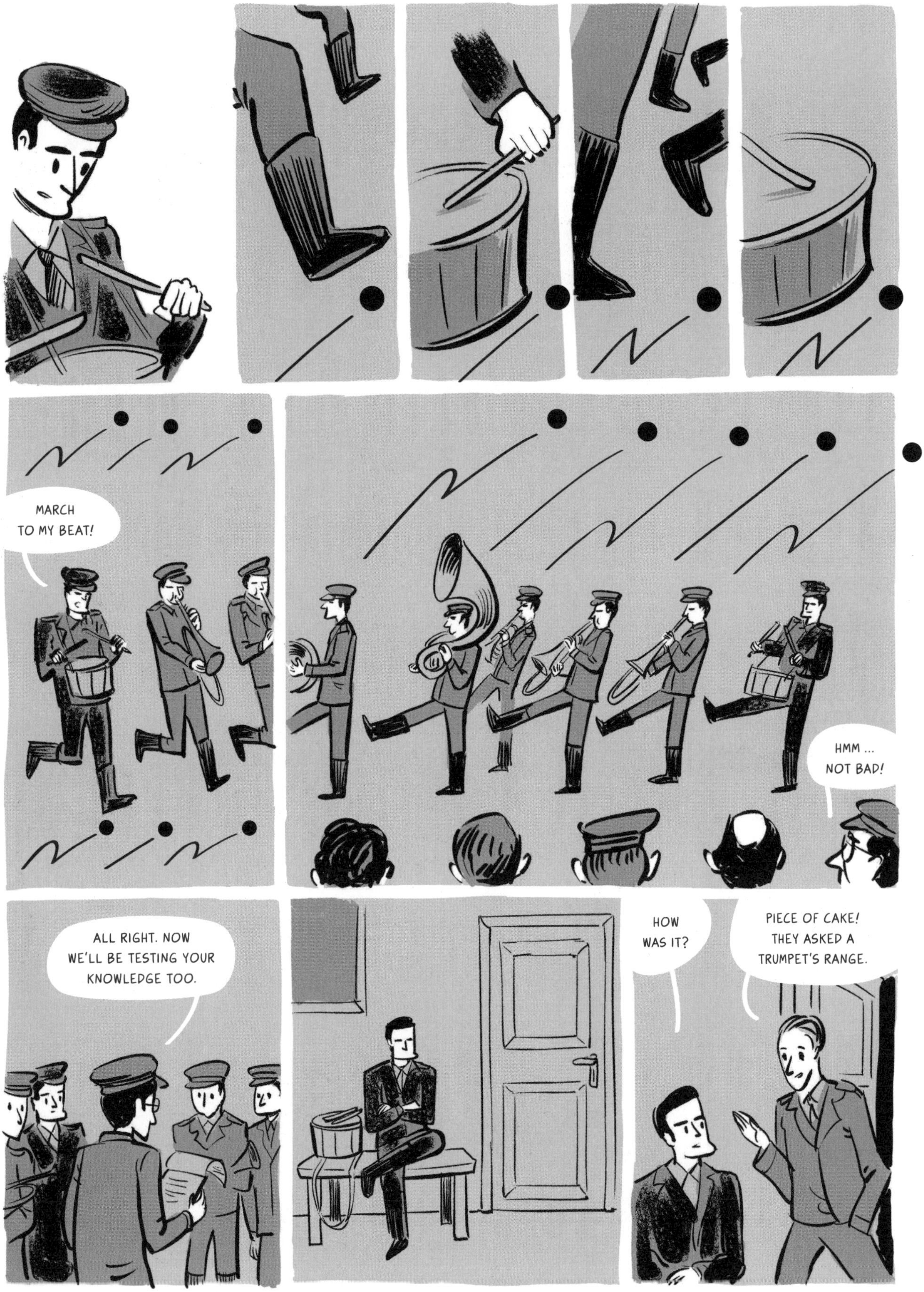
MARCH TO MY BEAT!
HMM ... NOT BAD!
ALL RIGHT. NOW WE'LL BE TESTING YOUR KNOWLEDGE TOO.
HOW WAS IT?
PIECE OF CAKE! THEY ASKED A TRUMPET'S RANGE.

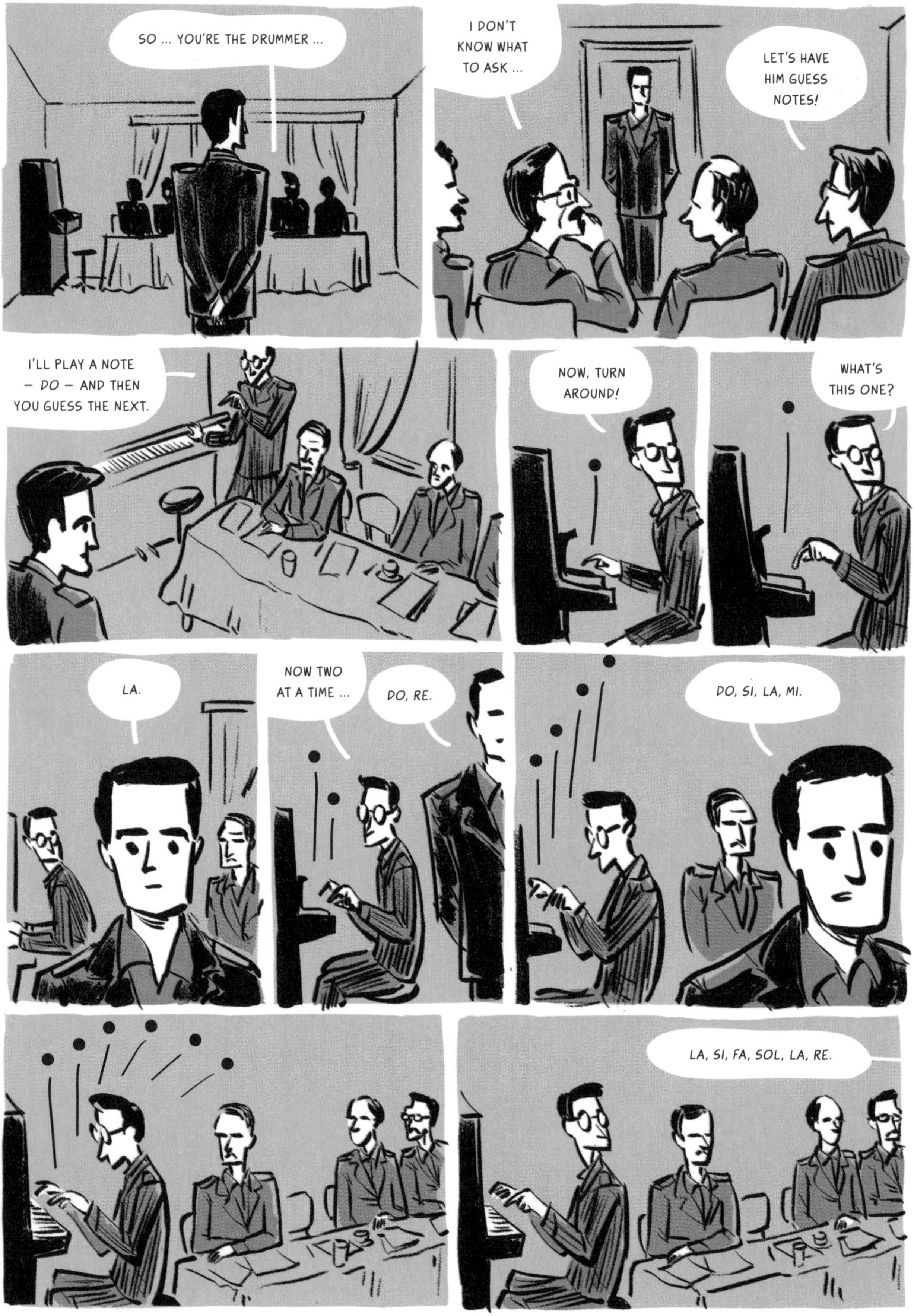
SO ... YOU'RE THE DRUMMER ...
I DON'T KNOW WHAT TO ASK ...
LET'S HAVE HIM GUESS NOTES!
I'LL PLAY A NOTE – DO – AND THEN YOU GUESS THE NEXT.
NOW, TURN AROUND!
WHAT'S THIS ONE?
LA.
NOW TWO AT A TIME ...
DO, RE.
DO, SI, LA, MI.
LA, SI, FA, SOL, LA, RE.

DO, SOL, SI, LA, RE ...

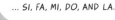

... SI, FA, MI, DO, AND LA.

YOU HAVE PERFECT PITCH!

NOT QUITE. I HAVE RELATIVE PITCH.

BUT WHY ARE YOU PLAYING A SNARE DRUM?

IT'S HARD TO MARCH WITH A PIANO.

HA HA HA HA HA HA HA

ARVO IS NAMED BEST DRUMMER OF THE BALTICS AT THE END OF THE COMPETITION.

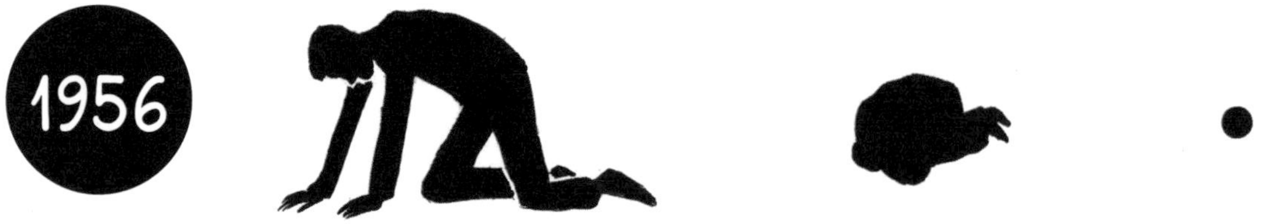
1956

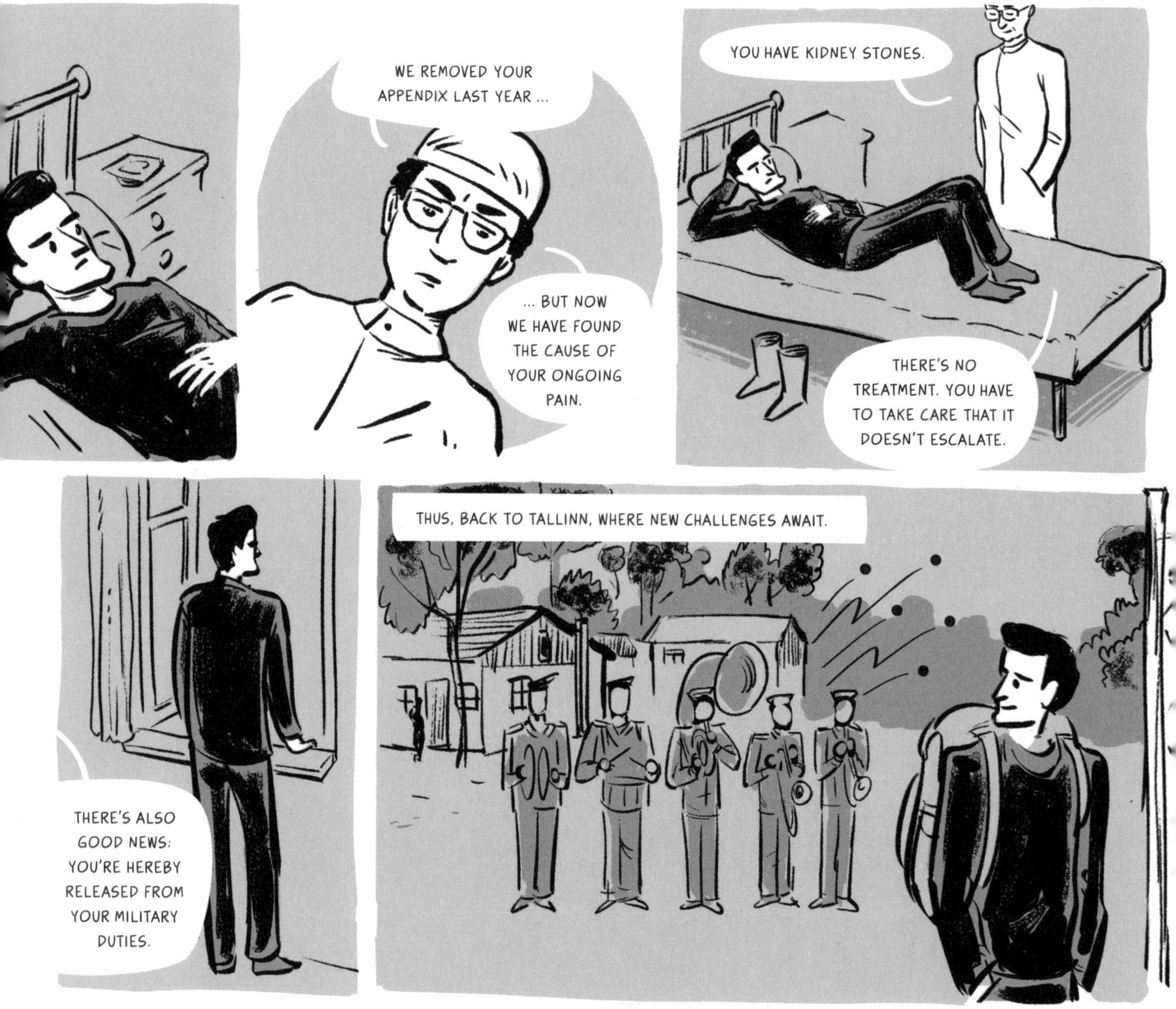
WE REMOVED YOUR APPENDIX LAST YEAR ...
... BUT NOW WE HAVE FOUND THE CAUSE OF YOUR ONGOING PAIN.
YOU HAVE KIDNEY STONES.
THERE'S NO TREATMENT. YOU HAVE TO TAKE CARE THAT IT DOESN'T ESCALATE.
THERE'S ALSO GOOD NEWS: YOU'RE HEREBY RELEASED FROM YOUR MILITARY DUTIES.
THUS, BACK TO TALLINN, WHERE NEW CHALLENGES AWAIT.

1957

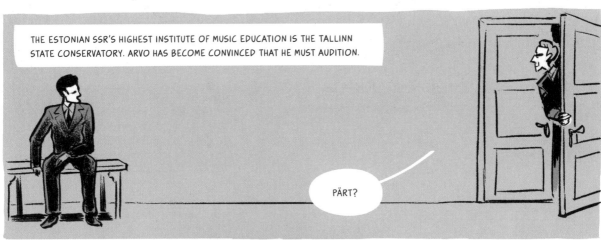

THE ESTONIAN SSR'S HIGHEST INSTITUTE OF MUSIC EDUCATION IS THE TALLINN STATE CONSERVATORY. ARVO HAS BECOME CONVINCED THAT HE MUST AUDITION.

PÄRT?

COULD YOU PLAY US THE BEGINNING OF BEETHOVEN'S "SONATA PATHÉTIQUE"?

OF COURSE.

WHEN THE TASK IS COMPLETE, PROFESSOR OF MUSIC HEIMAR ILVES ISSUES THE NEXT REQUEST.

NOW, PLAY IT FOR US AN AUGMENTED FOURTH HIGHER.

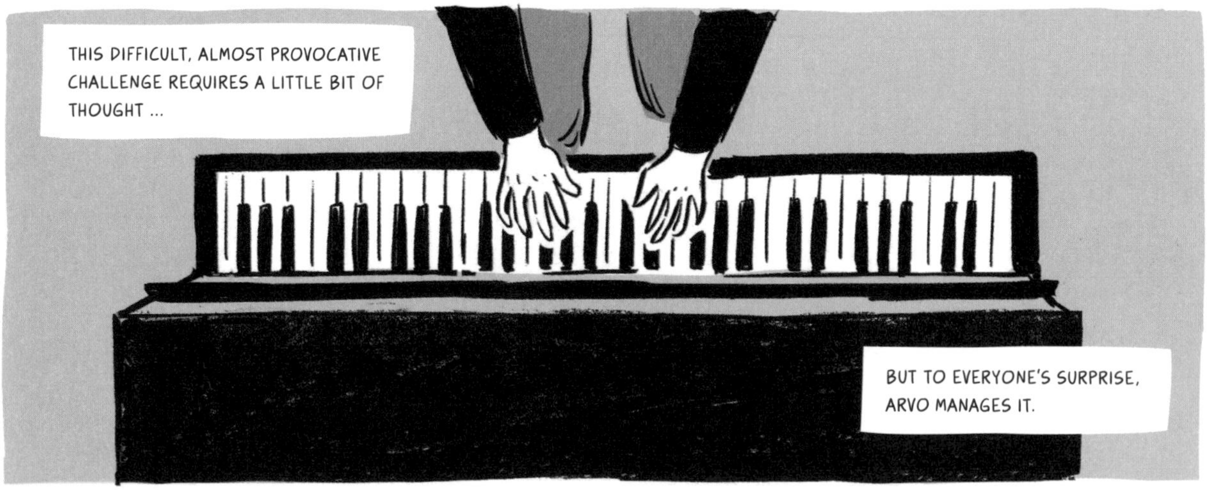
THIS DIFFICULT, ALMOST PROVOCATIVE CHALLENGE REQUIRES A LITTLE BIT OF THOUGHT ...
BUT TO EVERYONE'S SURPRISE, ARVO MANAGES IT.

THE AUDITION IS ALSO ATTENDED BY THE DIRECTOR OF THE DEPARTMENT OF COMPOSITION, PROFESSOR HEINO ELLER. HOLDING A DEGREE FROM THE ST. PETERSBURG CONSERVATORY, HE IS ONE OF THE PILLARS OF ESTONIAN SYMPHONIC MUSIC.

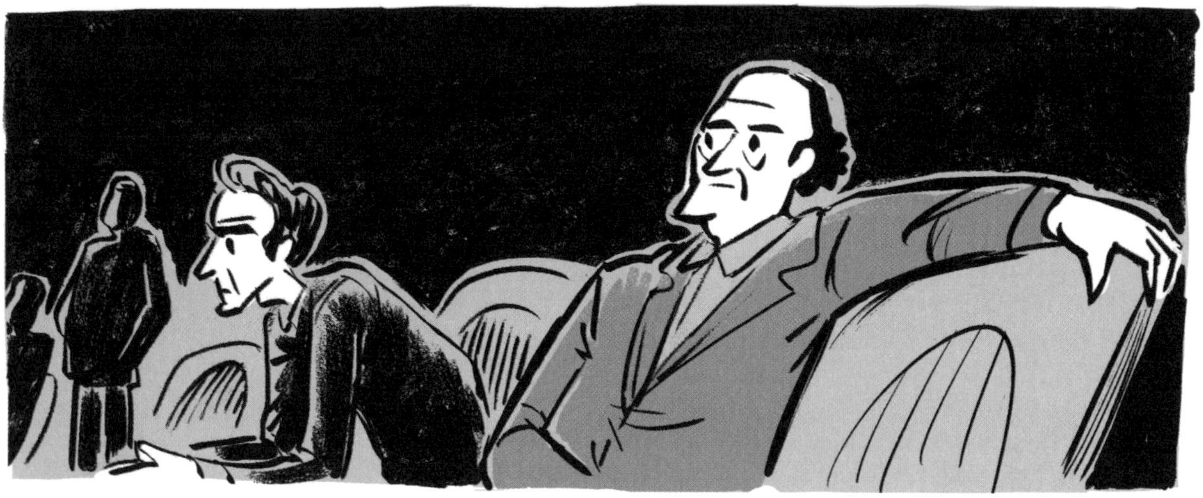

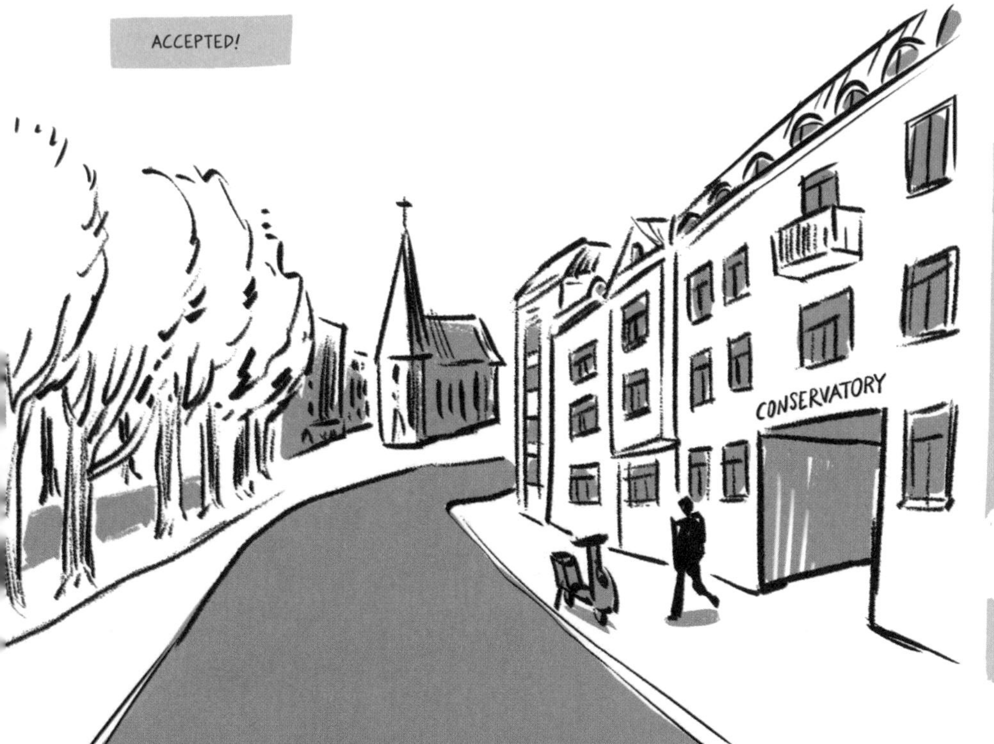
ACCEPTED!
CONSERVATORY

AND NOT ONLY THAT – AN EXTRA SPOT IN THE DEPARTMENT OF COMPOSITION IS ADDED JUST FOR ARVO PÄRT.

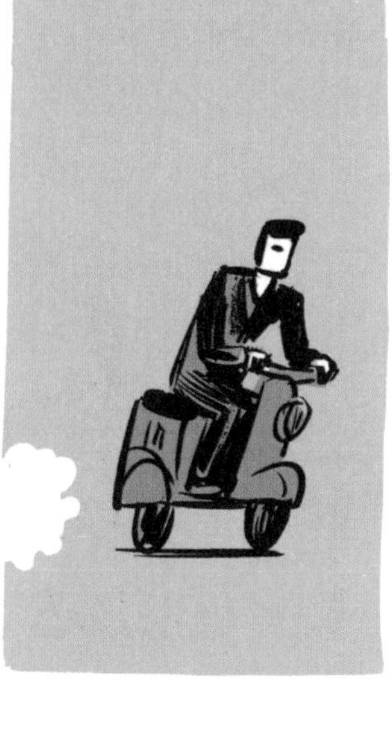

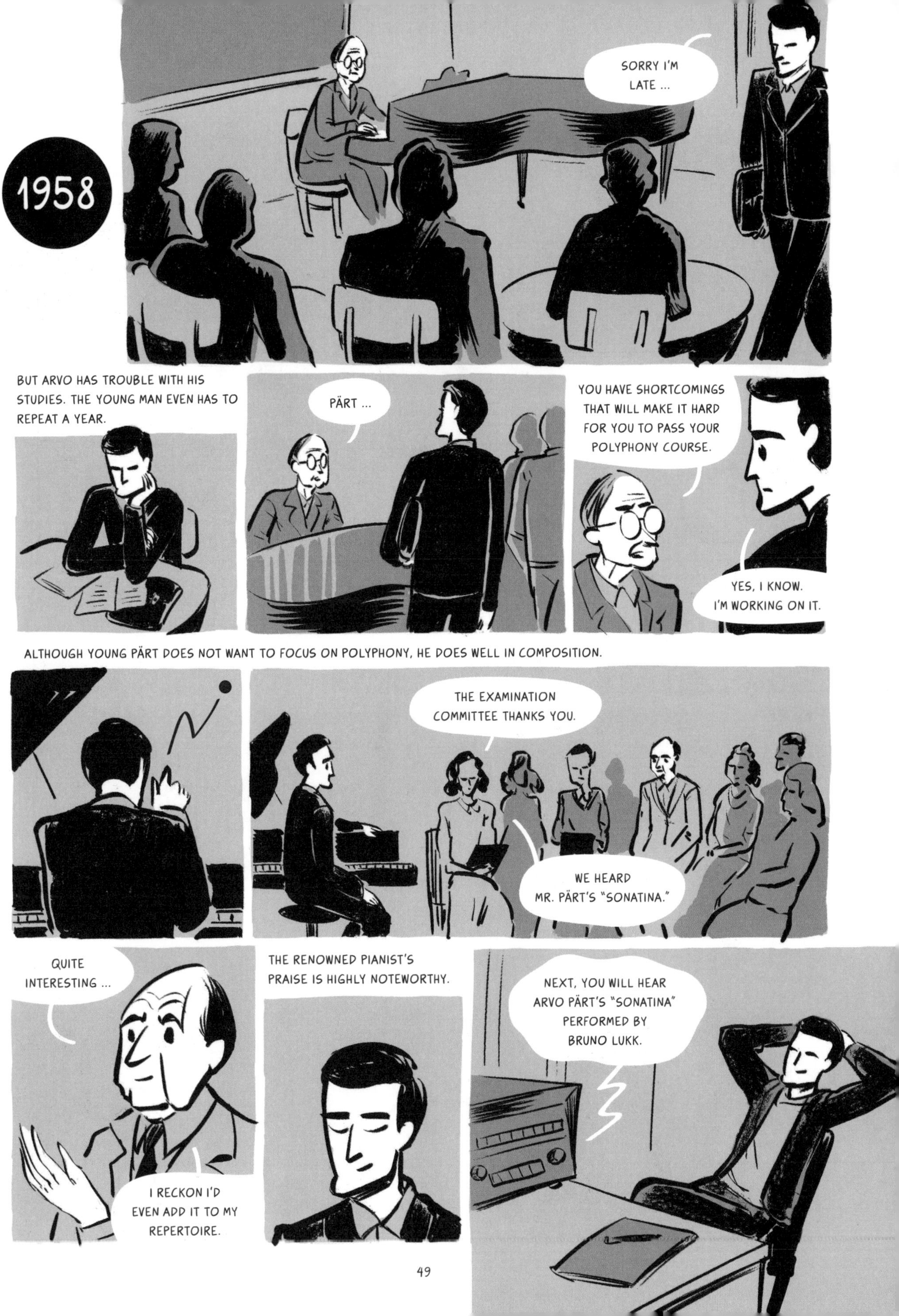
1958
SORRY I'M LATE ...
BUT ARVO HAS TROUBLE WITH HIS STUDIES. THE YOUNG MAN EVEN HAS TO REPEAT A YEAR.
PÄRT ...
YOU HAVE SHORTCOMINGS THAT WILL MAKE IT HARD FOR YOU TO PASS YOUR POLYPHONY COURSE.
YES, I KNOW. I'M WORKING ON IT.
ALTHOUGH YOUNG PÄRT DOES NOT WANT TO FOCUS ON POLYPHONY, HE DOES WELL IN COMPOSITION.
THE EXAMINATION COMMITTEE THANKS YOU.
WE HEARD MR. PÄRT'S "SONATINA."
QUITE INTERESTING ...
I RECKON I'D EVEN ADD IT TO MY REPERTOIRE.
THE RENOWNED PIANIST'S PRAISE IS HIGHLY NOTEWORTHY.
NEXT, YOU WILL HEAR ARVO PÄRT'S "SONATINA" PERFORMED BY BRUNO LUKK.

PROFESSOR HEINO ELLER GIVES ARVO EXTRA POLYPHONY LESSONS AT HIS OWN HOME.
THE MEETINGS ALSO ALLOW HIM TO BE MORE CANDID THAN HE COULD BE AT SCHOOL.

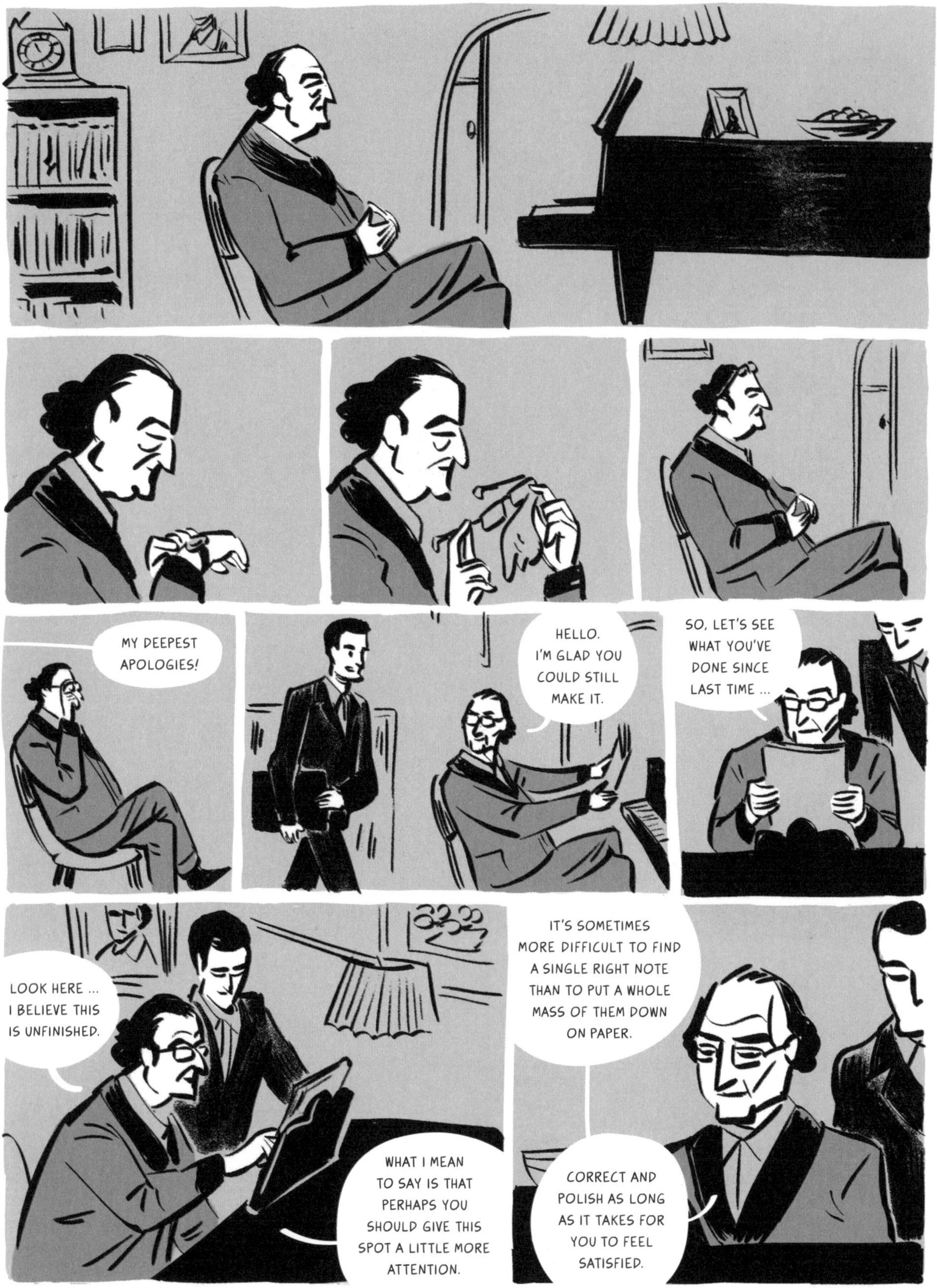
MY DEEPEST APOLOGIES!
HELLO. I'M GLAD YOU COULD STILL MAKE IT.
SO, LET'S SEE WHAT YOU'VE DONE SINCE LAST TIME ...
LOOK HERE ... I BELIEVE THIS IS UNFINISHED.
WHAT I MEAN TO SAY IS THAT PERHAPS YOU SHOULD GIVE THIS SPOT A LITTLE MORE ATTENTION.
IT'S SOMETIMES MORE DIFFICULT TO FIND A SINGLE RIGHT NOTE THAN TO PUT A WHOLE MASS OF THEM DOWN ON PAPER.
CORRECT AND POLISH AS LONG AS IT TAKES FOR YOU TO FEEL SATISFIED.

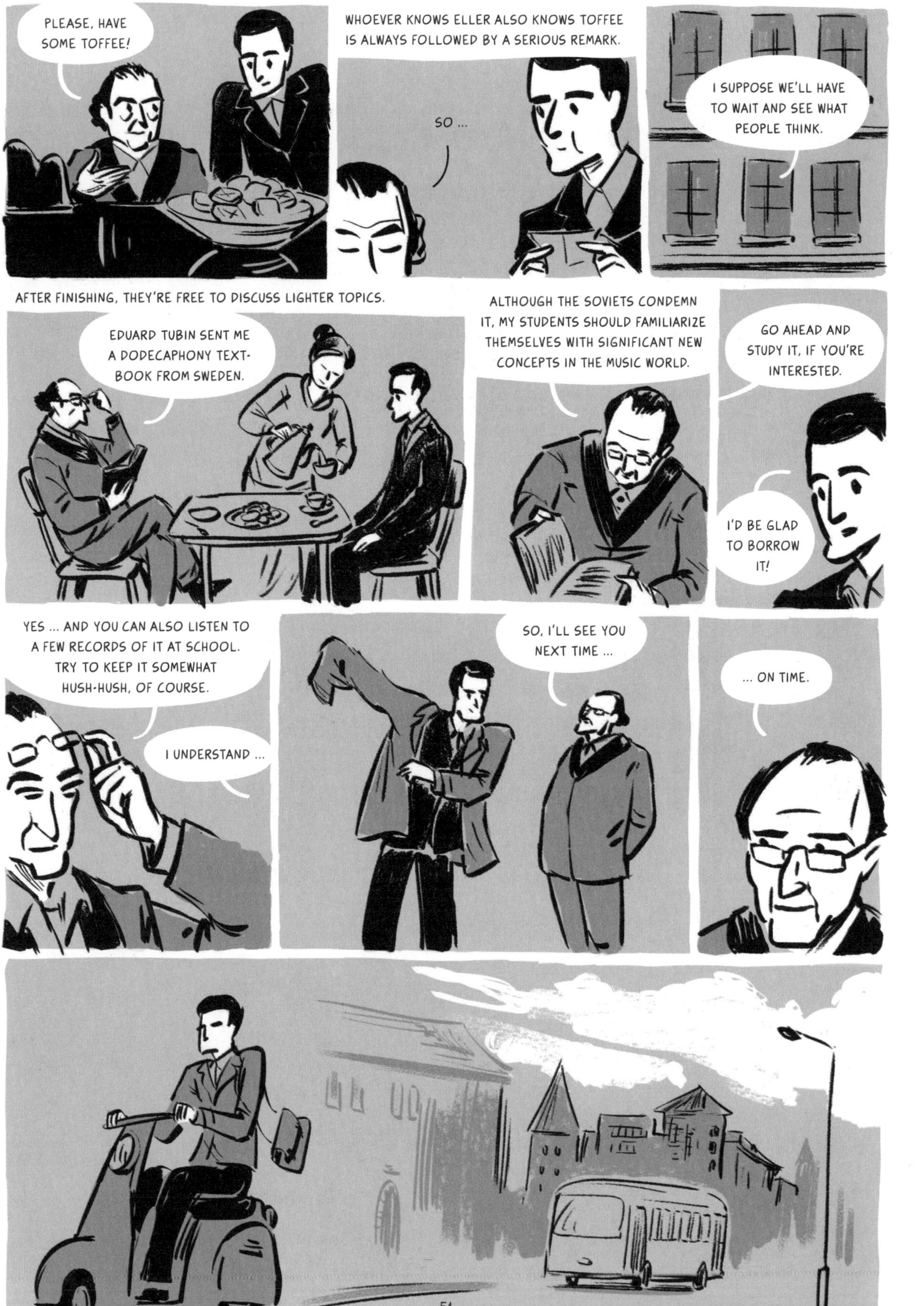
PLEASE, HAVE SOME TOFFEE!
WHOEVER KNOWS ELLER ALSO KNOWS TOFFEE IS ALWAYS FOLLOWED BY A SERIOUS REMARK.
SO ...
I SUPPOSE WE'LL HAVE TO WAIT AND SEE WHAT PEOPLE THINK.
AFTER FINISHING, THEY'RE FREE TO DISCUSS LIGHTER TOPICS.
EDUARD TUBIN SENT ME A DODECAPHONY TEXT-BOOK FROM SWEDEN.
ALTHOUGH THE SOVIETS CONDEMN IT, MY STUDENTS SHOULD FAMILIARIZE THEMSELVES WITH SIGNIFICANT NEW CONCEPTS IN THE MUSIC WORLD.
GO AHEAD AND STUDY IT, IF YOU'RE INTERESTED.
I'D BE GLAD TO BORROW IT!
YES ... AND YOU CAN ALSO LISTEN TO A FEW RECORDS OF IT AT SCHOOL. TRY TO KEEP IT SOMEWHAT HUSH-HUSH, OF COURSE.
I UNDERSTAND ...
SO, I'LL SEE YOU NEXT TIME ...
... ON TIME.

ESTONIAN RADIO. THE "FREEST" AND MOST PROGRESSIVE RADIO STATION IN THE ENTIRE USSR. THE HEART OF THE ESTONIAN MUSIC SCENE.

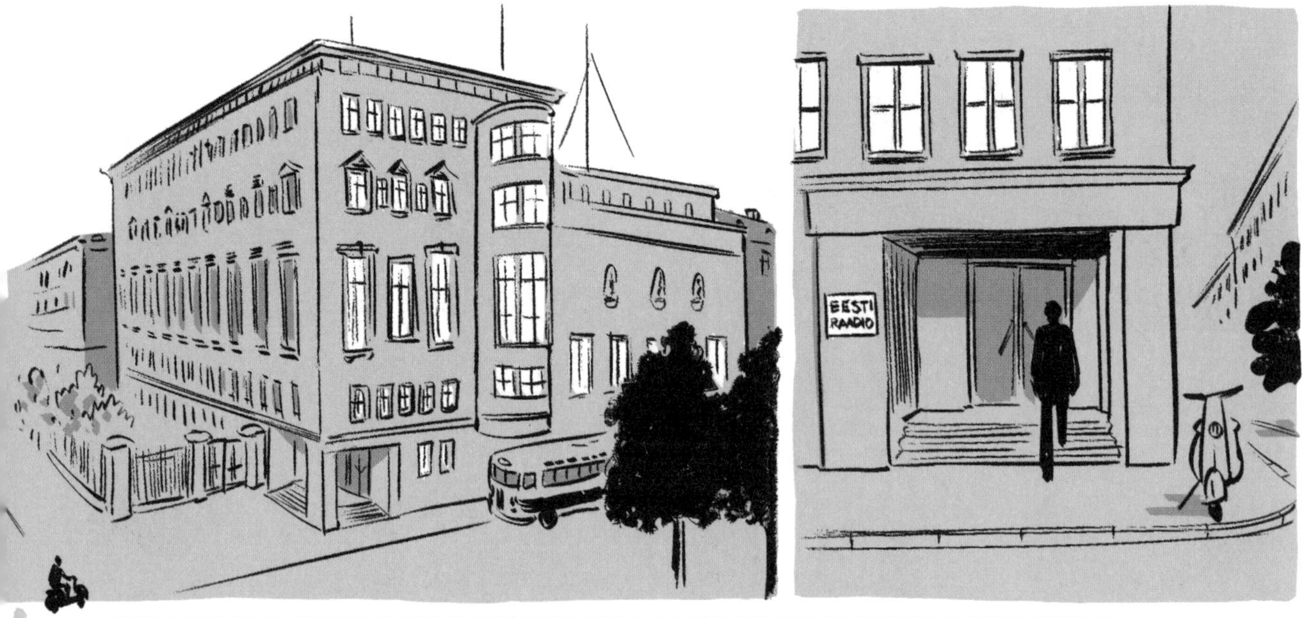

EESTI RAADIO

MANY YOUNG COMPOSERS END UP HERE AT SOME POINT. ARVO HAS PASSED THE TEST AND RECEIVED AN ENVIED POSITION ...

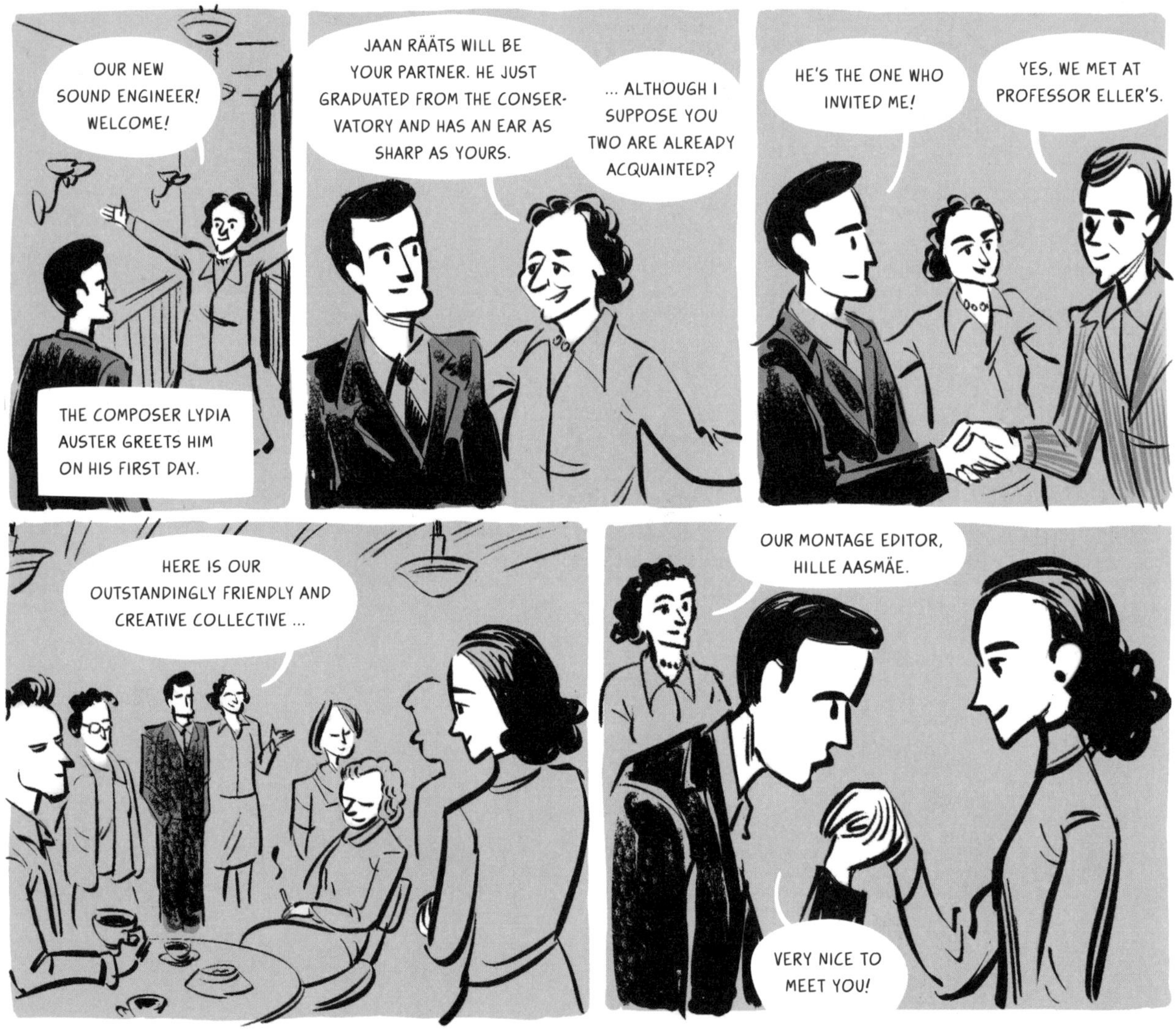

OUR NEW SOUND ENGINEER! WELCOME!
THE COMPOSER LYDIA AUSTER GREETS HIM ON HIS FIRST DAY.
JAAN RÄÄTS WILL BE YOUR PARTNER. HE JUST GRADUATED FROM THE CONSERVATORY AND HAS AN EAR AS SHARP AS YOURS.
... ALTHOUGH I SUPPOSE YOU TWO ARE ALREADY ACQUAINTED?
HE'S THE ONE WHO INVITED ME!
YES, WE MET AT PROFESSOR ELLER'S.
HERE IS OUR OUTSTANDINGLY FRIENDLY AND CREATIVE COLLECTIVE ...
OUR MONTAGE EDITOR, HILLE AASMÄE.
VERY NICE TO MEET YOU!

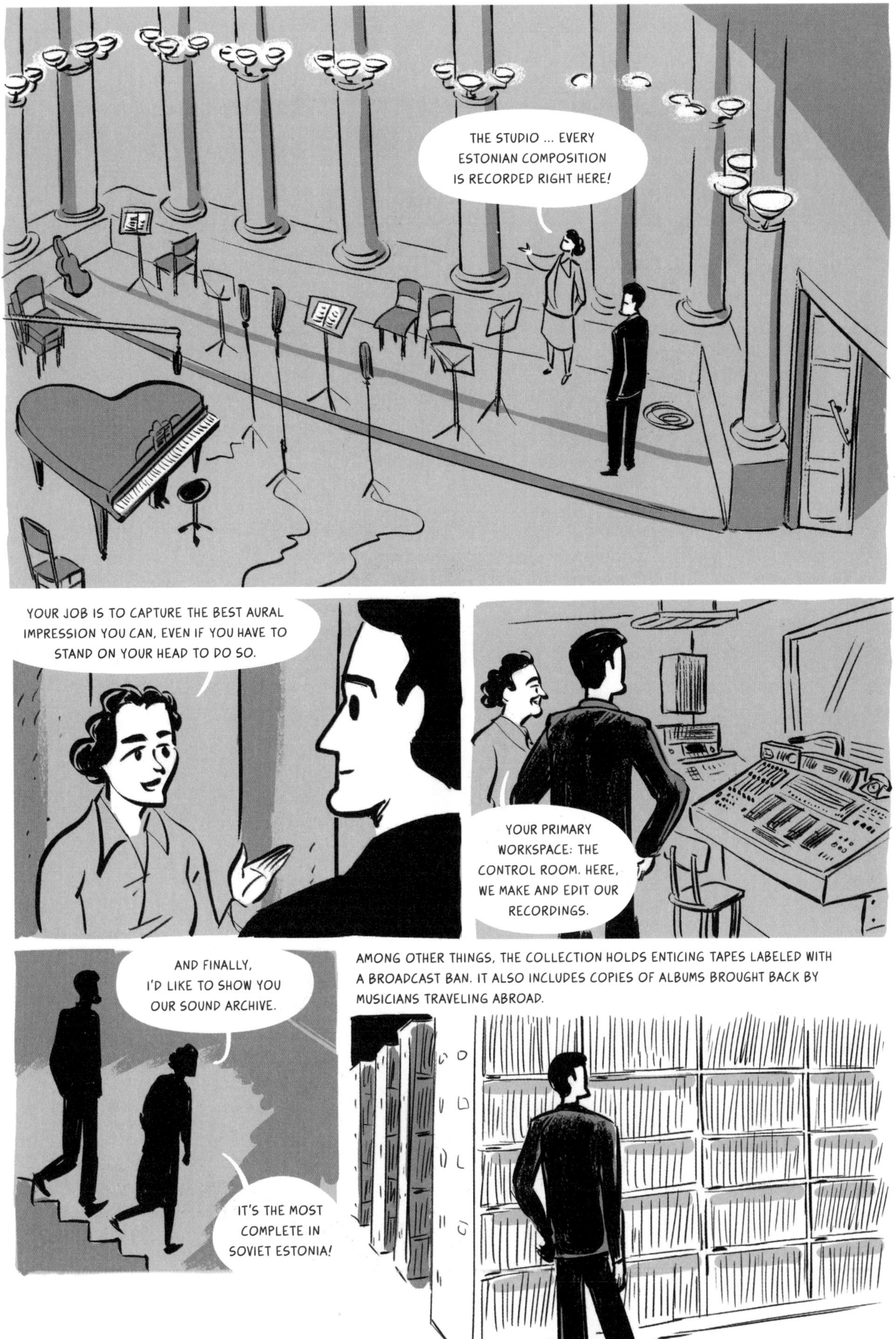
THE STUDIO ... EVERY ESTONIAN COMPOSITION IS RECORDED RIGHT HERE!
YOUR JOB IS TO CAPTURE THE BEST AURAL IMPRESSION YOU CAN, EVEN IF YOU HAVE TO STAND ON YOUR HEAD TO DO SO.
YOUR PRIMARY WORKSPACE: THE CONTROL ROOM. HERE, WE MAKE AND EDIT OUR RECORDINGS.
AND FINALLY, I'D LIKE TO SHOW YOU OUR SOUND ARCHIVE.
IT'S THE MOST COMPLETE IN SOVIET ESTONIA!
AMONG OTHER THINGS, THE COLLECTION HOLDS ENTICING TAPES LABELED WITH A BROADCAST BAN. IT ALSO INCLUDES COPIES OF ALBUMS BROUGHT BACK BY MUSICIANS TRAVELING ABROAD.

ACHIEVING IDEAL SOUND IN A RECORDING OFTEN TURNS OUT TO BE A COMPLICATED PROCESS.
ON HAND TO ASSIST IS MODERN RECORDING EQUIPMENT THAT ALLOWS SOUNDS TO BE FILTERED.
ARVO IS FACED WITH THE DILEMMA OF WHETHER OR NOT TO USE IT WHEN RECORDING HIS OWN PIECES.

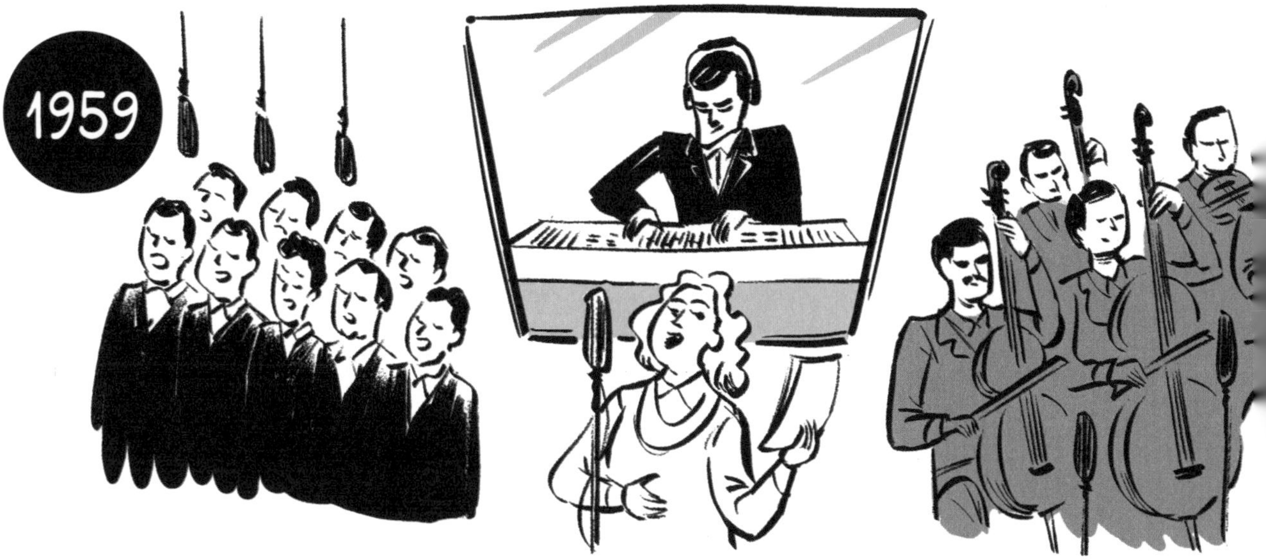
1959

FREE TIME CAN BE SPENT GETTING ACQUAINTED WITH THE RECORDING LIBRARY. SOMETIMES VERY LOUDLY!

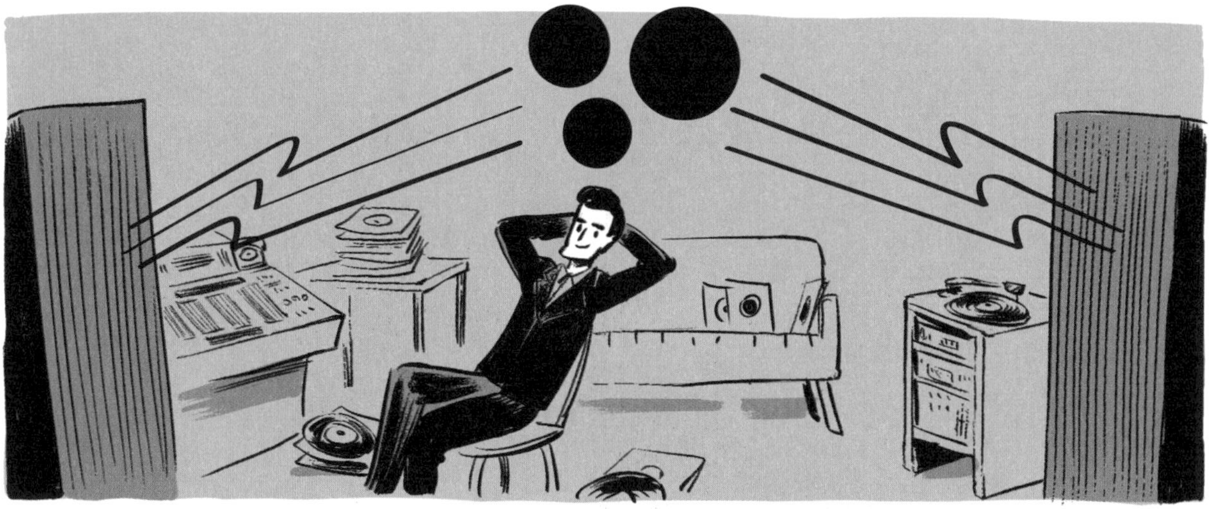

UNOCCUPIED SPACES IN THE RADIO HOUSE CAN ALSO BE USED FOR COMPOSING OR IMPROVISING. OR SIMPLY GETTING ACQUAINTED.

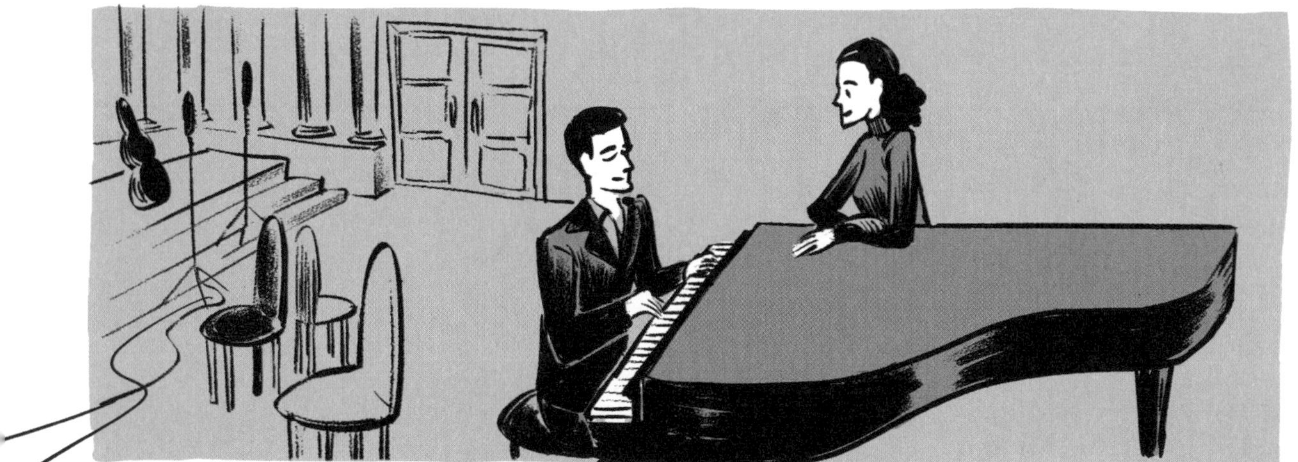

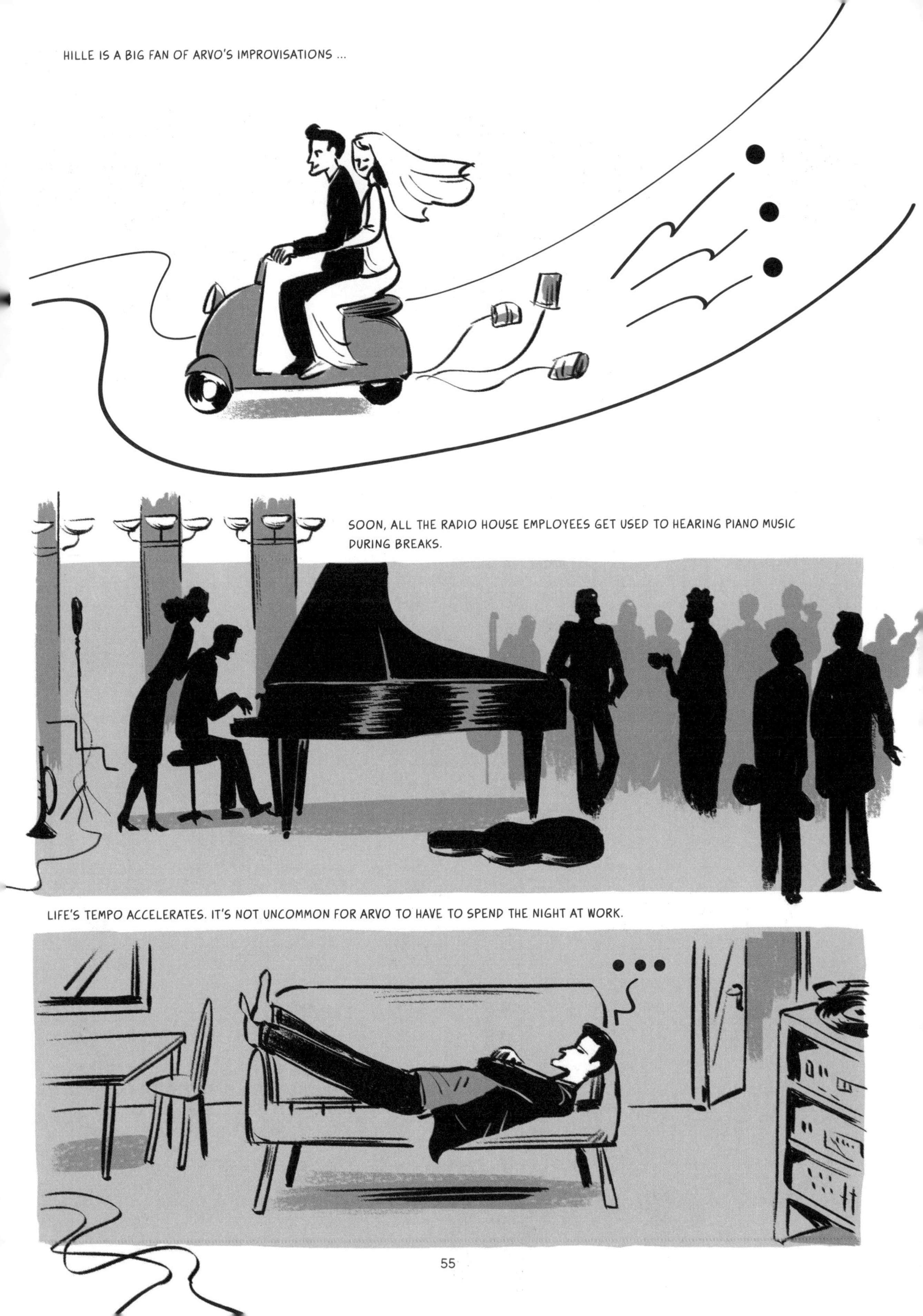
HILLE IS A BIG FAN OF ARVO'S IMPROVISATIONS ...
SOON, ALL THE RADIO HOUSE EMPLOYEES GET USED TO HEARING PIANO MUSIC DURING BREAKS.
LIFE'S TEMPO ACCELERATES. IT'S NOT UNCOMMON FOR ARVO TO HAVE TO SPEND THE NIGHT AT WORK.

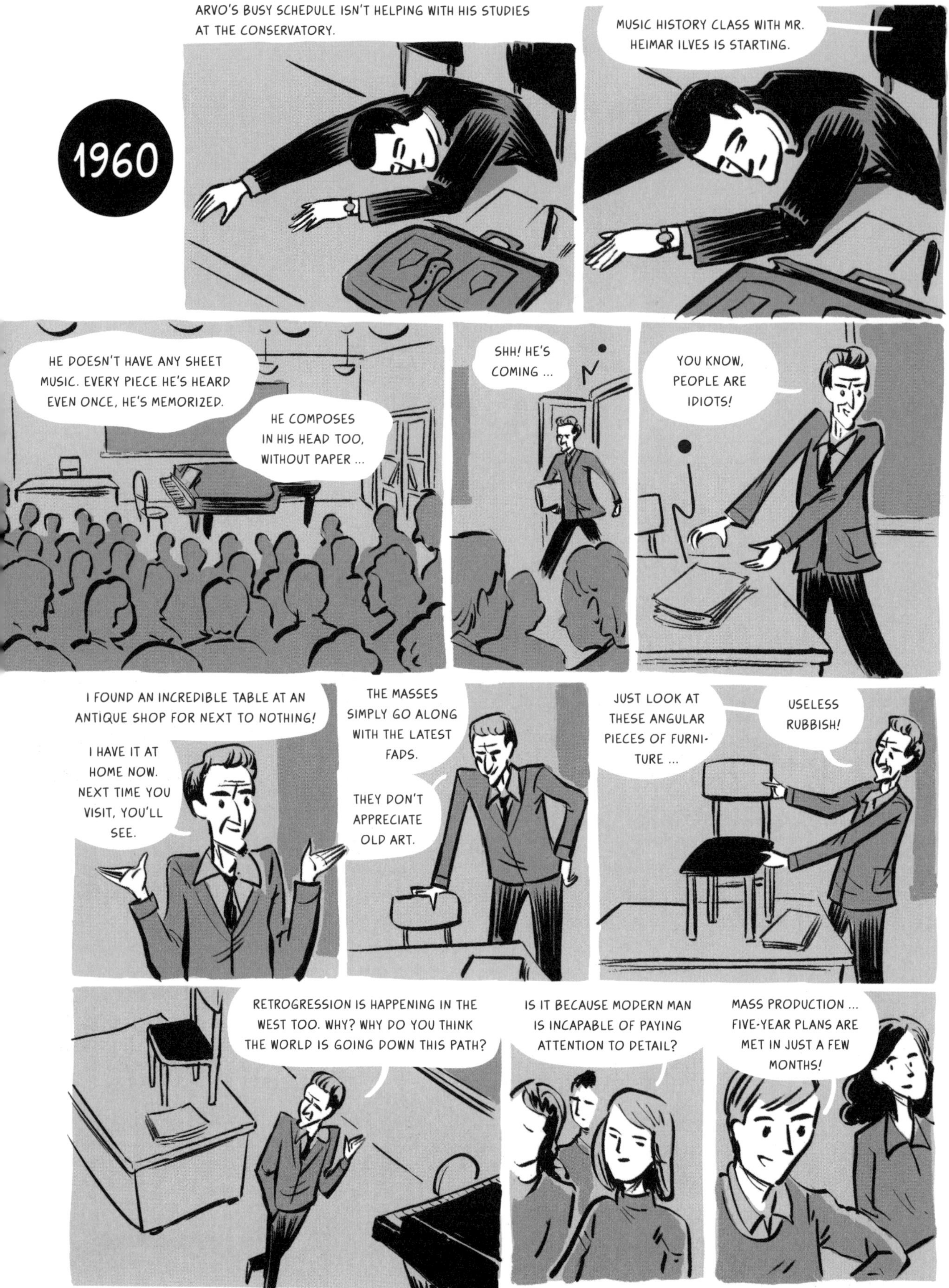
1960
ARVO'S BUSY SCHEDULE ISN'T HELPING WITH HIS STUDIES AT THE CONSERVATORY.
MUSIC HISTORY CLASS WITH MR. HEIMAR ILVES IS STARTING.
HE DOESN'T HAVE ANY SHEET MUSIC. EVERY PIECE HE'S HEARD EVEN ONCE, HE'S MEMORIZED.
HE COMPOSES IN HIS HEAD TOO, WITHOUT PAPER ...
SHH! HE'S COMING ...
YOU KNOW, PEOPLE ARE IDIOTS!
I FOUND AN INCREDIBLE TABLE AT AN ANTIQUE SHOP FOR NEXT TO NOTHING!
I HAVE IT AT HOME NOW. NEXT TIME YOU VISIT, YOU'LL SEE.
THE MASSES SIMPLY GO ALONG WITH THE LATEST FADS.
THEY DON'T APPRECIATE OLD ART.
JUST LOOK AT THESE ANGULAR PIECES OF FURNI-TURE ...
USELESS RUBBISH!
RETROGRESSION IS HAPPENING IN THE WEST TOO. WHY? WHY DO YOU THINK THE WORLD IS GOING DOWN THIS PATH?
IS IT BECAUSE MODERN MAN IS INCAPABLE OF PAYING ATTENTION TO DETAIL?
MASS PRODUCTION ... FIVE-YEAR PLANS ARE MET IN JUST A FEW MONTHS!

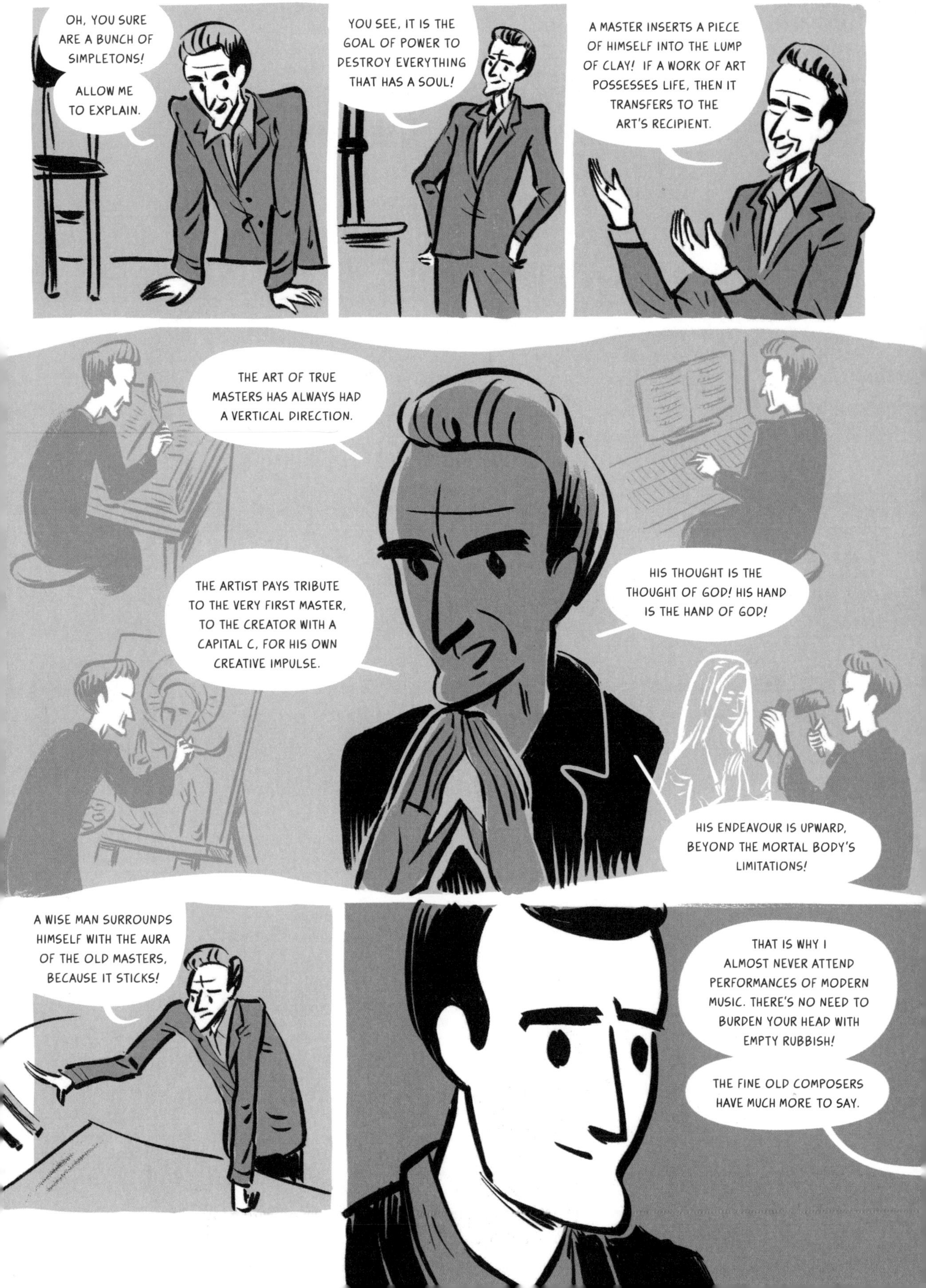
OH, YOU SURE ARE A BUNCH OF SIMPLETONS!
ALLOW ME TO EXPLAIN.
YOU SEE, IT IS THE GOAL OF POWER TO DESTROY EVERYTHING THAT HAS A SOUL!
A MASTER INSERTS A PIECE OF HIMSELF INTO THE LUMP OF CLAY! IF A WORK OF ART POSSESSES LIFE, THEN IT TRANSFERS TO THE ART'S RECIPIENT.
THE ART OF TRUE MASTERS HAS ALWAYS HAD A VERTICAL DIRECTION.
THE ARTIST PAYS TRIBUTE TO THE VERY FIRST MASTER, TO THE CREATOR WITH A CAPITAL C, FOR HIS OWN CREATIVE IMPULSE.
HIS THOUGHT IS THE THOUGHT OF GOD! HIS HAND IS THE HAND OF GOD!
HIS ENDEAVOUR IS UPWARD, BEYOND THE MORTAL BODY'S LIMITATIONS!
A WISE MAN SURROUNDS HIMSELF WITH THE AURA OF THE OLD MASTERS, BECAUSE IT STICKS!
THAT IS WHY I ALMOST NEVER ATTEND PERFORMANCES OF MODERN MUSIC. THERE'S NO NEED TO BURDEN YOUR HEAD WITH EMPTY RUBBISH!
THE FINE OLD COMPOSERS HAVE MUCH MORE TO SAY.

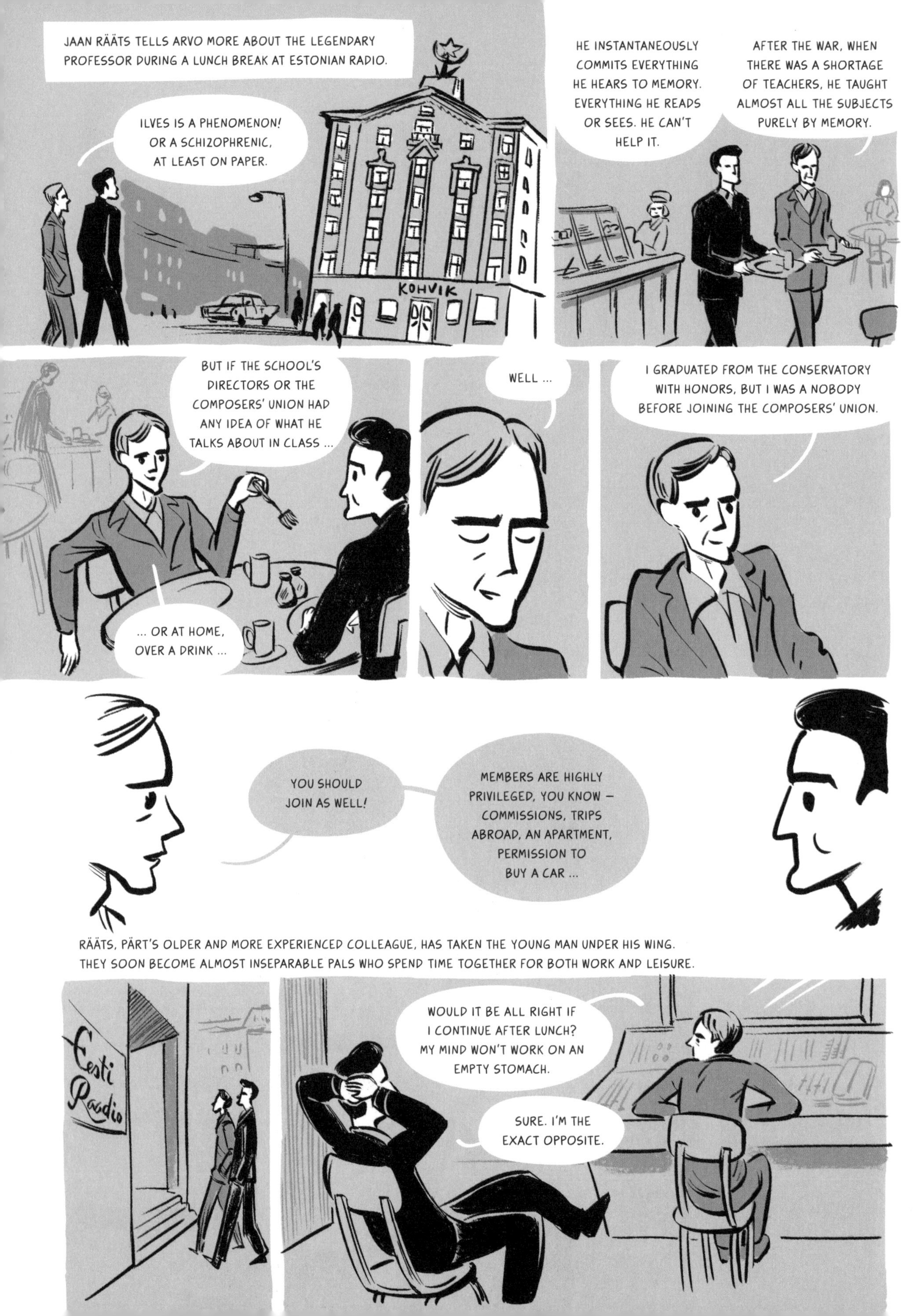
JAAN RÄÄTS TELLS ARVO MORE ABOUT THE LEGENDARY PROFESSOR DURING A LUNCH BREAK AT ESTONIAN RADIO.
ILVES IS A PHENOMENON! OR A SCHIZOPHRENIC, AT LEAST ON PAPER.
KOHVIK
HE INSTANTANEOUSLY COMMITS EVERYTHING HE HEARS TO MEMORY. EVERYTHING HE READS OR SEES. HE CAN'T HELP IT.
AFTER THE WAR, WHEN THERE WAS A SHORTAGE OF TEACHERS, HE TAUGHT ALMOST ALL THE SUBJECTS PURELY BY MEMORY.
BUT IF THE SCHOOL'S DIRECTORS OR THE COMPOSERS' UNION HAD ANY IDEA OF WHAT HE TALKS ABOUT IN CLASS ...
... OR AT HOME, OVER A DRINK ...
WELL ...
I GRADUATED FROM THE CONSERVATORY WITH HONORS, BUT I WAS A NOBODY BEFORE JOINING THE COMPOSERS' UNION.
YOU SHOULD JOIN AS WELL!
MEMBERS ARE HIGHLY PRIVILEGED, YOU KNOW – COMMISSIONS, TRIPS ABROAD, AN APARTMENT, PERMISSION TO BUY A CAR ...
RÄÄTS, PÄRT'S OLDER AND MORE EXPERIENCED COLLEAGUE, HAS TAKEN THE YOUNG MAN UNDER HIS WING. THEY SOON BECOME ALMOST INSEPARABLE PALS WHO SPEND TIME TOGETHER FOR BOTH WORK AND LEISURE.
Eesti Raadio
WOULD IT BE ALL RIGHT IF I CONTINUE AFTER LUNCH? MY MIND WON'T WORK ON AN EMPTY STOMACH.
SURE. I'M THE EXACT OPPOSITE.

BENEATH THE TALLINN ART HOUSE IS THE LEGENDARY KUKU CLUB, WHERE CONVERSATION USUALLY BUZZES TILL THE MORNING HOURS.

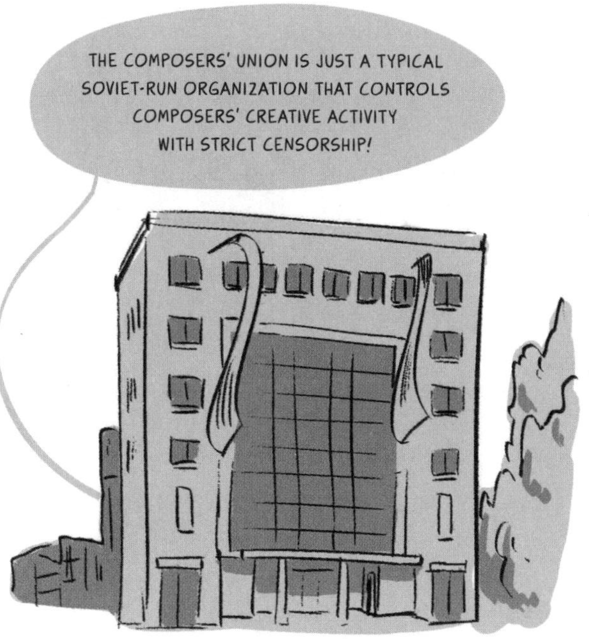
THE COMPOSERS' UNION IS JUST A TYPICAL SOVIET-RUN ORGANIZATION THAT CONTROLS COMPOSERS' CREATIVE ACTIVITY WITH STRICT CENSORSHIP!

THE TERM "UNDERGROUND" IS QUITE LITERAL, AS THE CLUB IS RUN IN A CELLAR SPACE.

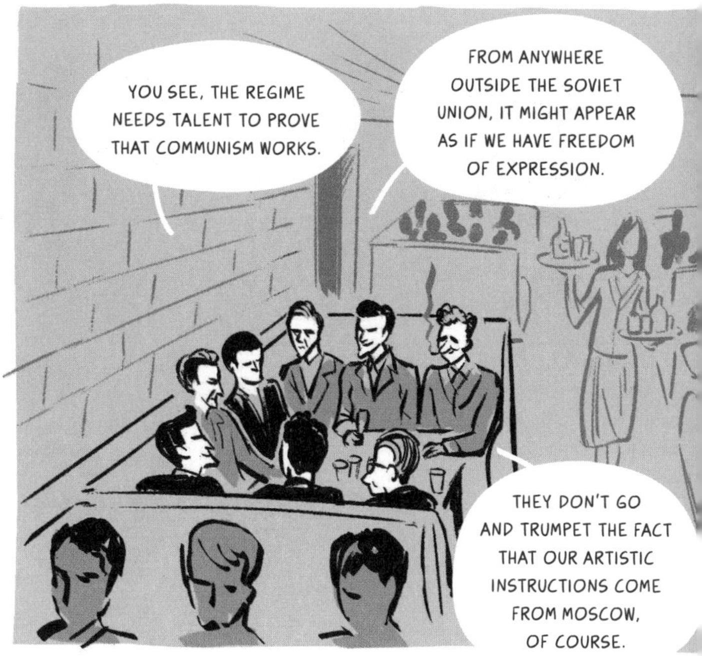
YOU SEE, THE REGIME NEEDS TALENT TO PROVE THAT COMMUNISM WORKS.
FROM ANYWHERE OUTSIDE THE SOVIET UNION, IT MIGHT APPEAR AS IF WE HAVE FREEDOM OF EXPRESSION.
THEY DON'T GO AND TRUMPET THE FACT THAT OUR ARTISTIC INSTRUCTIONS COME FROM MOSCOW, OF COURSE.

THE CLUB IS FREQUENTED BY ARTISTS, MUSICIANS, RESEARCHERS ...
IT IS LIKE A STATE WITHIN A STATE, WHERE FREEDOM OF THOUGHT SMOLDERS BENEATH THE ASHES.

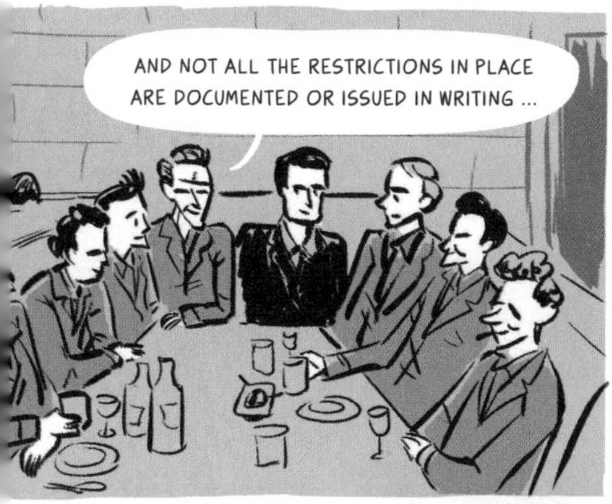
AND NOT ALL THE RESTRICTIONS IN PLACE ARE DOCUMENTED OR ISSUED IN WRITING ...

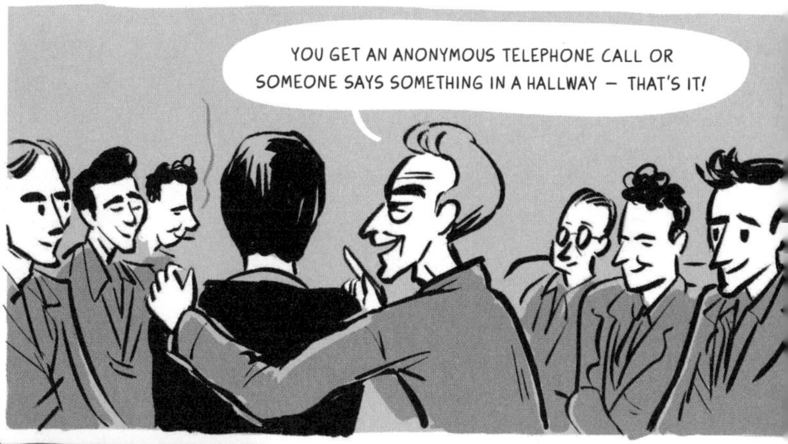
YOU GET AN ANONYMOUS TELEPHONE CALL OR SOMEONE SAYS SOMETHING IN A HALLWAY – THAT'S IT!

ARVO HAS BEEN WELCOMED HERE WARMLY TOO.

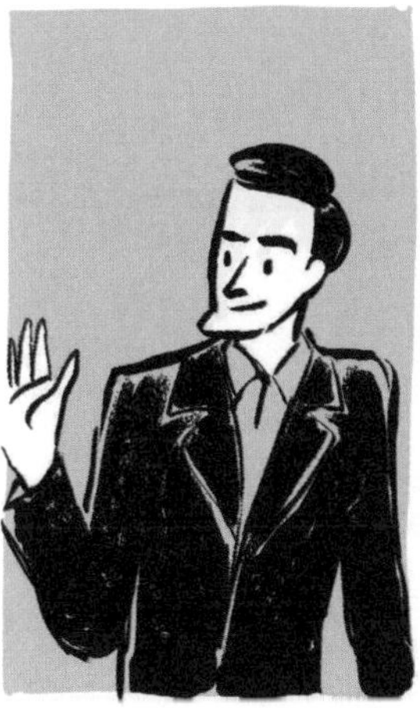

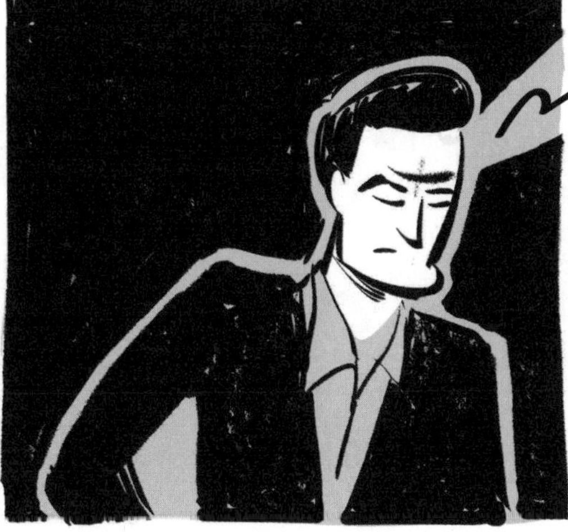

FEW ARE AWARE THAT INCREASINGLY ACUTE KIDNEY PAINS SOUR THE YOUNG STUDENT'S DAYS.

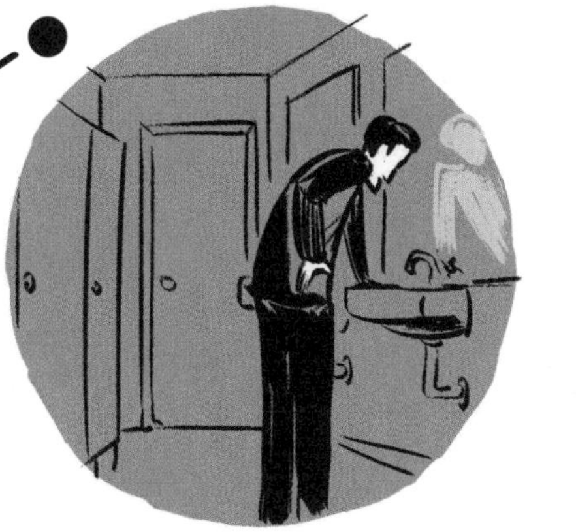

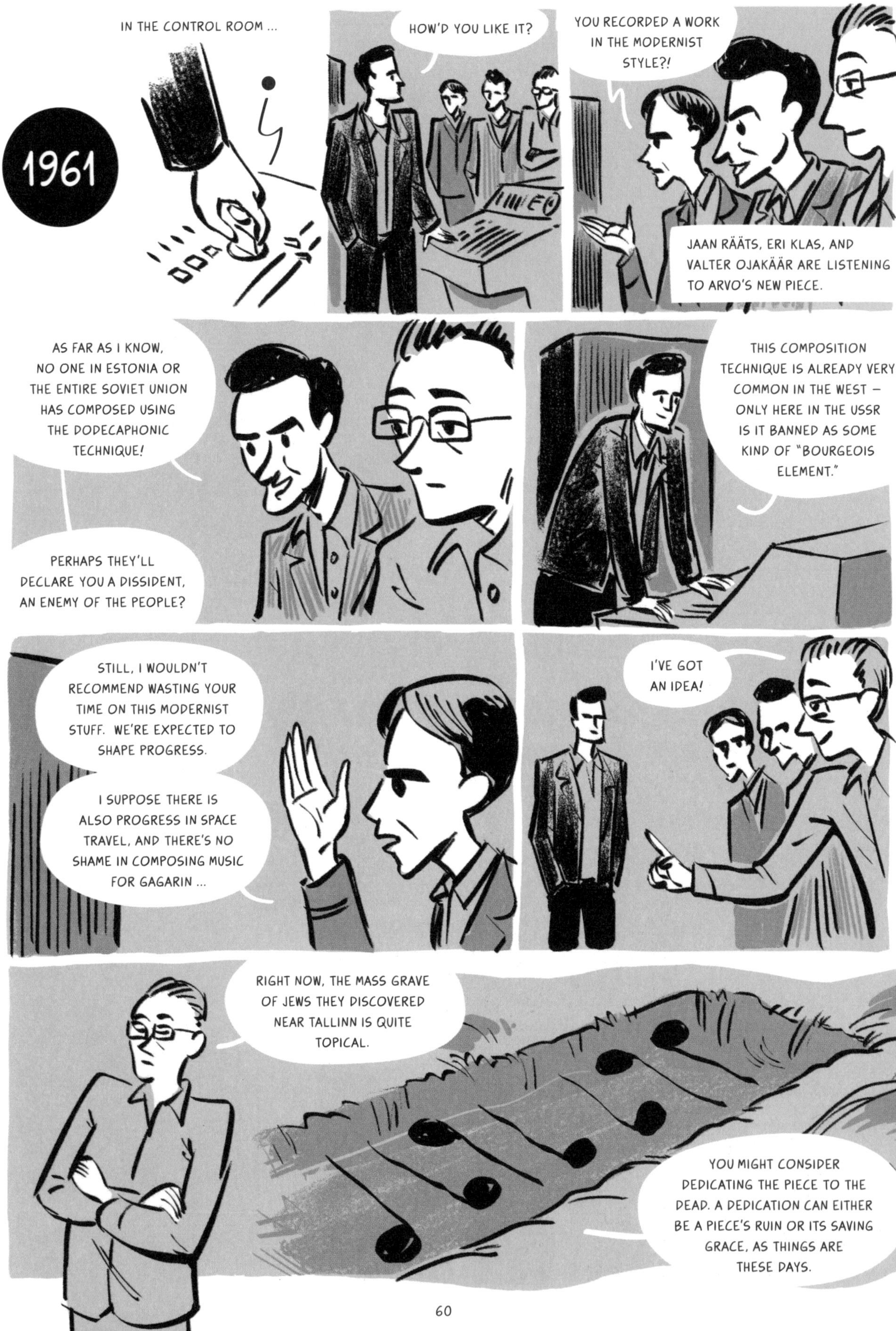
1961
IN THE CONTROL ROOM ...
HOW'D YOU LIKE IT?
YOU RECORDED A WORK IN THE MODERNIST STYLE?!
JAAN RÄÄTS, ERI KLAS, AND VALTER OJAKÄÄR ARE LISTENING TO ARVO'S NEW PIECE.
AS FAR AS I KNOW, NO ONE IN ESTONIA OR THE ENTIRE SOVIET UNION HAS COMPOSED USING THE DODECAPHONIC TECHNIQUE!
PERHAPS THEY'LL DECLARE YOU A DISSIDENT, AN ENEMY OF THE PEOPLE?
THIS COMPOSITION TECHNIQUE IS ALREADY VERY COMMON IN THE WEST – ONLY HERE IN THE USSR IS IT BANNED AS SOME KIND OF "BOURGEOIS ELEMENT."
STILL, I WOULDN'T RECOMMEND WASTING YOUR TIME ON THIS MODERNIST STUFF. WE'RE EXPECTED TO SHAPE PROGRESS.
I SUPPOSE THERE IS ALSO PROGRESS IN SPACE TRAVEL, AND THERE'S NO SHAME IN COMPOSING MUSIC FOR GAGARIN ...
I'VE GOT AN IDEA!
RIGHT NOW, THE MASS GRAVE OF JEWS THEY DISCOVERED NEAR TALLINN IS QUITE TOPICAL.
YOU MIGHT CONSIDER DEDICATING THE PIECE TO THE DEAD. A DEDICATION CAN EITHER BE A PIECE'S RUIN OR ITS SAVING GRACE, AS THINGS ARE THESE DAYS.

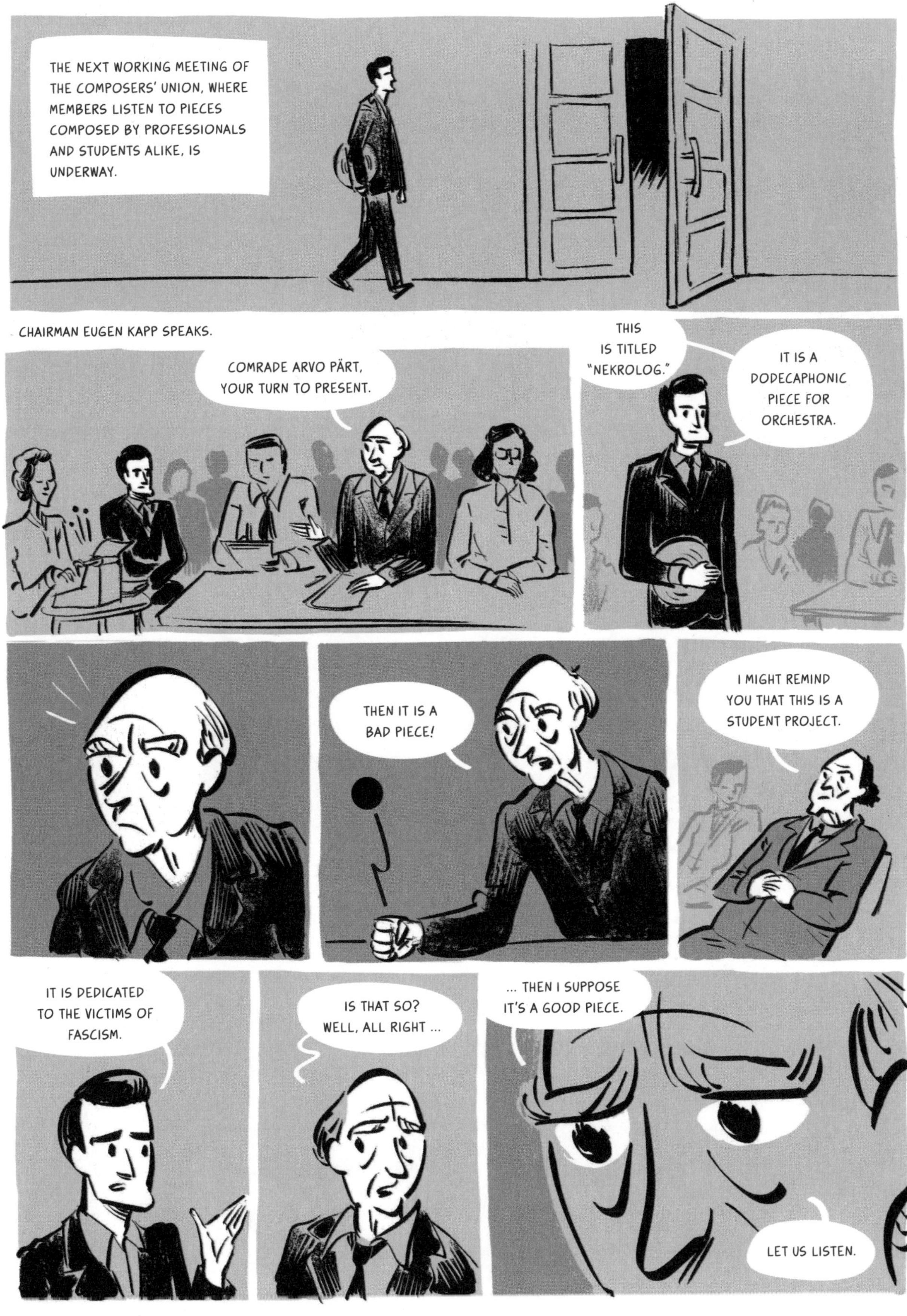
THE NEXT WORKING MEETING OF THE COMPOSERS' UNION, WHERE MEMBERS LISTEN TO PIECES COMPOSED BY PROFESSIONALS AND STUDENTS ALIKE, IS UNDERWAY.
CHAIRMAN EUGEN KAPP SPEAKS.
COMRADE ARVO PÄRT, YOUR TURN TO PRESENT.
THIS IS TITLED "NEKROLOG."
IT IS A DODECAPHONIC PIECE FOR ORCHESTRA.
THEN IT IS A BAD PIECE!
I MIGHT REMIND YOU THAT THIS IS A STUDENT PROJECT.
IT IS DEDICATED TO THE VICTIMS OF FASCISM.
IS THAT SO? WELL, ALL RIGHT ...
... THEN I SUPPOSE IT'S A GOOD PIECE.
LET US LISTEN.

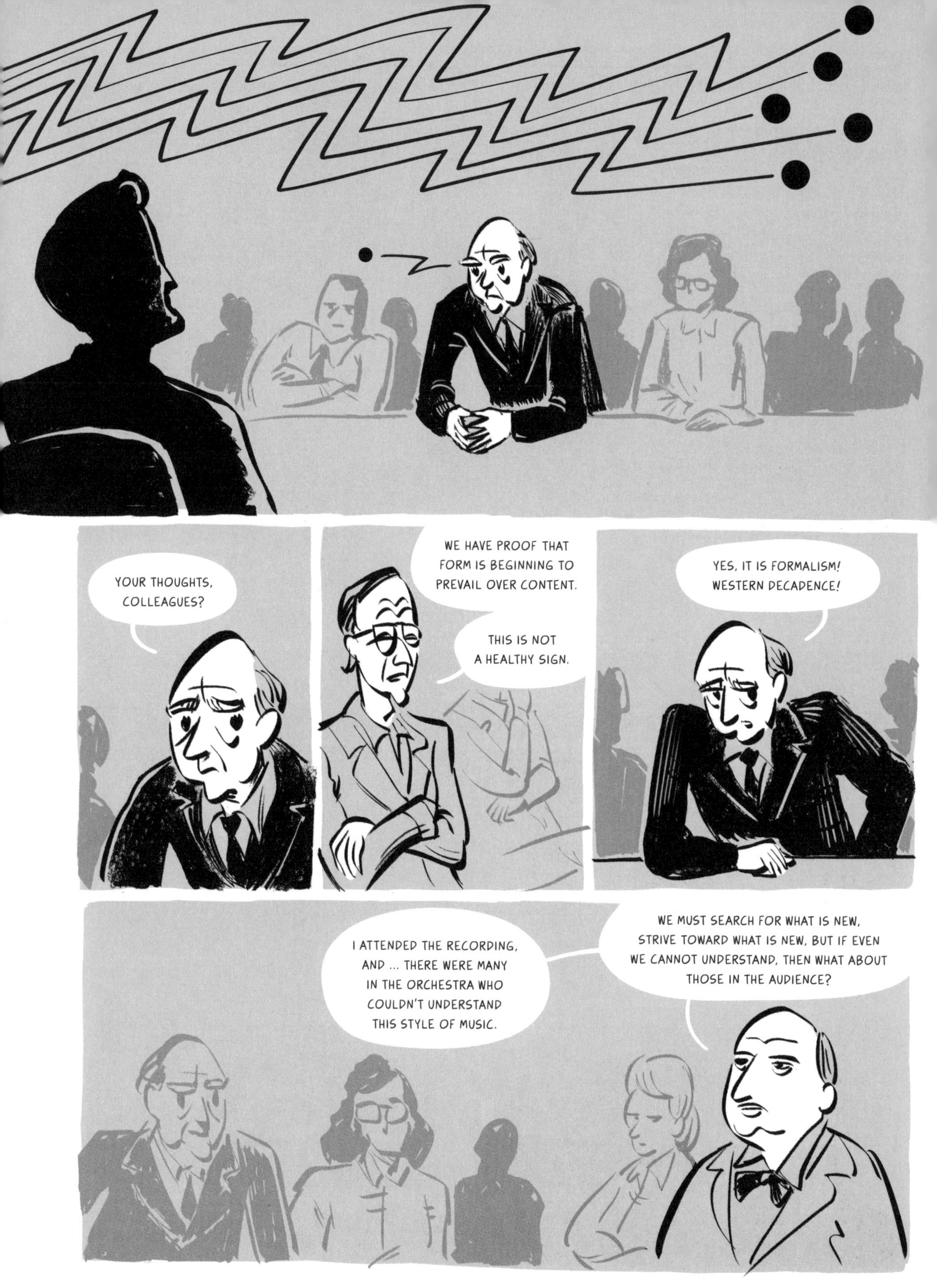
YOUR THOUGHTS, COLLEAGUES?
WE HAVE PROOF THAT FORM IS BEGINNING TO PREVAIL OVER CONTENT.
THIS IS NOT A HEALTHY SIGN.
YES, IT IS FORMALISM! WESTERN DECADENCE!
I ATTENDED THE RECORDING, AND ... THERE WERE MANY IN THE ORCHESTRA WHO COULDN'T UNDERSTAND THIS STYLE OF MUSIC.
WE MUST SEARCH FOR WHAT IS NEW, STRIVE TOWARD WHAT IS NEW, BUT IF EVEN WE CANNOT UNDERSTAND, THEN WHAT ABOUT THOSE IN THE AUDIENCE?

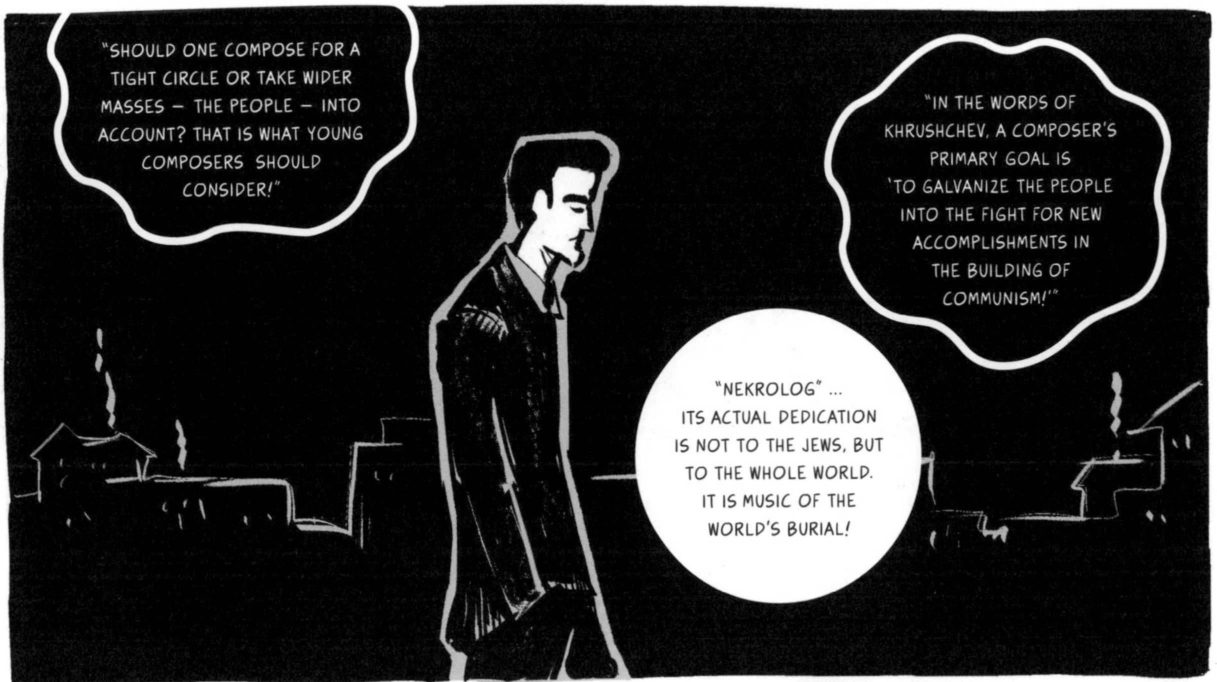
"SHOULD ONE COMPOSE FOR A TIGHT CIRCLE OR TAKE WIDER MASSES – THE PEOPLE – INTO ACCOUNT? THAT IS WHAT YOUNG COMPOSERS SHOULD CONSIDER!"
"IN THE WORDS OF KHRUSHCHEV, A COMPOSER'S PRIMARY GOAL IS 'TO GALVANIZE THE PEOPLE INTO THE FIGHT FOR NEW ACCOMPLISHMENTS IN THE BUILDING OF COMMUNISM!'"
"NEKROLOG" ... ITS ACTUAL DEDICATION IS NOT TO THE JEWS, BUT TO THE WHOLE WORLD. IT IS MUSIC OF THE WORLD'S BURIAL!

THE NEXT MEETING IS IN A WEEK'S TIME. HOW TO REACT?

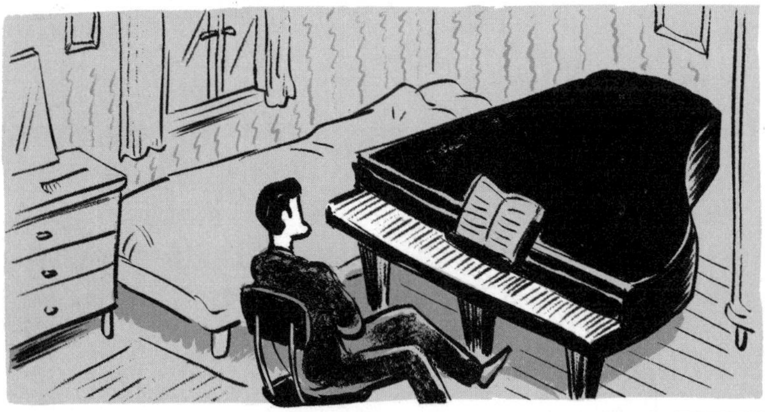

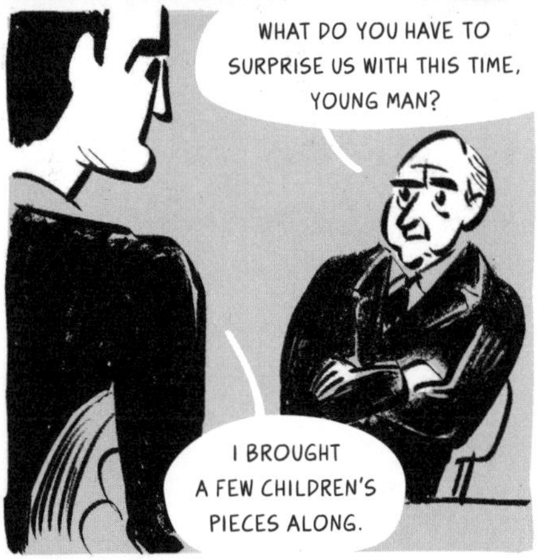
WHAT DO YOU HAVE TO SURPRISE US WITH THIS TIME, YOUNG MAN?
I BROUGHT A FEW CHILDREN'S PIECES ALONG.

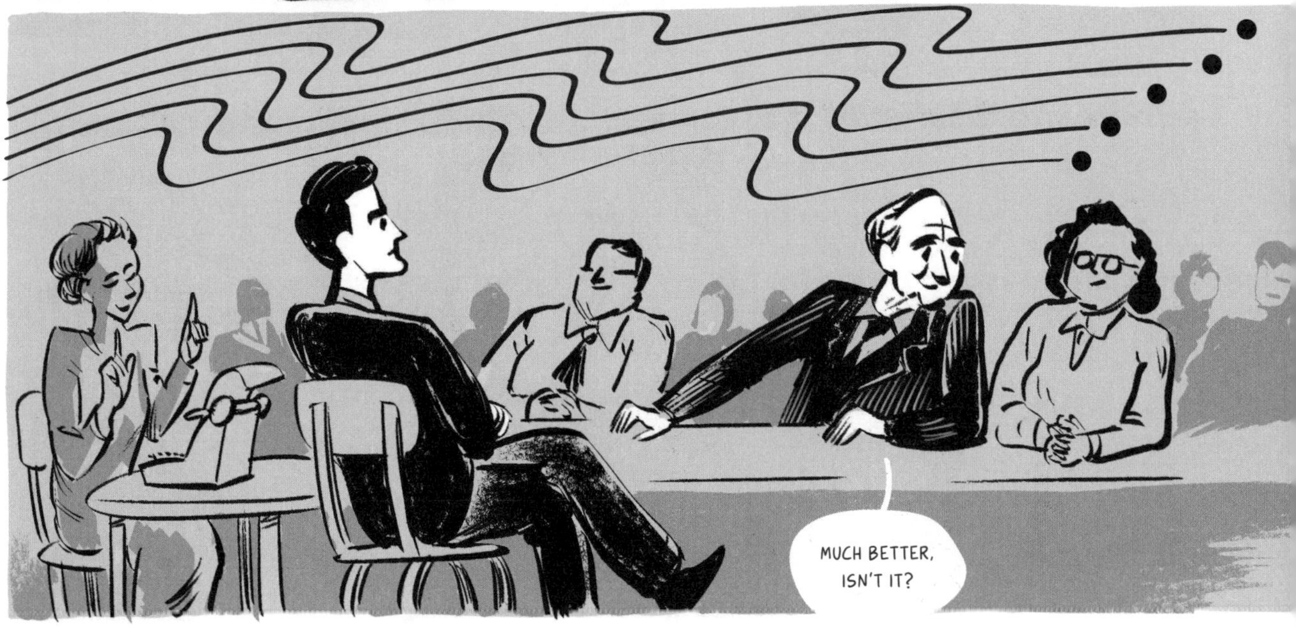
MUCH BETTER, ISN'T IT?

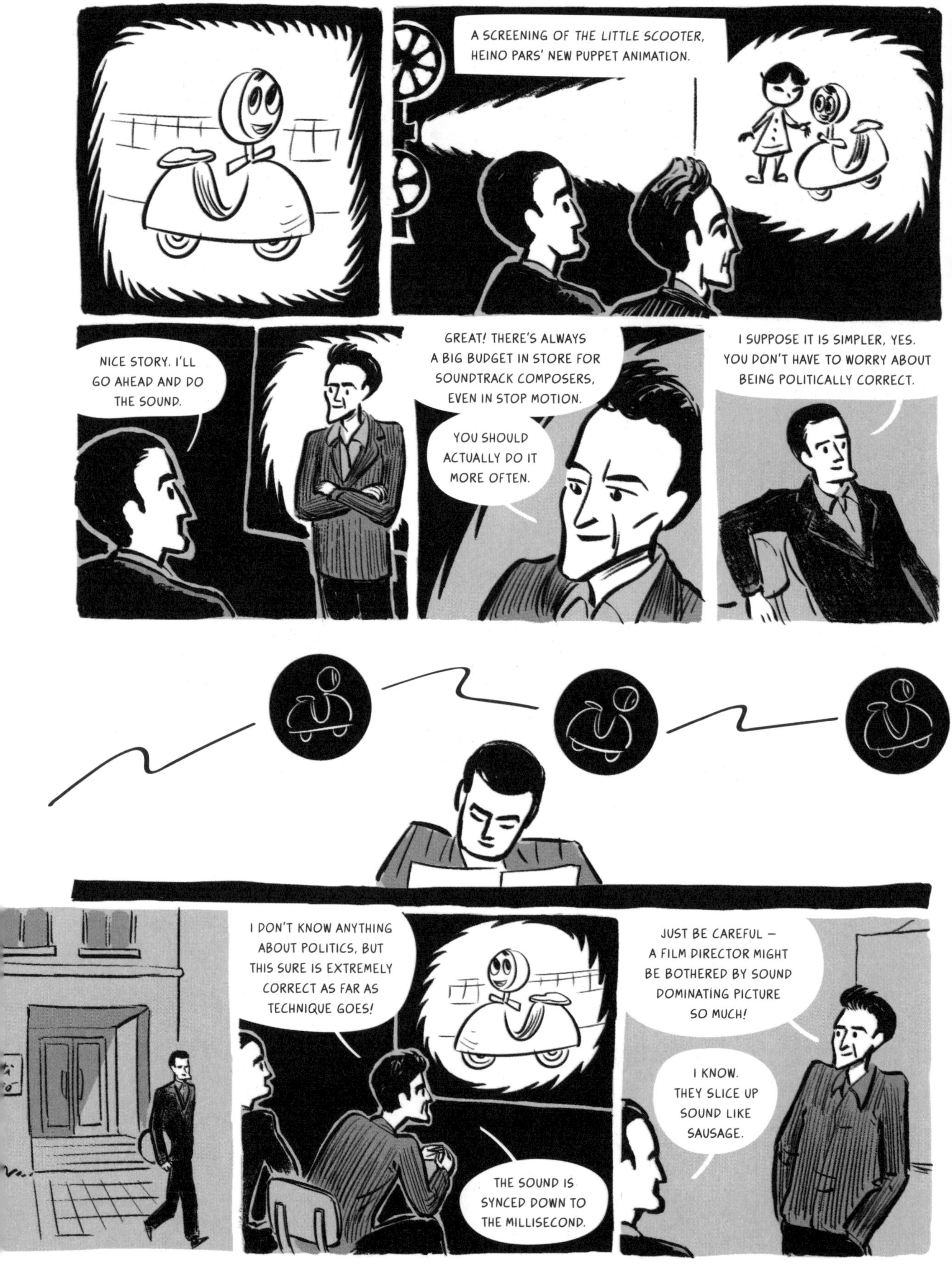

A SCREENING OF THE LITTLE SCOOTER, HEINO PARS' NEW PUPPET ANIMATION.
NICE STORY. I'LL GO AHEAD AND DO THE SOUND.
GREAT! THERE'S ALWAYS A BIG BUDGET IN STORE FOR SOUNDTRACK COMPOSERS, EVEN IN STOP MOTION.
YOU SHOULD ACTUALLY DO IT MORE OFTEN.
I SUPPOSE IT IS SIMPLER, YES. YOU DON'T HAVE TO WORRY ABOUT BEING POLITICALLY CORRECT.
I DON'T KNOW ANYTHING ABOUT POLITICS, BUT THIS SURE IS EXTREMELY CORRECT AS FAR AS TECHNIQUE GOES!
THE SOUND IS SYNCED DOWN TO THE MILLISECOND.
JUST BE CAREFUL – A FILM DIRECTOR MIGHT BE BOTHERED BY SOUND DOMINATING PICTURE SO MUCH!
I KNOW. THEY SLICE UP SOUND LIKE SAUSAGE.

IN ADDITION TO COMPOSING FOR ANIMATED FILMS, ARVO ENTERTAINS CHILDREN AT THE PIONEER PALACE WITH HIS PIANO ACCOMPANIMENT.

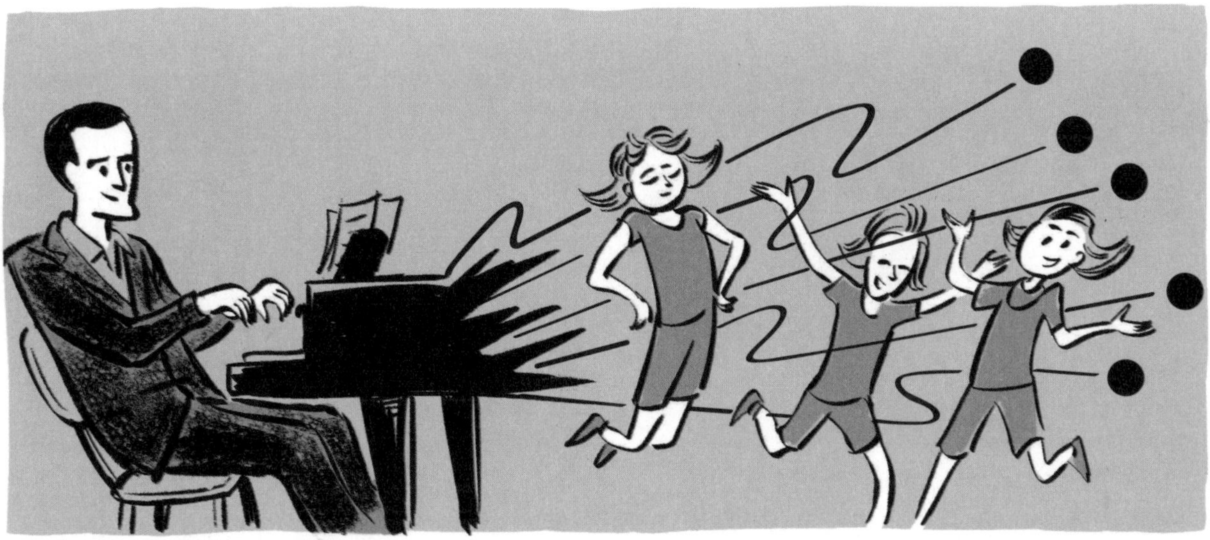

HE ALSO ACCOMPANIES THE ESTONIAN RADIO CHILDREN'S CHOIR ON PIANO, THOUGH IT'S NOT UNUSUAL FOR THEM TO SIMPLY HORSE AROUND ...

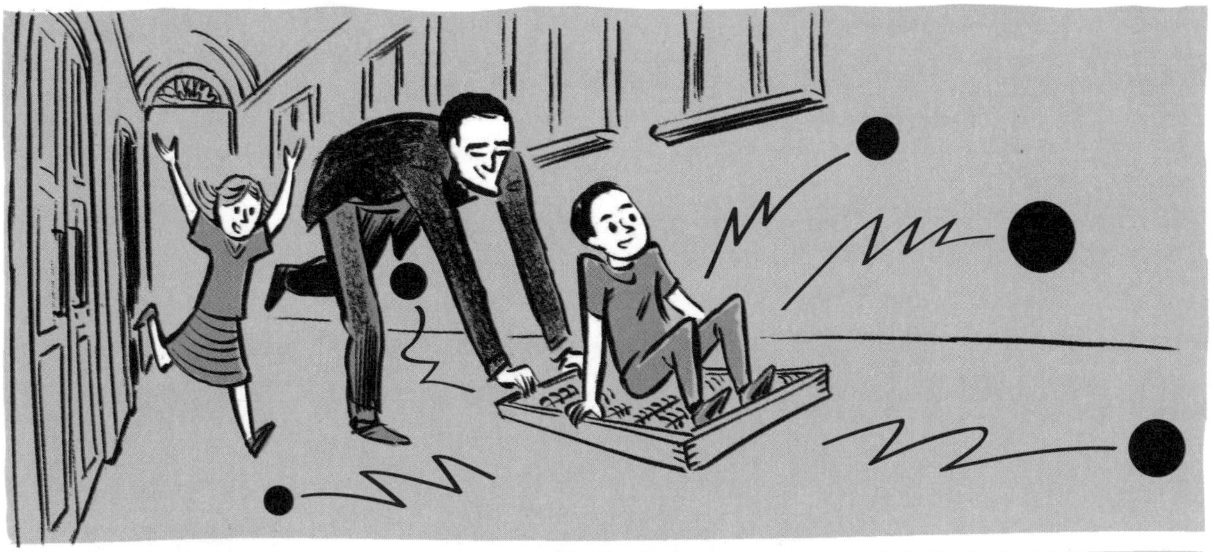

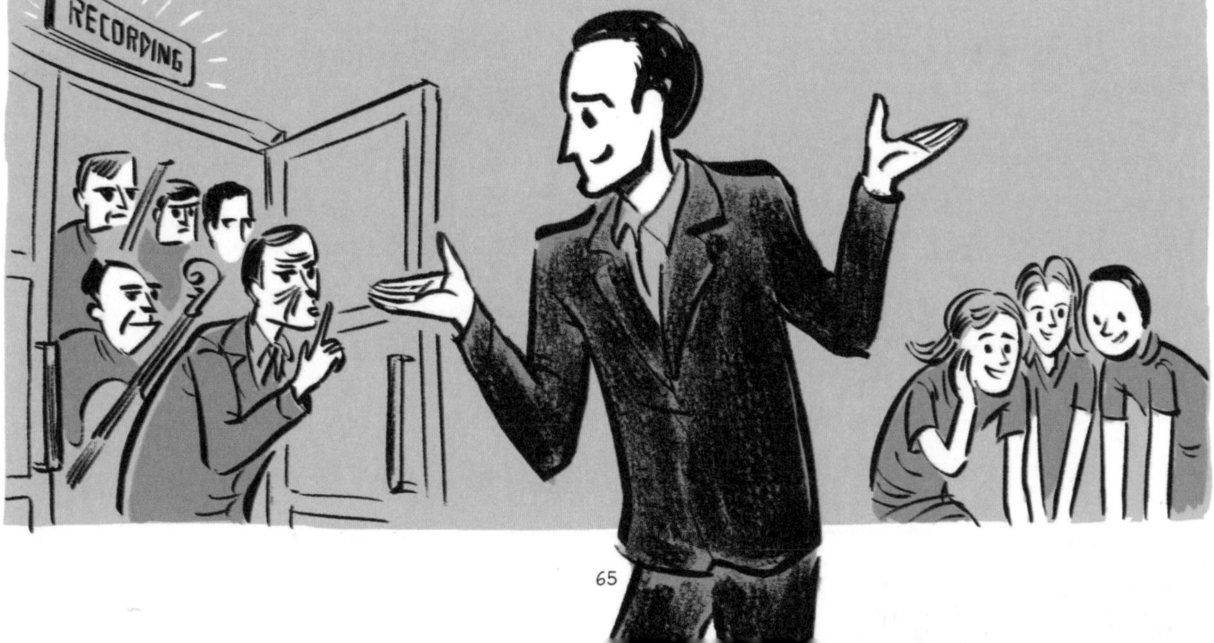
RECORDING

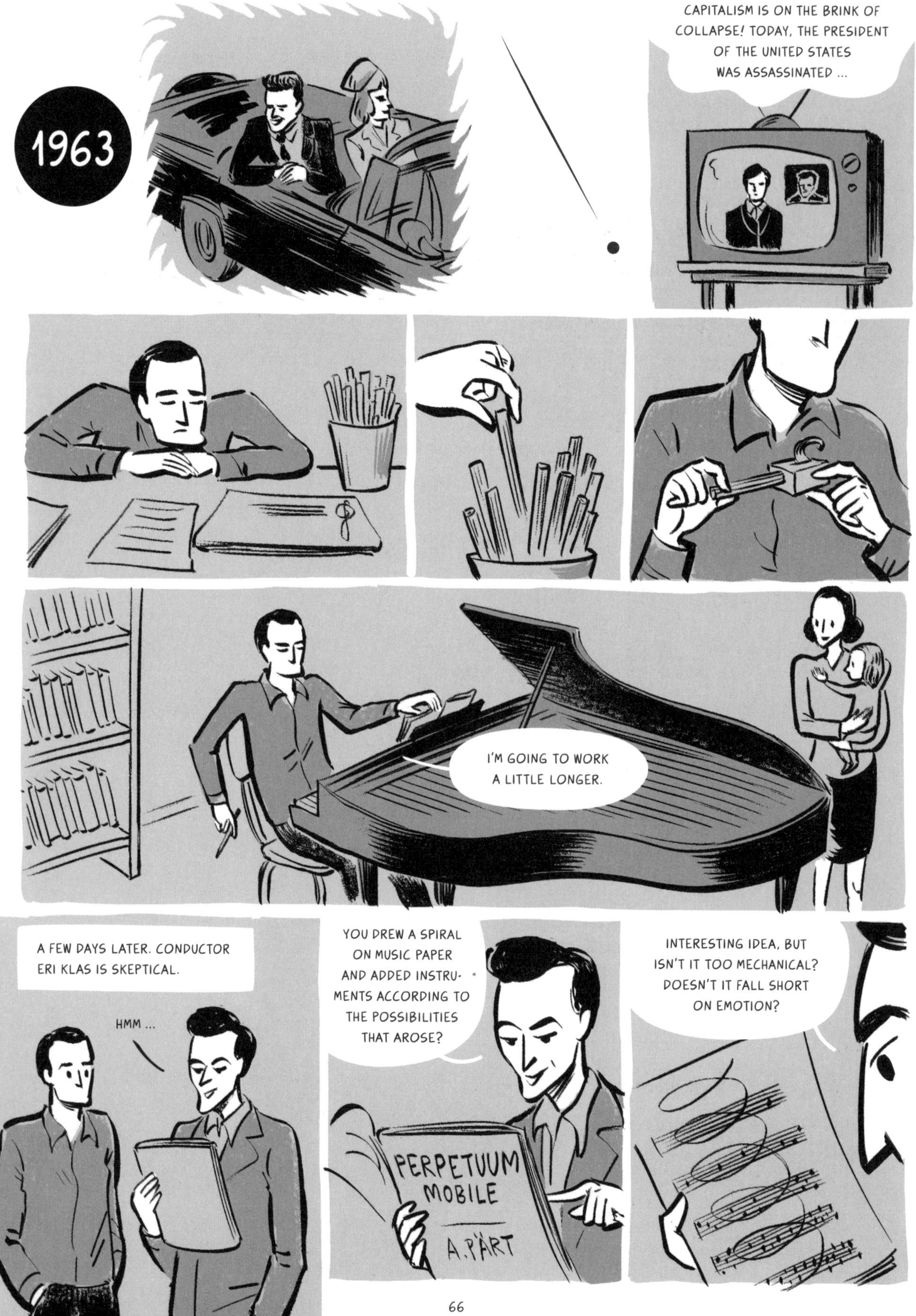
1963
CAPITALISM IS ON THE BRINK OF COLLAPSE! TODAY, THE PRESIDENT OF THE UNITED STATES WAS ASSASSINATED ...
I'M GOING TO WORK A LITTLE LONGER.
A FEW DAYS LATER. CONDUCTOR ERI KLAS IS SKEPTICAL.
HMM ...
YOU DREW A SPIRAL ON MUSIC PAPER AND ADDED INSTRUMENTS ACCORDING TO THE POSSIBILITIES THAT AROSE?
PERPETUUM MOBILE
A. PÄRT
INTERESTING IDEA, BUT ISN'T IT TOO MECHANICAL? DOESN'T IT FALL SHORT ON EMOTION?

ESTONIA CONCERT HALL. ARVO'S PREMIERE IS ON THE PROGRAM.
HE'S ALREADY ACHIEVED A CERTAIN LEVEL OF FAME, MOSTLY AMONG YOUNG LISTENERS.

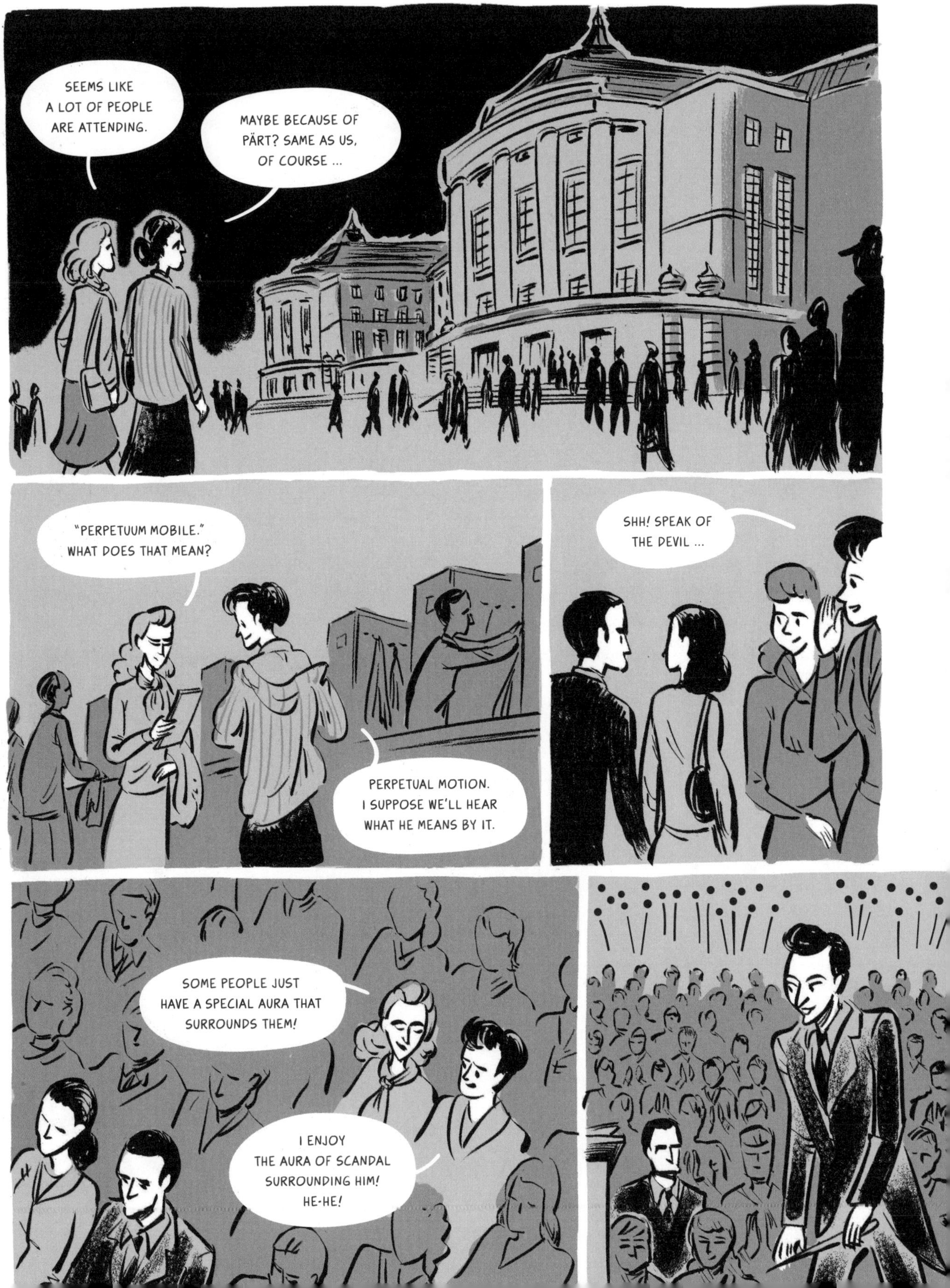
SEEMS LIKE A LOT OF PEOPLE ARE ATTENDING.
MAYBE BECAUSE OF PÄRT? SAME AS US, OF COURSE ...
"PERPETUUM MOBILE." WHAT DOES THAT MEAN?
PERPETUAL MOTION. I SUPPOSE WE'LL HEAR WHAT HE MEANS BY IT.
SHH! SPEAK OF THE DEVIL ...
SOME PEOPLE JUST HAVE A SPECIAL AURA THAT SURROUNDS THEM!
I ENJOY THE AURA OF SCANDAL SURROUNDING HIM! HE-HE!

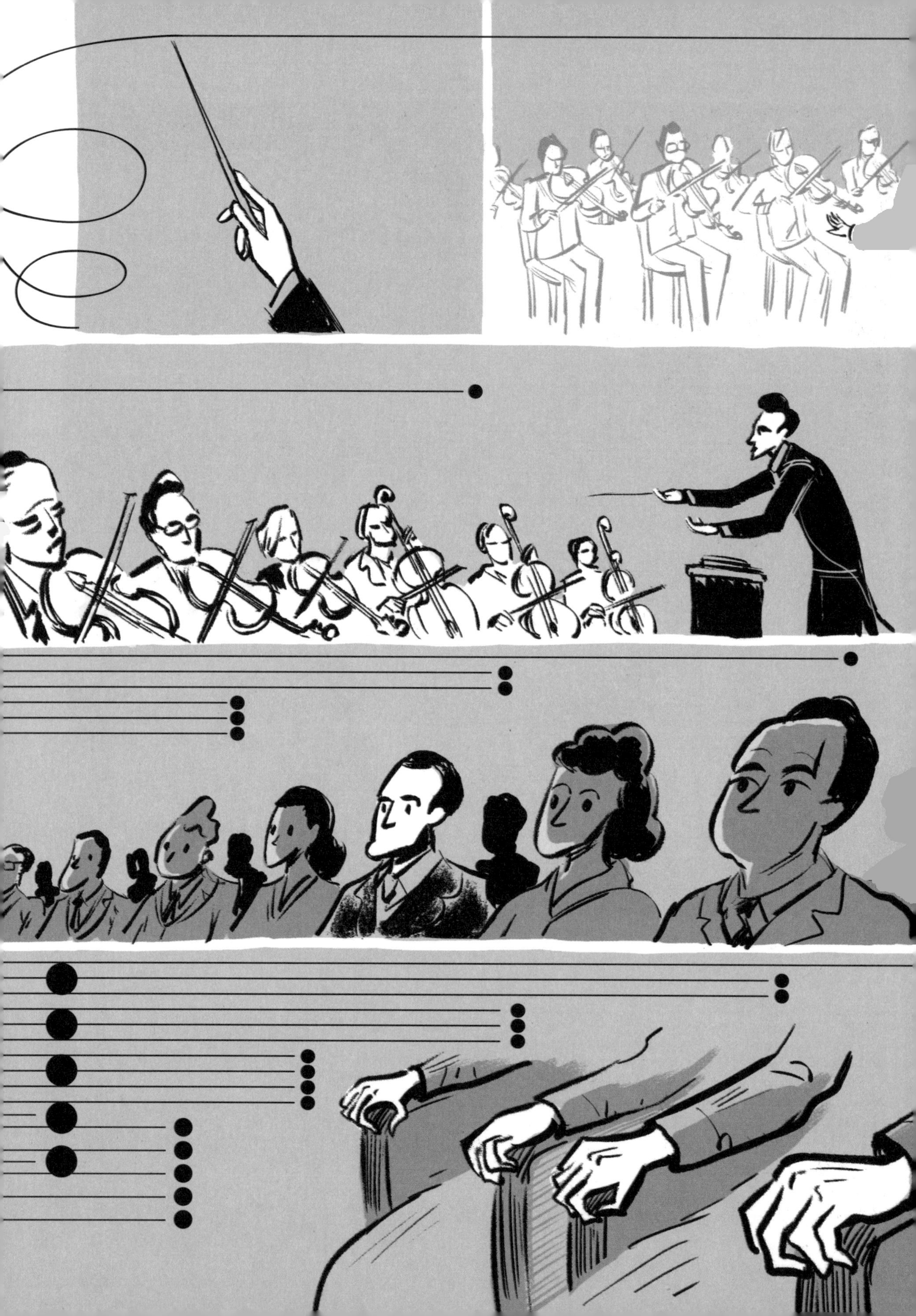

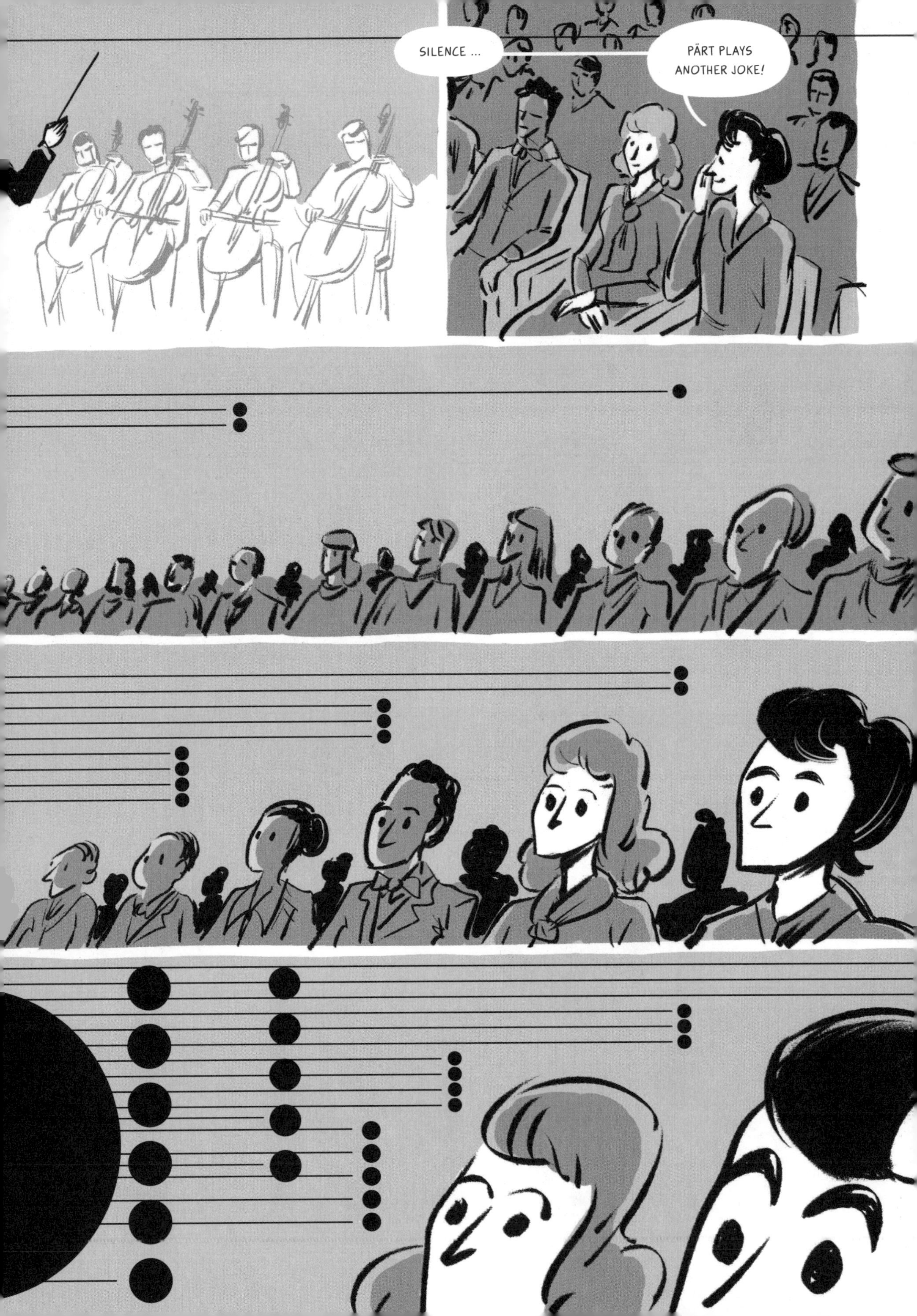
SILENCE ...
PÄRT PLAYS ANOTHER JOKE!

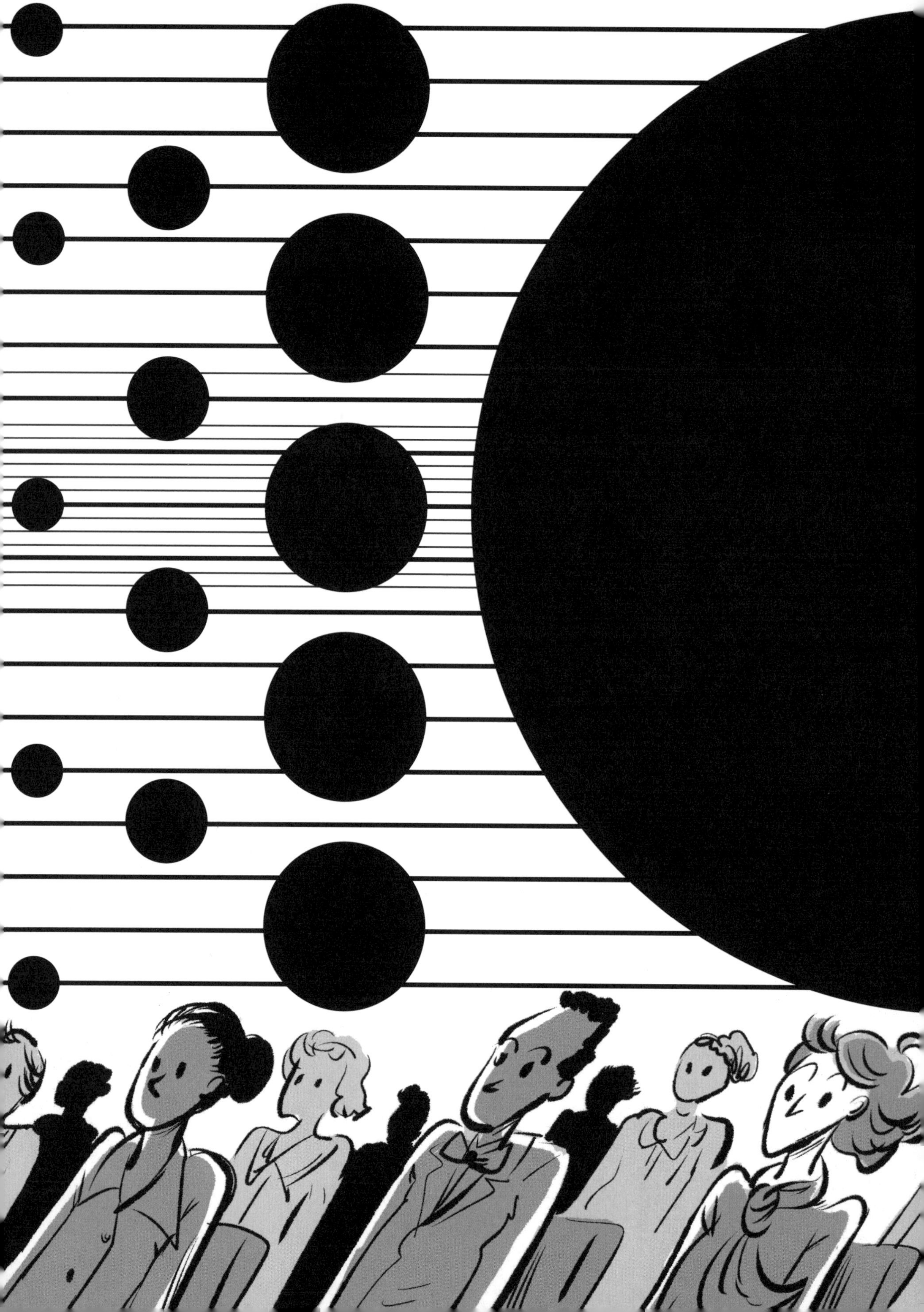

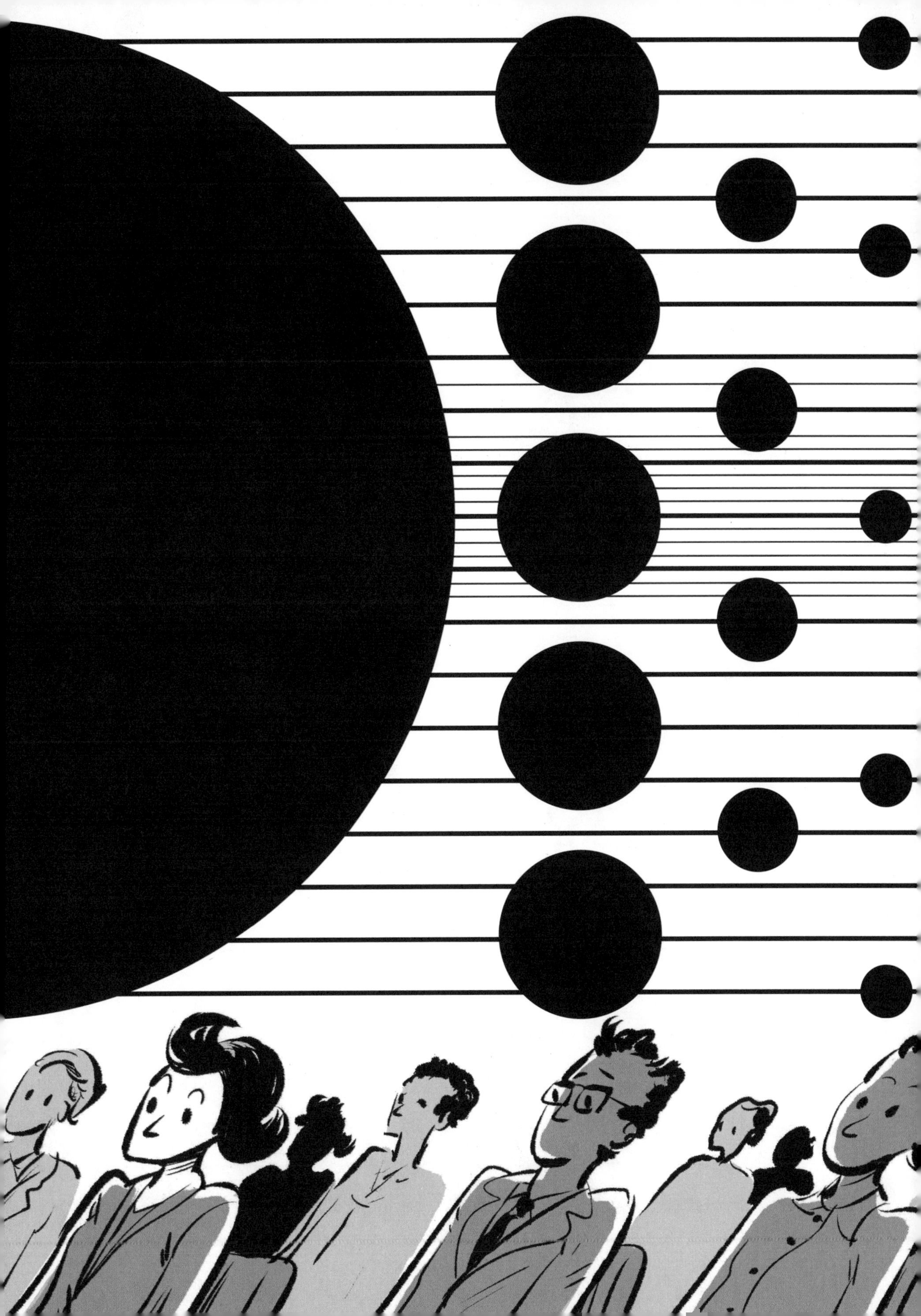

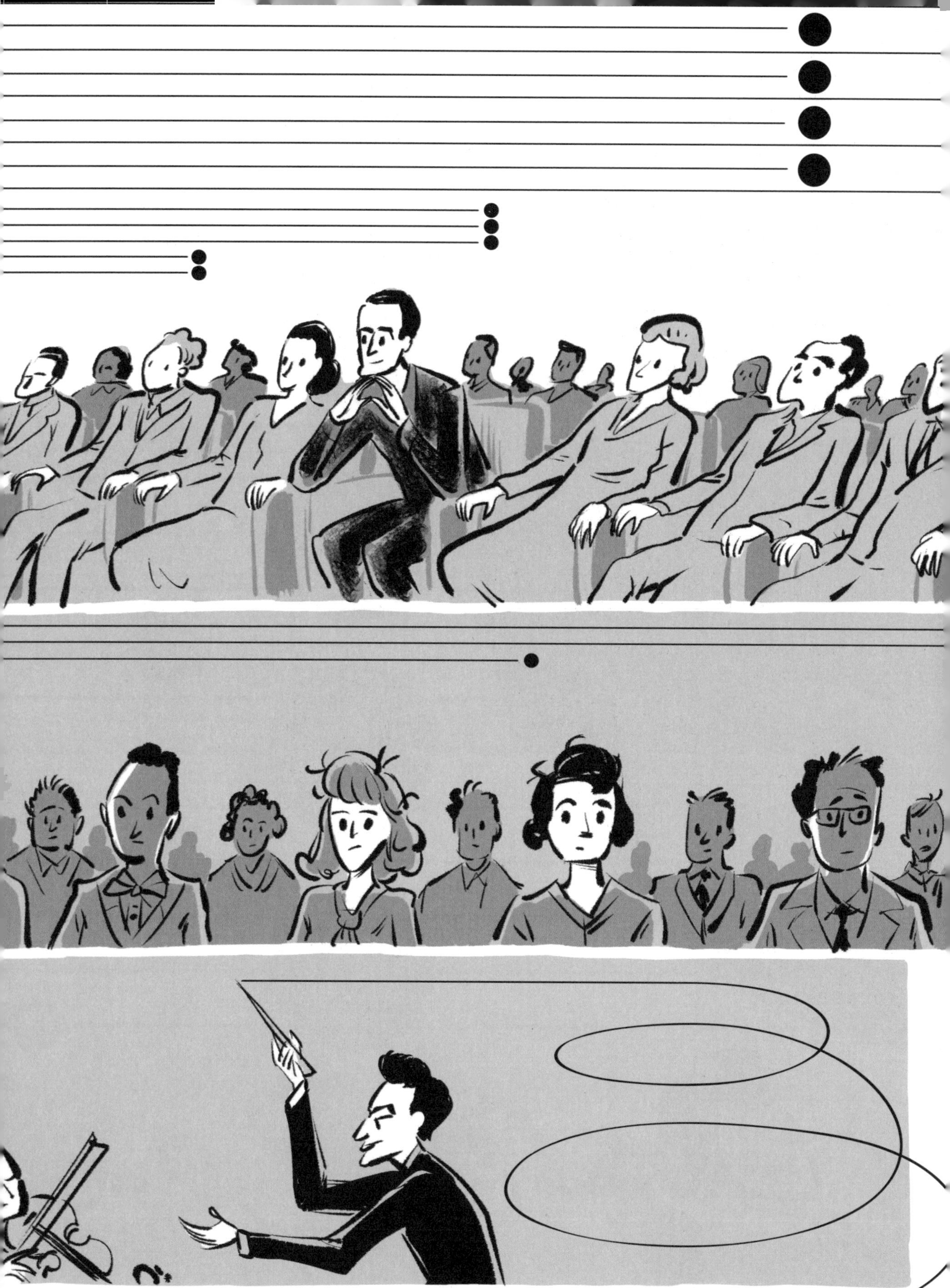

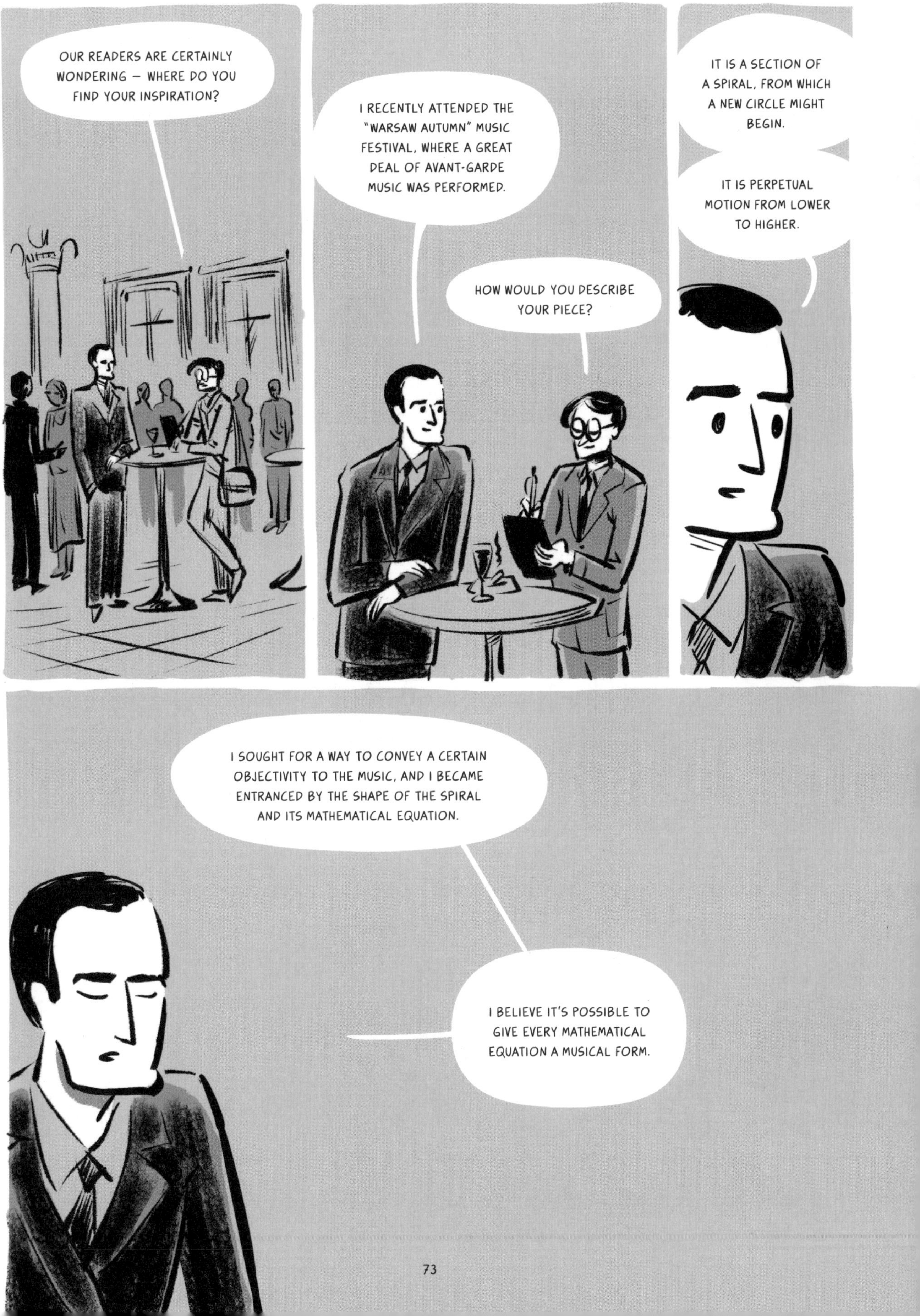
OUR READERS ARE CERTAINLY WONDERING – WHERE DO YOU FIND YOUR INSPIRATION?
I RECENTLY ATTENDED THE "WARSAW AUTUMN" MUSIC FESTIVAL, WHERE A GREAT DEAL OF AVANT-GARDE MUSIC WAS PERFORMED.
HOW WOULD YOU DESCRIBE YOUR PIECE?
IT IS A SECTION OF A SPIRAL, FROM WHICH A NEW CIRCLE MIGHT BEGIN.
IT IS PERPETUAL MOTION FROM LOWER TO HIGHER.
I SOUGHT FOR A WAY TO CONVEY A CERTAIN OBJECTIVITY TO THE MUSIC, AND I BECAME ENTRANCED BY THE SHAPE OF THE SPIRAL AND ITS MATHEMATICAL EQUATION.
I BELIEVE IT'S POSSIBLE TO GIVE EVERY MATHEMATICAL EQUATION A MUSICAL FORM.

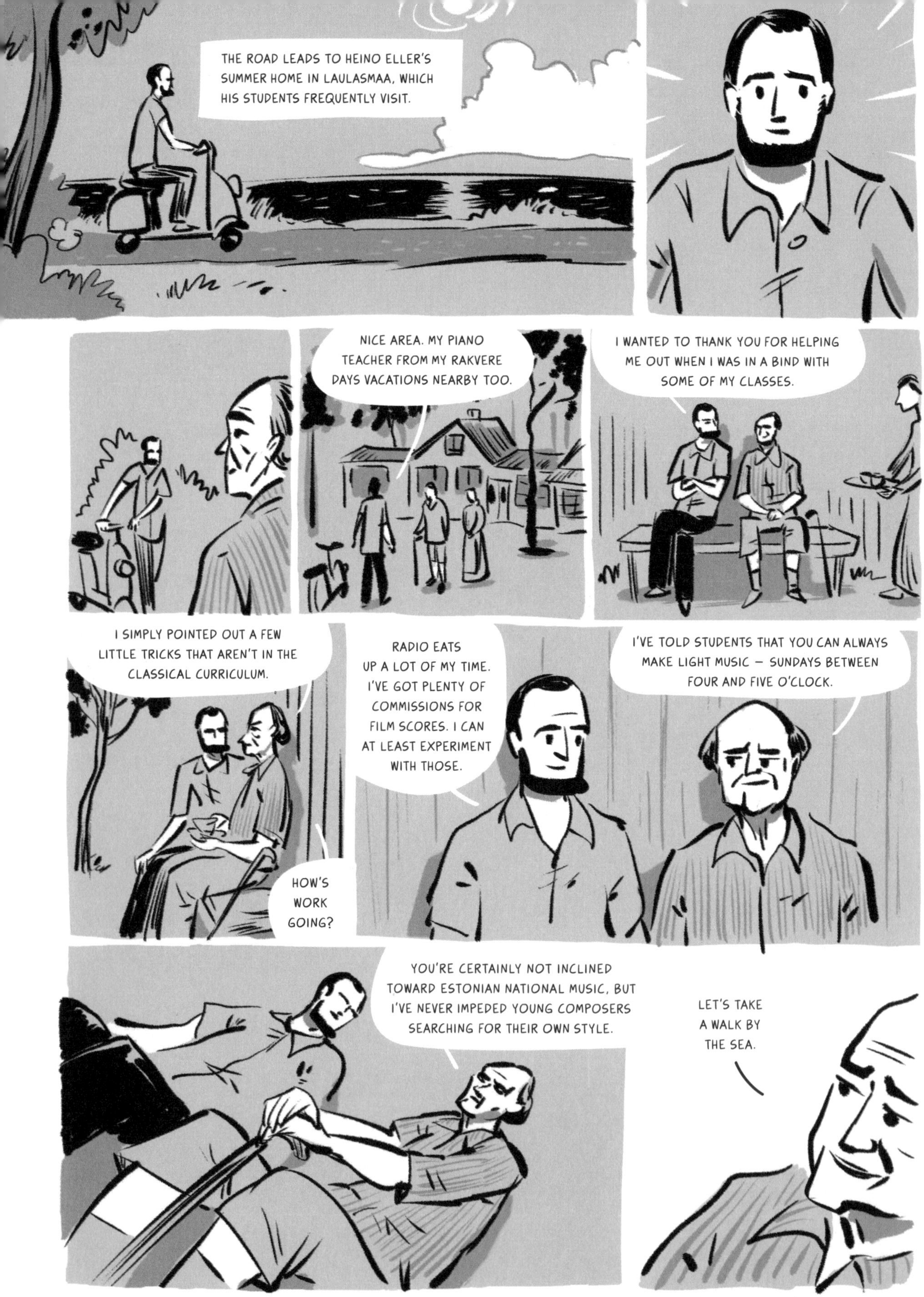
THE ROAD LEADS TO HEINO ELLER'S SUMMER HOME IN LAULASMAA, WHICH HIS STUDENTS FREQUENTLY VISIT.
NICE AREA. MY PIANO TEACHER FROM MY RAKVERE DAYS VACATIONS NEARBY TOO.
I WANTED TO THANK YOU FOR HELPING ME OUT WHEN I WAS IN A BIND WITH SOME OF MY CLASSES.
I SIMPLY POINTED OUT A FEW LITTLE TRICKS THAT AREN'T IN THE CLASSICAL CURRICULUM.
HOW'S WORK GOING?
RADIO EATS UP A LOT OF MY TIME. I'VE GOT PLENTY OF COMMISSIONS FOR FILM SCORES. I CAN AT LEAST EXPERIMENT WITH THOSE.
I'VE TOLD STUDENTS THAT YOU CAN ALWAYS MAKE LIGHT MUSIC – SUNDAYS BETWEEN FOUR AND FIVE O'CLOCK.
YOU'RE CERTAINLY NOT INCLINED TOWARD ESTONIAN NATIONAL MUSIC, BUT I'VE NEVER IMPEDED YOUNG COMPOSERS SEARCHING FOR THEIR OWN STYLE.
LET'S TAKE A WALK BY THE SEA.

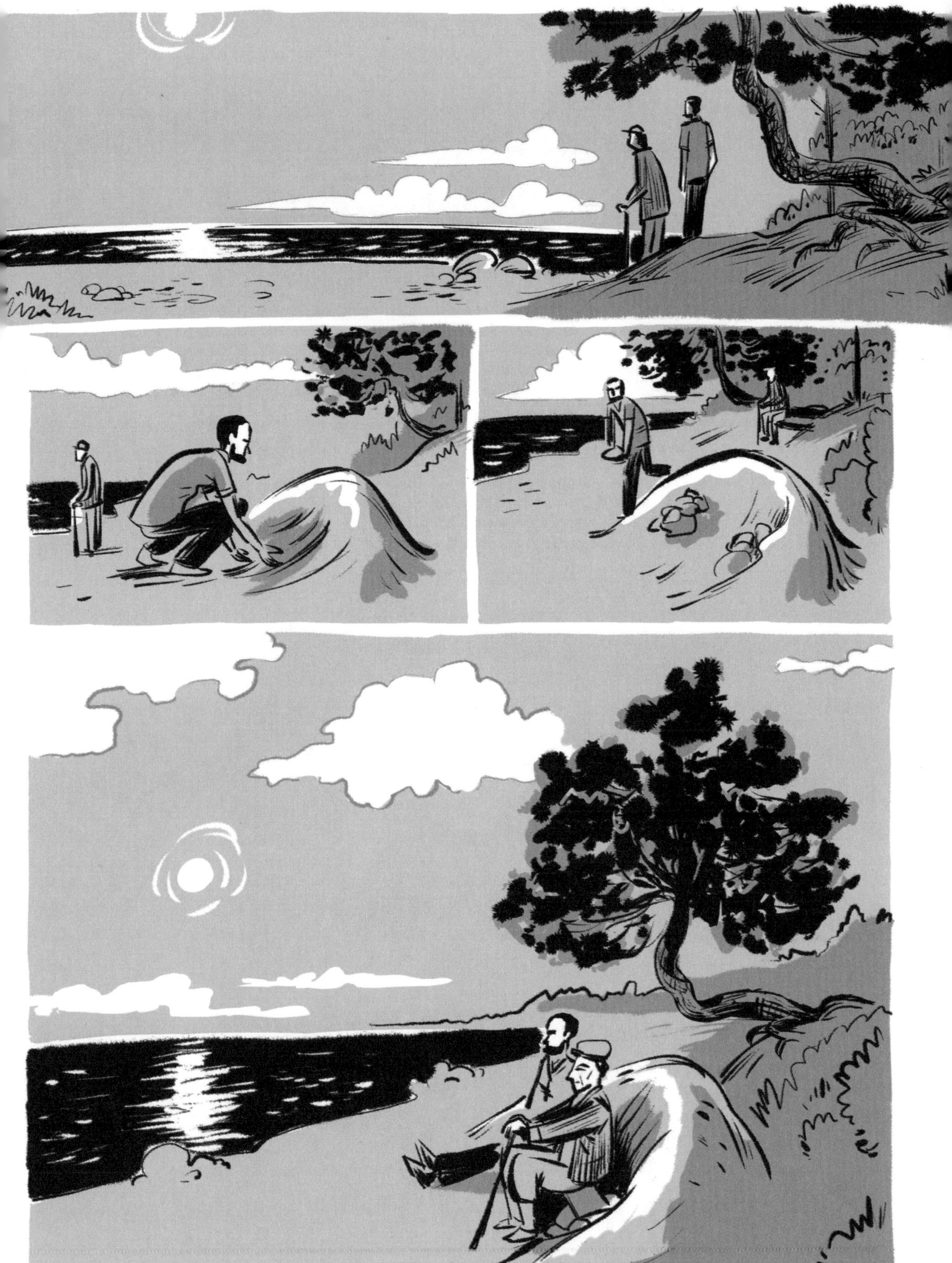

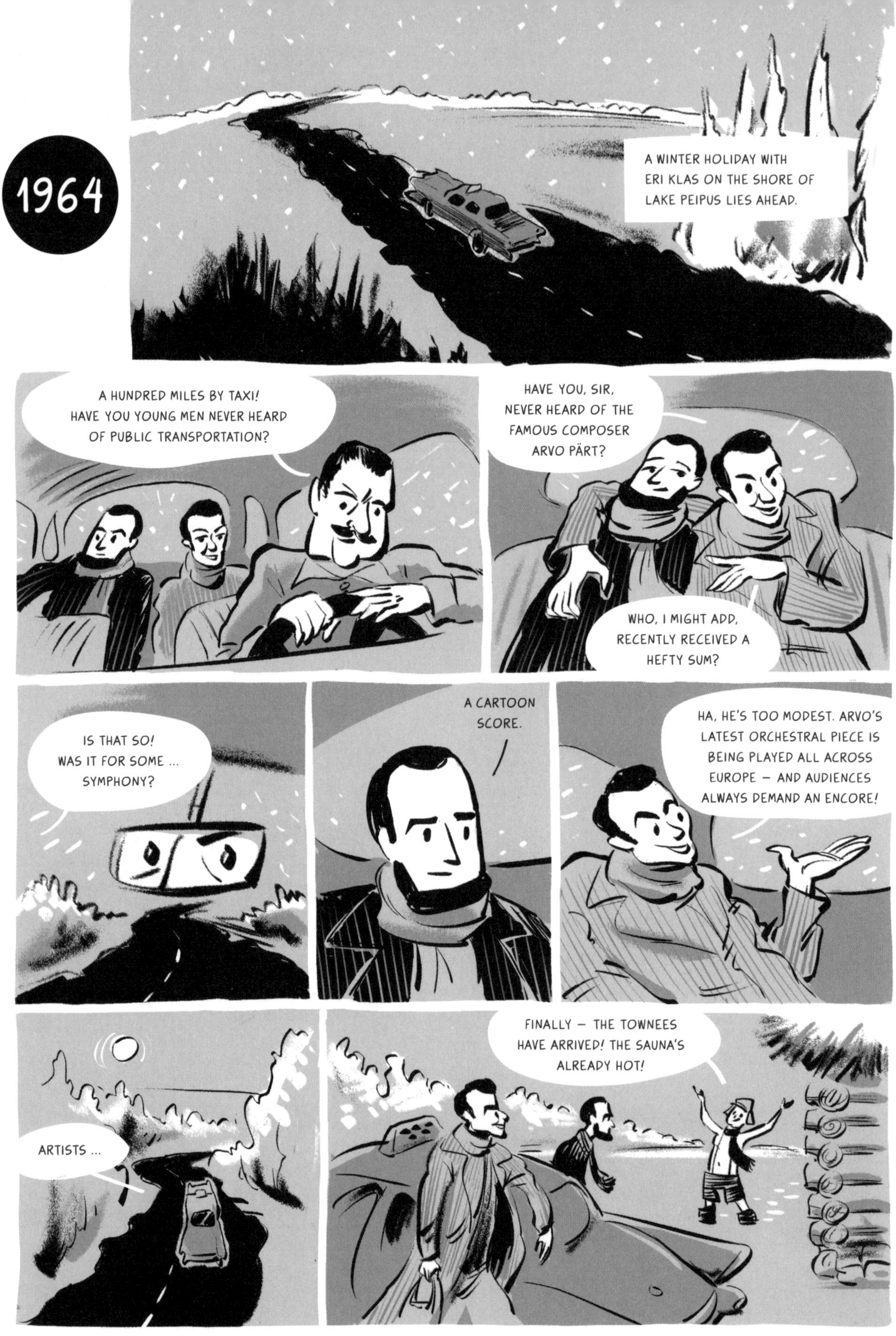
1964
A WINTER HOLIDAY WITH ERI KLAS ON THE SHORE OF LAKE PEIPUS LIES AHEAD.
A HUNDRED MILES BY TAXI! HAVE YOU YOUNG MEN NEVER HEARD OF PUBLIC TRANSPORTATION?
HAVE YOU, SIR, NEVER HEARD OF THE FAMOUS COMPOSER ARVO PÄRT?
WHO, I MIGHT ADD, RECENTLY RECEIVED A HEFTY SUM?
IS THAT SO! WAS IT FOR SOME ... SYMPHONY?
A CARTOON SCORE.
HA, HE'S TOO MODEST. ARVO'S LATEST ORCHESTRAL PIECE IS BEING PLAYED ALL ACROSS EUROPE – AND AUDIENCES ALWAYS DEMAND AN ENCORE!
ARTISTS ...
FINALLY – THE TOWNEES HAVE ARRIVED! THE SAUNA'S ALREADY HOT!

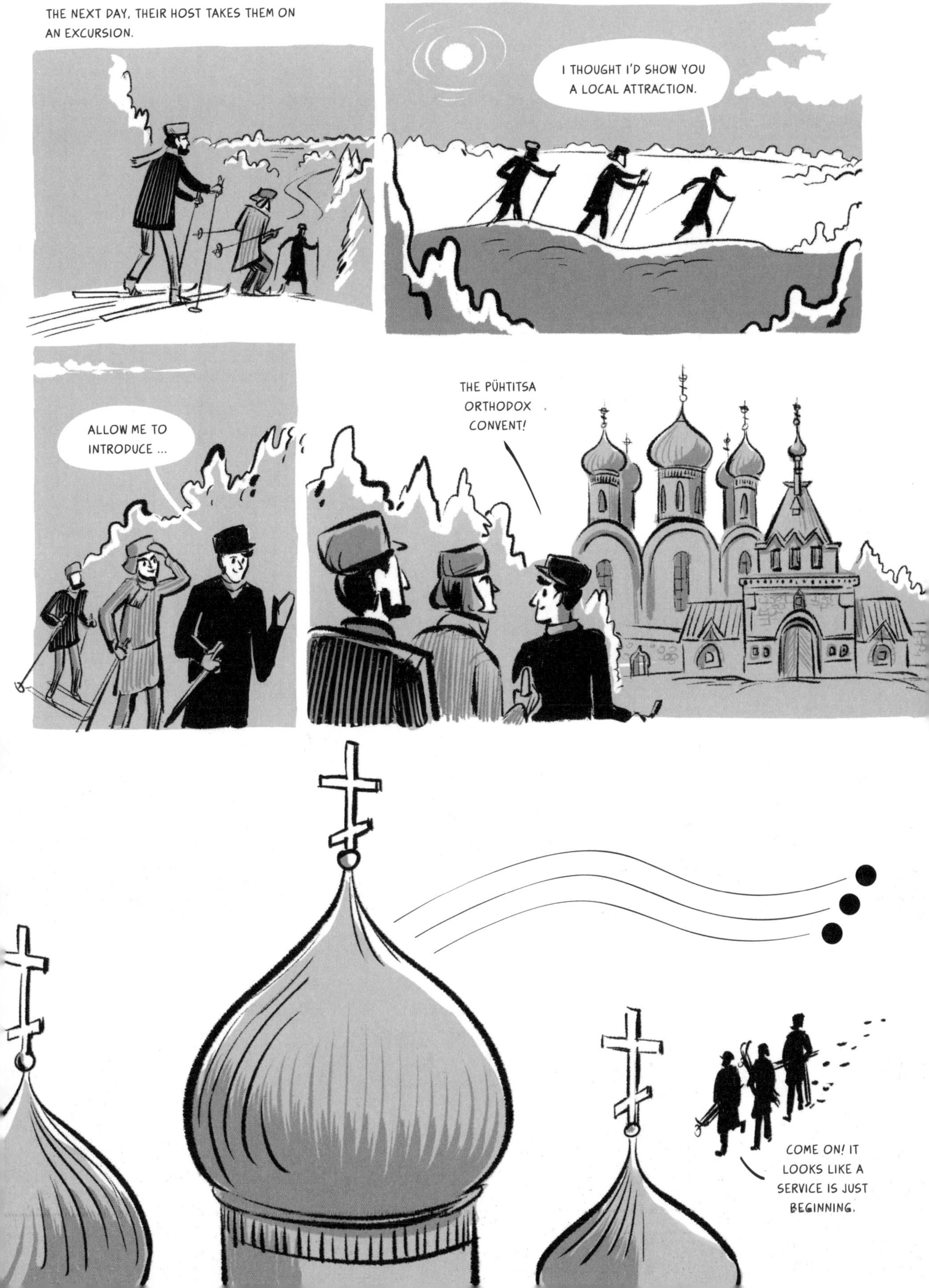
THE NEXT DAY, THEIR HOST TAKES THEM ON AN EXCURSION.
I THOUGHT I'D SHOW YOU A LOCAL ATTRACTION.
ALLOW ME TO INTRODUCE ...
THE PÜHTITSA ORTHODOX CONVENT!
COME ON! IT LOOKS LIKE A SERVICE IS JUST BEGINNING.

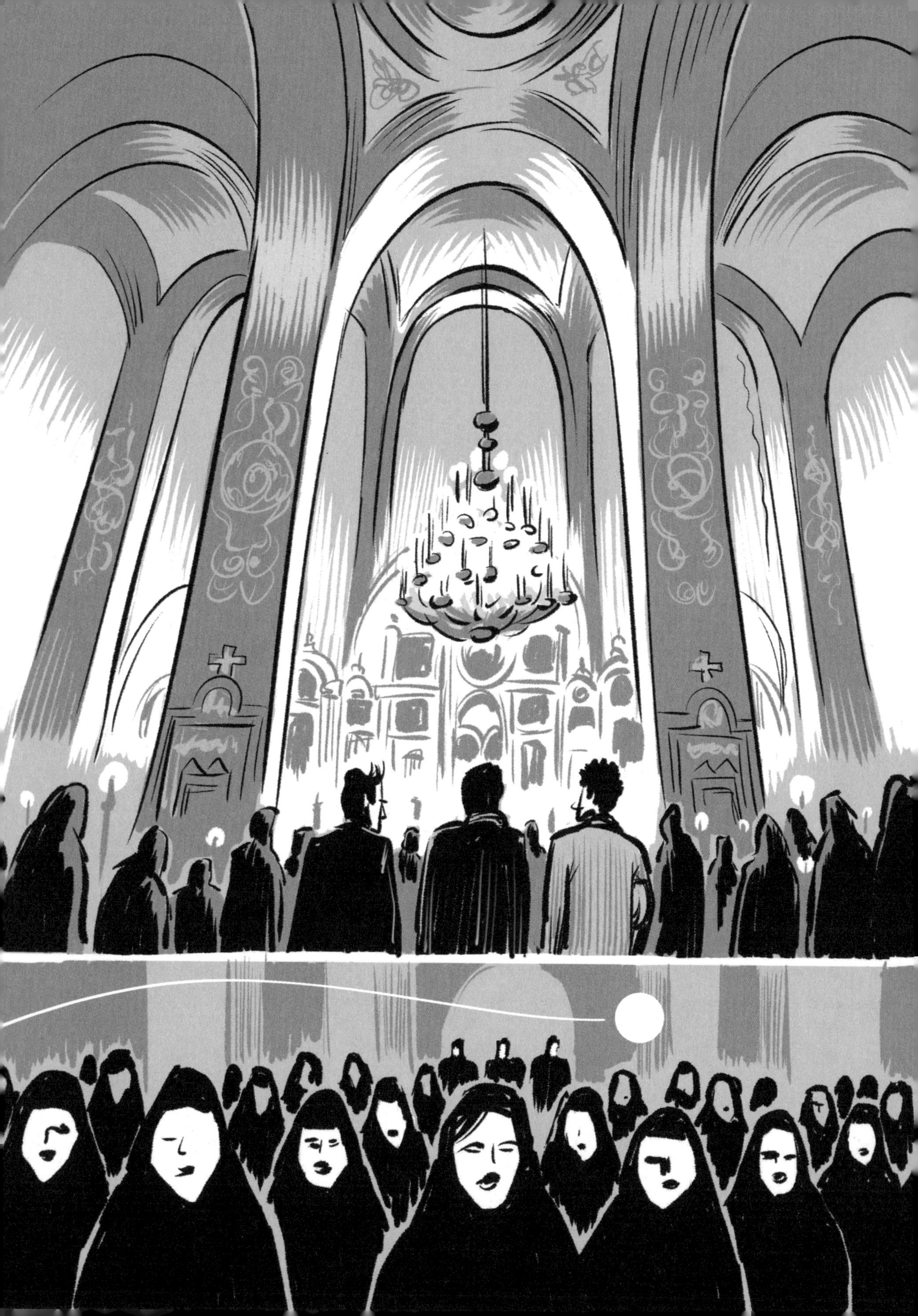

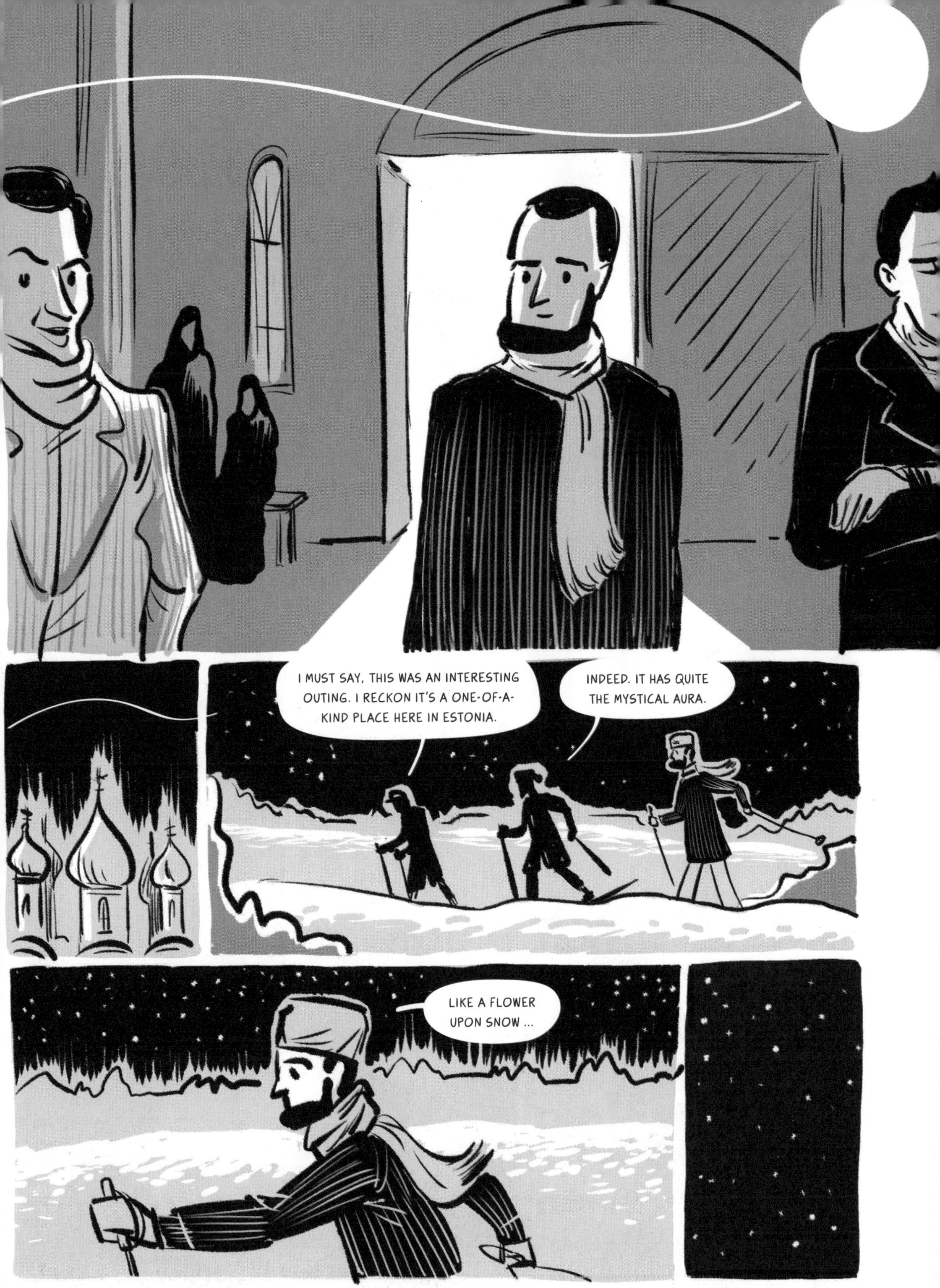
I MUST SAY, THIS WAS AN INTERESTING OUTING. I RECKON IT'S A ONE-OF-A-KIND PLACE HERE IN ESTONIA.
INDEED. IT HAS QUITE THE MYSTICAL AURA.
LIKE A FLOWER UPON SNOW ...

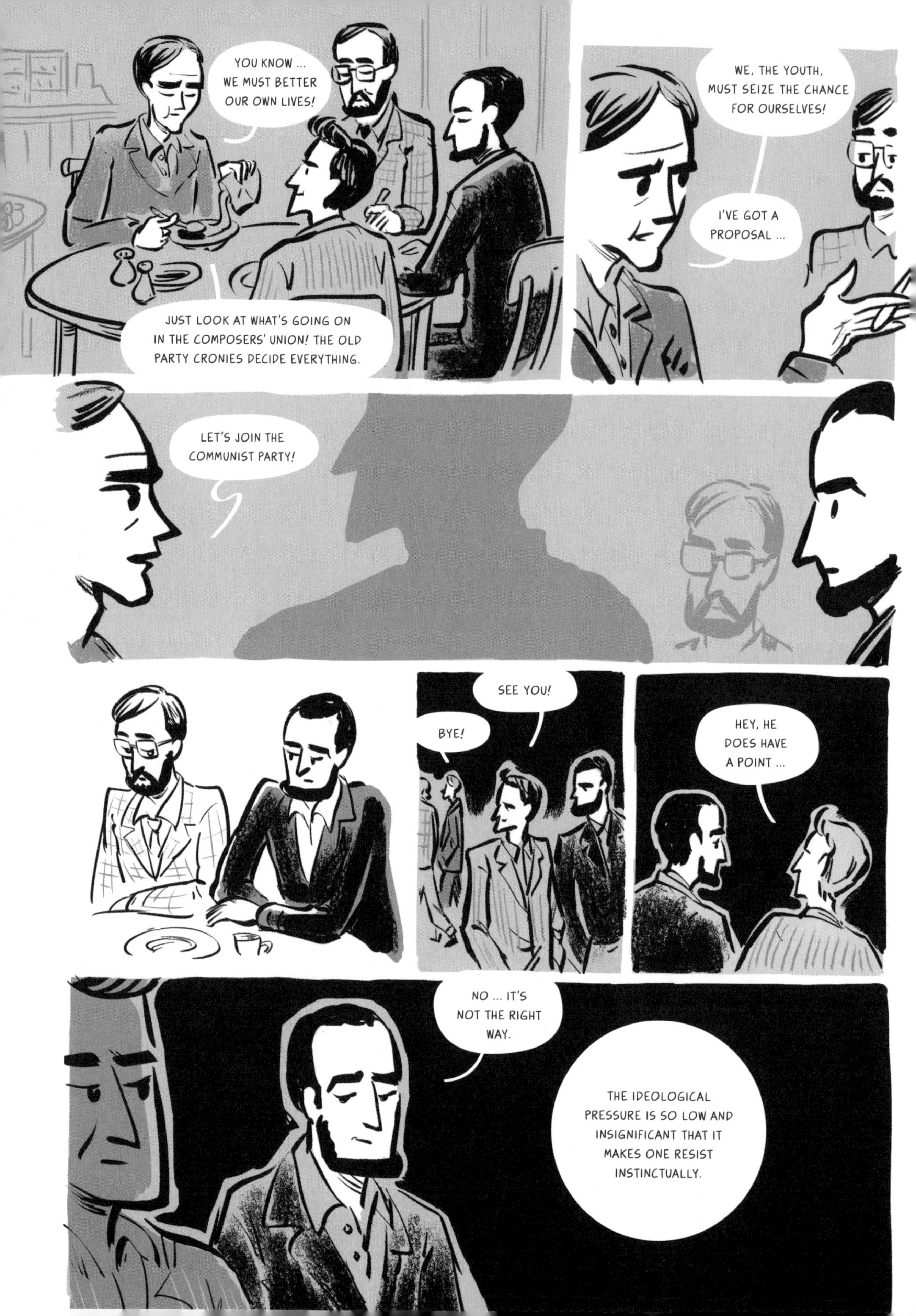
YOU KNOW ... WE MUST BETTER OUR OWN LIVES!
JUST LOOK AT WHAT'S GOING ON IN THE COMPOSERS' UNION! THE OLD PARTY CRONIES DECIDE EVERYTHING.
WE, THE YOUTH, MUST SEIZE THE CHANCE FOR OURSELVES!
I'VE GOT A PROPOSAL ...
LET'S JOIN THE COMMUNIST PARTY!
SEE YOU!
BYE!
HEY, HE DOES HAVE A POINT ...
NO ... IT'S NOT THE RIGHT WAY.
THE IDEOLOGICAL PRESSURE IS SO LOW AND INSIGNIFICANT THAT IT MAKES ONE RESIST INSTINCTUALLY.

BUT WHAT IS THE RIGHT WAY? AND HOW TO FIND THE MEANS TO EMBARK UPON IT?

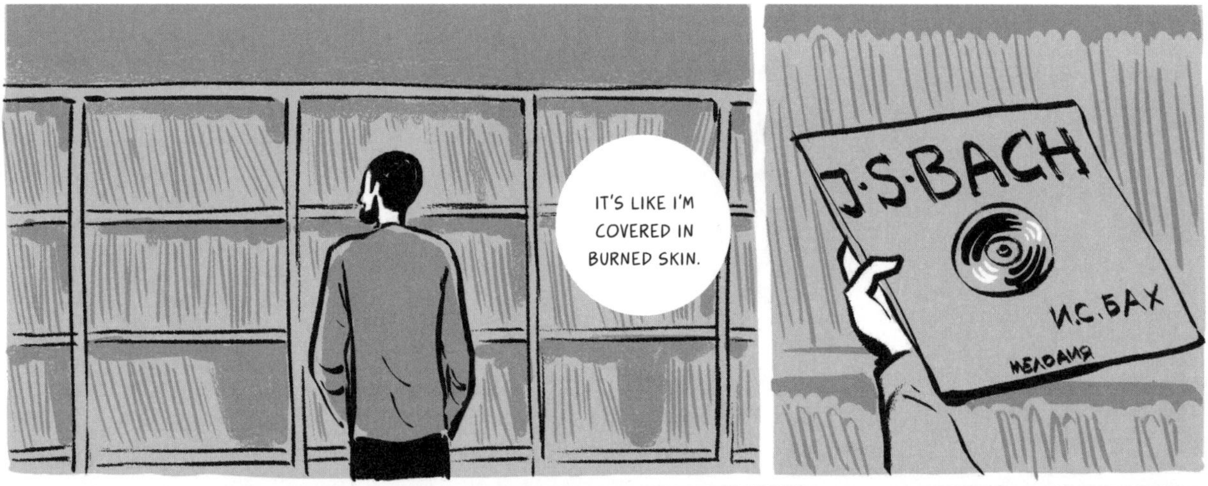
IT'S LIKE I'M COVERED IN BURNED SKIN.
J·S·BACH
И.С.БАХ
МЕЛОДИЯ

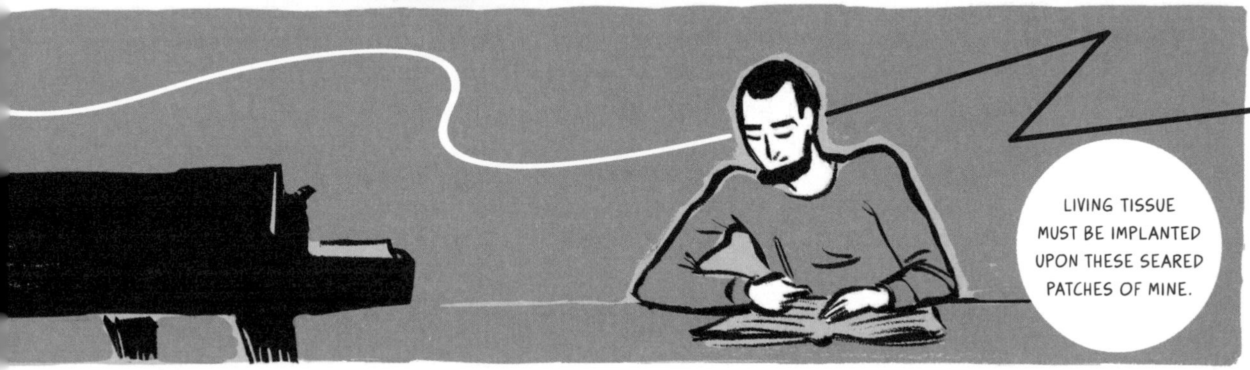
LIVING TISSUE MUST BE IMPLANTED UPON THESE SEARED PATCHES OF MINE.

BY PLACING THE CHAOS OF HIS OWN MODERNIST COMPOSITION AND BACH'S CALM AND ORDER SIDE BY SIDE, ARVO CREATES COLLAGES.

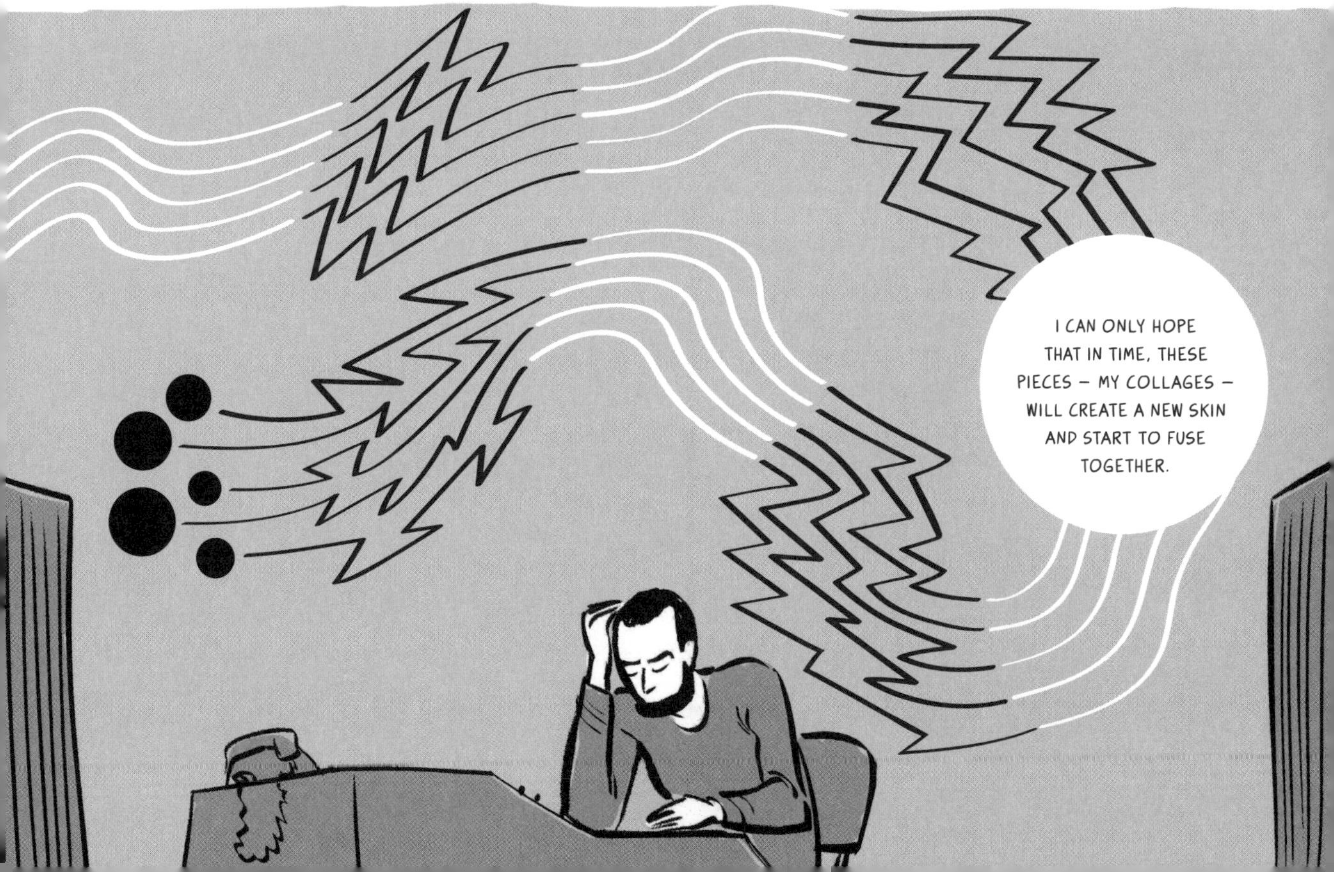
I CAN ONLY HOPE THAT IN TIME, THESE PIECES – MY COLLAGES – WILL CREATE A NEW SKIN AND START TO FUSE TOGETHER.

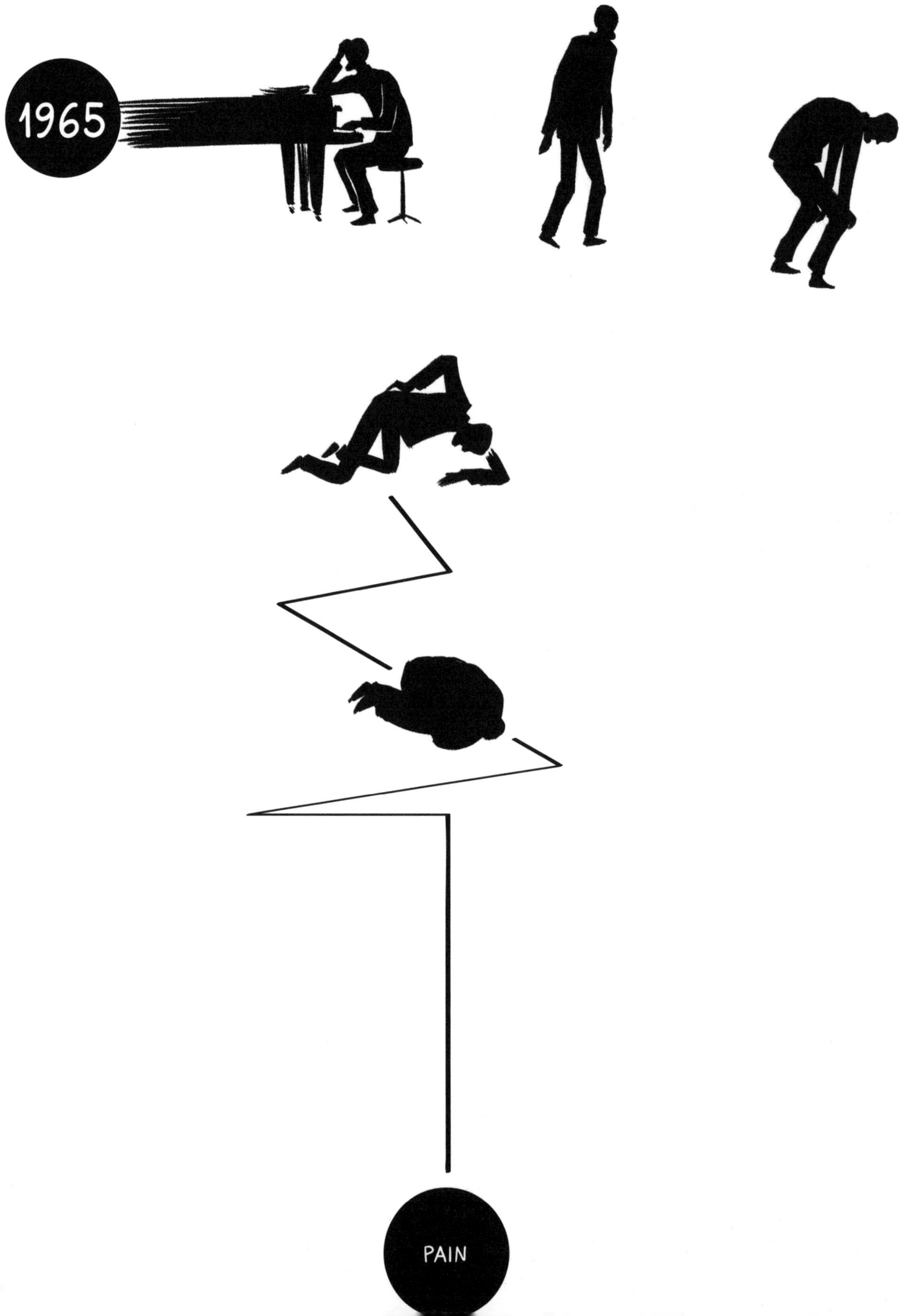
1965
PAIN

ARVO'S KIDNEY STONES INFLICT INCREDIBLE PAIN AND HIS HEALTH CONTINUES TO DECLINE.

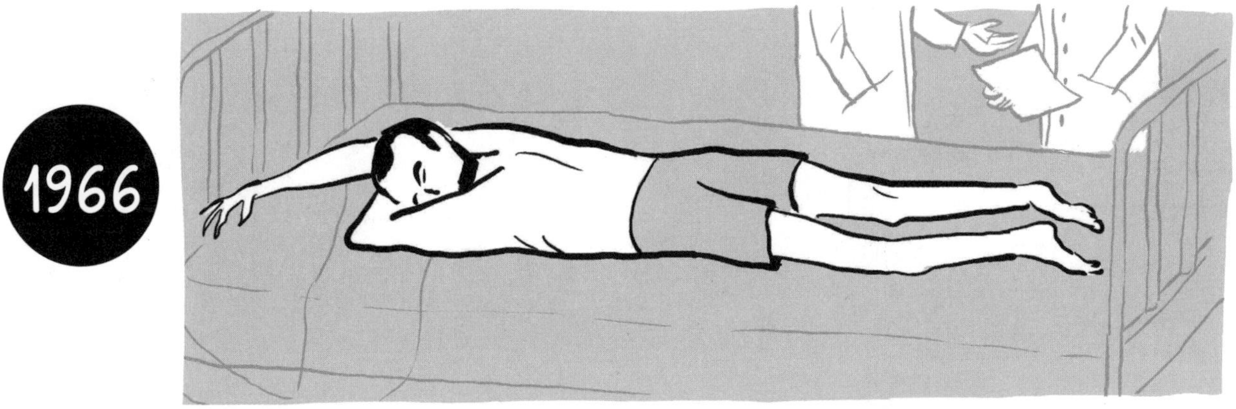
1966

HE HASN'T COMPOSED IN AN ENTIRE YEAR. NOT EVEN AN OPERATION ALLEVIATES THE SITUATION – HIS HEALTH ONLY DETERIORATES.

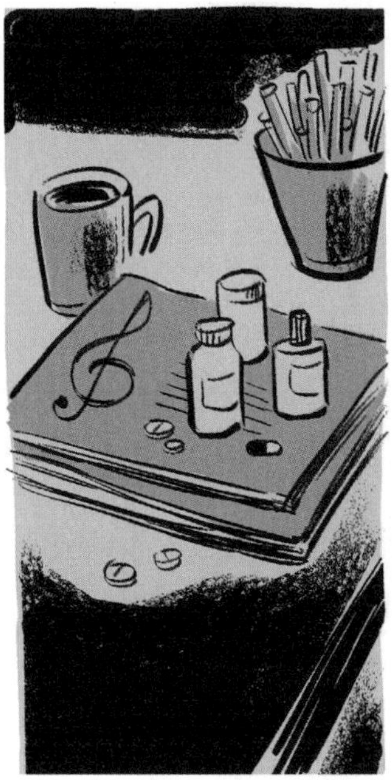

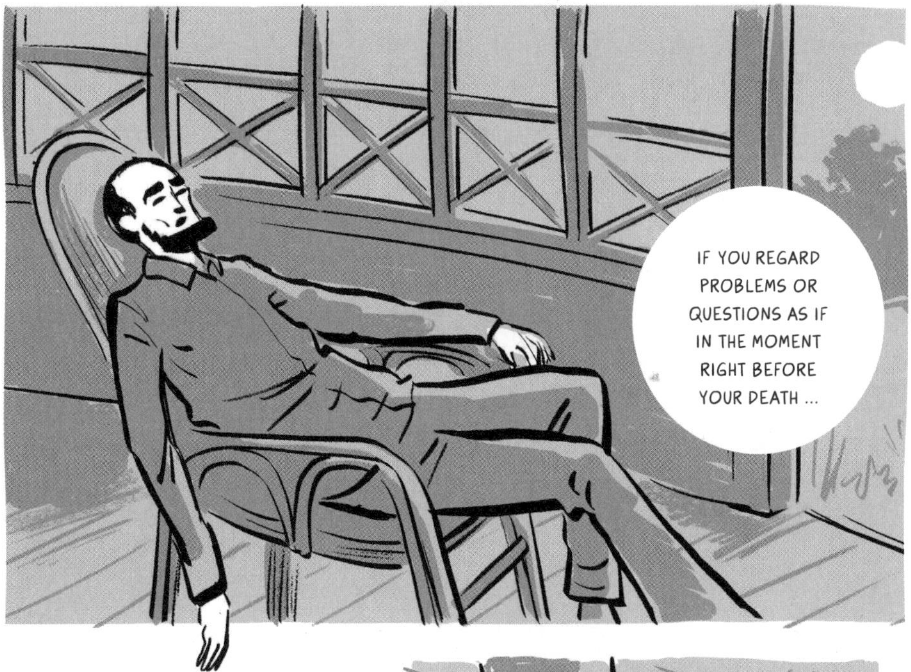
IF YOU REGARD PROBLEMS OR QUESTIONS AS IF IN THE MOMENT RIGHT BEFORE YOUR DEATH ...

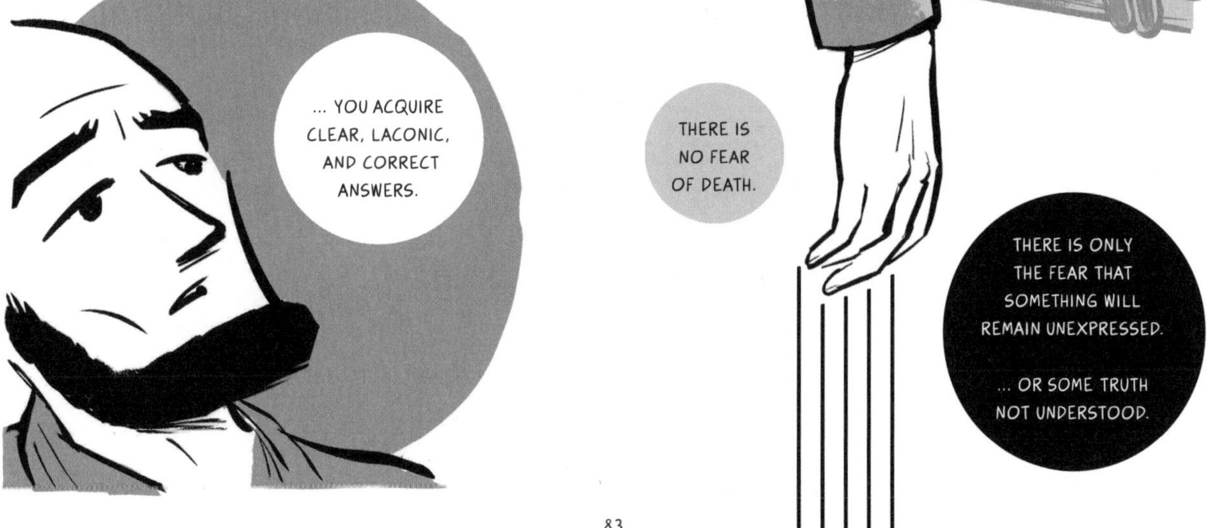
... YOU ACQUIRE CLEAR, LACONIC, AND CORRECT ANSWERS.
THERE IS NO FEAR OF DEATH.
THERE IS ONLY THE FEAR THAT SOMETHING WILL REMAIN UNEXPRESSED.
... OR SOME TRUTH NOT UNDERSTOOD.

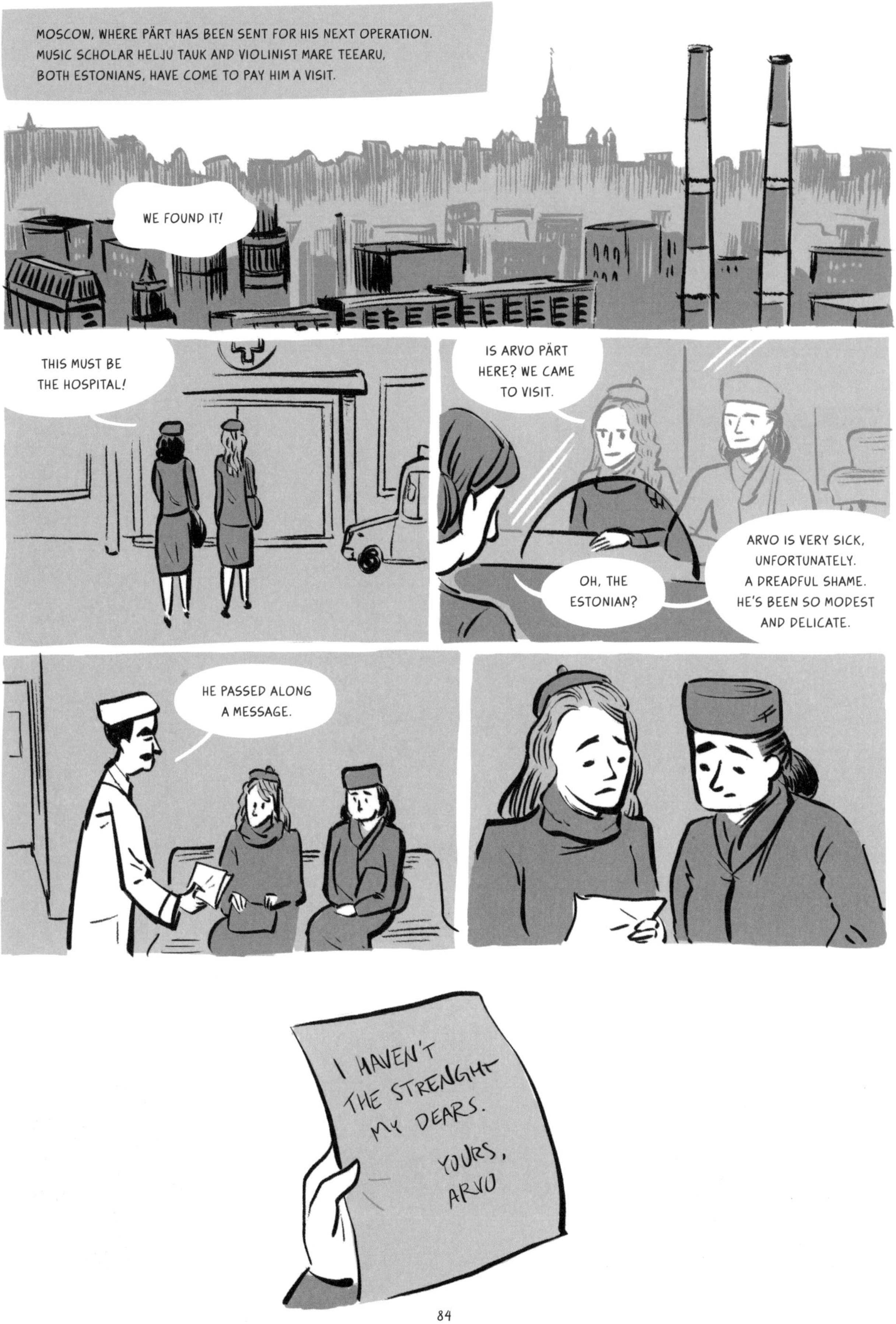
MOSCOW, WHERE PÄRT HAS BEEN SENT FOR HIS NEXT OPERATION.
MUSIC SCHOLAR HELJU TAUK AND VIOLINIST MARE TEEARU,
BOTH ESTONIANS, HAVE COME TO PAY HIM A VISIT.
WE FOUND IT!
THIS MUST BE THE HOSPITAL!
IS ARVO PÄRT HERE? WE CAME TO VISIT.
OH, THE ESTONIAN?
ARVO IS VERY SICK, UNFORTUNATELY. A DREADFUL SHAME. HE'S BEEN SO MODEST AND DELICATE.
HE PASSED ALONG A MESSAGE.
I HAVEN'T THE STRENGHT MY DEARS.
YOURS, ARVO

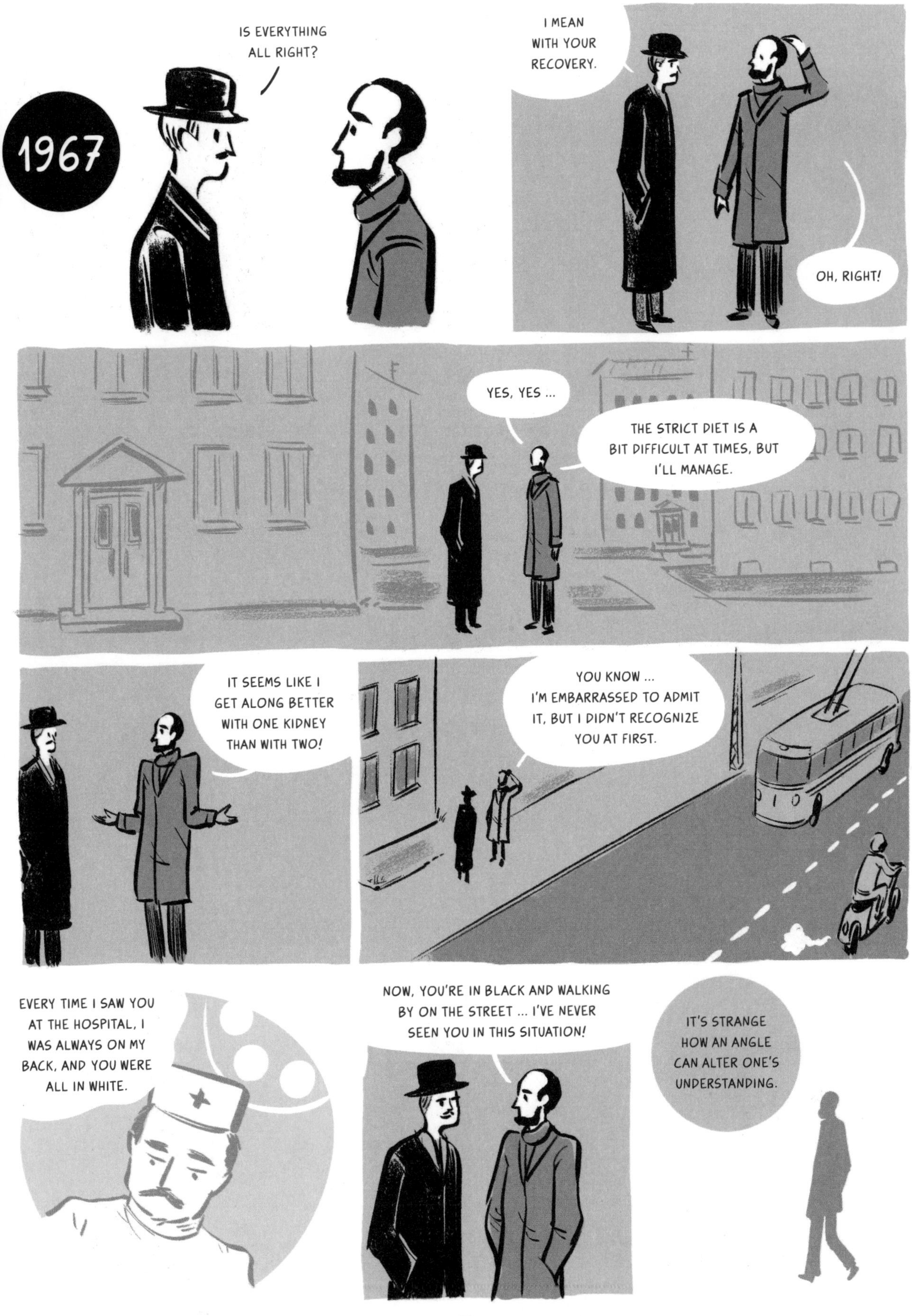
1967
IS EVERYTHING ALL RIGHT?
I MEAN WITH YOUR RECOVERY.
OH, RIGHT!
YES, YES ...
THE STRICT DIET IS A BIT DIFFICULT AT TIMES, BUT I'LL MANAGE.
IT SEEMS LIKE I GET ALONG BETTER WITH ONE KIDNEY THAN WITH TWO!
YOU KNOW ... I'M EMBARRASSED TO ADMIT IT, BUT I DIDN'T RECOGNIZE YOU AT FIRST.
EVERY TIME I SAW YOU AT THE HOSPITAL, I WAS ALWAYS ON MY BACK, AND YOU WERE ALL IN WHITE.
NOW, YOU'RE IN BLACK AND WALKING BY ON THE STREET ... I'VE NEVER SEEN YOU IN THIS SITUATION!
IT'S STRANGE HOW AN ANGLE CAN ALTER ONE'S UNDERSTANDING.

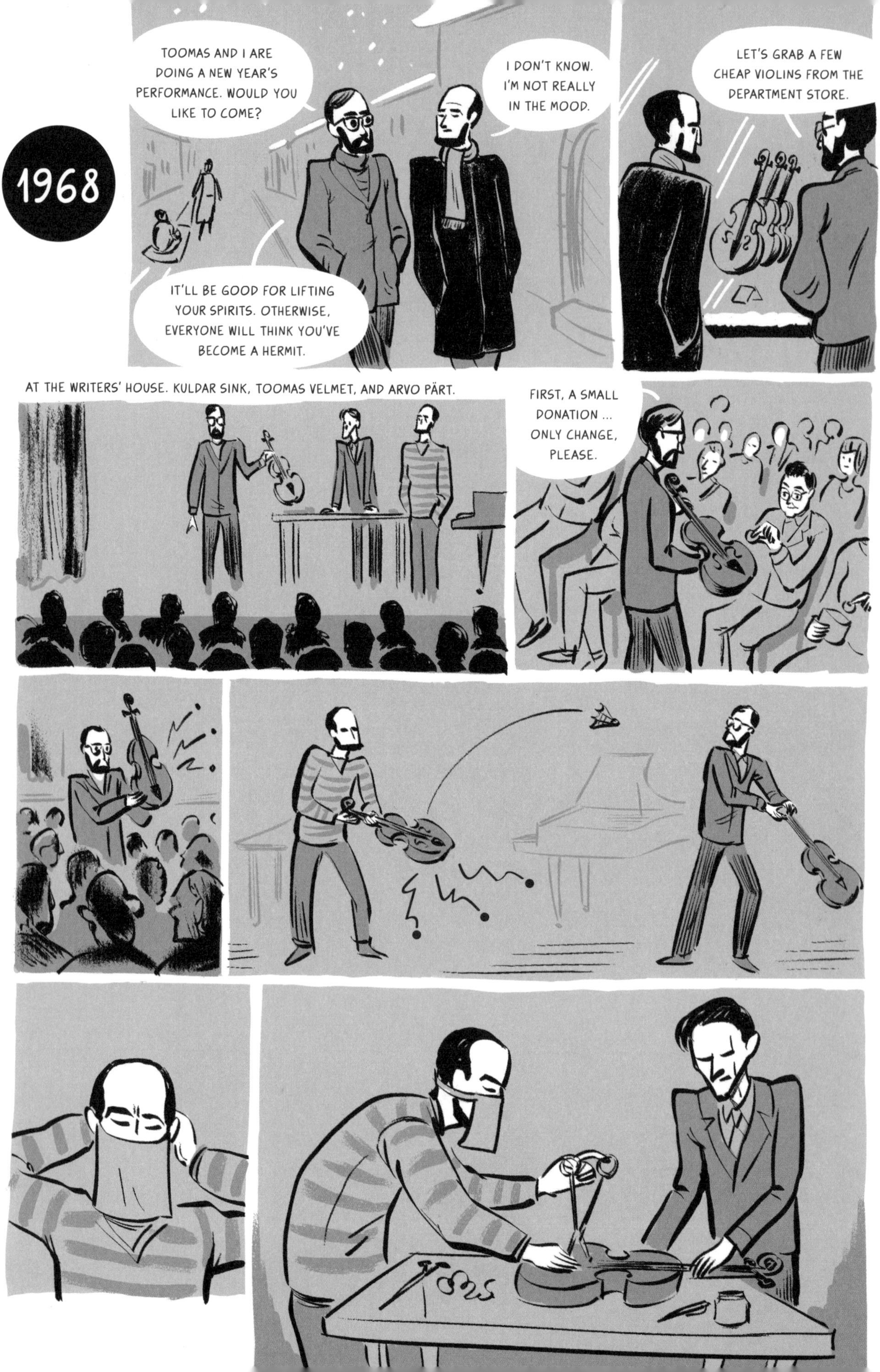
1968
TOOMAS AND I ARE DOING A NEW YEAR'S PERFORMANCE. WOULD YOU LIKE TO COME?
I DON'T KNOW. I'M NOT REALLY IN THE MOOD.
IT'LL BE GOOD FOR LIFTING YOUR SPIRITS. OTHERWISE, EVERYONE WILL THINK YOU'VE BECOME A HERMIT.
LET'S GRAB A FEW CHEAP VIOLINS FROM THE DEPARTMENT STORE.
AT THE WRITERS' HOUSE. KULDAR SINK, TOOMAS VELMET, AND ARVO PÄRT.
FIRST, A SMALL DONATION ... ONLY CHANGE, PLEASE.

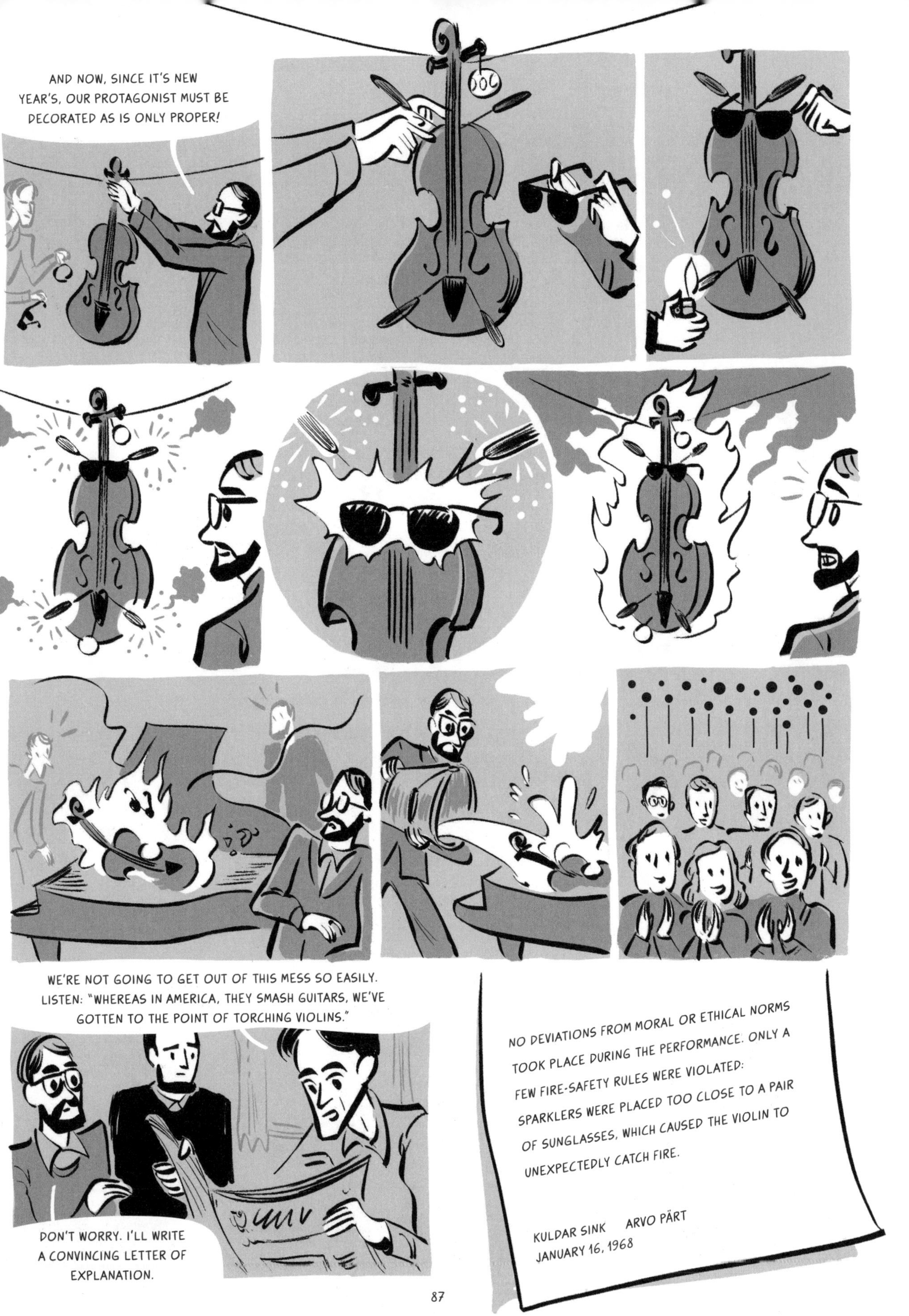
AND NOW, SINCE IT'S NEW YEAR'S, OUR PROTAGONIST MUST BE DECORATED AS IS ONLY PROPER!
WE'RE NOT GOING TO GET OUT OF THIS MESS SO EASILY. LISTEN: "WHEREAS IN AMERICA, THEY SMASH GUITARS, WE'VE GOTTEN TO THE POINT OF TORCHING VIOLINS."
DON'T WORRY. I'LL WRITE A CONVINCING LETTER OF EXPLANATION.
NO DEVIATIONS FROM MORAL OR ETHICAL NORMS TOOK PLACE DURING THE PERFORMANCE. ONLY A FEW FIRE-SAFETY RULES WERE VIOLATED: SPARKLERS WERE PLACED TOO CLOSE TO A PAIR OF SUNGLASSES, WHICH CAUSED THE VIOLIN TO UNEXPECTEDLY CATCH FIRE.
KULDAR SINK ARVO PÄRT
JANUARY 16, 1968

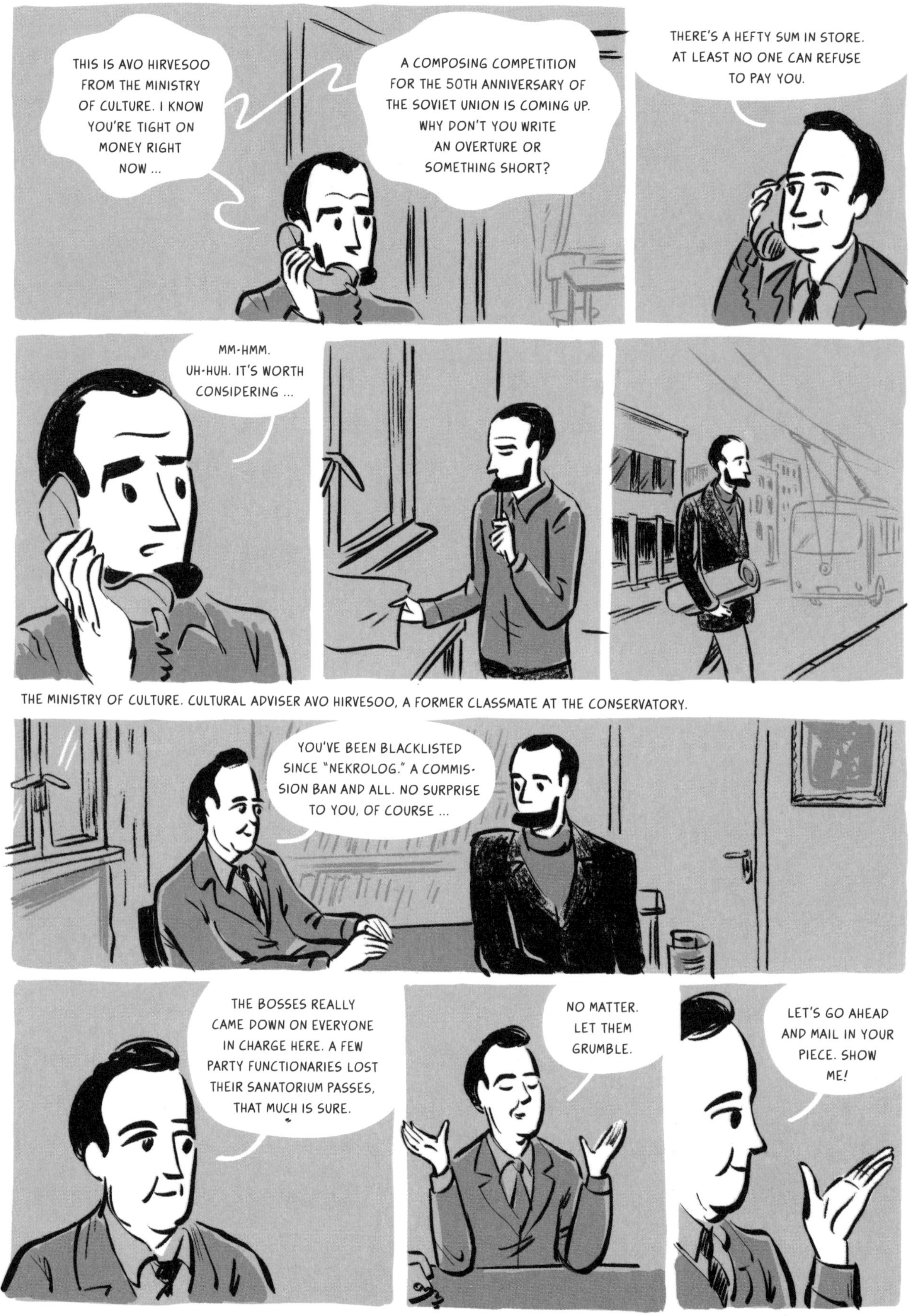
THIS IS AVO HIRVESOO FROM THE MINISTRY OF CULTURE. I KNOW YOU'RE TIGHT ON MONEY RIGHT NOW ...
A COMPOSING COMPETITION FOR THE 50TH ANNIVERSARY OF THE SOVIET UNION IS COMING UP. WHY DON'T YOU WRITE AN OVERTURE OR SOMETHING SHORT?
THERE'S A HEFTY SUM IN STORE. AT LEAST NO ONE CAN REFUSE TO PAY YOU.
MM-HMM. UH-HUH. IT'S WORTH CONSIDERING ...
THE MINISTRY OF CULTURE. CULTURAL ADVISER AVO HIRVESOO, A FORMER CLASSMATE AT THE CONSERVATORY.
YOU'VE BEEN BLACKLISTED SINCE "NEKROLOG." A COMMIS-SION BAN AND ALL. NO SURPRISE TO YOU, OF COURSE ...
THE BOSSES REALLY CAME DOWN ON EVERYONE IN CHARGE HERE. A FEW PARTY FUNCTIONARIES LOST THEIR SANATORIUM PASSES, THAT MUCH IS SURE.
NO MATTER. LET THEM GRUMBLE.
LET'S GO AHEAD AND MAIL IN YOUR PIECE. SHOW ME!

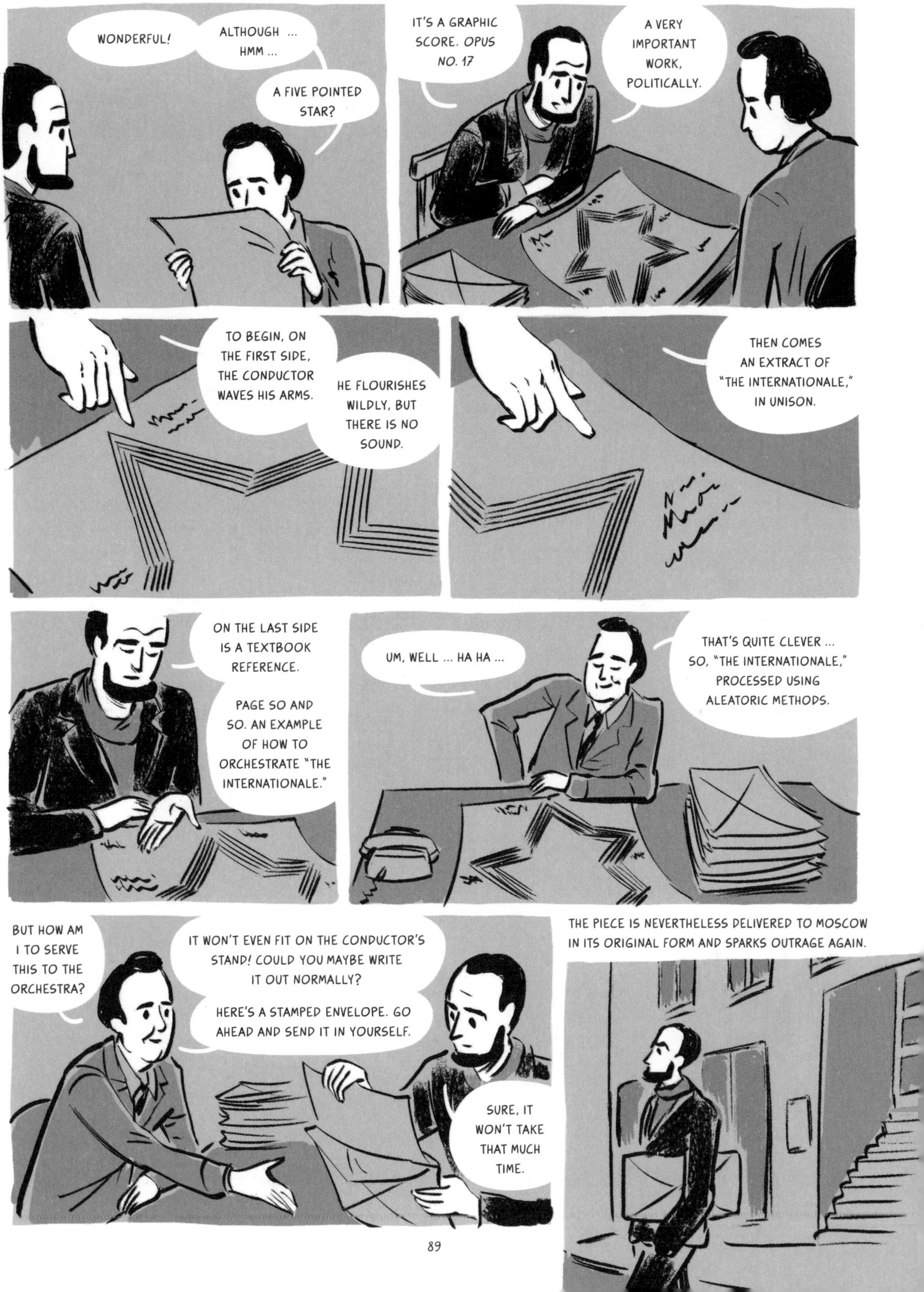
WONDERFUL!
ALTHOUGH ... HMM ...
A FIVE POINTED STAR?
IT'S A GRAPHIC SCORE. OPUS NO. 17
A VERY IMPORTANT WORK, POLITICALLY.
TO BEGIN, ON THE FIRST SIDE, THE CONDUCTOR WAVES HIS ARMS.
HE FLOURISHES WILDLY, BUT THERE IS NO SOUND.
THEN COMES AN EXTRACT OF "THE INTERNATIONALE," IN UNISON.
ON THE LAST SIDE IS A TEXTBOOK REFERENCE.
PAGE SO AND SO. AN EXAMPLE OF HOW TO ORCHESTRATE "THE INTERNATIONALE."
UM, WELL ... HA HA ...
THAT'S QUITE CLEVER ... SO, "THE INTERNATIONALE," PROCESSED USING ALEATORIC METHODS.
BUT HOW AM I TO SERVE THIS TO THE ORCHESTRA?
IT WON'T EVEN FIT ON THE CONDUCTOR'S STAND! COULD YOU MAYBE WRITE IT OUT NORMALLY?
HERE'S A STAMPED ENVELOPE. GO AHEAD AND SEND IT IN YOURSELF.
SURE, IT WON'T TAKE THAT MUCH TIME.
THE PIECE IS NEVERTHELESS DELIVERED TO MOSCOW IN ITS ORIGINAL FORM AND SPARKS OUTRAGE AGAIN.

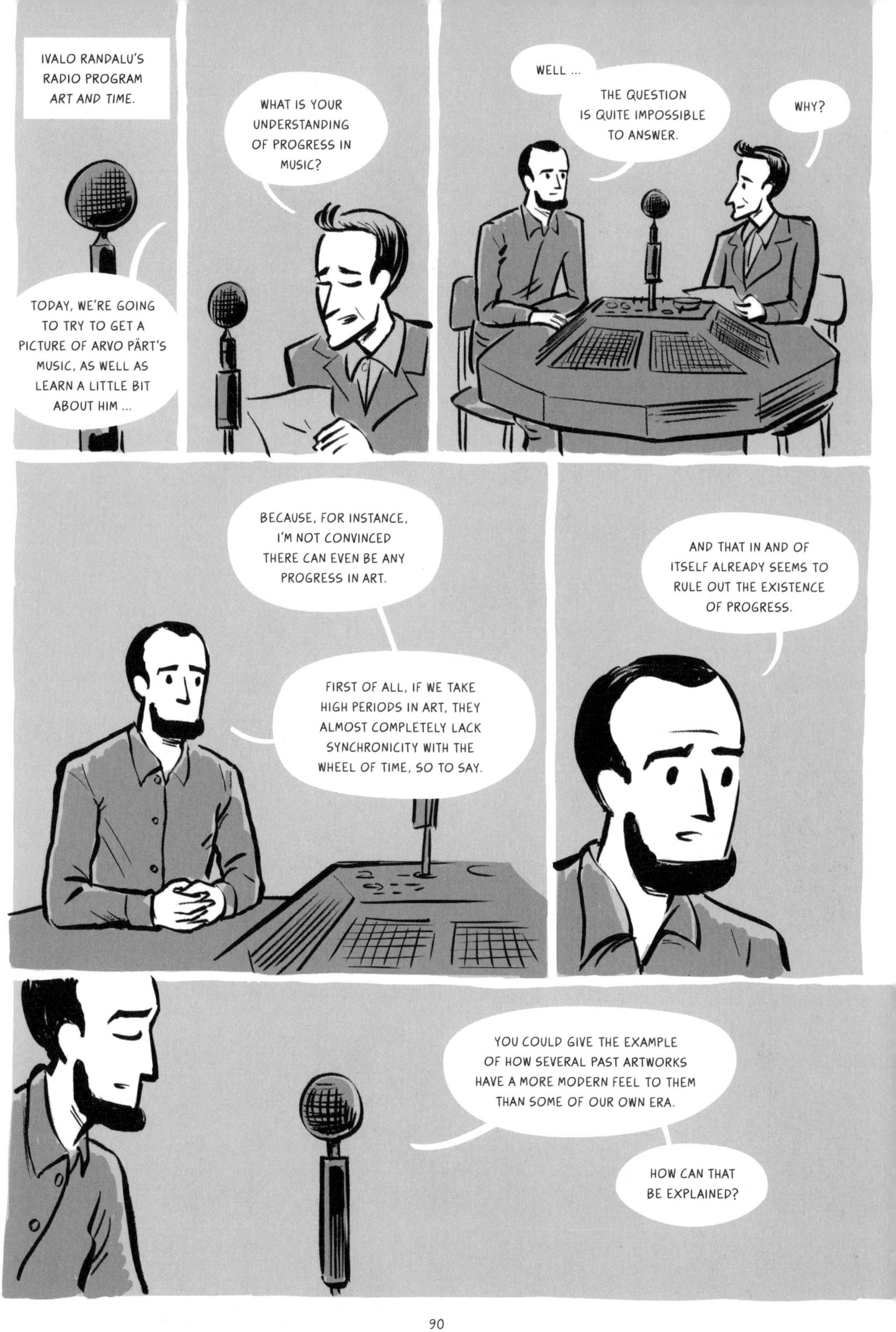
IVALO RANDALU'S RADIO PROGRAM ART AND TIME.
TODAY, WE'RE GOING TO TRY TO GET A PICTURE OF ARVO PÄRT'S MUSIC, AS WELL AS LEARN A LITTLE BIT ABOUT HIM ...
WHAT IS YOUR UNDERSTANDING OF PROGRESS IN MUSIC?
WELL ...
THE QUESTION IS QUITE IMPOSSIBLE TO ANSWER.
WHY?
BECAUSE, FOR INSTANCE, I'M NOT CONVINCED THERE CAN EVEN BE ANY PROGRESS IN ART.
FIRST OF ALL, IF WE TAKE HIGH PERIODS IN ART, THEY ALMOST COMPLETELY LACK SYNCHRONICITY WITH THE WHEEL OF TIME, SO TO SAY.
AND THAT IN AND OF ITSELF ALREADY SEEMS TO RULE OUT THE EXISTENCE OF PROGRESS.
YOU COULD GIVE THE EXAMPLE OF HOW SEVERAL PAST ARTWORKS HAVE A MORE MODERN FEEL TO THEM THAN SOME OF OUR OWN ERA.
HOW CAN THAT BE EXPLAINED?

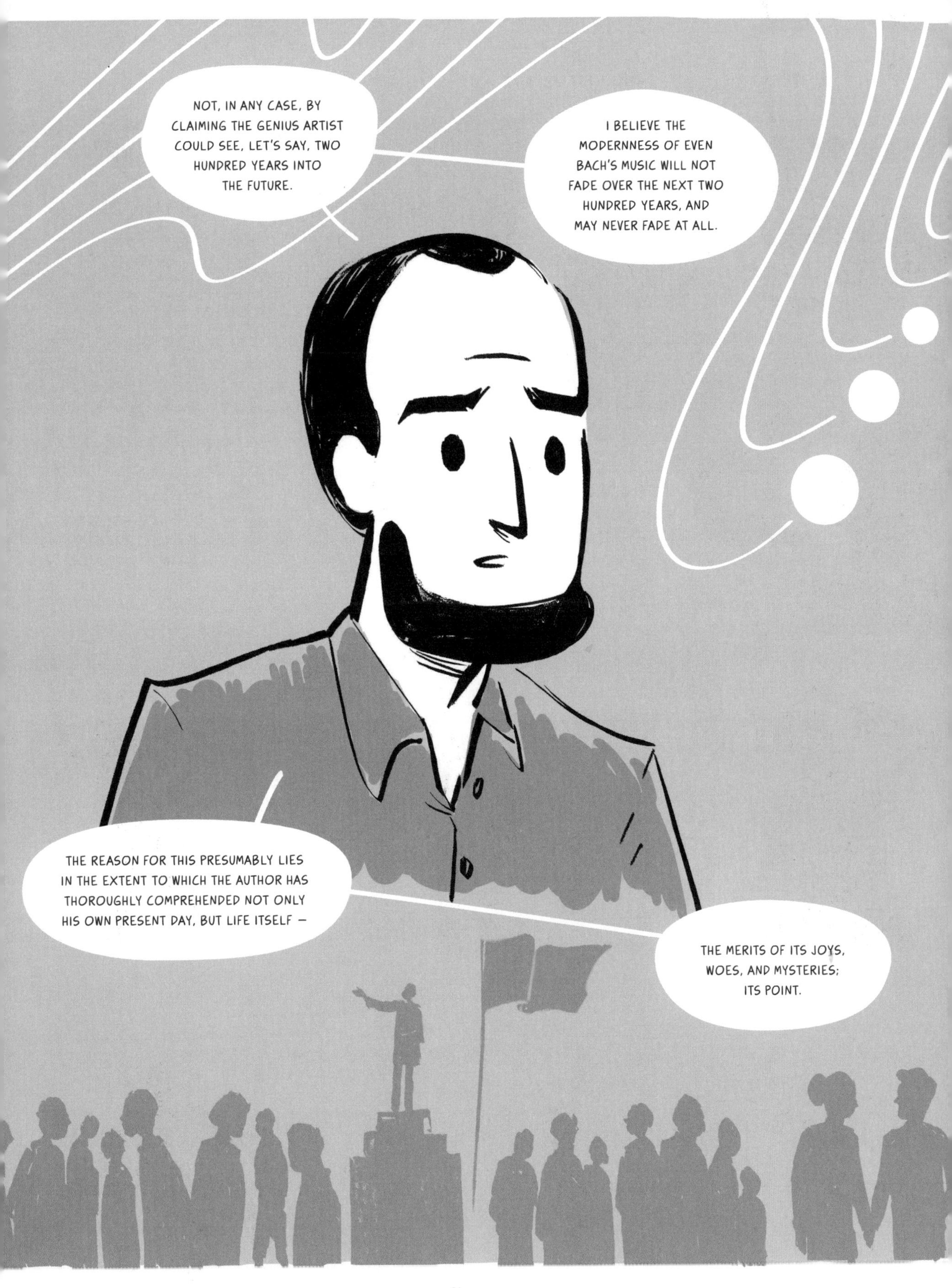
NOT, IN ANY CASE, BY CLAIMING THE GENIUS ARTIST COULD SEE, LET'S SAY, TWO HUNDRED YEARS INTO THE FUTURE.
I BELIEVE THE MODERNNESS OF EVEN BACH'S MUSIC WILL NOT FADE OVER THE NEXT TWO HUNDRED YEARS, AND MAY NEVER FADE AT ALL.
THE REASON FOR THIS PRESUMABLY LIES IN THE EXTENT TO WHICH THE AUTHOR HAS THOROUGHLY COMPREHENDED NOT ONLY HIS OWN PRESENT DAY, BUT LIFE ITSELF –
THE MERITS OF ITS JOYS, WOES, AND MYSTERIES; ITS POINT.

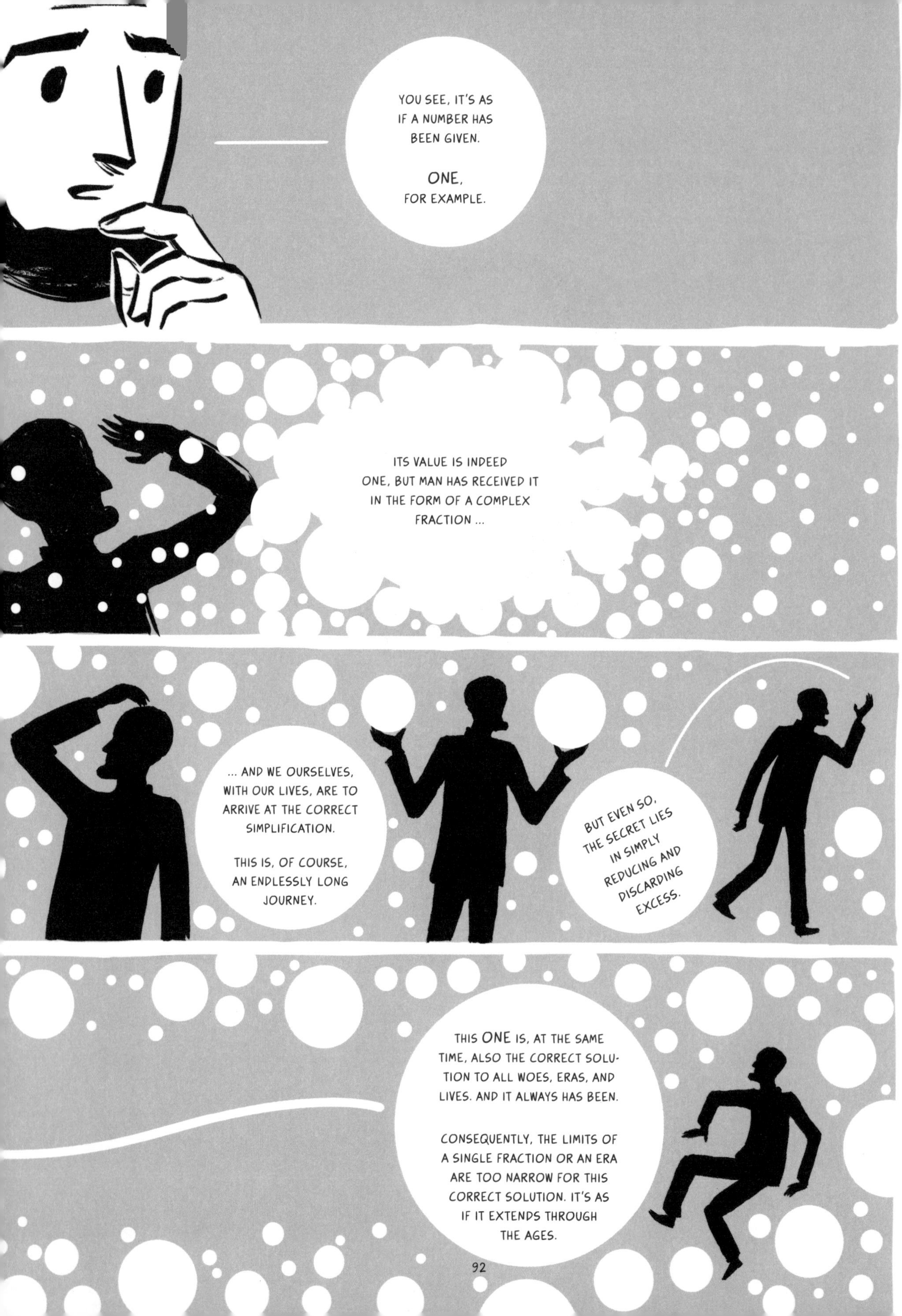
YOU SEE, IT'S AS IF A NUMBER HAS BEEN GIVEN.
ONE, FOR EXAMPLE.
ITS VALUE IS INDEED ONE, BUT MAN HAS RECEIVED IT IN THE FORM OF A COMPLEX FRACTION ...
... AND WE OURSELVES, WITH OUR LIVES, ARE TO ARRIVE AT THE CORRECT SIMPLIFICATION.
THIS IS, OF COURSE, AN ENDLESSLY LONG JOURNEY.
BUT EVEN SO, THE SECRET LIES IN SIMPLY REDUCING AND DISCARDING EXCESS.
THIS ONE IS, AT THE SAME TIME, ALSO THE CORRECT SOLUTION TO ALL WOES, ERAS, AND LIVES. AND IT ALWAYS HAS BEEN.
CONSEQUENTLY, THE LIMITS OF A SINGLE FRACTION OR AN ERA ARE TOO NARROW FOR THIS CORRECT SOLUTION. IT'S AS IF IT EXTENDS THROUGH THE AGES.

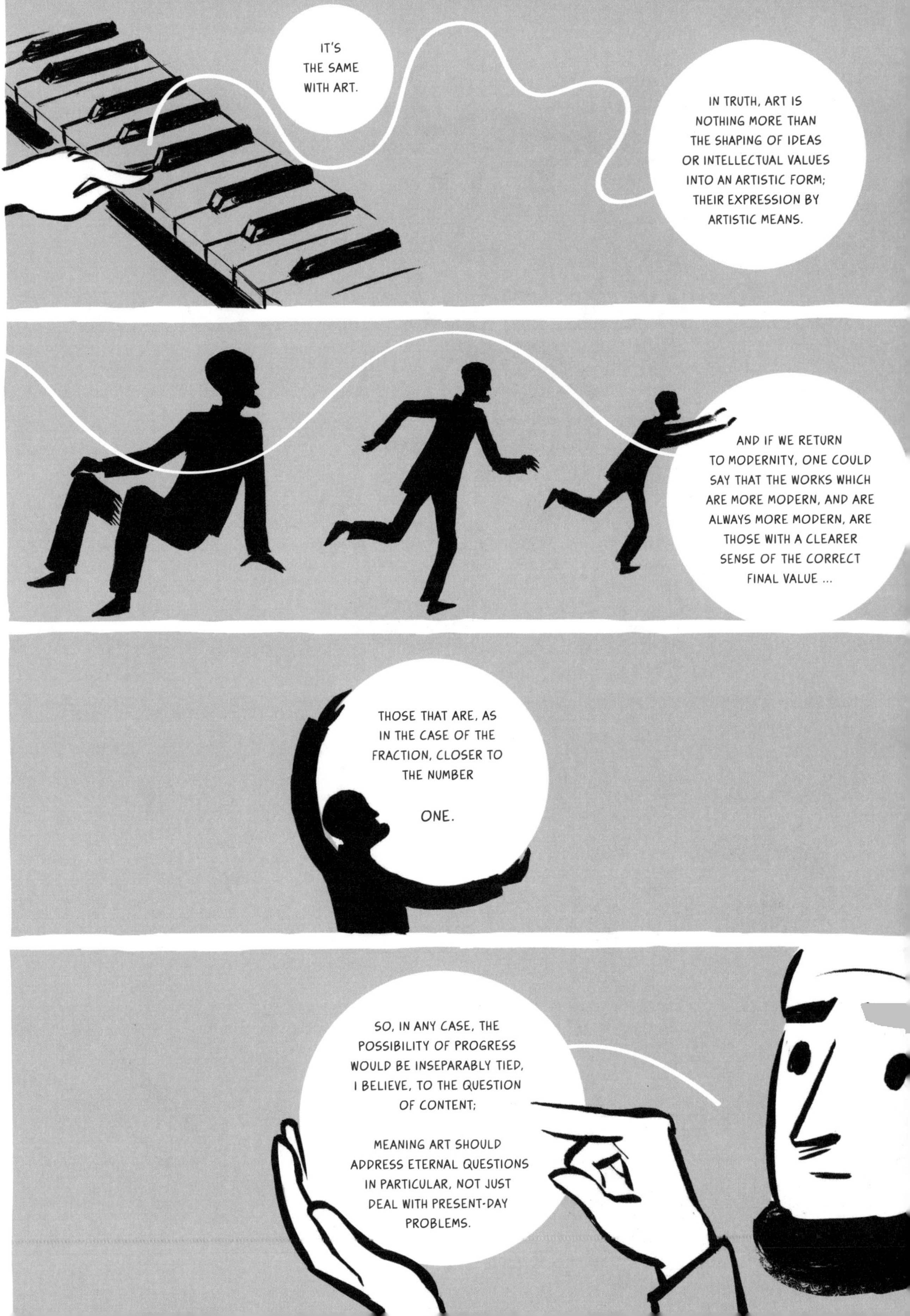
IT'S THE SAME WITH ART.
IN TRUTH, ART IS NOTHING MORE THAN THE SHAPING OF IDEAS OR INTELLECTUAL VALUES INTO AN ARTISTIC FORM; THEIR EXPRESSION BY ARTISTIC MEANS.
AND IF WE RETURN TO MODERNITY, ONE COULD SAY THAT THE WORKS WHICH ARE MORE MODERN, AND ARE ALWAYS MORE MODERN, ARE THOSE WITH A CLEARER SENSE OF THE CORRECT FINAL VALUE ...
THOSE THAT ARE, AS IN THE CASE OF THE FRACTION, CLOSER TO THE NUMBER
ONE.
SO, IN ANY CASE, THE POSSIBILITY OF PROGRESS WOULD BE INSEPARABLY TIED, I BELIEVE, TO THE QUESTION OF CONTENT;
MEANING ART SHOULD ADDRESS ETERNAL QUESTIONS IN PARTICULAR, NOT JUST DEAL WITH PRESENT-DAY PROBLEMS.

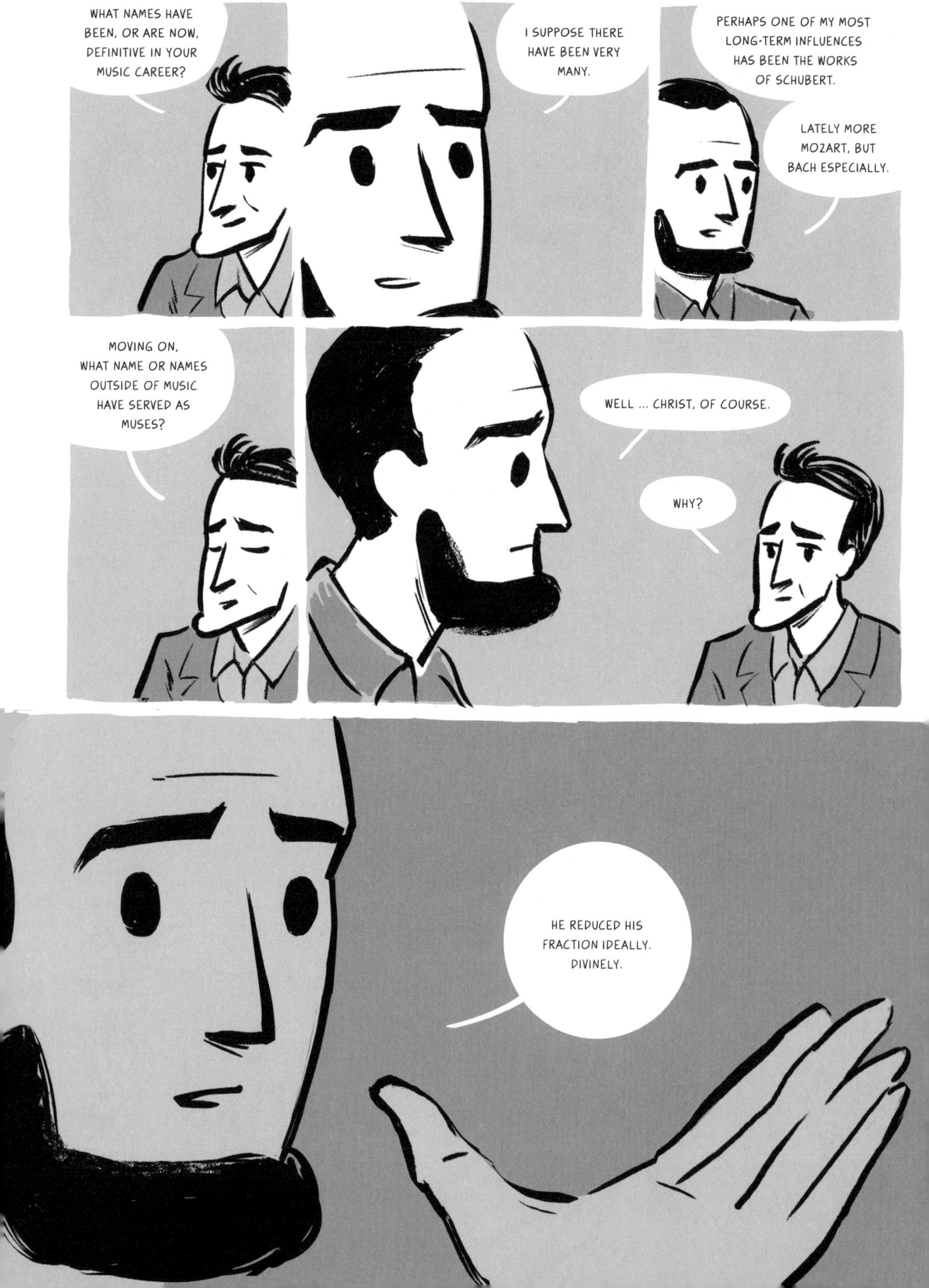
WHAT NAMES HAVE BEEN, OR ARE NOW, DEFINITIVE IN YOUR MUSIC CAREER?
I SUPPOSE THERE HAVE BEEN VERY MANY.
PERHAPS ONE OF MY MOST LONG-TERM INFLUENCES HAS BEEN THE WORKS OF SCHUBERT.
LATELY MORE MOZART, BUT BACH ESPECIALLY.
MOVING ON, WHAT NAME OR NAMES OUTSIDE OF MUSIC HAVE SERVED AS MUSES?
WELL ... CHRIST, OF COURSE.
WHY?
HE REDUCED HIS FRACTION IDEALLY. DIVINELY.

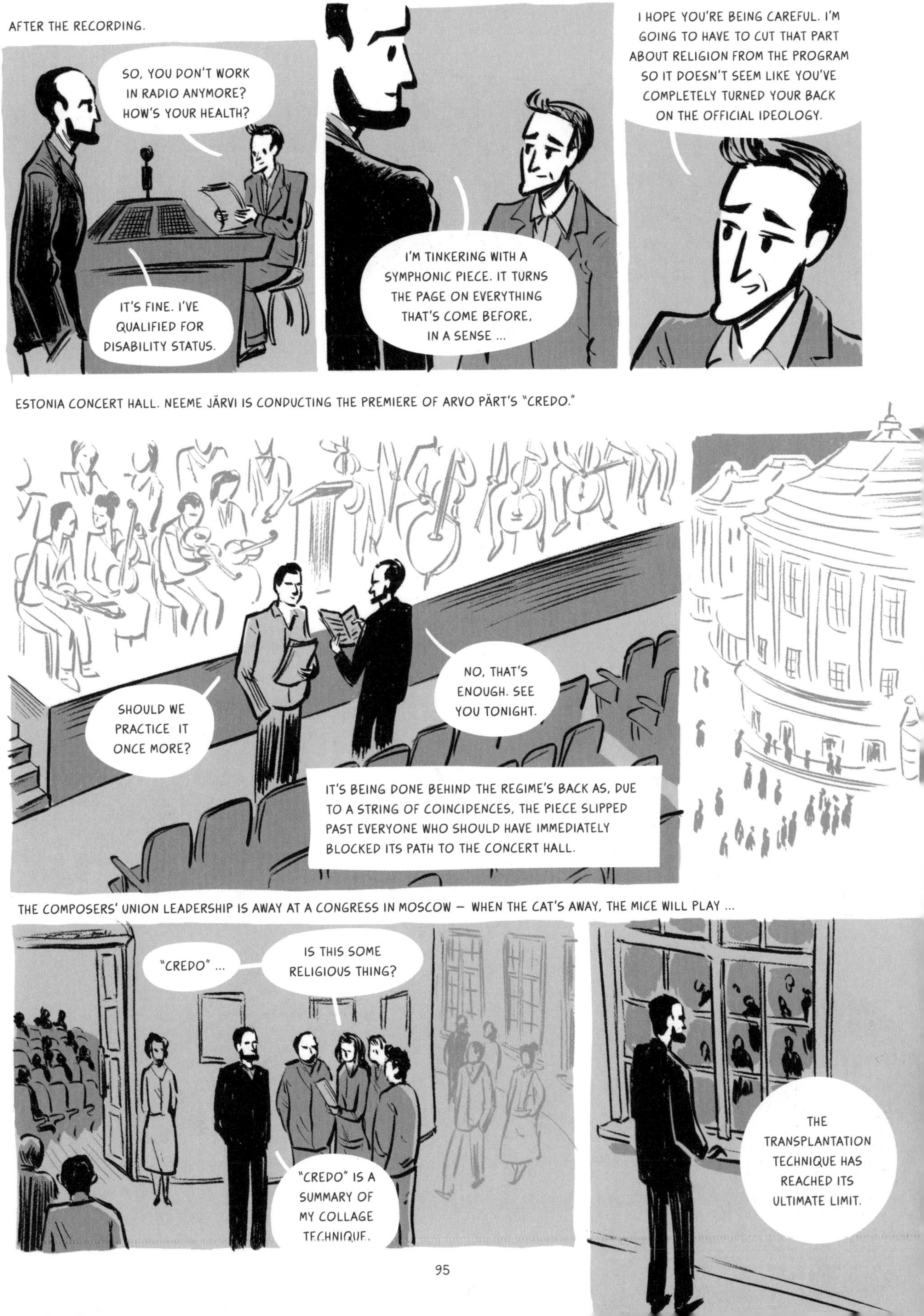
AFTER THE RECORDING.
SO, YOU DON'T WORK IN RADIO ANYMORE? HOW'S YOUR HEALTH?
IT'S FINE. I'VE QUALIFIED FOR DISABILITY STATUS.
I'M TINKERING WITH A SYMPHONIC PIECE. IT TURNS THE PAGE ON EVERYTHING THAT'S COME BEFORE, IN A SENSE ...
I HOPE YOU'RE BEING CAREFUL. I'M GOING TO HAVE TO CUT THAT PART ABOUT RELIGION FROM THE PROGRAM SO IT DOESN'T SEEM LIKE YOU'VE COMPLETELY TURNED YOUR BACK ON THE OFFICIAL IDEOLOGY.
ESTONIA CONCERT HALL. NEEME JÄRVI IS CONDUCTING THE PREMIERE OF ARVO PÄRT'S "CREDO."
SHOULD WE PRACTICE IT ONCE MORE?
NO, THAT'S ENOUGH. SEE YOU TONIGHT.
IT'S BEING DONE BEHIND THE REGIME'S BACK AS, DUE TO A STRING OF COINCIDENCES, THE PIECE SLIPPED PAST EVERYONE WHO SHOULD HAVE IMMEDIATELY BLOCKED ITS PATH TO THE CONCERT HALL.
THE COMPOSERS' UNION LEADERSHIP IS AWAY AT A CONGRESS IN MOSCOW – WHEN THE CAT'S AWAY, THE MICE WILL PLAY ...
"CREDO" ...
IS THIS SOME RELIGIOUS THING?
"CREDO" IS A SUMMARY OF MY COLLAGE TECHNIQUE.
THE TRANSPLANTATION TECHNIQUE HAS REACHED ITS ULTIMATE LIMIT.

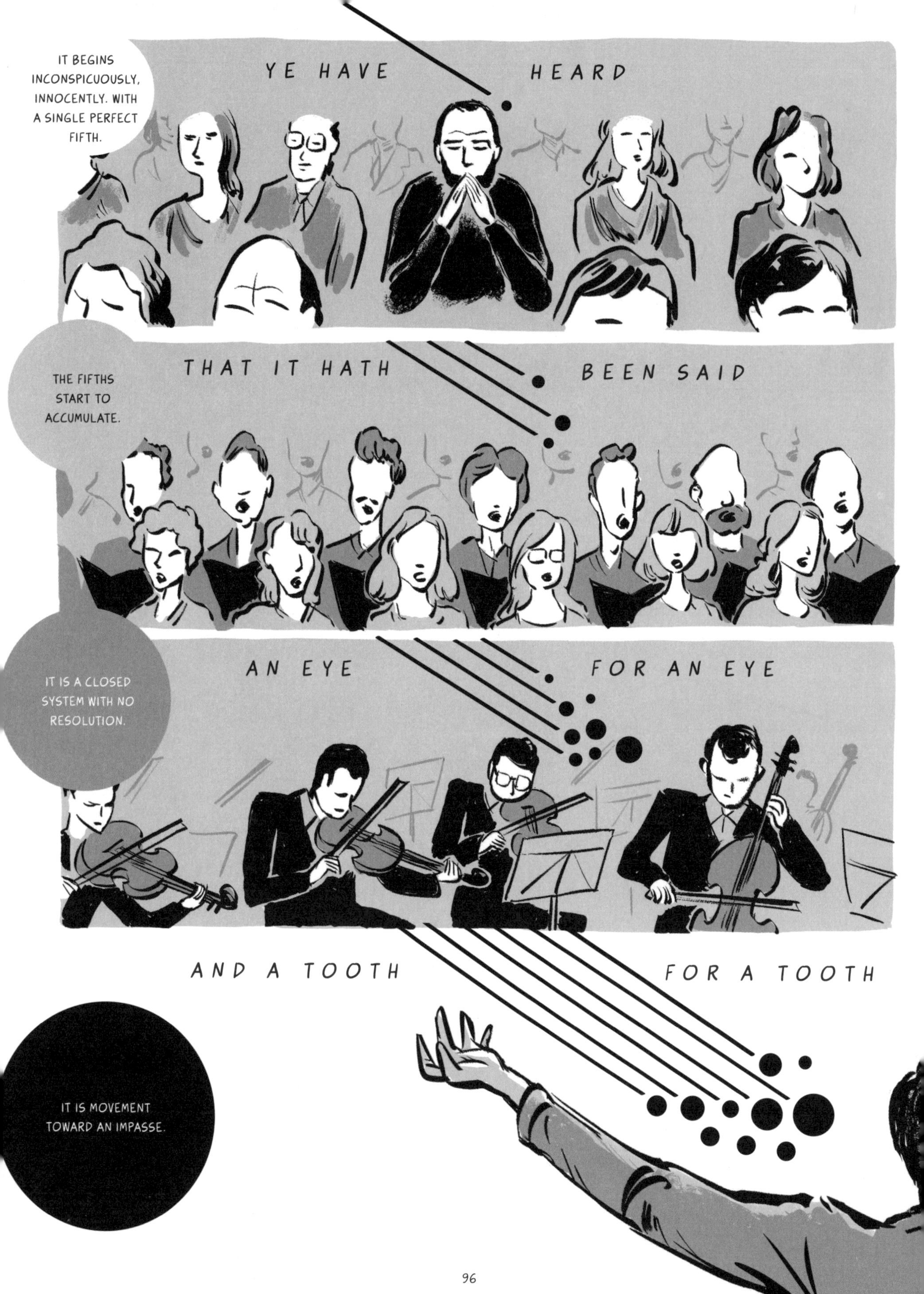
IT BEGINS INCONSPICUOUSLY, INNOCENTLY. WITH A SINGLE PERFECT FIFTH.
YE HAVE
HEARD
THE FIFTHS START TO ACCUMULATE.
THAT IT HATH
BEEN SAID
IT IS A CLOSED SYSTEM WITH NO RESOLUTION.
AN EYE
FOR AN EYE
AND A TOOTH
FOR A TOOTH
IT IS MOVEMENT TOWARD AN IMPASSE.

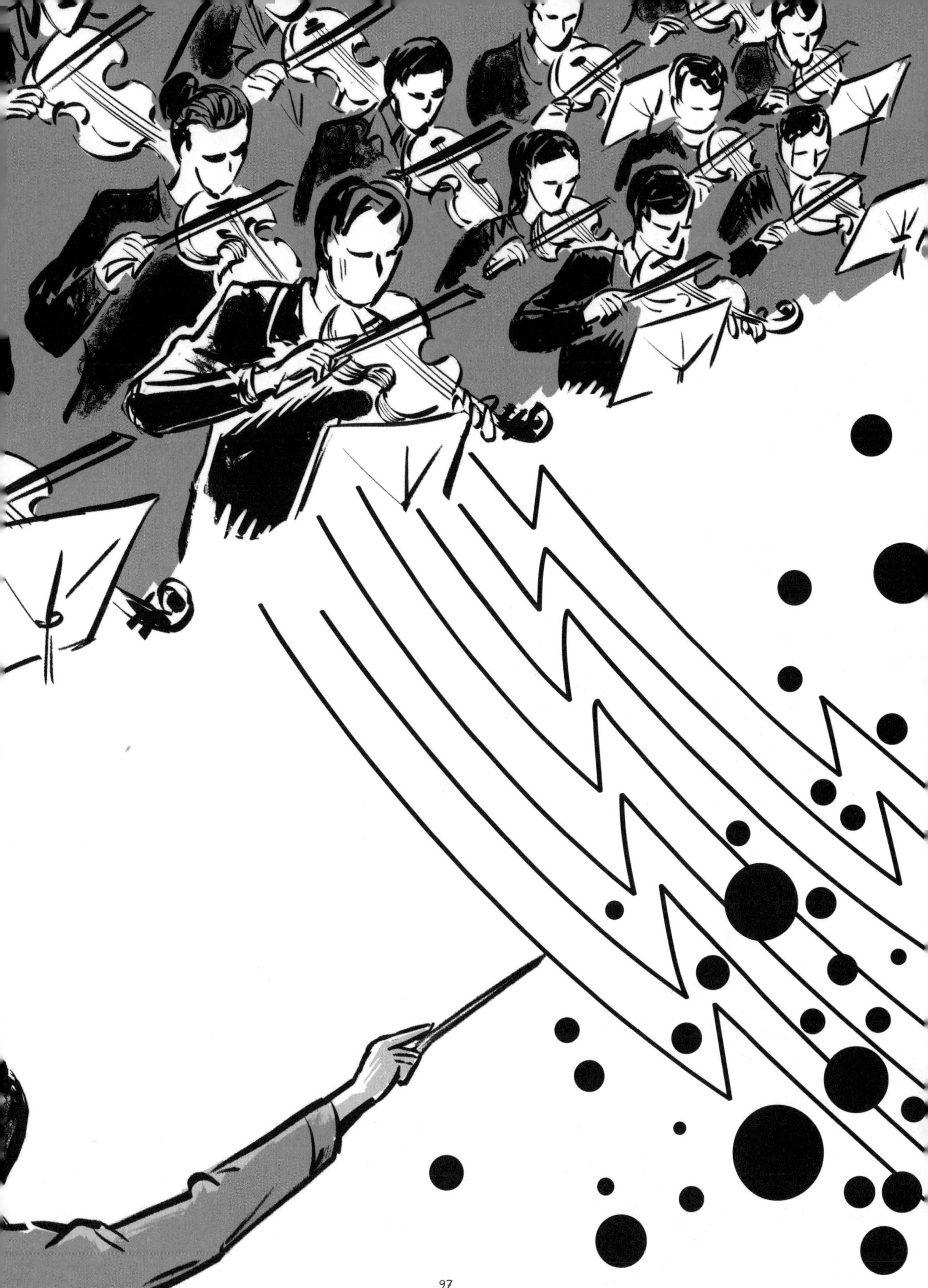

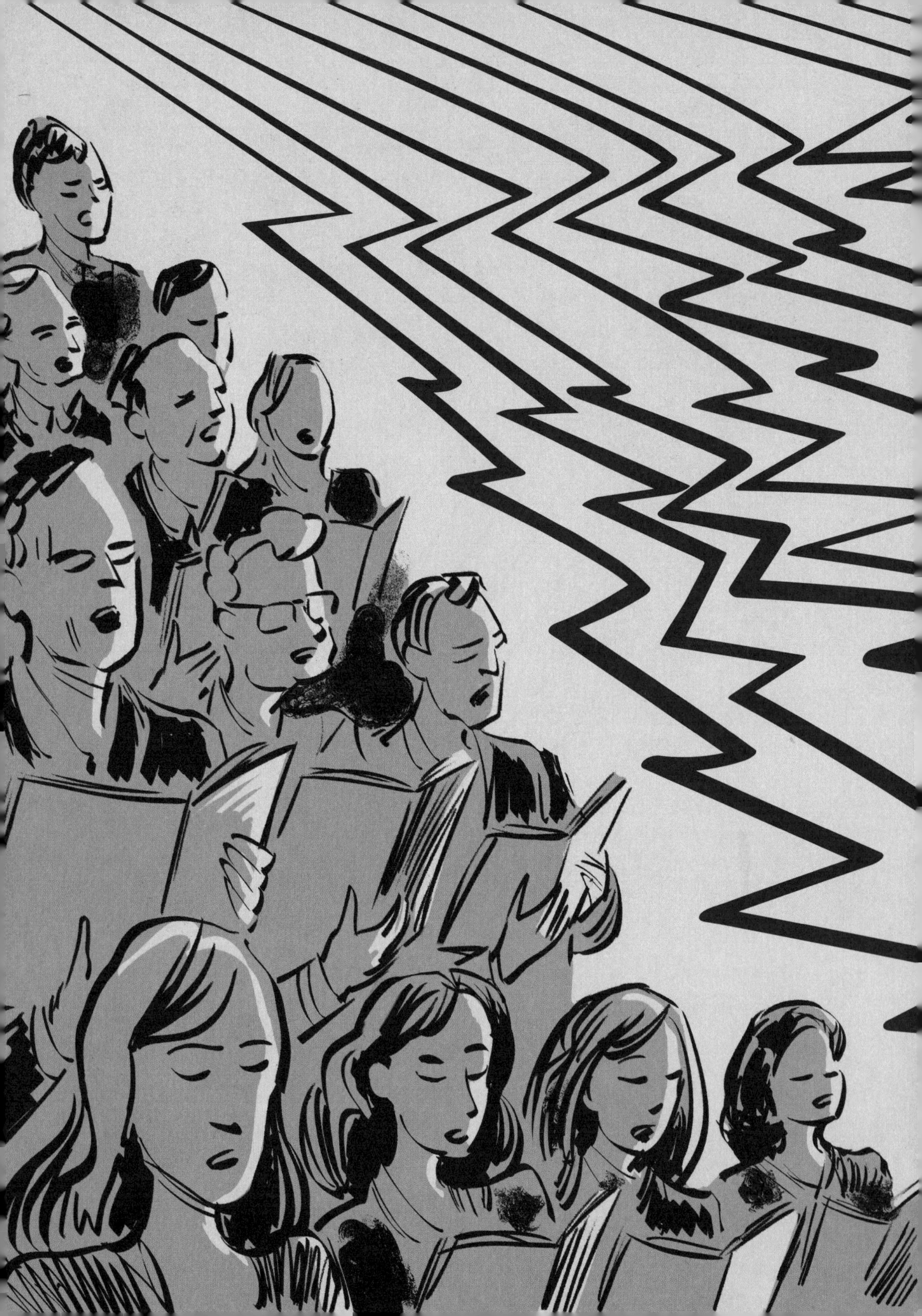

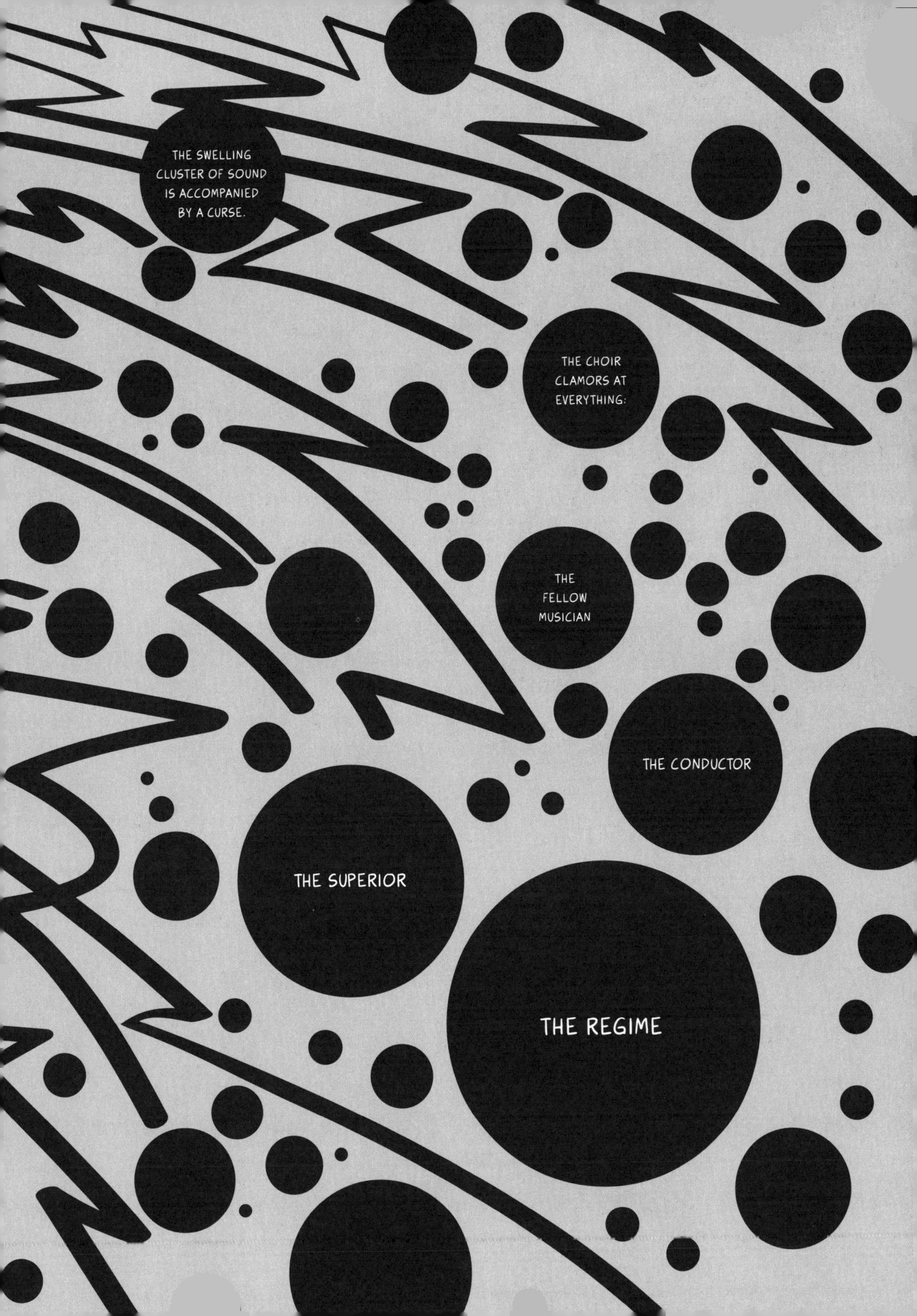
THE SWELLING CLUSTER OF SOUND IS ACCOMPANIED BY A CURSE.
THE CHOIR CLAMORS AT EVERYTHING:
THE FELLOW MUSICIAN
THE CONDUCTOR
THE SUPERIOR
THE REGIME

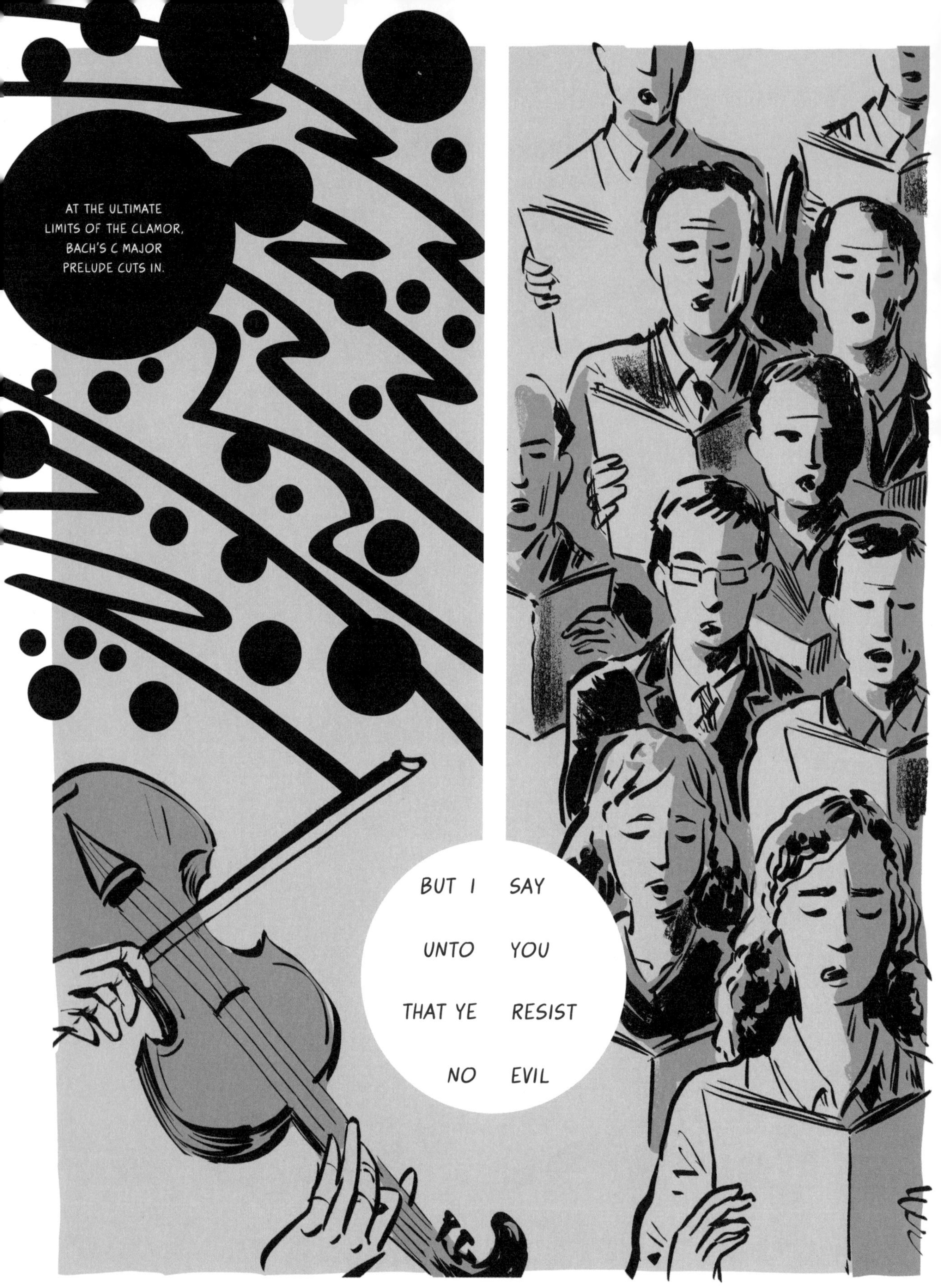
AT THE ULTIMATE LIMITS OF THE CLAMOR, BACH'S C MAJOR PRELUDE CUTS IN.
BUT I SAY UNTO YOU THAT YE RESIST NO EVIL

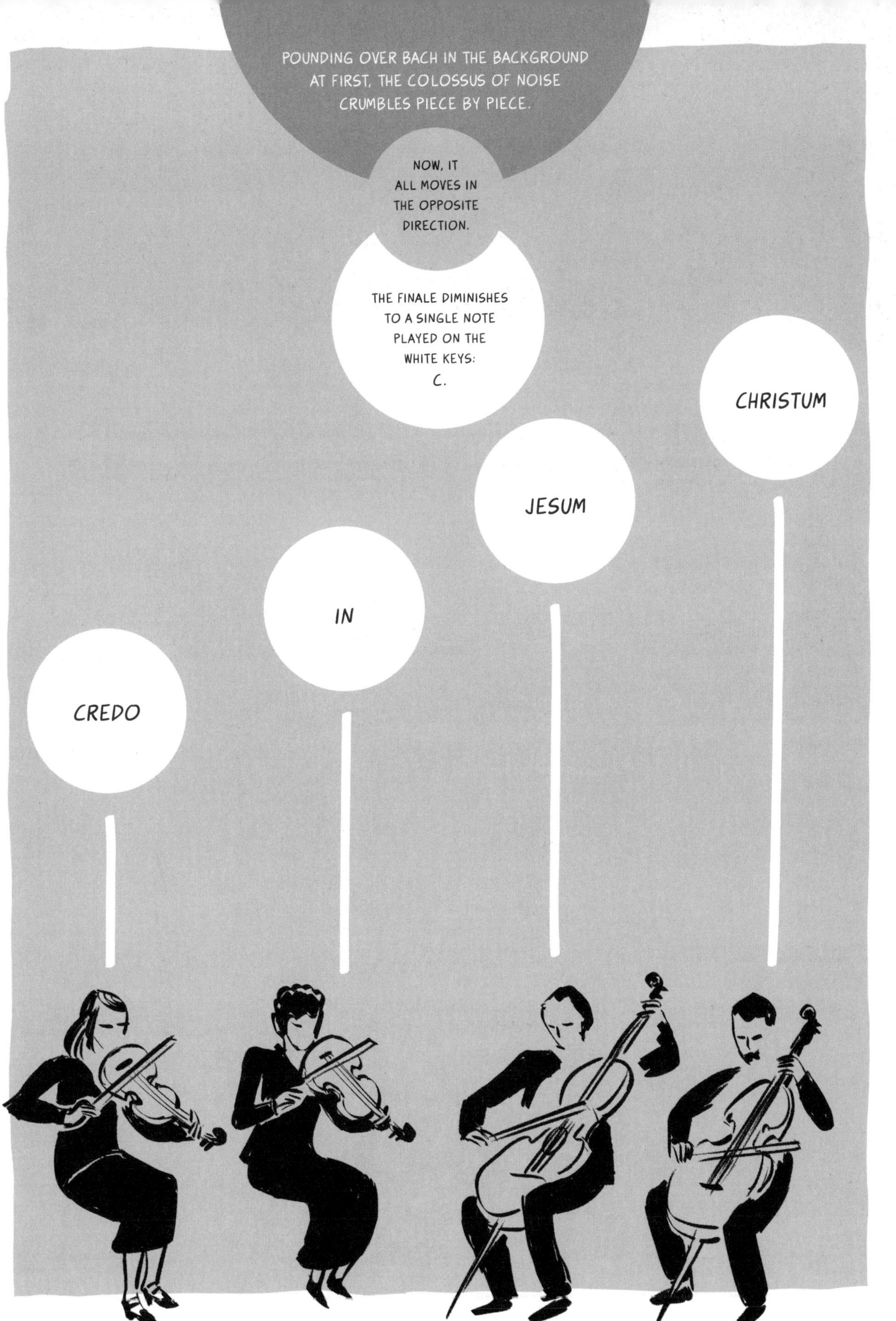
POUNDING OVER BACH IN THE BACKGROUND AT FIRST, THE COLOSSUS OF NOISE CRUMBLES PIECE BY PIECE.
NOW, IT ALL MOVES IN THE OPPOSITE DIRECTION.
THE FINALE DIMINISHES TO A SINGLE NOTE PLAYED ON THE WHITE KEYS: C.
CREDO
IN
JESUM
CHRISTUM

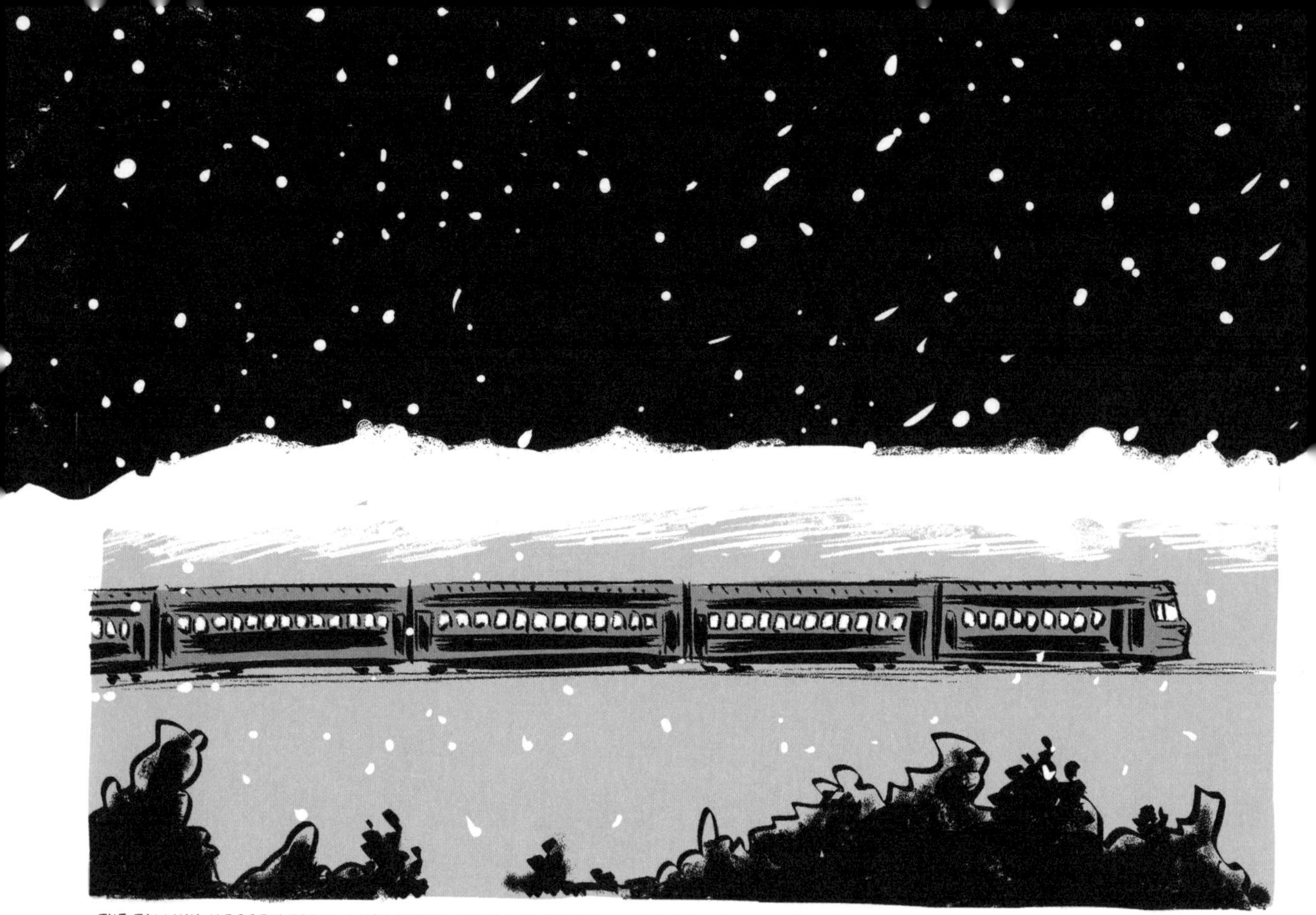

THE TALLINN-MOSCOW TRAIN, A FEW WEEKS AFTER THE PREMIERE OF "CREDO." A COMPOSERS' UNION DELEGATION IS EN ROUTE TO A CONGRESS.

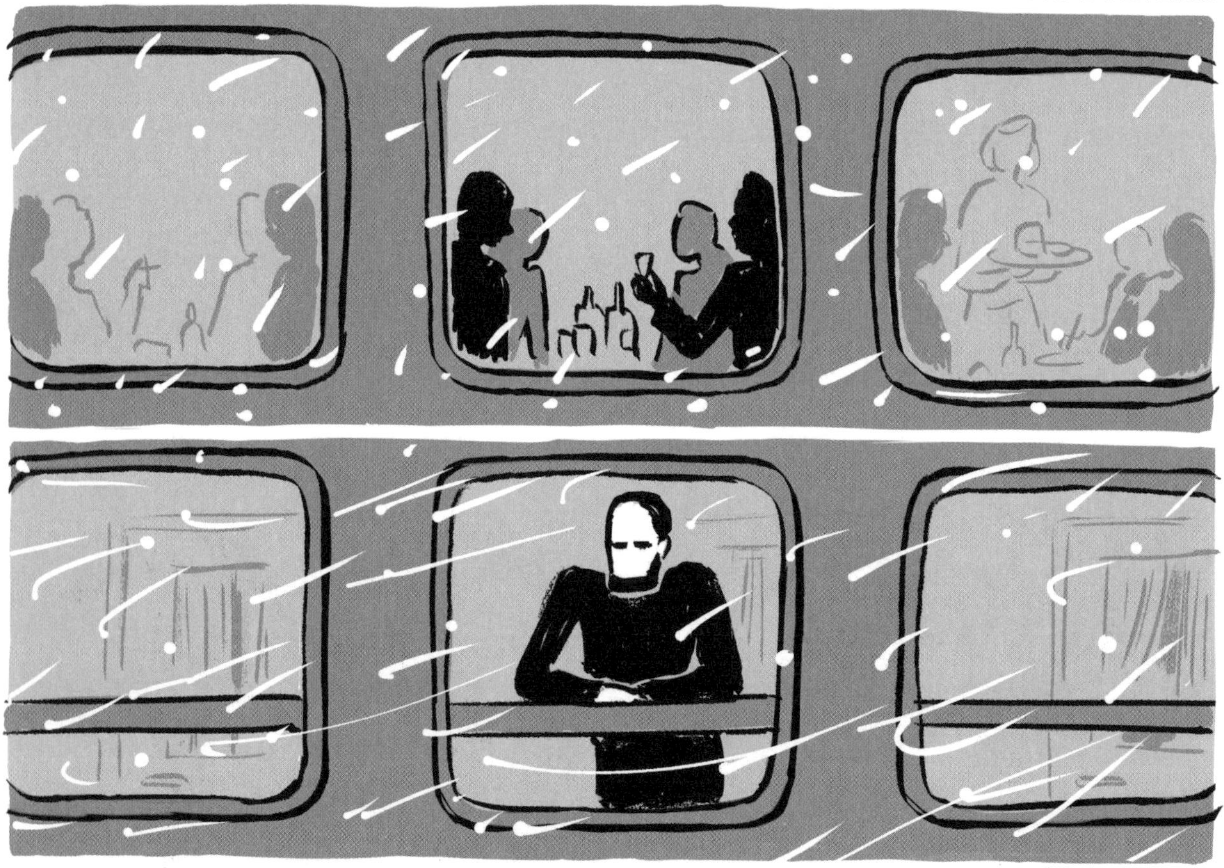

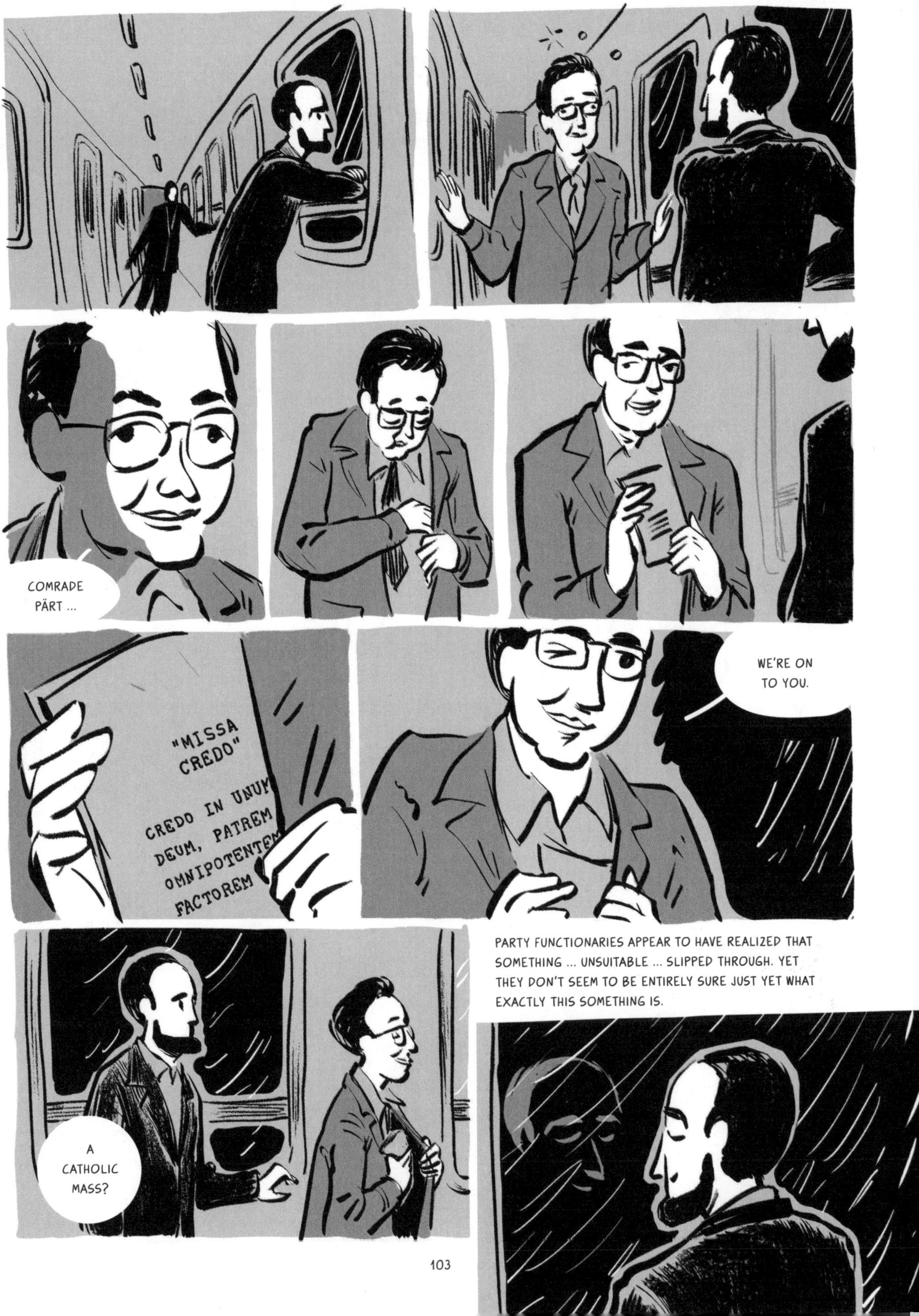
COMRADE PÄRT ...
"MISSA CREDO"
CREDO IN UNUM DEUM, PATREM OMNIPOTENTEM FACTOREM
WE'RE ON TO YOU.
A CATHOLIC MASS?
PARTY FUNCTIONARIES APPEAR TO HAVE REALIZED THAT SOMETHING ... UNSUITABLE ... SLIPPED THROUGH. YET THEY DON'T SEEM TO BE ENTIRELY SURE JUST YET WHAT EXACTLY THIS SOMETHING IS.

A FEW MONTHS LATER, ARVO IS CALLED IN FOR ANOTHER MEETING WITH OLAF UTT, SECRETARY OF CULTURE OF THE CENTRAL COMMITTEE OF THE COMMUNIST PARTY.

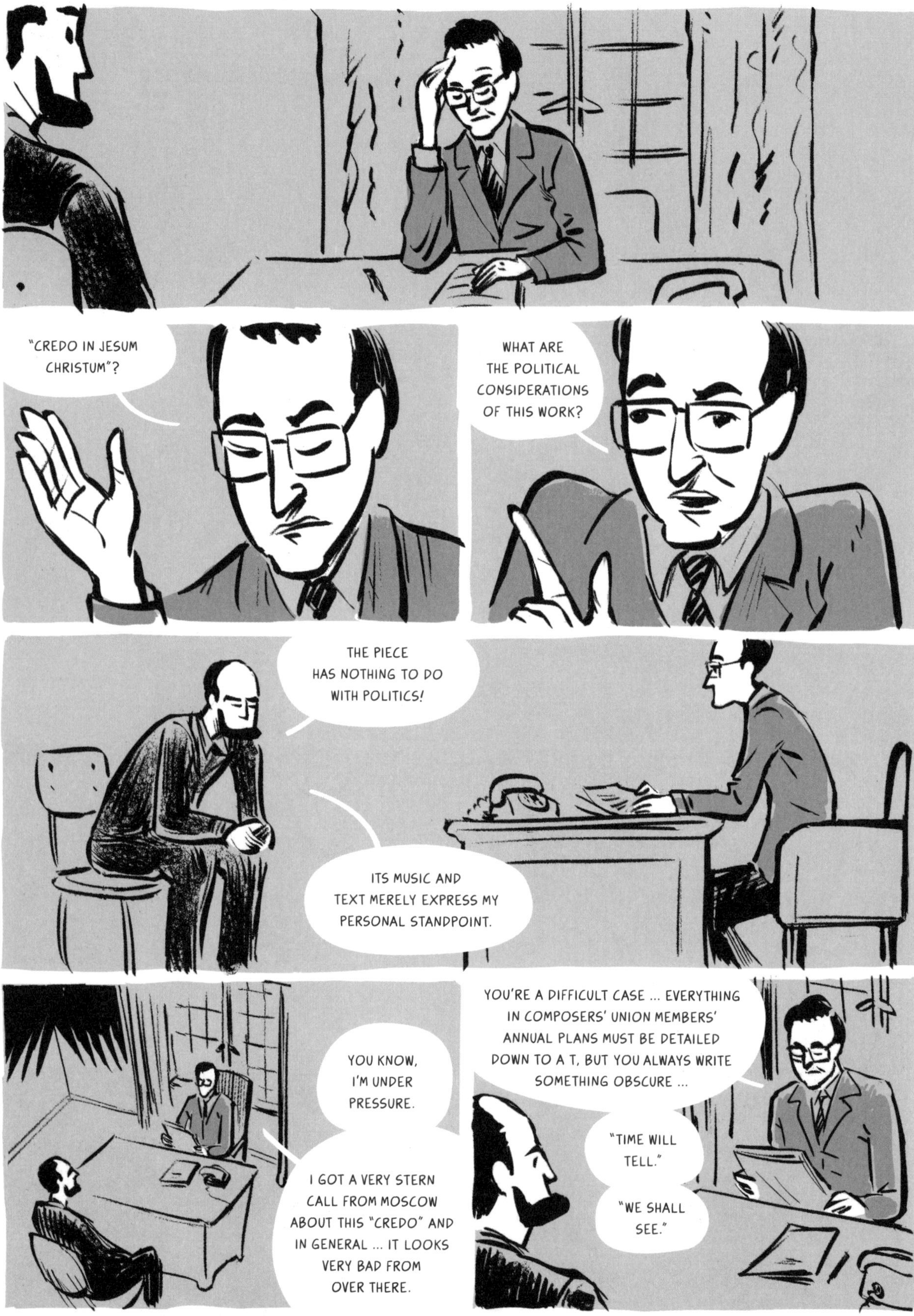

"CREDO IN JESUM CHRISTUM"?
WHAT ARE THE POLITICAL CONSIDERATIONS OF THIS WORK?
THE PIECE HAS NOTHING TO DO WITH POLITICS!
ITS MUSIC AND TEXT MERELY EXPRESS MY PERSONAL STANDPOINT.
YOU KNOW, I'M UNDER PRESSURE.
I GOT A VERY STERN CALL FROM MOSCOW ABOUT THIS "CREDO" AND IN GENERAL ... IT LOOKS VERY BAD FROM OVER THERE.
YOU'RE A DIFFICULT CASE ... EVERYTHING IN COMPOSERS' UNION MEMBERS' ANNUAL PLANS MUST BE DETAILED DOWN TO A T, BUT YOU ALWAYS WRITE SOMETHING OBSCURE ...
"TIME WILL TELL."
"WE SHALL SEE."

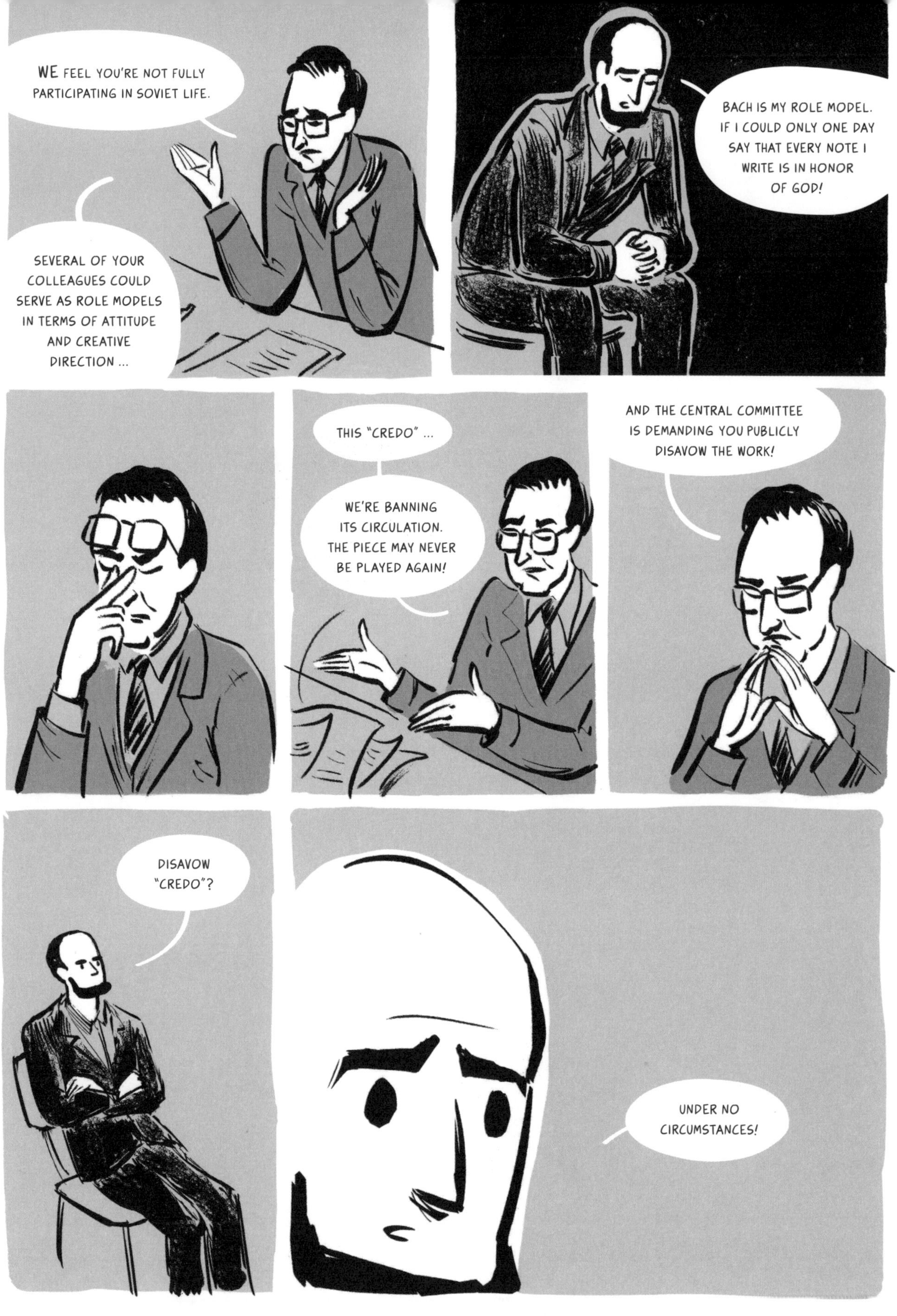
WE FEEL YOU'RE NOT FULLY PARTICIPATING IN SOVIET LIFE.
SEVERAL OF YOUR COLLEAGUES COULD SERVE AS ROLE MODELS IN TERMS OF ATTITUDE AND CREATIVE DIRECTION ...
BACH IS MY ROLE MODEL. IF I COULD ONLY ONE DAY SAY THAT EVERY NOTE I WRITE IS IN HONOR OF GOD!
THIS "CREDO" ...
WE'RE BANNING ITS CIRCULATION. THE PIECE MAY NEVER BE PLAYED AGAIN!
AND THE CENTRAL COMMITTEE IS DEMANDING YOU PUBLICLY DISAVOW THE WORK!
DISAVOW "CREDO"?
UNDER NO CIRCUMSTANCES!

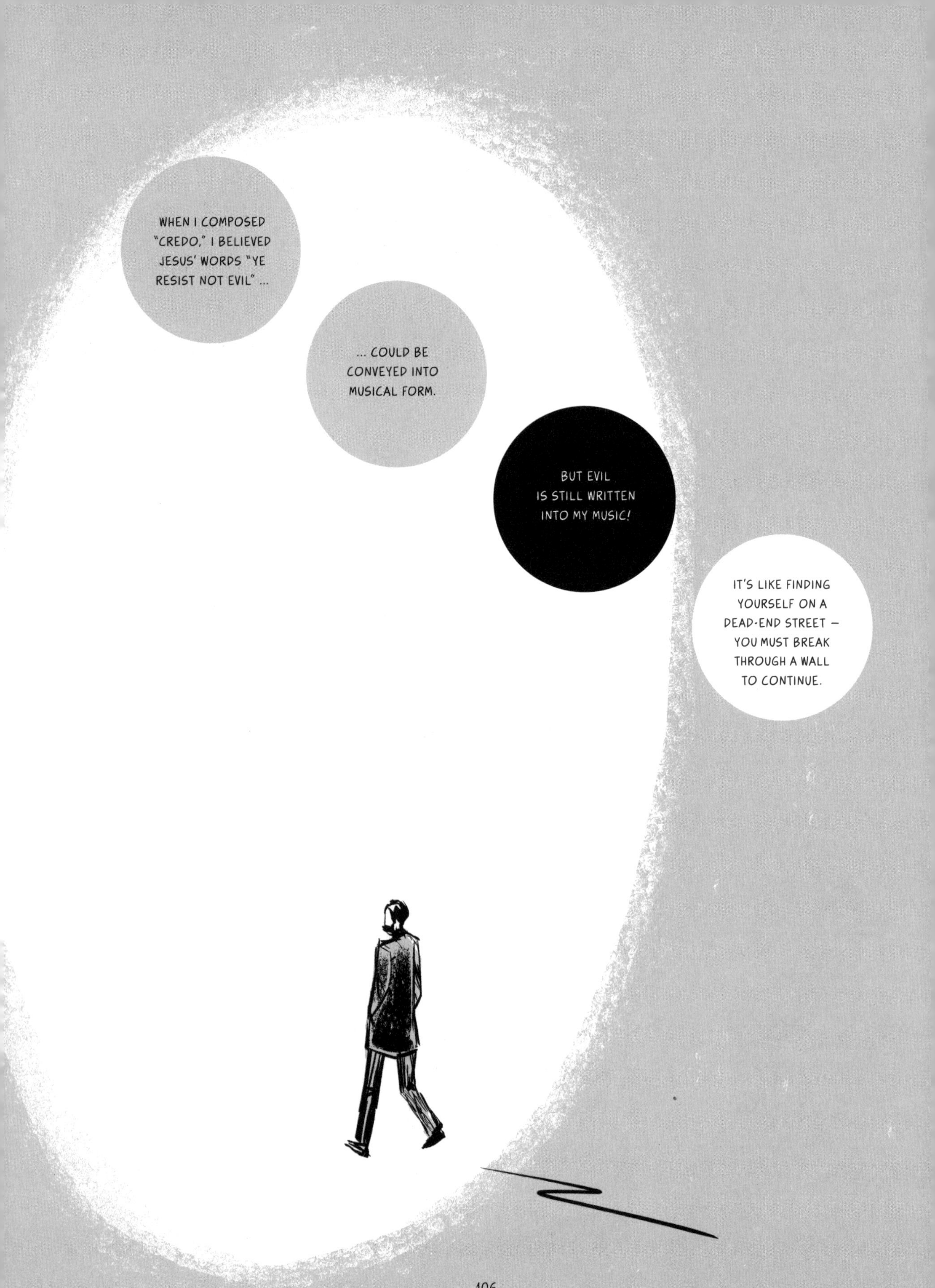
WHEN I COMPOSED "CREDO," I BELIEVED JESUS' WORDS "YE RESIST NOT EVIL" ...
... COULD BE CONVEYED INTO MUSICAL FORM.
BUT EVIL IS STILL WRITTEN INTO MY MUSIC!
IT'S LIKE FINDING YOURSELF ON A DEAD-END STREET — YOU MUST BREAK THROUGH A WALL TO CONTINUE.

II

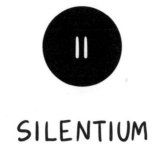

SILENTIUM

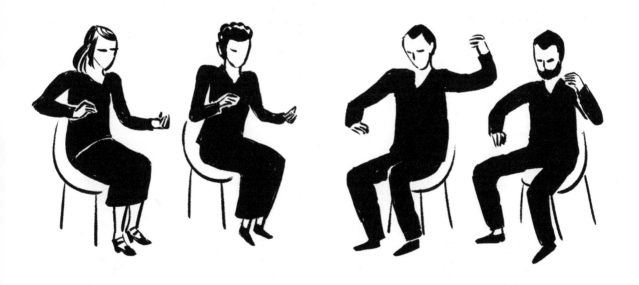

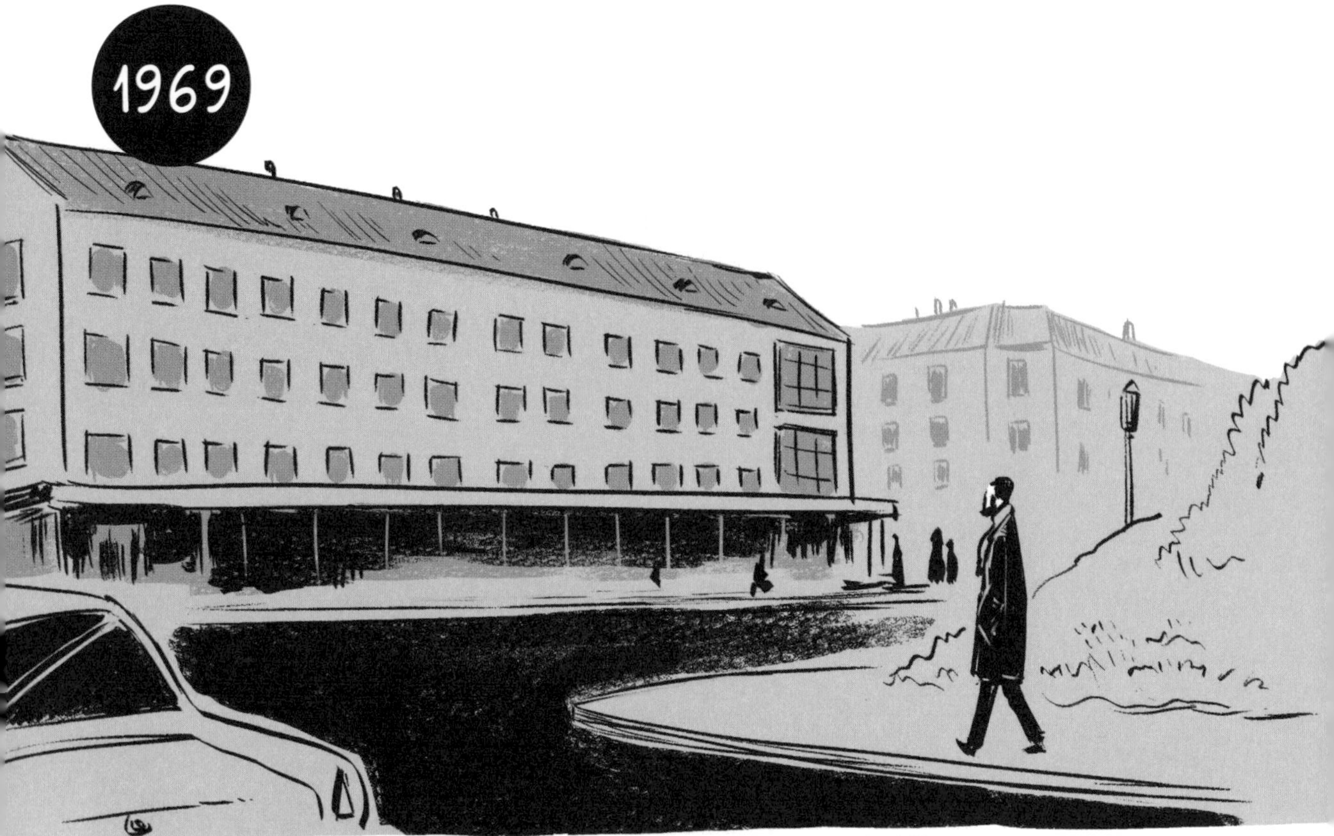
1969

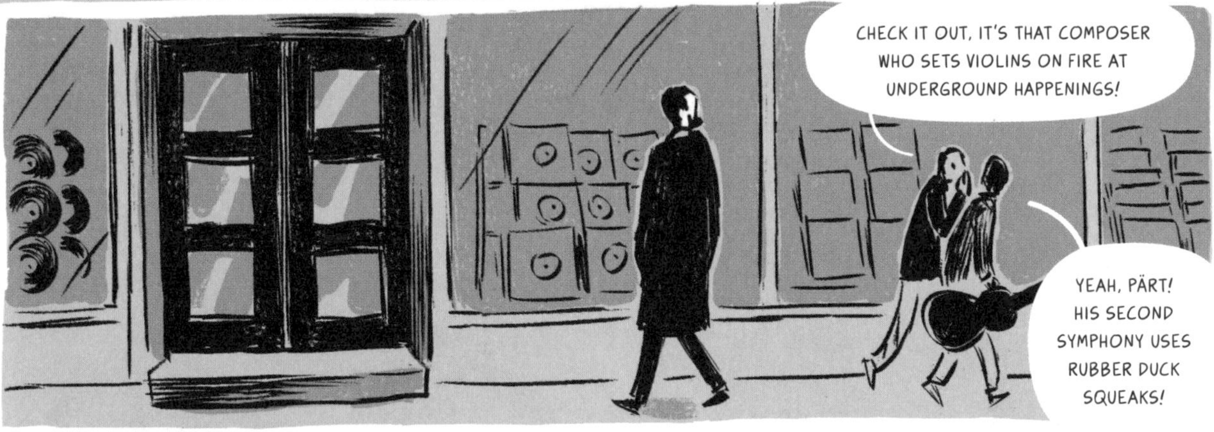
CHECK IT OUT, IT'S THAT COMPOSER WHO SETS VIOLINS ON FIRE AT UNDERGROUND HAPPENINGS!
YEAH, PÄRT! HIS SECOND SYMPHONY USES RUBBER DUCK SQUEAKS!

ON THE GROUND FLOOR OF TALLINN'S WRITERS' HOUSE IS ONE OF THE LARGEST RECORD STORES IN THE ESTONIAN SSR.

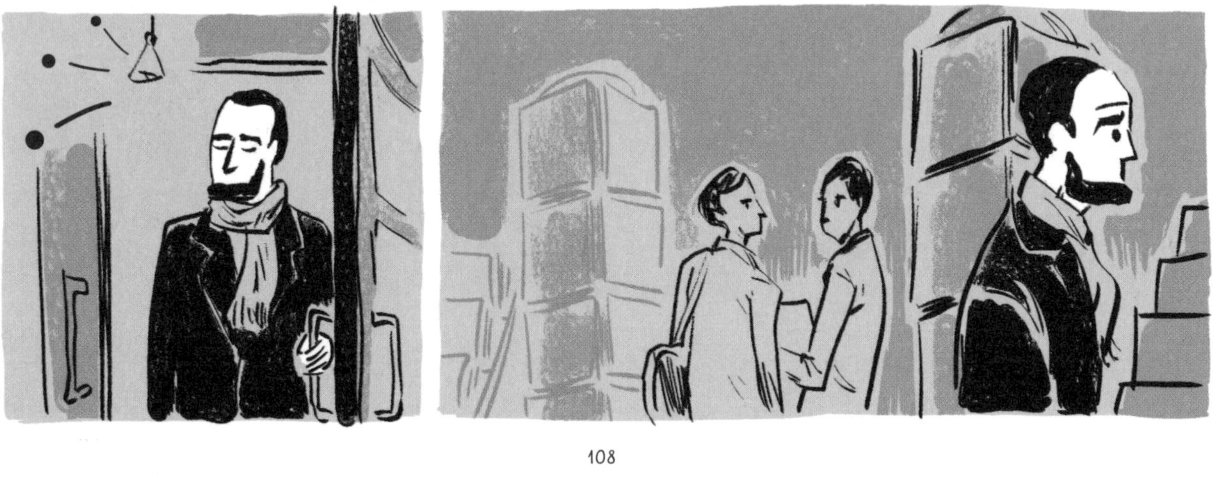

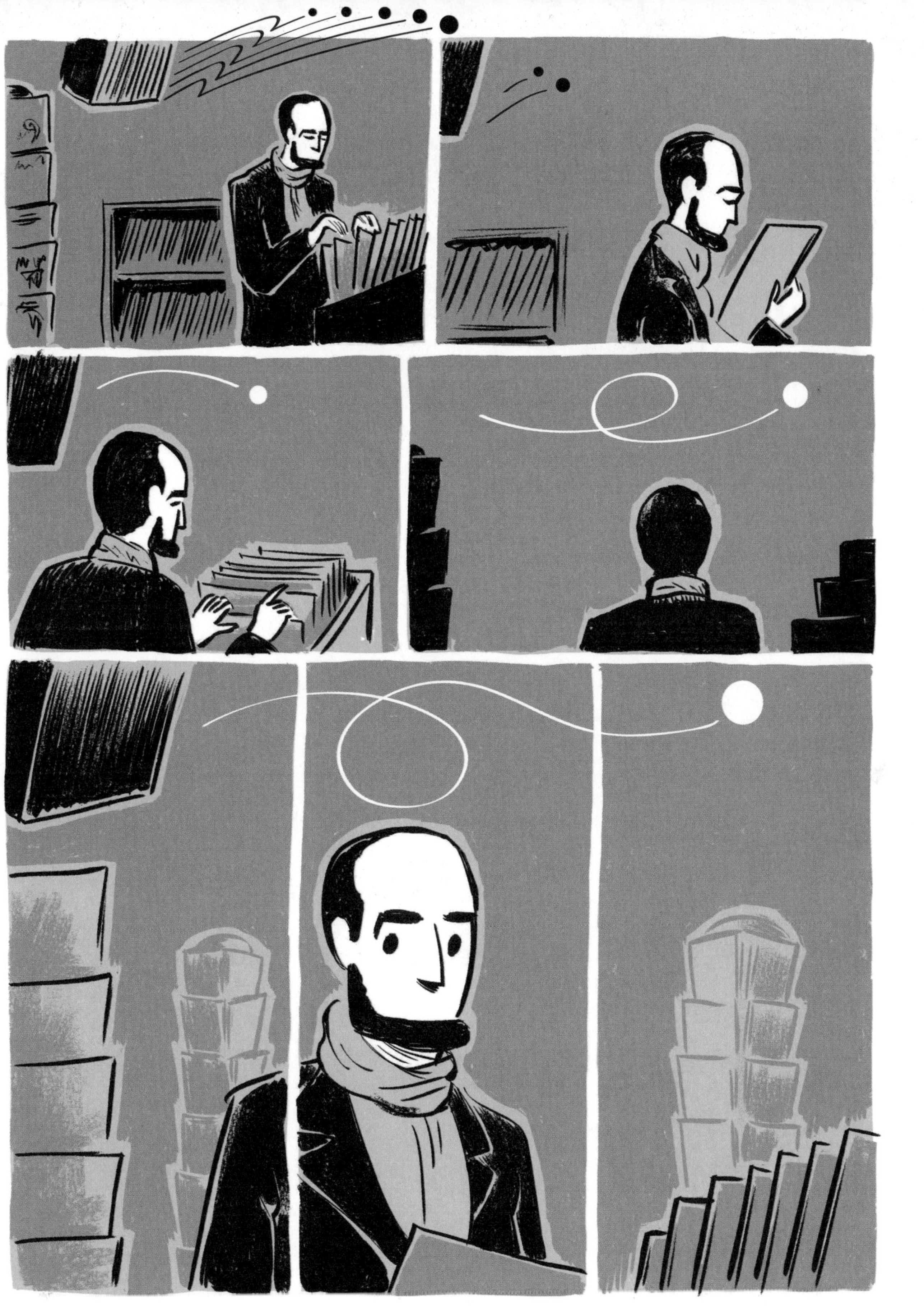

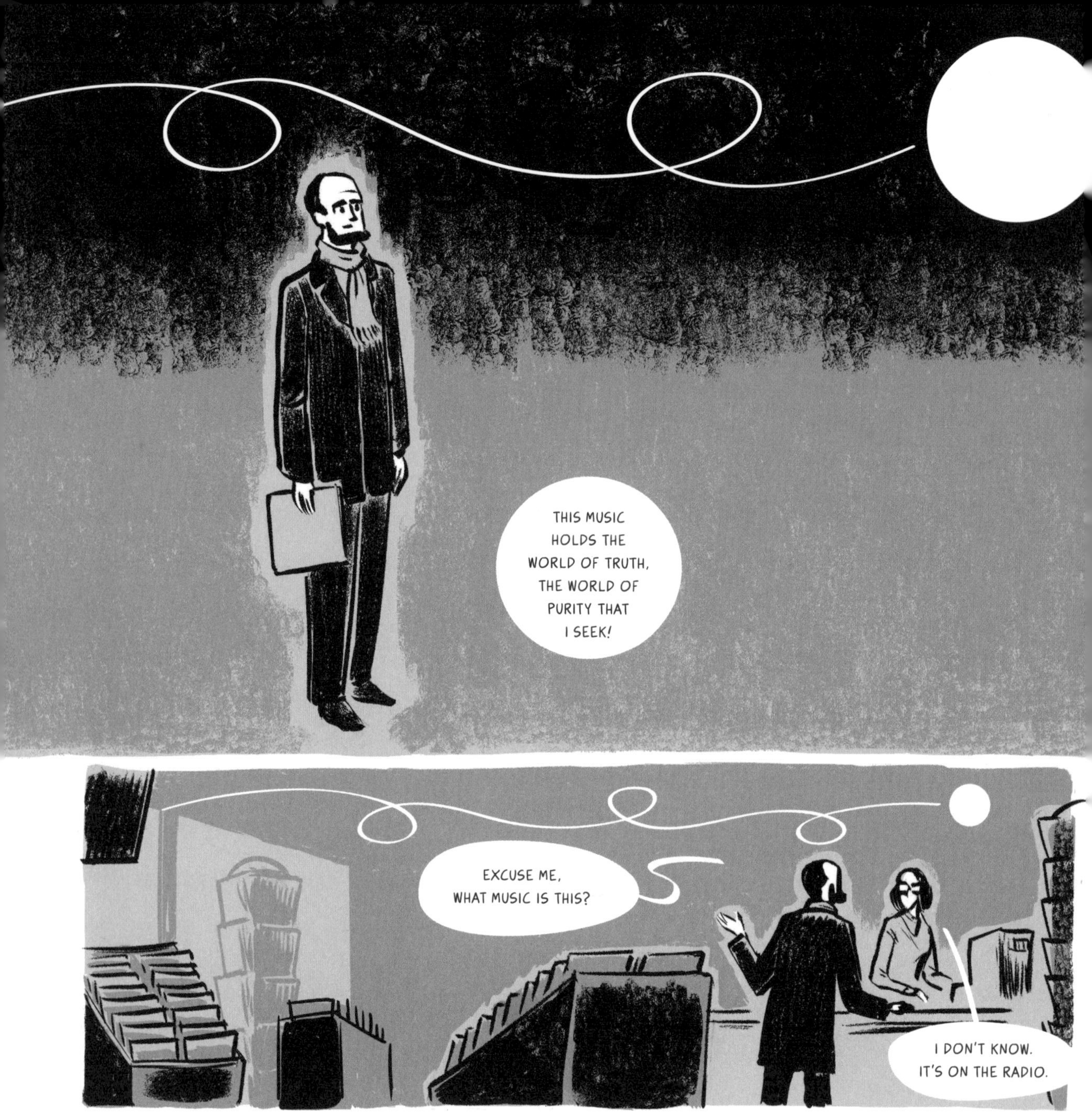
THIS MUSIC HOLDS THE WORLD OF TRUTH, THE WORLD OF PURITY THAT I SEEK!
EXCUSE ME, WHAT MUSIC IS THIS?
I DON'T KNOW. IT'S ON THE RADIO.

ARVO HEARS SOMETHING THAT FUNDAMENTALLY CHANGES HIS CONCEPTION OF MUSIC.
IT TAKES A WHILE, BUT HE EVENTUALLY FINDS OUT IT WAS THE "EARLY MUSIC HOUR" PROGRAM FEATURING GREGORIAN CHANT.

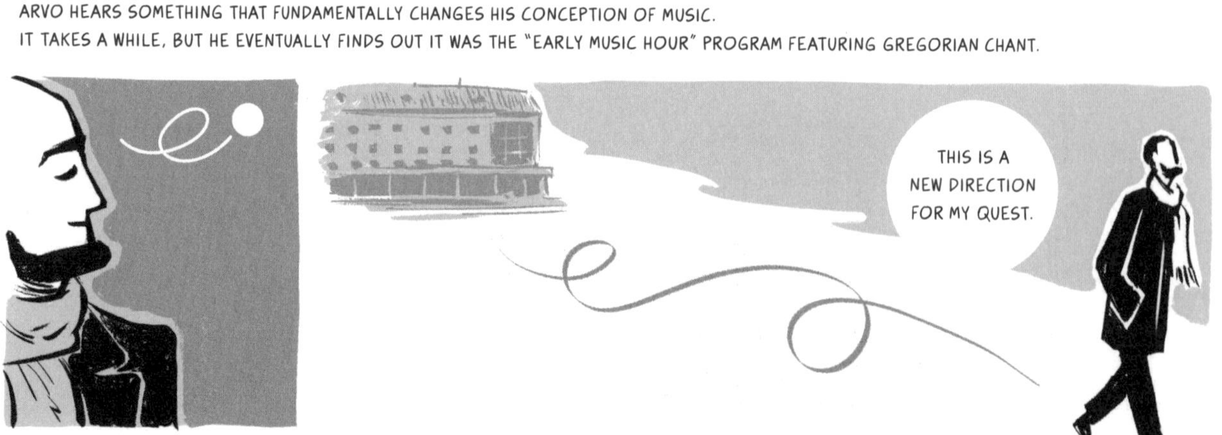
THIS IS A NEW DIRECTION FOR MY QUEST.

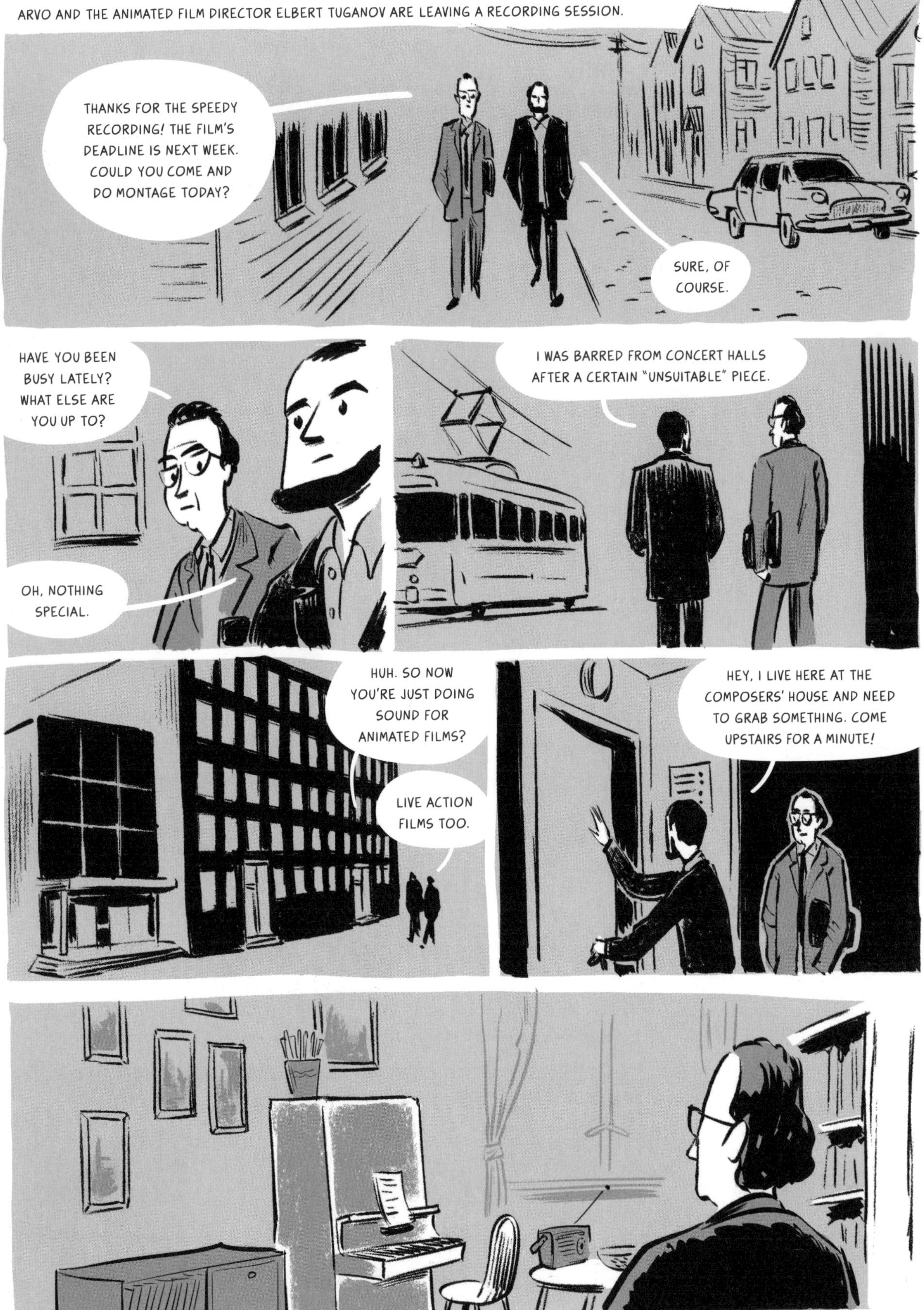
ARVO AND THE ANIMATED FILM DIRECTOR ELBERT TUGANOV ARE LEAVING A RECORDING SESSION.
THANKS FOR THE SPEEDY RECORDING! THE FILM'S DEADLINE IS NEXT WEEK. COULD YOU COME AND DO MONTAGE TODAY?
SURE, OF COURSE.
HAVE YOU BEEN BUSY LATELY? WHAT ELSE ARE YOU UP TO?
OH, NOTHING SPECIAL.
I WAS BARRED FROM CONCERT HALLS AFTER A CERTAIN "UNSUITABLE" PIECE.
HUH. SO NOW YOU'RE JUST DOING SOUND FOR ANIMATED FILMS?
LIVE ACTION FILMS TOO.
HEY, I LIVE HERE AT THE COMPOSERS' HOUSE AND NEED TO GRAB SOMETHING. COME UPSTAIRS FOR A MINUTE!

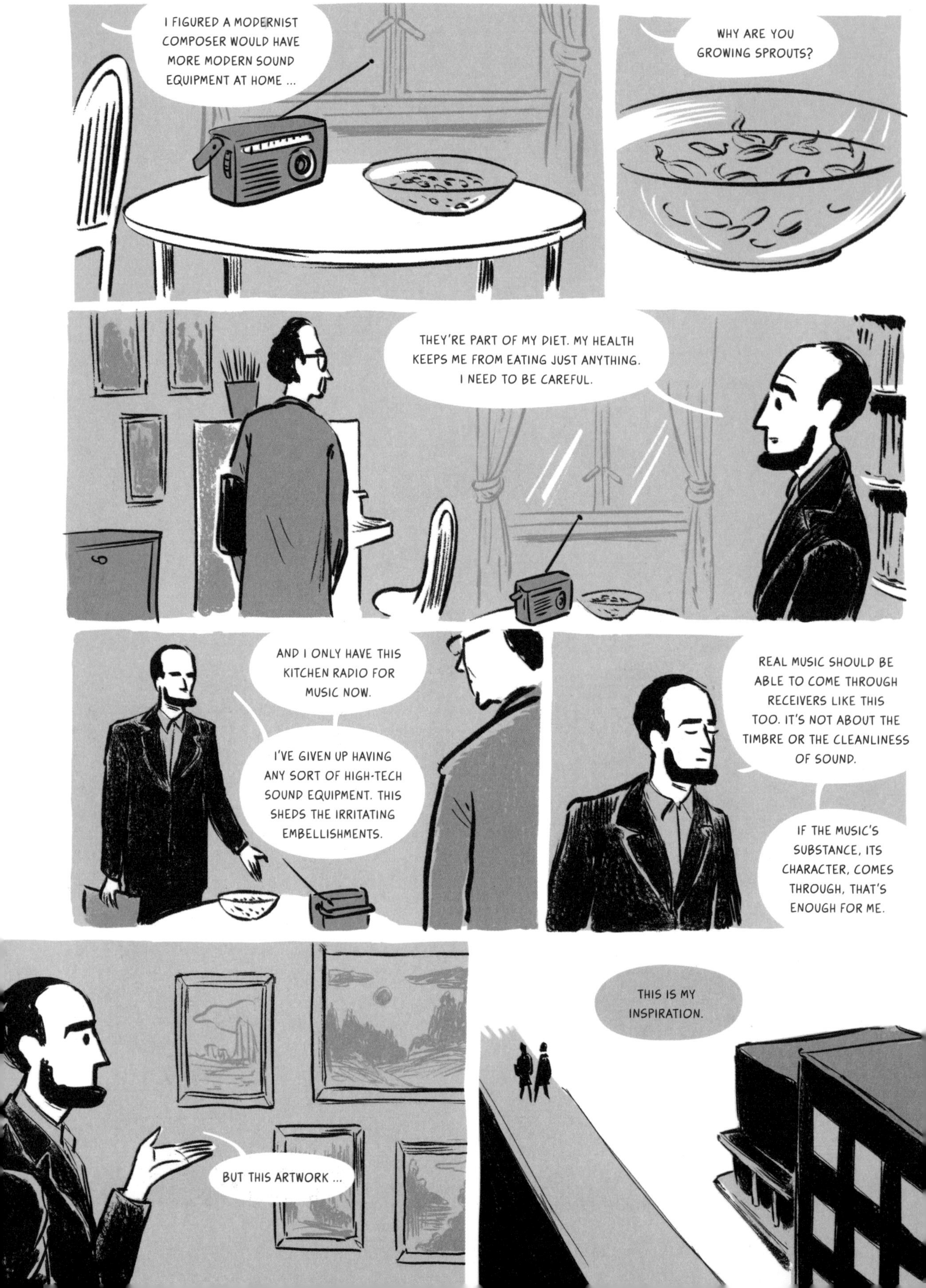
I FIGURED A MODERNIST COMPOSER WOULD HAVE MORE MODERN SOUND EQUIPMENT AT HOME ...
WHY ARE YOU GROWING SPROUTS?
THEY'RE PART OF MY DIET. MY HEALTH KEEPS ME FROM EATING JUST ANYTHING. I NEED TO BE CAREFUL.
AND I ONLY HAVE THIS KITCHEN RADIO FOR MUSIC NOW.
I'VE GIVEN UP HAVING ANY SORT OF HIGH-TECH SOUND EQUIPMENT. THIS SHEDS THE IRRITATING EMBELLISHMENTS.
REAL MUSIC SHOULD BE ABLE TO COME THROUGH RECEIVERS LIKE THIS TOO. IT'S NOT ABOUT THE TIMBRE OR THE CLEANLINESS OF SOUND.
IF THE MUSIC'S SUBSTANCE, ITS CHARACTER, COMES THROUGH, THAT'S ENOUGH FOR ME.
BUT THIS ARTWORK ...
THIS IS MY INSPIRATION.

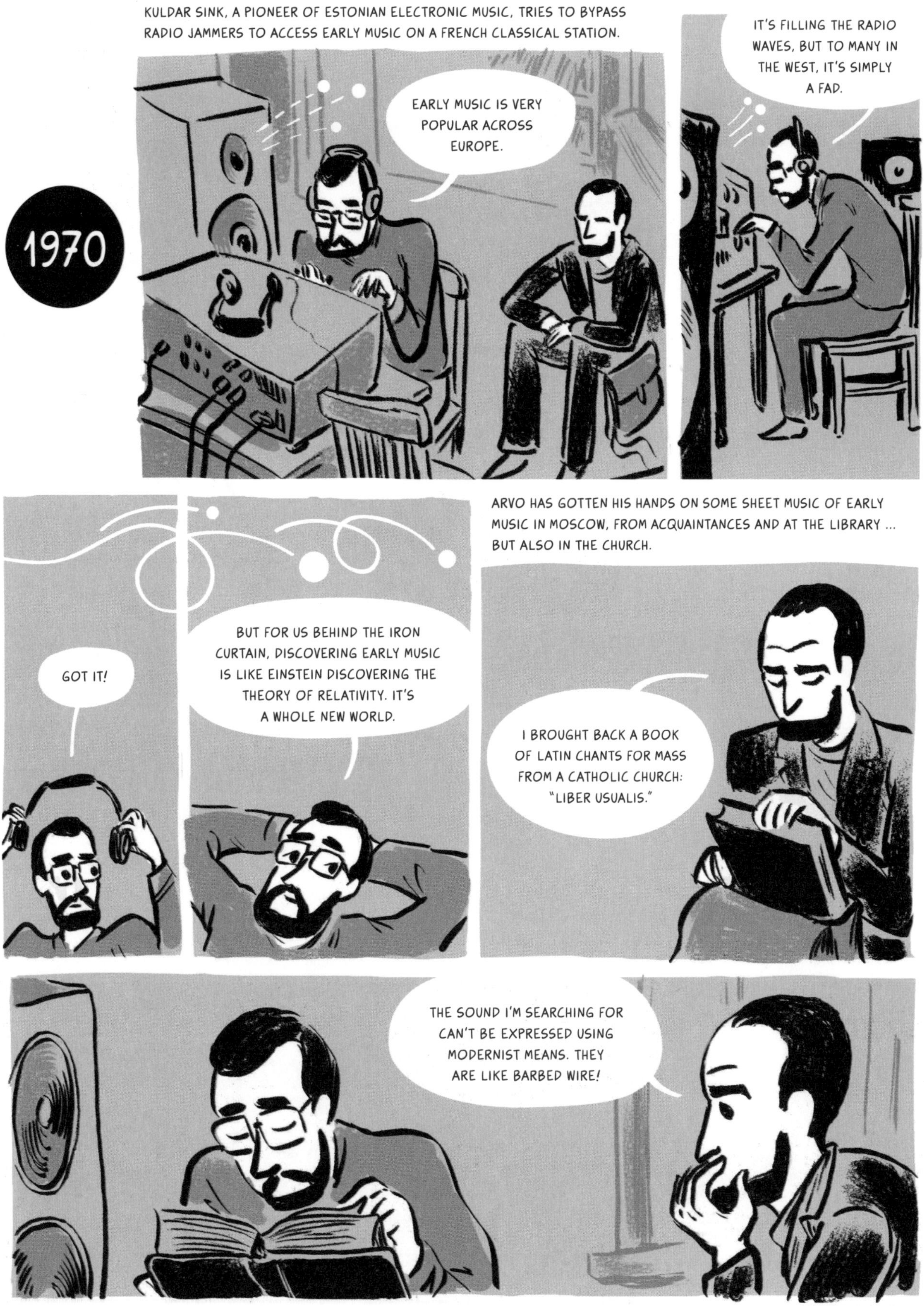
1970
KULDAR SINK, A PIONEER OF ESTONIAN ELECTRONIC MUSIC, TRIES TO BYPASS RADIO JAMMERS TO ACCESS EARLY MUSIC ON A FRENCH CLASSICAL STATION.
EARLY MUSIC IS VERY POPULAR ACROSS EUROPE.
IT'S FILLING THE RADIO WAVES, BUT TO MANY IN THE WEST, IT'S SIMPLY A FAD.
GOT IT!
BUT FOR US BEHIND THE IRON CURTAIN, DISCOVERING EARLY MUSIC IS LIKE EINSTEIN DISCOVERING THE THEORY OF RELATIVITY. IT'S A WHOLE NEW WORLD.
ARVO HAS GOTTEN HIS HANDS ON SOME SHEET MUSIC OF EARLY MUSIC IN MOSCOW, FROM ACQUAINTANCES AND AT THE LIBRARY ... BUT ALSO IN THE CHURCH.
I BROUGHT BACK A BOOK OF LATIN CHANTS FOR MASS FROM A CATHOLIC CHURCH: "LIBER USUALIS."
THE SOUND I'M SEARCHING FOR CAN'T BE EXPRESSED USING MODERNIST MEANS. THEY ARE LIKE BARBED WIRE!

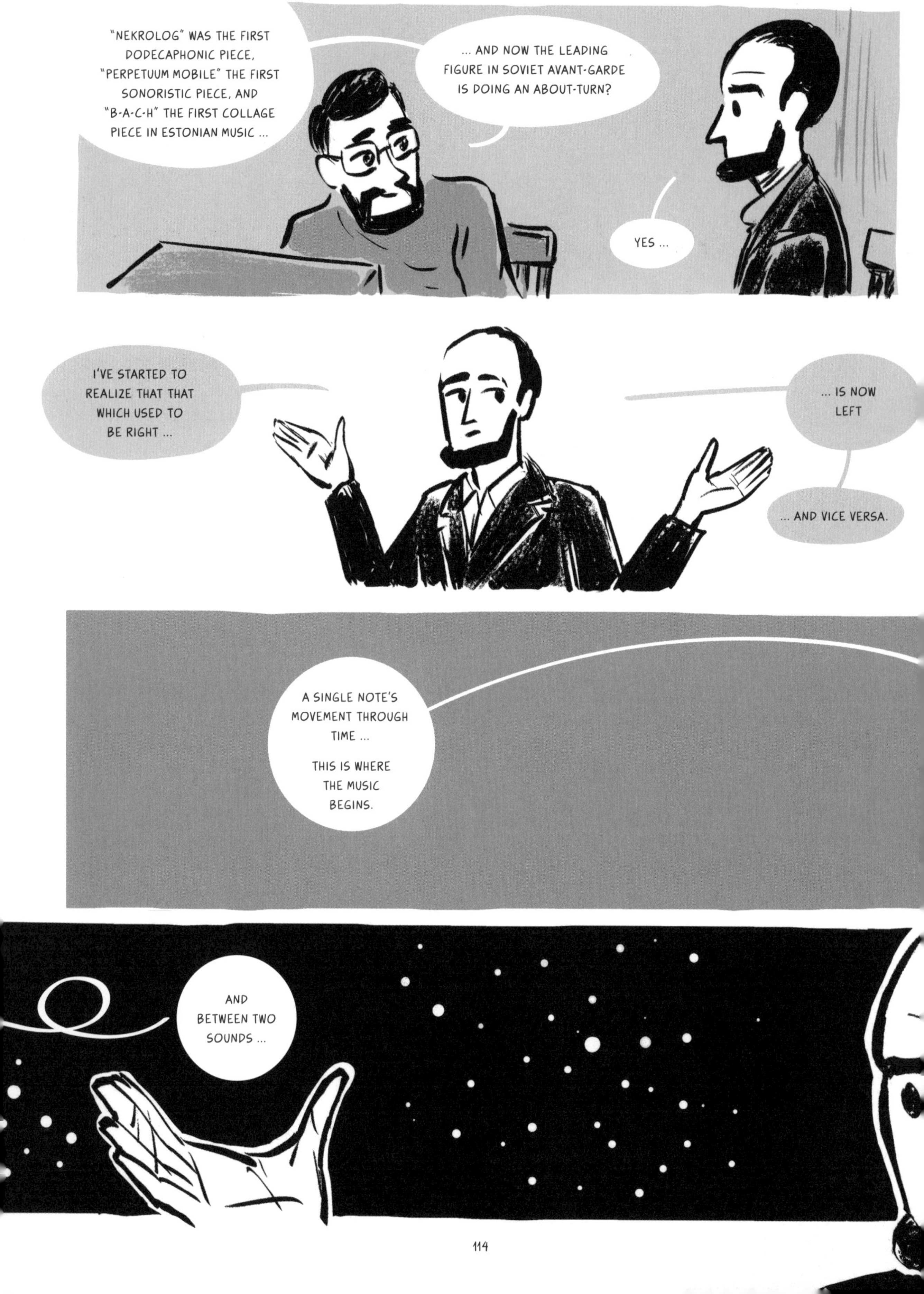

"NEKROLOG" WAS THE FIRST DODECAPHONIC PIECE, "PERPETUUM MOBILE" THE FIRST SONORISTIC PIECE, AND "B-A-C-H" THE FIRST COLLAGE PIECE IN ESTONIAN MUSIC ...
... AND NOW THE LEADING FIGURE IN SOVIET AVANT-GARDE IS DOING AN ABOUT-TURN?
YES ...
I'VE STARTED TO REALIZE THAT THAT WHICH USED TO BE RIGHT ...
... IS NOW LEFT
... AND VICE VERSA.
A SINGLE NOTE'S MOVEMENT THROUGH TIME ...
THIS IS WHERE THE MUSIC BEGINS.
AND BETWEEN TWO SOUNDS ...

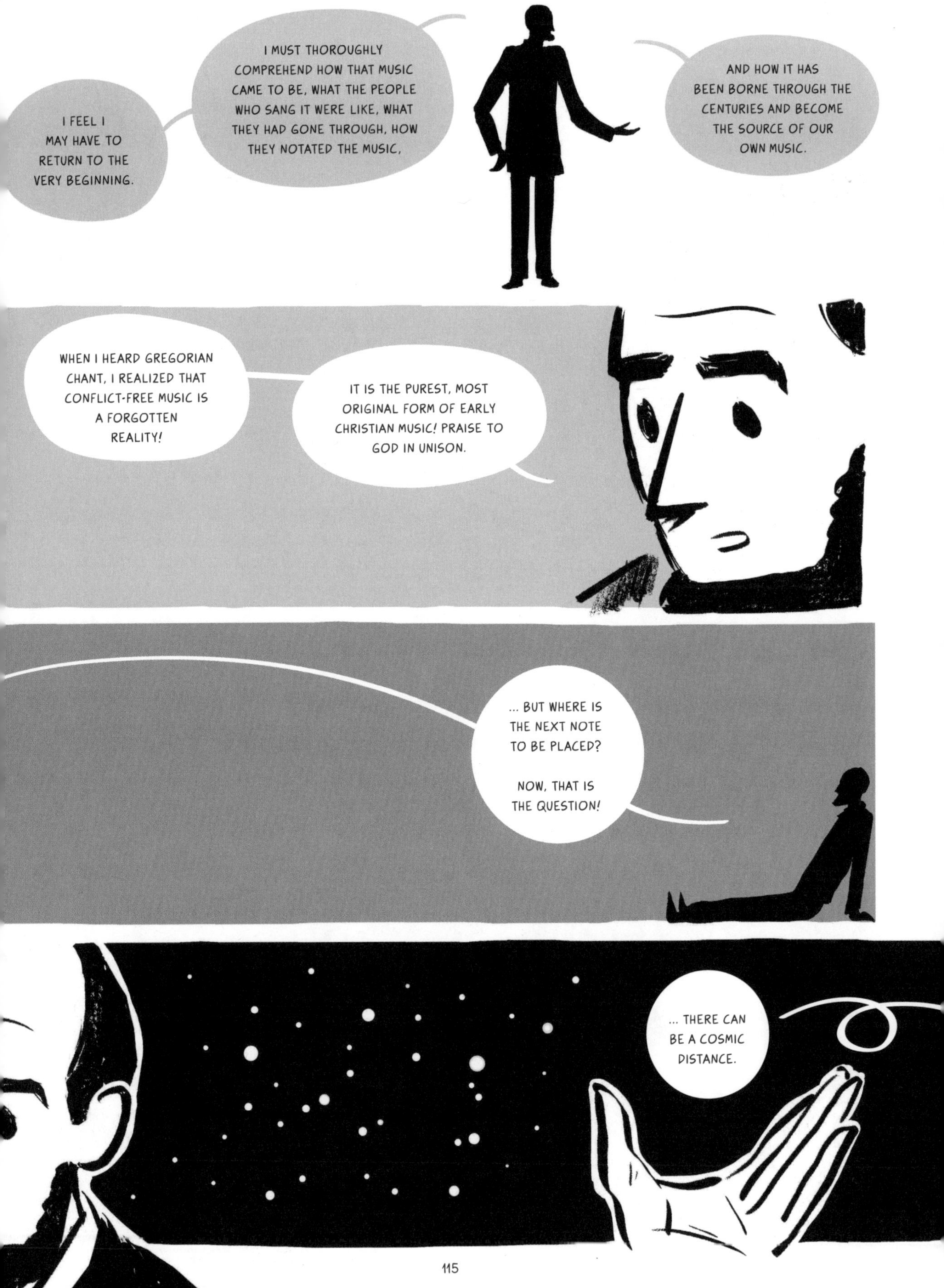
I FEEL I MAY HAVE TO RETURN TO THE VERY BEGINNING.
I MUST THOROUGHLY COMPREHEND HOW THAT MUSIC CAME TO BE, WHAT THE PEOPLE WHO SANG IT WERE LIKE, WHAT THEY HAD GONE THROUGH, HOW THEY NOTATED THE MUSIC,
AND HOW IT HAS BEEN BORNE THROUGH THE CENTURIES AND BECOME THE SOURCE OF OUR OWN MUSIC.
WHEN I HEARD GREGORIAN CHANT, I REALIZED THAT CONFLICT-FREE MUSIC IS A FORGOTTEN REALITY!
IT IS THE PUREST, MOST ORIGINAL FORM OF EARLY CHRISTIAN MUSIC! PRAISE TO GOD IN UNISON.
... BUT WHERE IS THE NEXT NOTE TO BE PLACED?
NOW, THAT IS THE QUESTION!
... THERE CAN BE A COSMIC DISTANCE.

HEIMAR ILVES, WHO NO LONGER TEACHES AT THE CONSERVATORY (THE RECTOR'S OFFICE GOT WIND OF HIS PRINCIPLES), STILL INTERACTS WITH CURRENT STUDENTS AND ALUMNI. ILVES AND ARVO HAVE BEEN ESPECIALLY CLOSE OVER THE LAST DECADE.

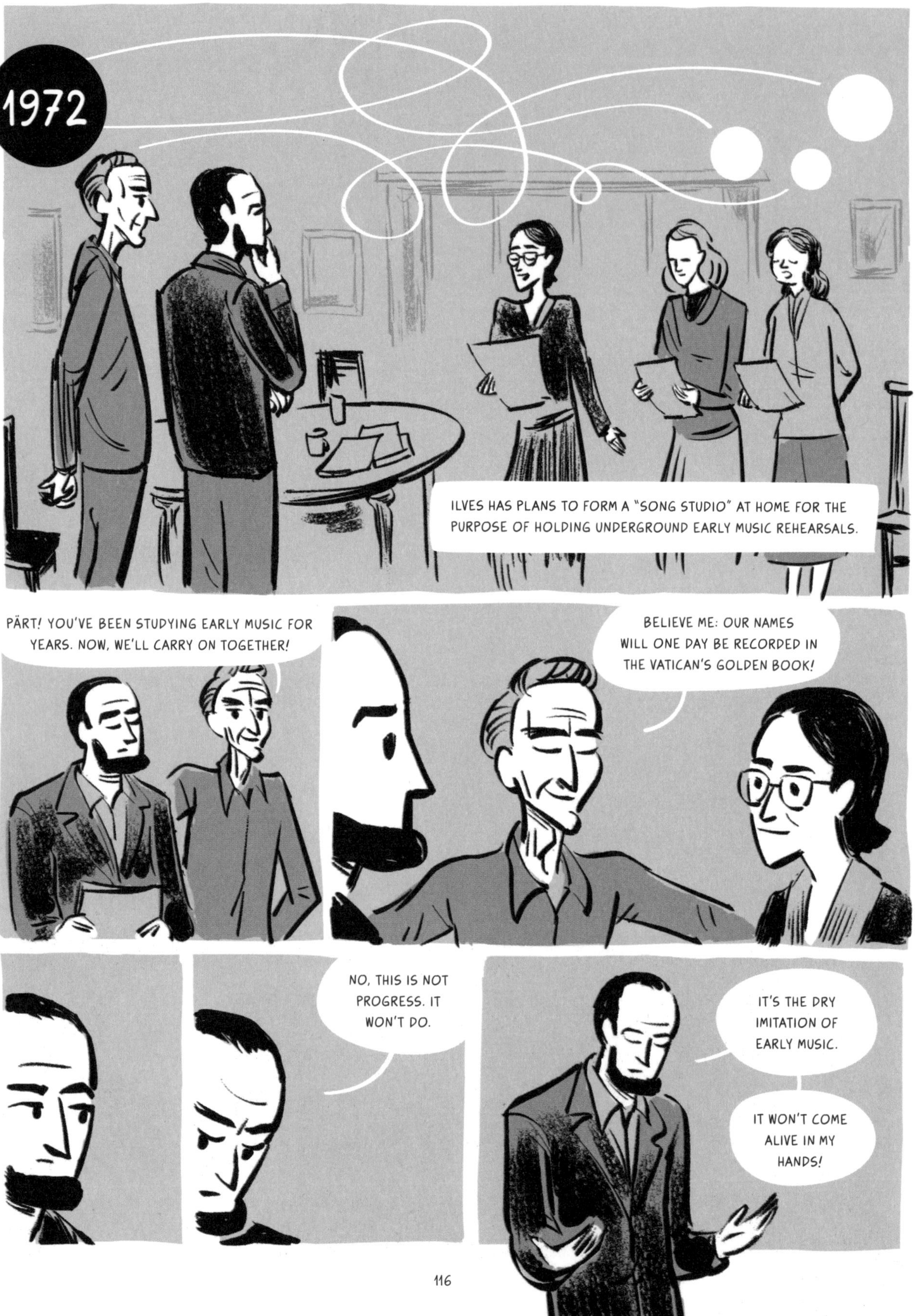
1972
ILVES HAS PLANS TO FORM A "SONG STUDIO" AT HOME FOR THE PURPOSE OF HOLDING UNDERGROUND EARLY MUSIC REHEARSALS.
PÄRT! YOU'VE BEEN STUDYING EARLY MUSIC FOR YEARS. NOW, WE'LL CARRY ON TOGETHER!
BELIEVE ME: OUR NAMES WILL ONE DAY BE RECORDED IN THE VATICAN'S GOLDEN BOOK!
NO, THIS IS NOT PROGRESS. IT WON'T DO.
IT'S THE DRY IMITATION OF EARLY MUSIC.
IT WON'T COME ALIVE IN MY HANDS!

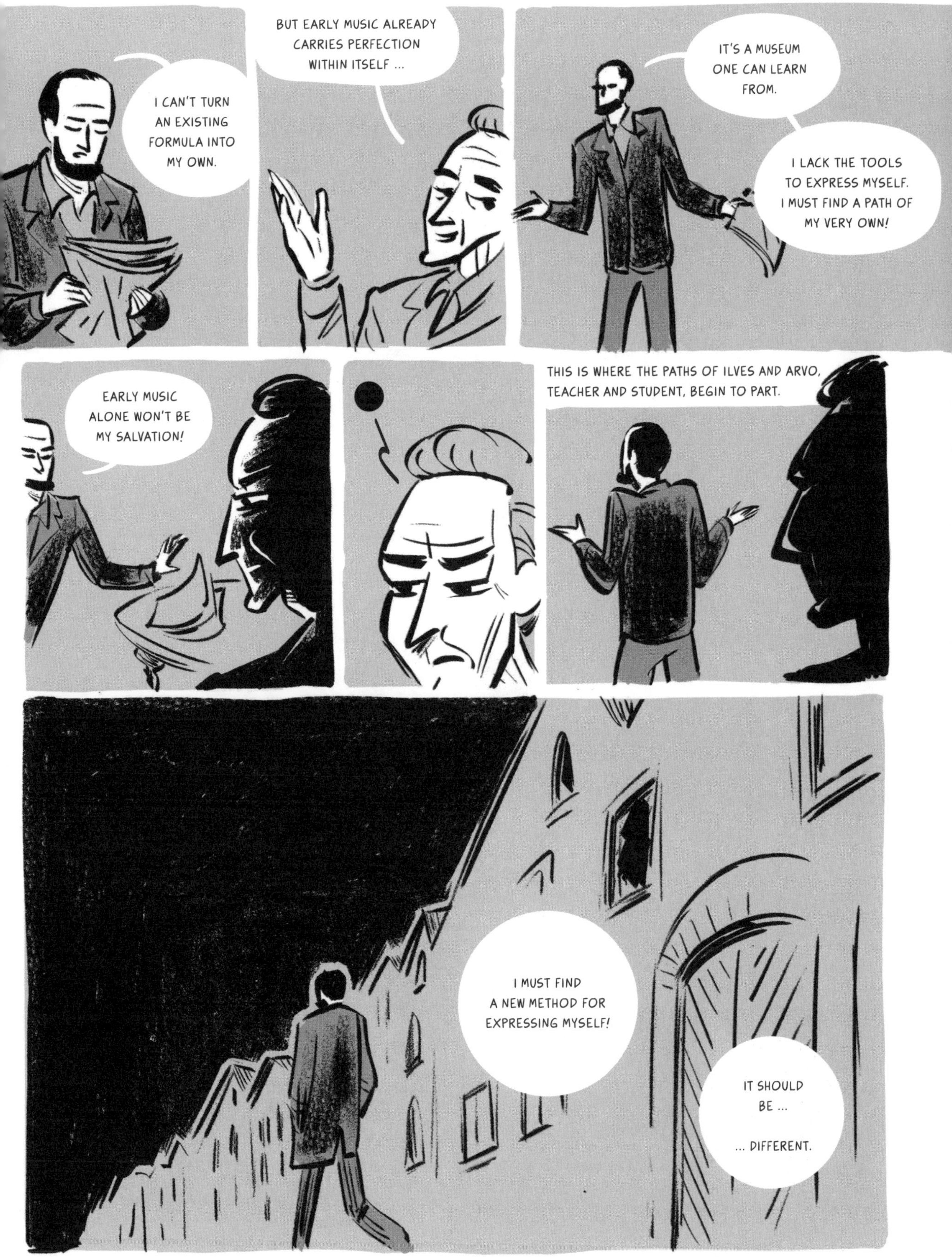

I CAN'T TURN AN EXISTING FORMULA INTO MY OWN.
BUT EARLY MUSIC ALREADY CARRIES PERFECTION WITHIN ITSELF ...
IT'S A MUSEUM ONE CAN LEARN FROM.
I LACK THE TOOLS TO EXPRESS MYSELF. I MUST FIND A PATH OF MY VERY OWN!
EARLY MUSIC ALONE WON'T BE MY SALVATION!
THIS IS WHERE THE PATHS OF ILVES AND ARVO, TEACHER AND STUDENT, BEGIN TO PART.
I MUST FIND A NEW METHOD FOR EXPRESSING MYSELF!
IT SHOULD BE ...
... DIFFERENT.

ARVO'S MARRIAGE IS OVER. WHILE SOME GROW DISTANT, OTHERS GROW CLOSER ...
HE MEETS ELEONORA SUPINA, NORA, AT ILVES'S SONG STUDIO — A YOUNG JEWISH WOMAN WHO STUDIED MUSIC AND CONDUCTING.
BOTH REALIZE THEIR QUESTS ARE SIMILAR AND THAT THEY ARE WALKING THE VERY SAME PATH.

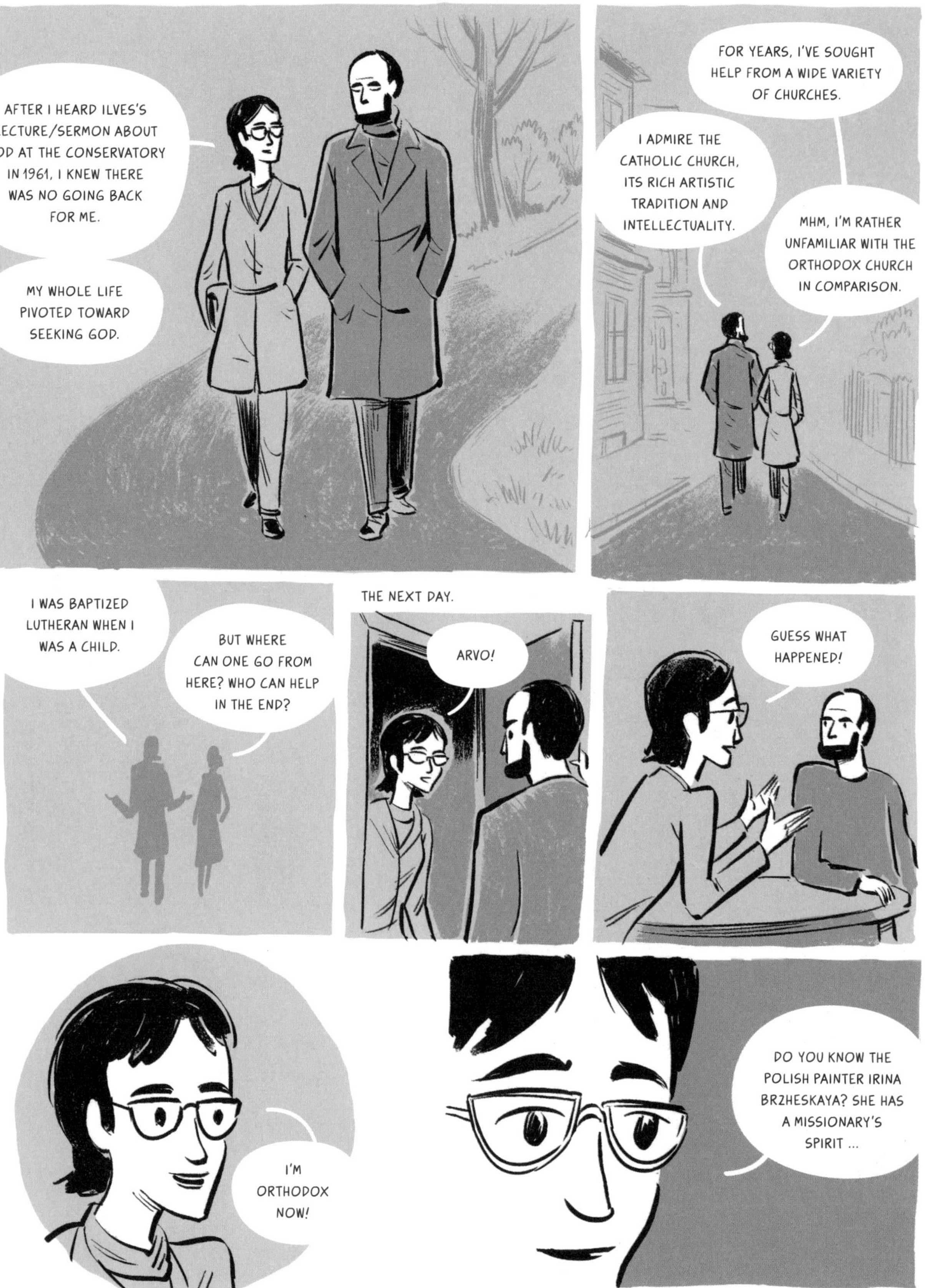
AFTER I HEARD ILVES'S LECTURE/SERMON ABOUT GOD AT THE CONSERVATORY IN 1961, I KNEW THERE WAS NO GOING BACK FOR ME.
MY WHOLE LIFE PIVOTED TOWARD SEEKING GOD.
FOR YEARS, I'VE SOUGHT HELP FROM A WIDE VARIETY OF CHURCHES.
I ADMIRE THE CATHOLIC CHURCH, ITS RICH ARTISTIC TRADITION AND INTELLECTUALITY.
MHM, I'M RATHER UNFAMILIAR WITH THE ORTHODOX CHURCH IN COMPARISON.
I WAS BAPTIZED LUTHERAN WHEN I WAS A CHILD.
BUT WHERE CAN ONE GO FROM HERE? WHO CAN HELP IN THE END?
THE NEXT DAY.
ARVO!
GUESS WHAT HAPPENED!
I'M ORTHODOX NOW!
DO YOU KNOW THE POLISH PAINTER IRINA BRZHESKAYA? SHE HAS A MISSIONARY'S SPIRIT ...

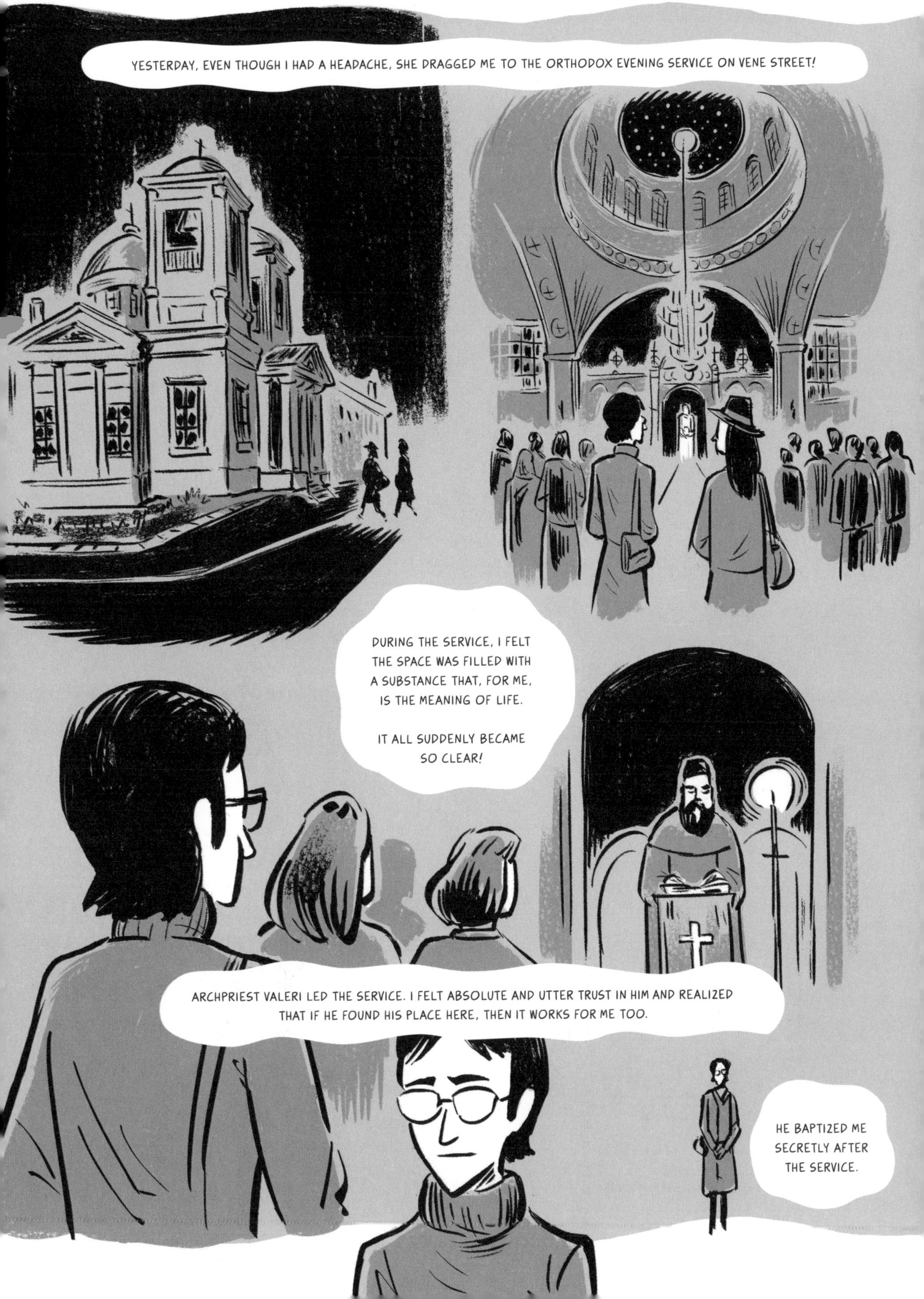
YESTERDAY, EVEN THOUGH I HAD A HEADACHE, SHE DRAGGED ME TO THE ORTHODOX EVENING SERVICE ON VENE STREET!
DURING THE SERVICE, I FELT THE SPACE WAS FILLED WITH A SUBSTANCE THAT, FOR ME, IS THE MEANING OF LIFE.
IT ALL SUDDENLY BECAME SO CLEAR!
ARCHPRIEST VALERI LED THE SERVICE. I FELT ABSOLUTE AND UTTER TRUST IN HIM AND REALIZED THAT IF HE FOUND HIS PLACE HERE, THEN IT WORKS FOR ME TOO.
HE BAPTIZED ME SECRETLY AFTER THE SERVICE.

ARVO ALSO STARTS FEELING HE IS READY TO RECEIVE THE BREAD OF THE ORTHODOX CHURCH ...

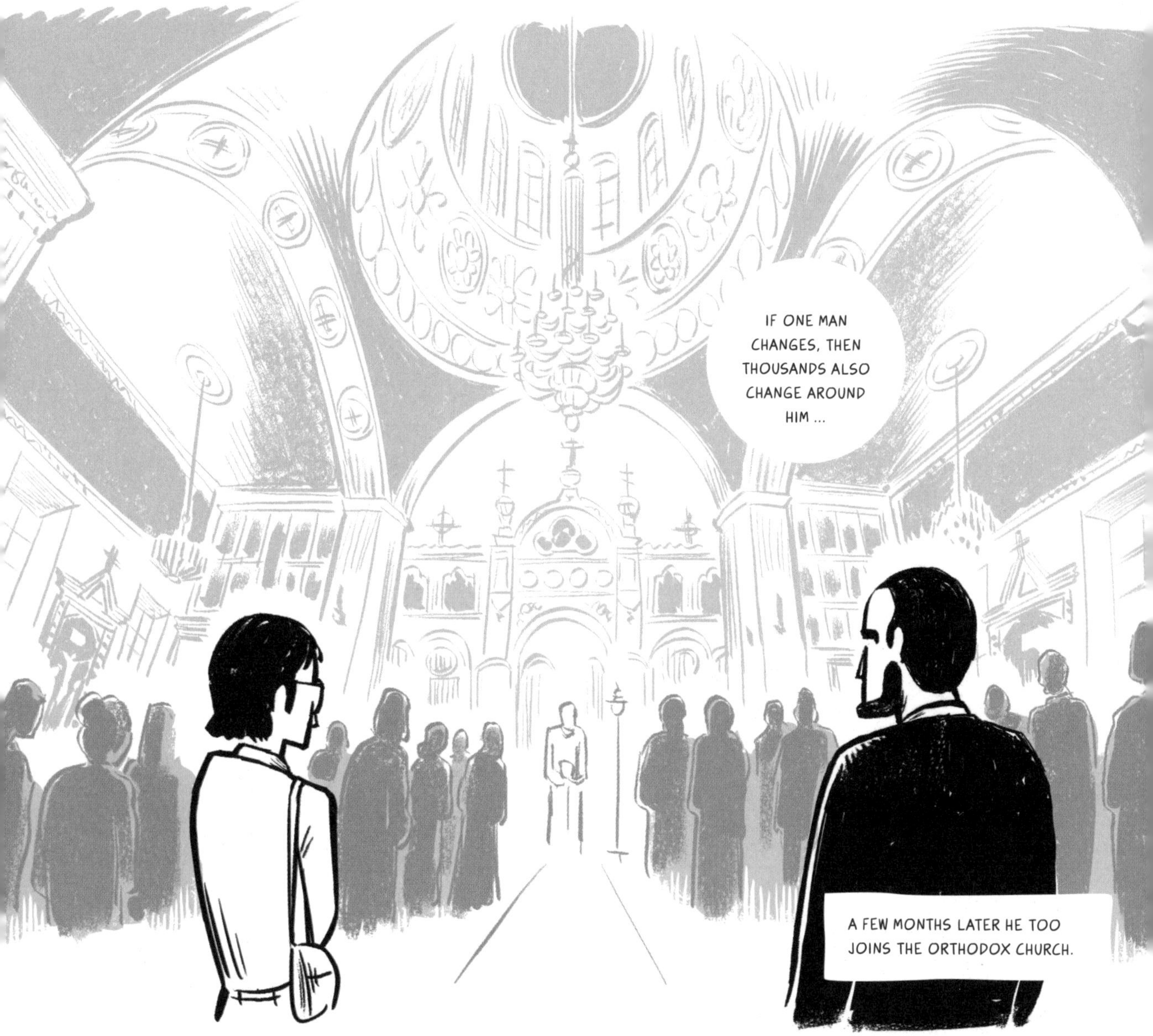
IF ONE MAN CHANGES, THEN THOUSANDS ALSO CHANGE AROUND HIM ...
A FEW MONTHS LATER HE TOO JOINS THE ORTHODOX CHURCH.

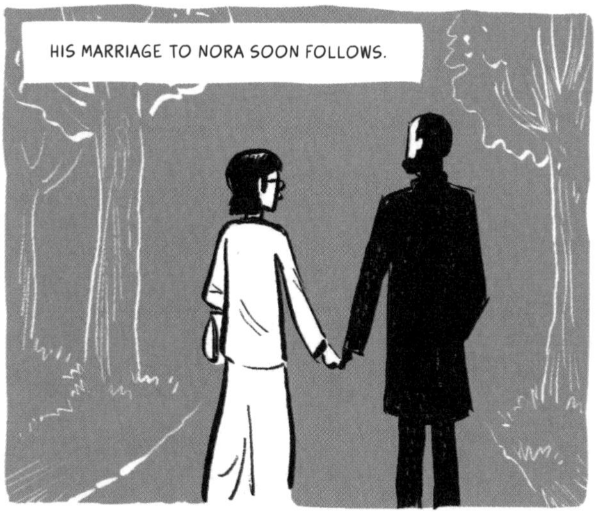
HIS MARRIAGE TO NORA SOON FOLLOWS.

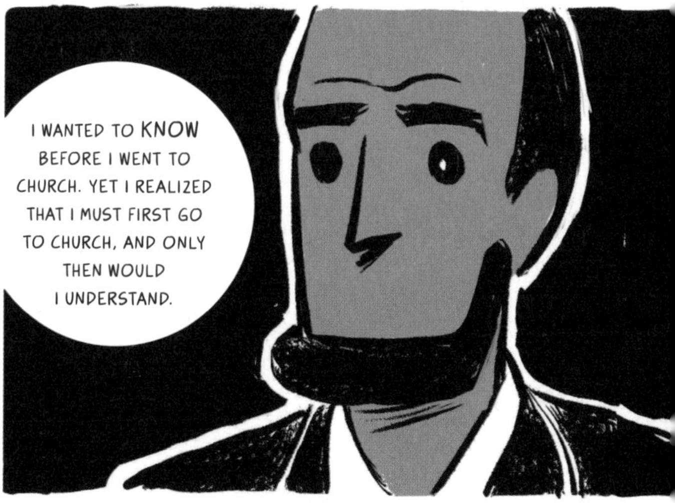
I WANTED TO KNOW BEFORE I WENT TO CHURCH. YET I REALIZED THAT I MUST FIRST GO TO CHURCH, AND ONLY THEN WOULD I UNDERSTAND.

THERE'S BEEN A VERY LONG BREAK IN ARVO'S COMPOSITION FOR PERFORMANCE. STILL, HE FILLS NOTEBOOK AFTER NOTEBOOK WITH EXPERIMENTATION. ONLY A SCANT FEW LATER TAKE SHAPE AS FULL PIECES. ONE OF THESE IS "SARAH WAS NINETY YEARS OLD."

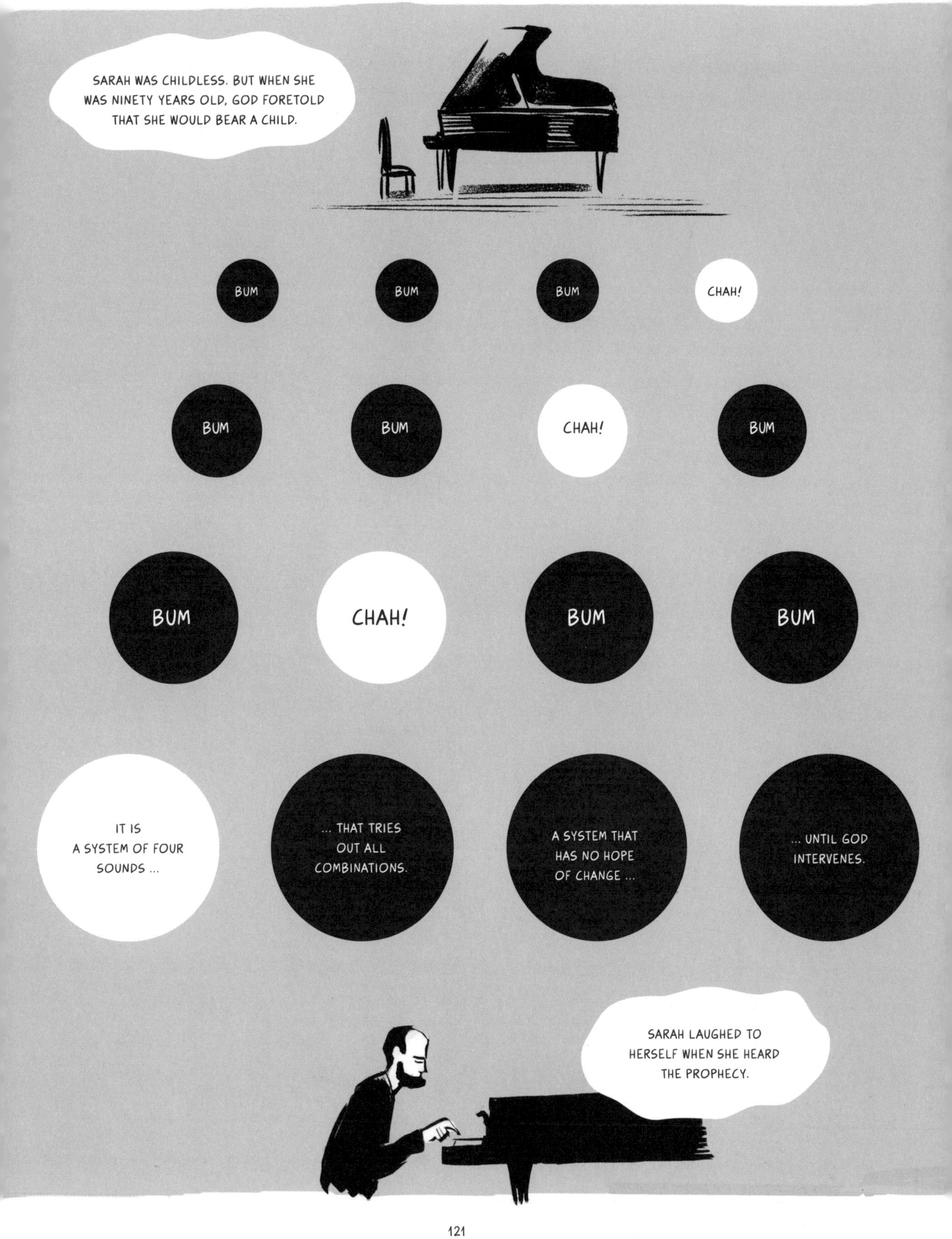
SARAH WAS CHILDLESS. BUT WHEN SHE WAS NINETY YEARS OLD, GOD FORETOLD THAT SHE WOULD BEAR A CHILD.
BUM
BUM
BUM
CHAH!
BUM
BUM
CHAH!
BUM
BUM
CHAH!
BUM
BUM
IT IS A SYSTEM OF FOUR SOUNDS ...
... THAT TRIES OUT ALL COMBINATIONS.
A SYSTEM THAT HAS NO HOPE OF CHANGE ...
... UNTIL GOD INTERVENES.
SARAH LAUGHED TO HERSELF WHEN SHE HEARD THE PROPHECY.

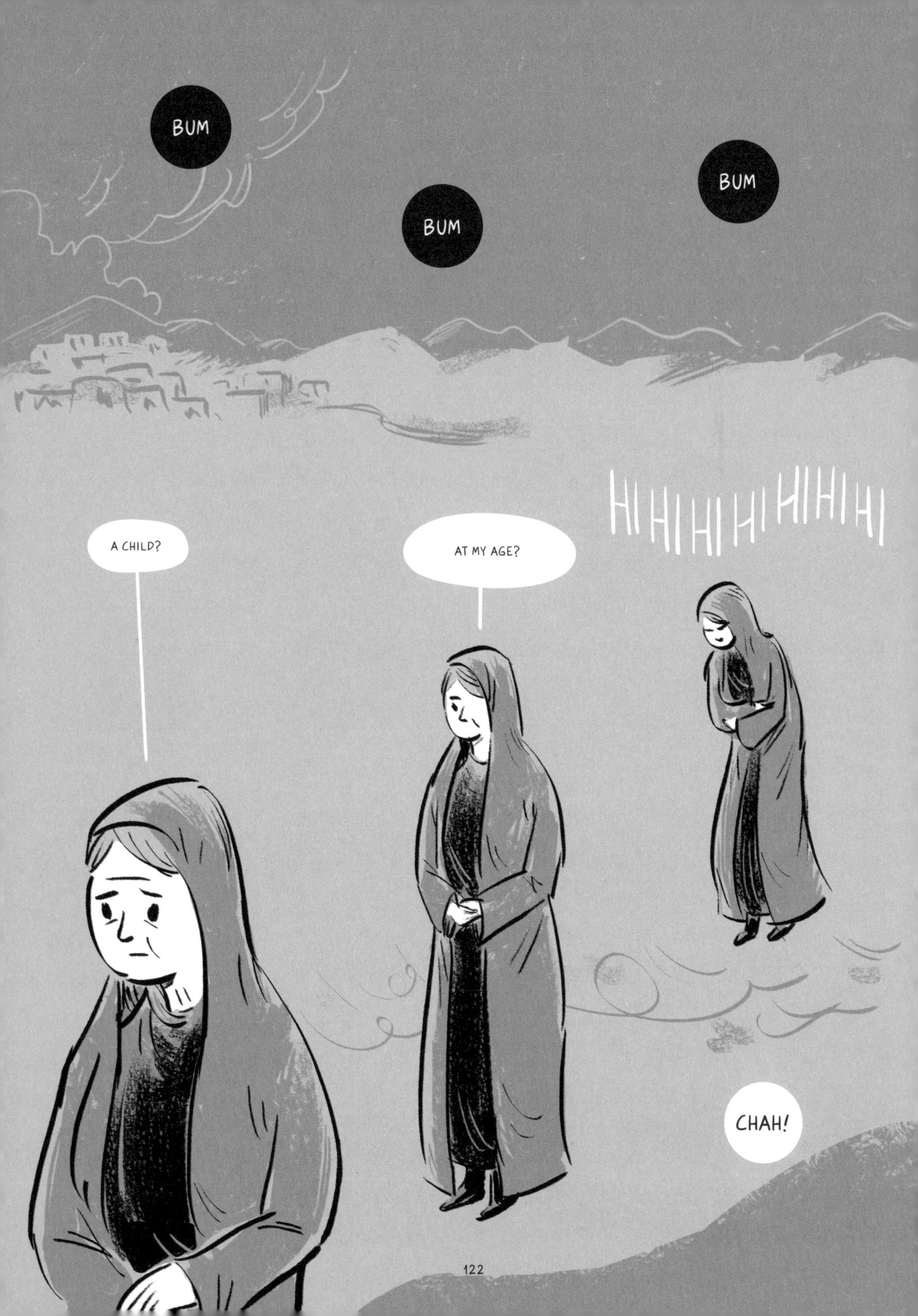
BUM
BUM
BUM
A CHILD?
AT MY AGE?
HIHIHIHIHIHIHIHI
CHAH!

THE NEWLYWEDS MOVE TO MUSTAMÄE, A NEW HOUSING DISTRICT LINED WITH IDENTICAL APARTMENT BLOCKS NICKNAMED "KHRUSHCHYOVKAS," AFTER KHRUSHCHEV, THE SOVIET PREMIER.

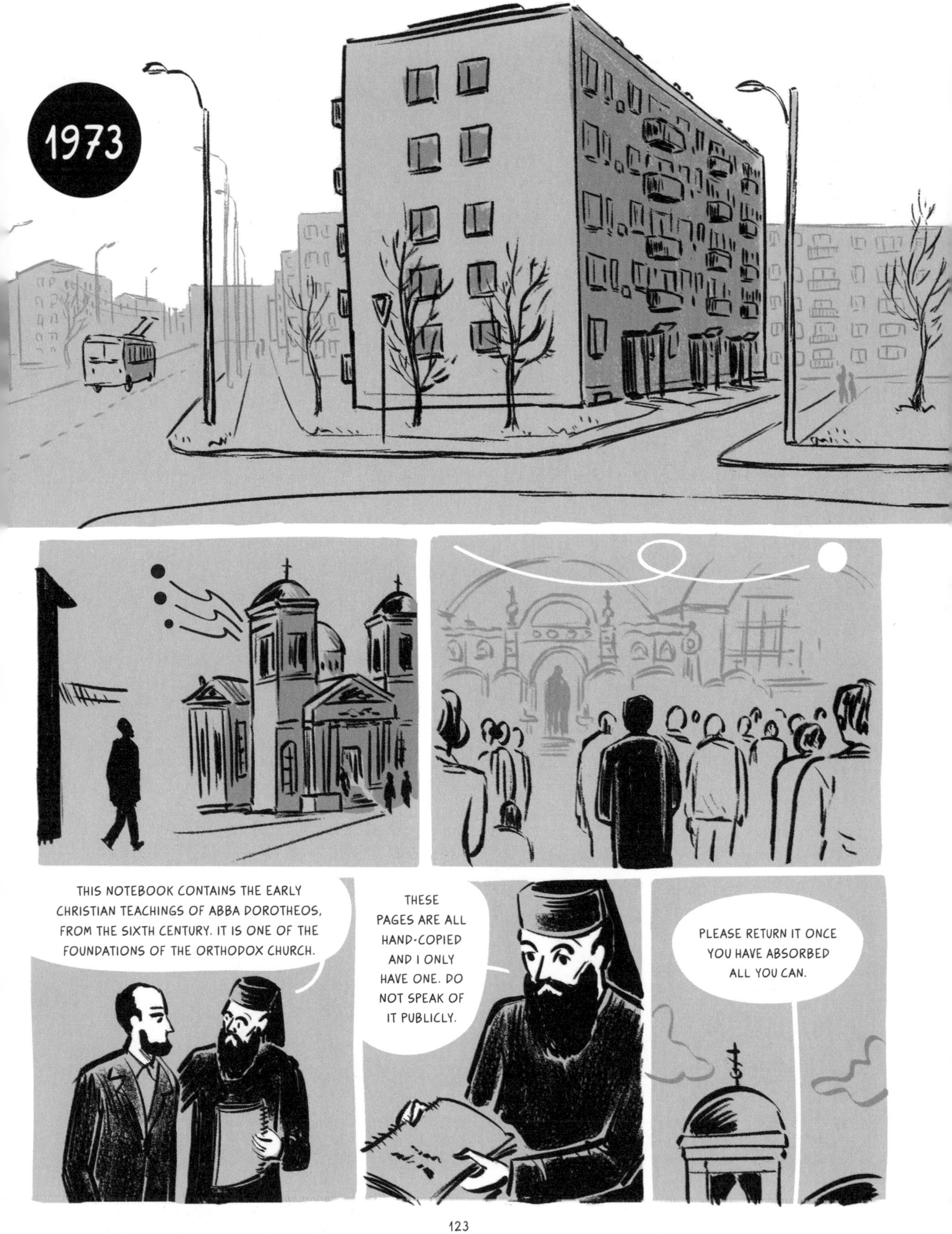
1973
THIS NOTEBOOK CONTAINS THE EARLY CHRISTIAN TEACHINGS OF ABBA DOROTHEOS, FROM THE SIXTH CENTURY. IT IS ONE OF THE FOUNDATIONS OF THE ORTHODOX CHURCH.
THESE PAGES ARE ALL HAND-COPIED AND I ONLY HAVE ONE. DO NOT SPEAK OF IT PUBLICLY.
PLEASE RETURN IT ONCE YOU HAVE ABSORBED ALL YOU CAN.

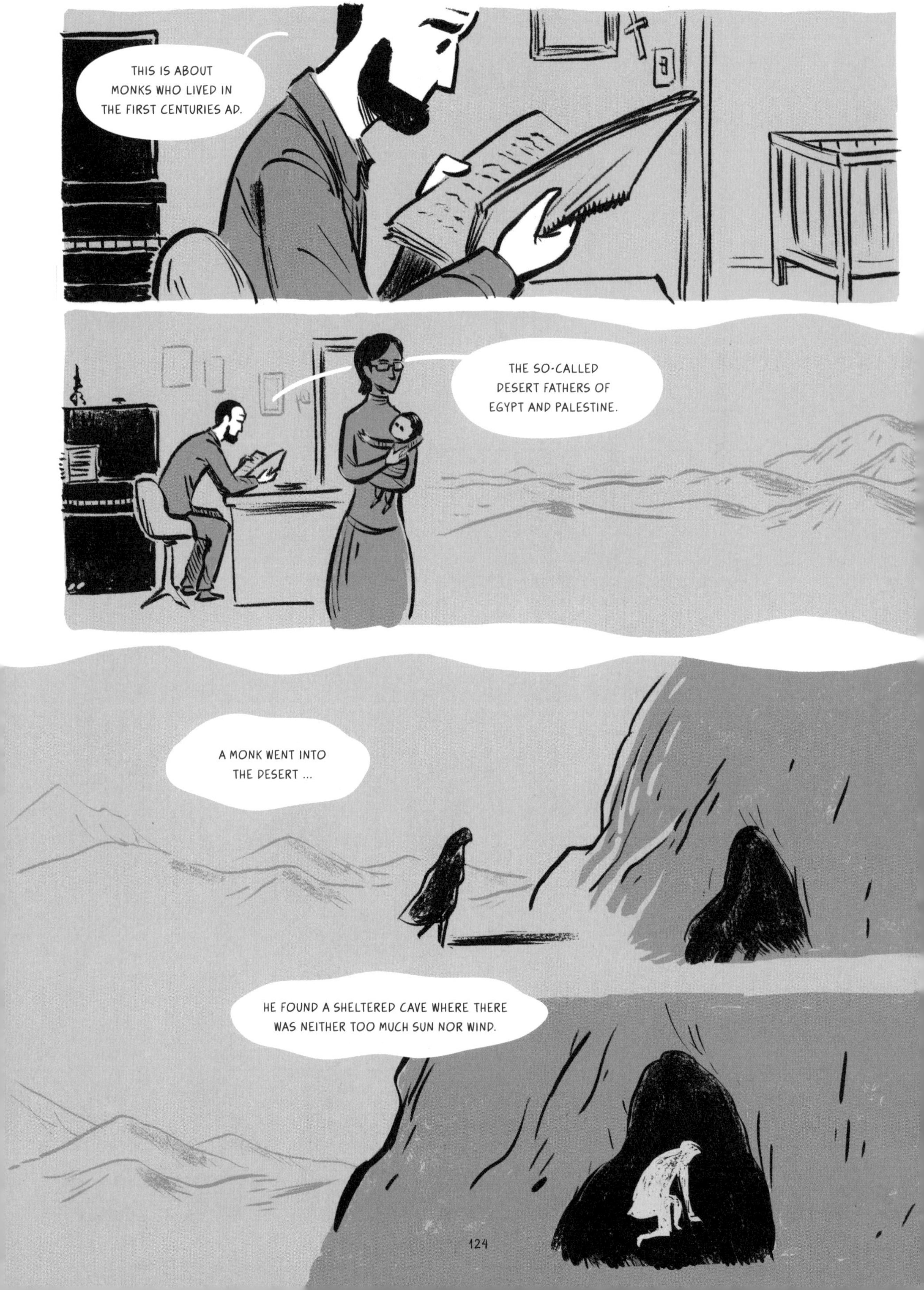
THIS IS ABOUT MONKS WHO LIVED IN THE FIRST CENTURIES AD.
THE SO-CALLED DESERT FATHERS OF EGYPT AND PALESTINE.
A MONK WENT INTO THE DESERT ...
HE FOUND A SHELTERED CAVE WHERE THERE WAS NEITHER TOO MUCH SUN NOR WIND.

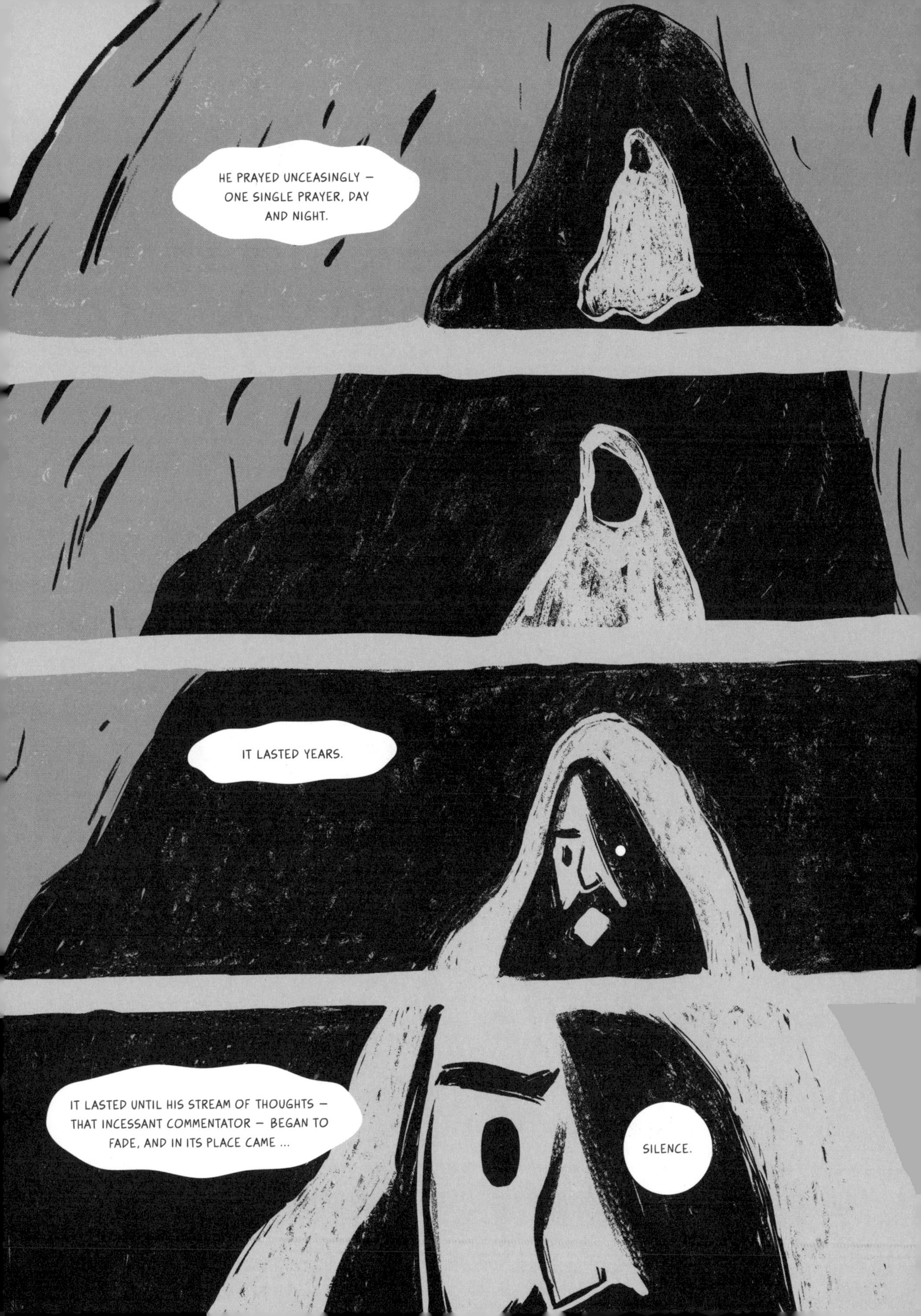
HE PRAYED UNCEASINGLY — ONE SINGLE PRAYER, DAY AND NIGHT.
IT LASTED YEARS.
IT LASTED UNTIL HIS STREAM OF THOUGHTS — THAT INCESSANT COMMENTATOR — BEGAN TO FADE, AND IN ITS PLACE CAME ...
SILENCE.

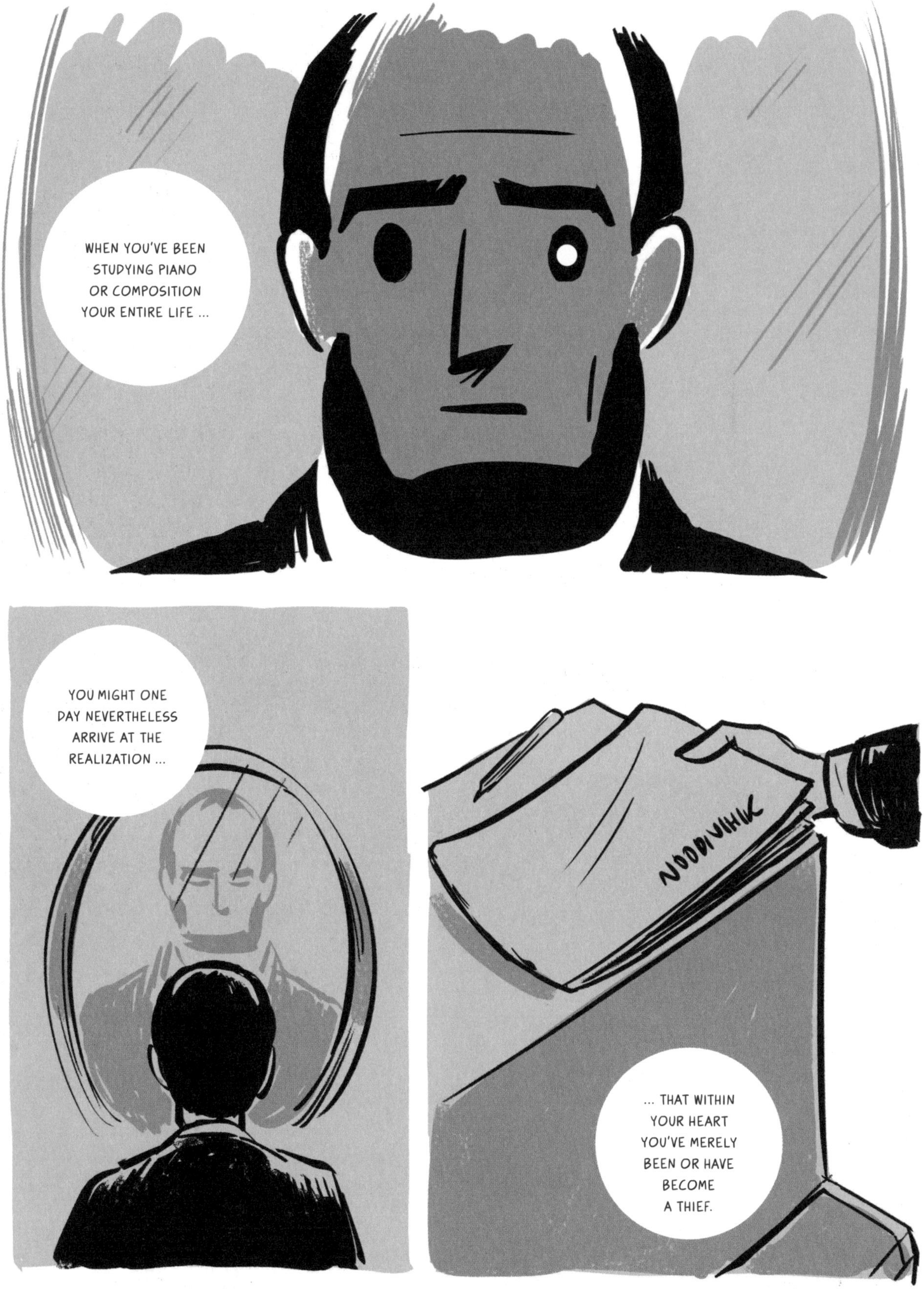
WHEN YOU'VE BEEN STUDYING PIANO OR COMPOSITION YOUR ENTIRE LIFE ...
YOU MIGHT ONE DAY NEVERTHELESS ARRIVE AT THE REALIZATION ...
... THAT WITHIN YOUR HEART YOU'VE MERELY BEEN OR HAVE BECOME A THIEF.

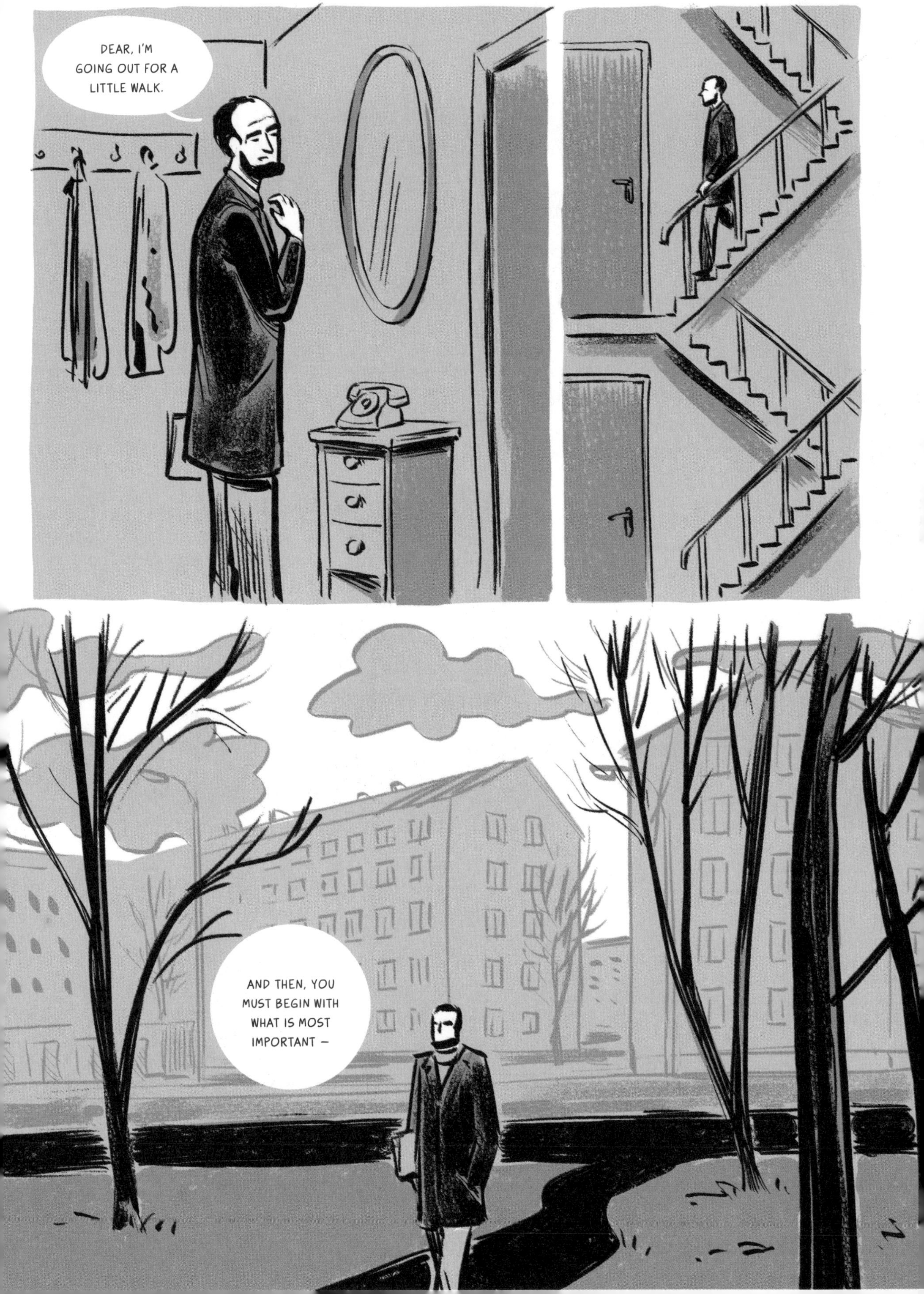
DEAR, I'M GOING OUT FOR A LITTLE WALK.
AND THEN, YOU MUST BEGIN WITH WHAT IS MOST IMPORTANT –

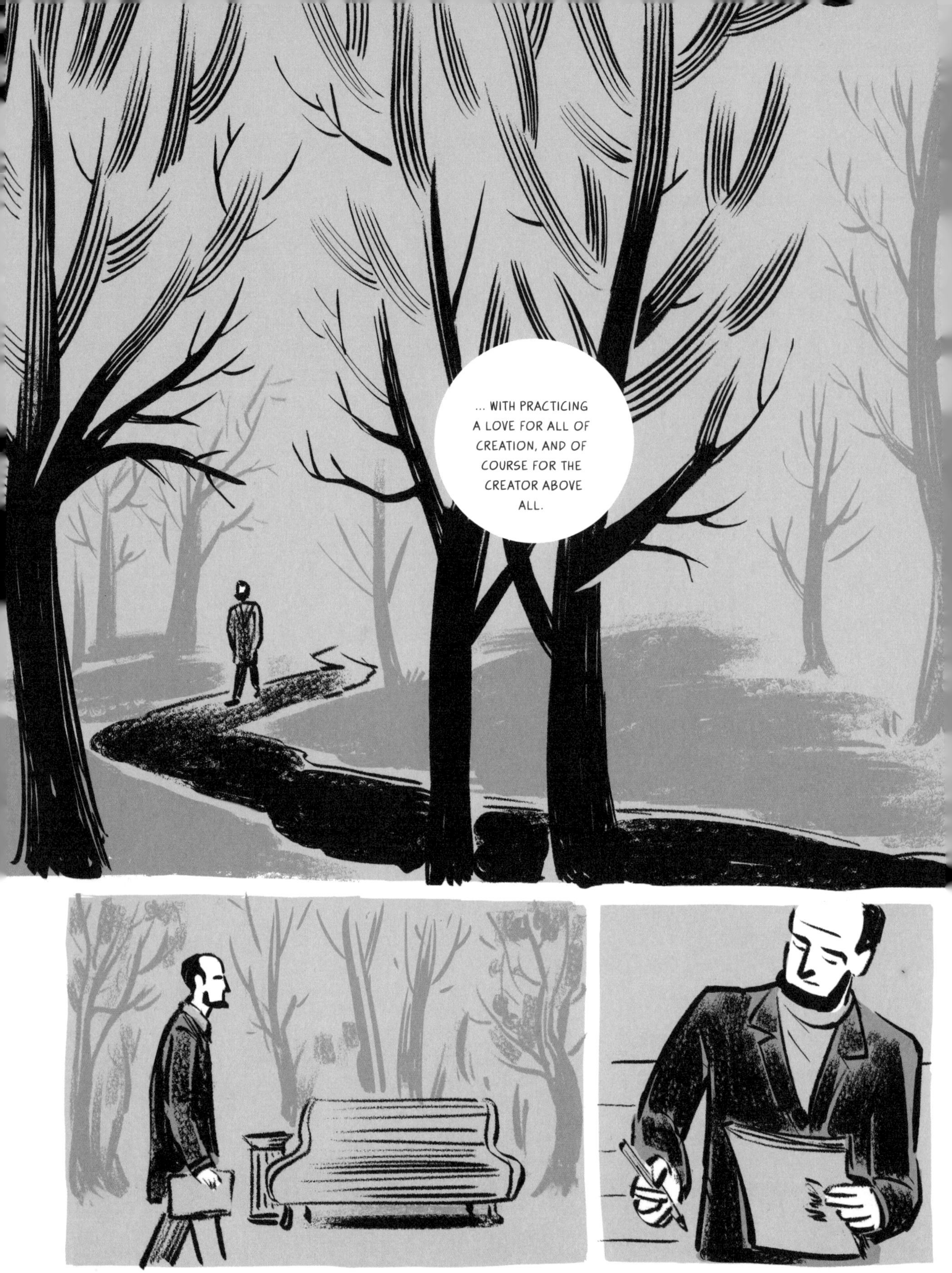
... WITH PRACTICING A LOVE FOR ALL OF CREATION, AND OF COURSE FOR THE CREATOR ABOVE ALL.

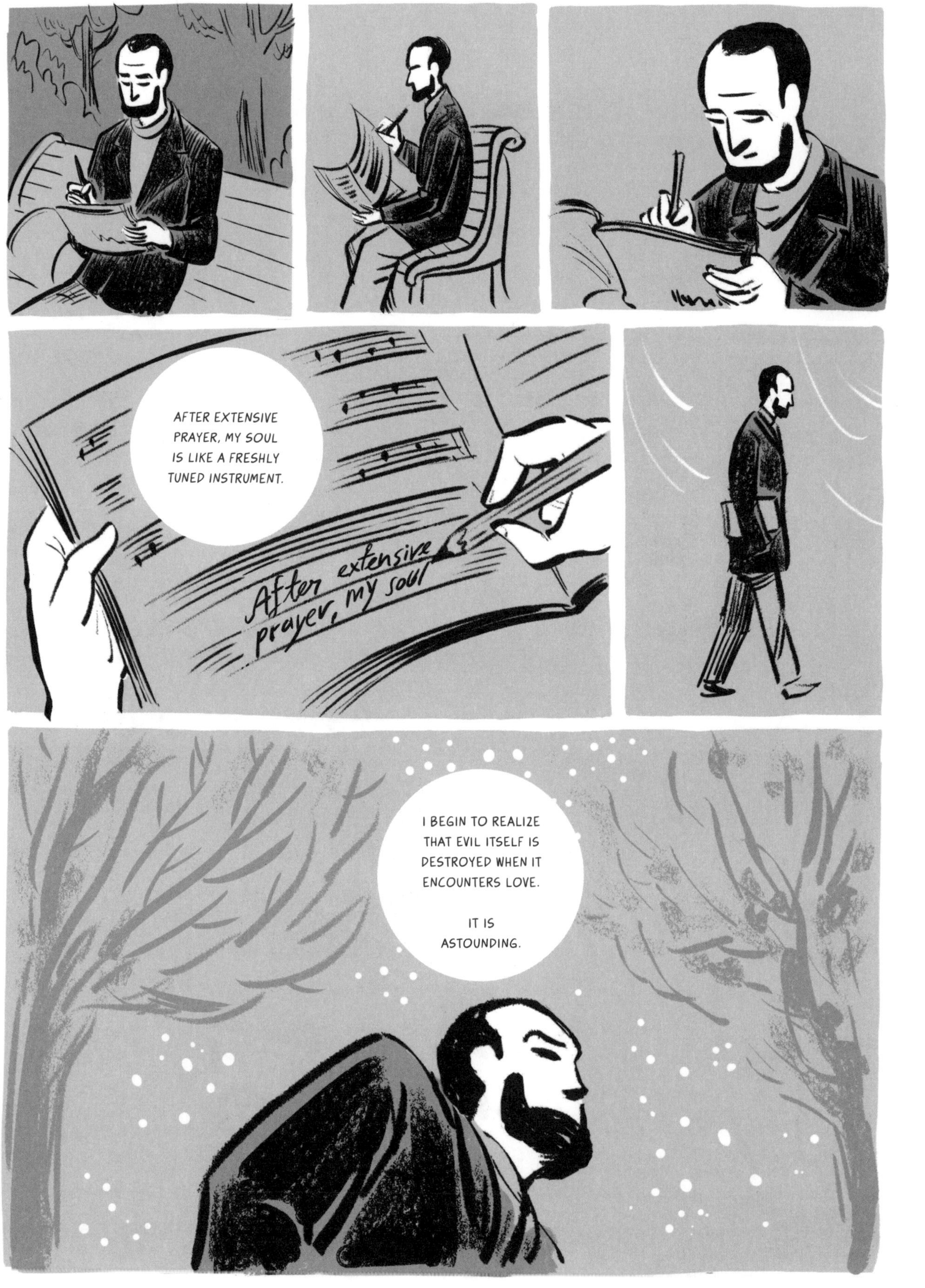
AFTER EXTENSIVE PRAYER, MY SOUL IS LIKE A FRESHLY TUNED INSTRUMENT.
After extensive prayer, my soul
I BEGIN TO REALIZE THAT EVIL ITSELF IS DESTROYED WHEN IT ENCOUNTERS LOVE.
IT IS ASTOUNDING.

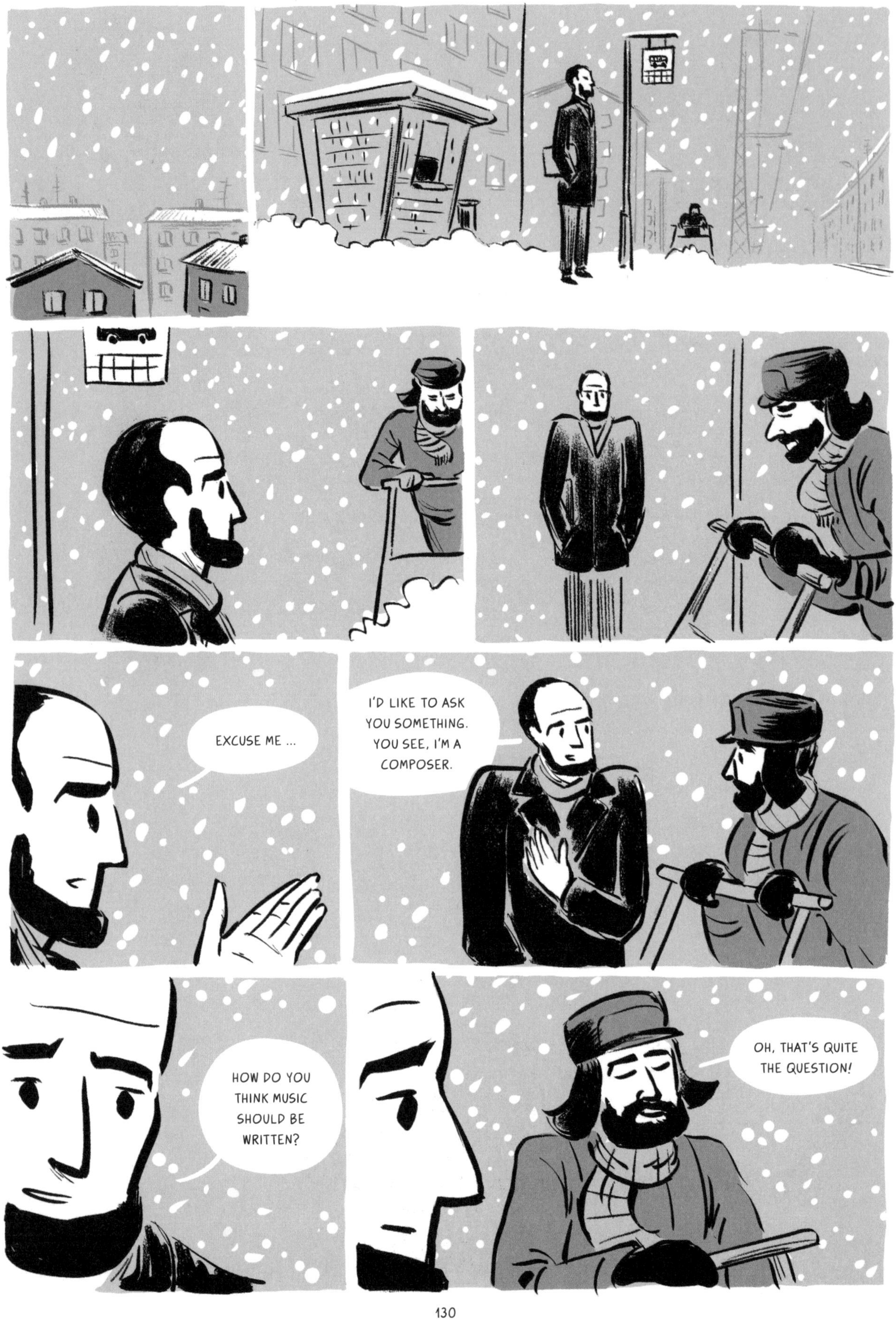
EXCUSE ME ...
I'D LIKE TO ASK YOU SOMETHING. YOU SEE, I'M A COMPOSER.
HOW DO YOU THINK MUSIC SHOULD BE WRITTEN?
OH, THAT'S QUITE THE QUESTION!

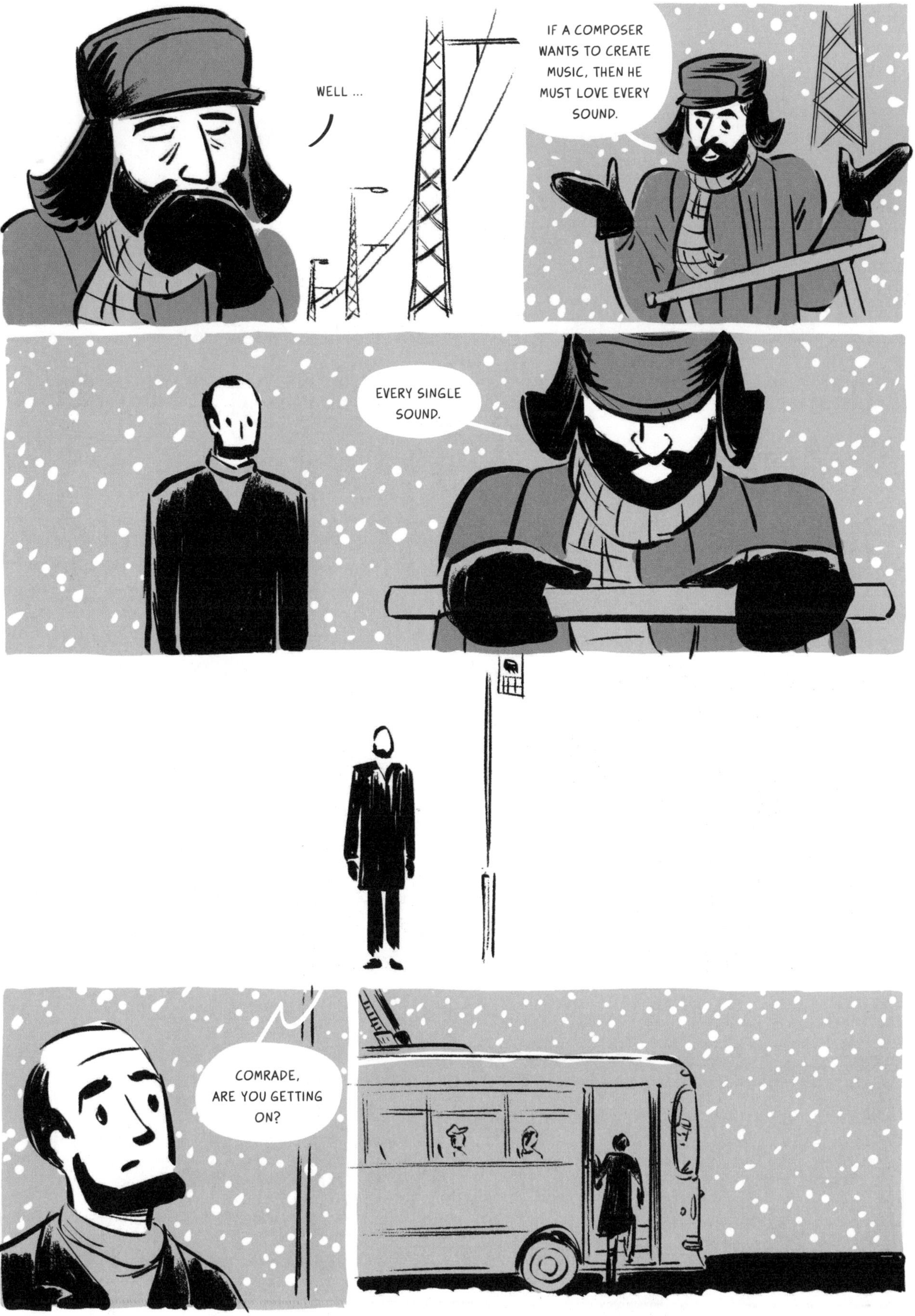
WELL ...
IF A COMPOSER WANTS TO CREATE MUSIC, THEN HE MUST LOVE EVERY SOUND.
EVERY SINGLE SOUND.
COMRADE, ARE YOU GETTING ON?

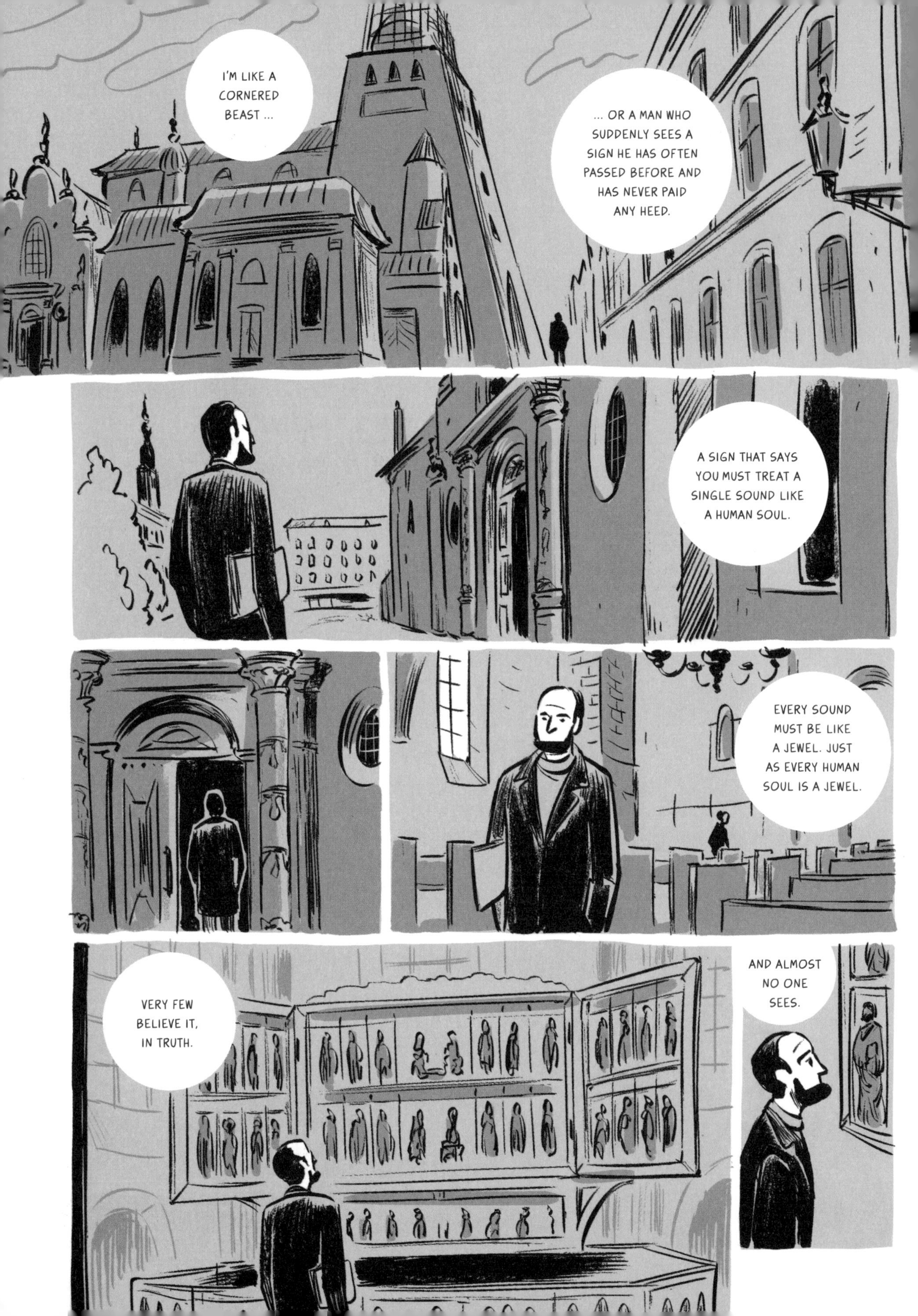
I'M LIKE A CORNERED BEAST ...
... OR A MAN WHO SUDDENLY SEES A SIGN HE HAS OFTEN PASSED BEFORE AND HAS NEVER PAID ANY HEED.
A SIGN THAT SAYS YOU MUST TREAT A SINGLE SOUND LIKE A HUMAN SOUL.
EVERY SOUND MUST BE LIKE A JEWEL. JUST AS EVERY HUMAN SOUL IS A JEWEL.
VERY FEW BELIEVE IT, IN TRUTH.
AND ALMOST NO ONE SEES.

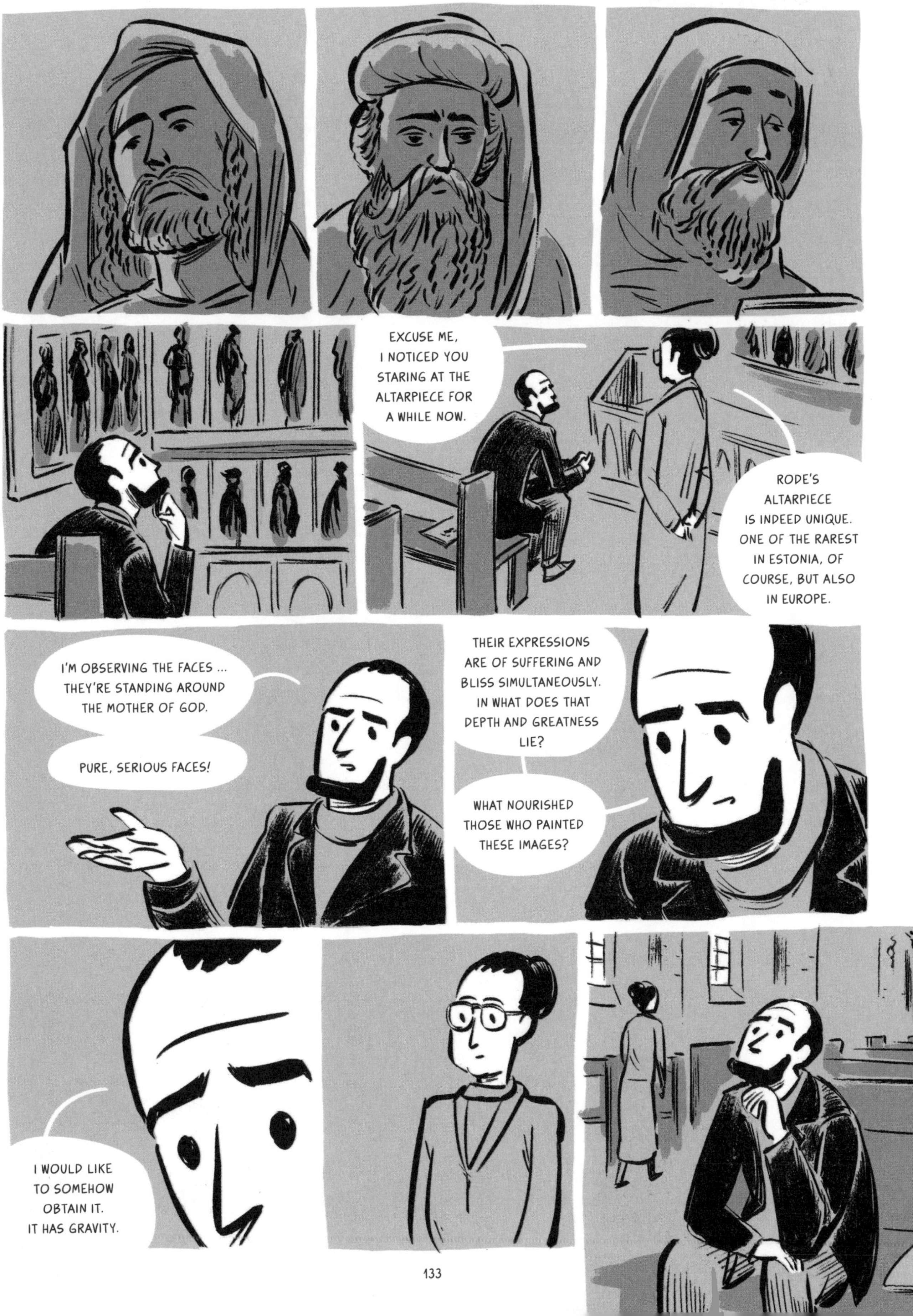
EXCUSE ME, I NOTICED YOU STARING AT THE ALTARPIECE FOR A WHILE NOW.
RODE'S ALTARPIECE IS INDEED UNIQUE. ONE OF THE RAREST IN ESTONIA, OF COURSE, BUT ALSO IN EUROPE.
I'M OBSERVING THE FACES ... THEY'RE STANDING AROUND THE MOTHER OF GOD.
PURE, SERIOUS FACES!
THEIR EXPRESSIONS ARE OF SUFFERING AND BLISS SIMULTANEOUSLY. IN WHAT DOES THAT DEPTH AND GREATNESS LIE?
WHAT NOURISHED THOSE WHO PAINTED THESE IMAGES?
I WOULD LIKE TO SOMEHOW OBTAIN IT. IT HAS GRAVITY.

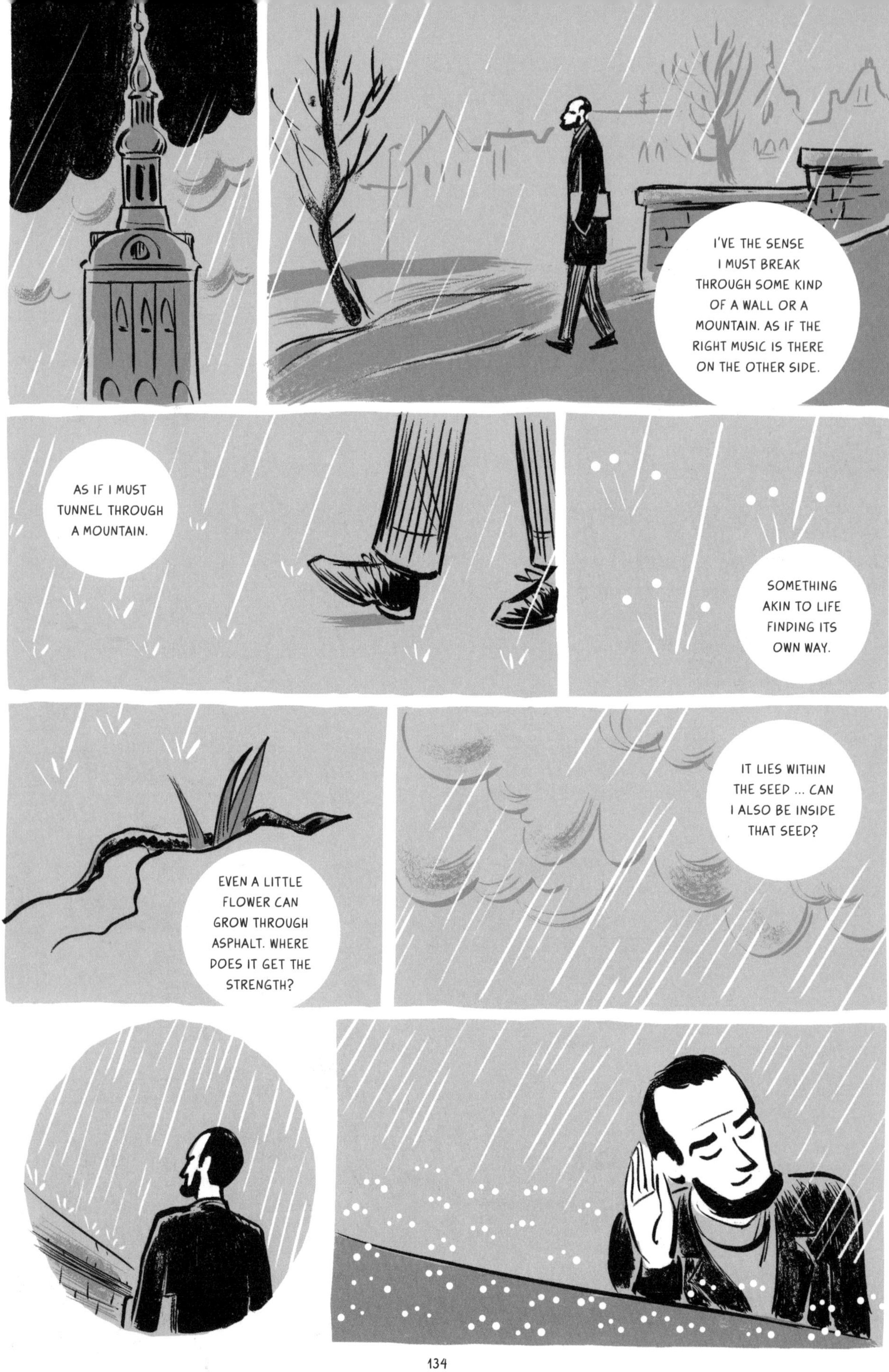
I'VE THE SENSE I MUST BREAK THROUGH SOME KIND OF A WALL OR A MOUNTAIN. AS IF THE RIGHT MUSIC IS THERE ON THE OTHER SIDE.
AS IF I MUST TUNNEL THROUGH A MOUNTAIN.
SOMETHING AKIN TO LIFE FINDING ITS OWN WAY.
EVEN A LITTLE FLOWER CAN GROW THROUGH ASPHALT. WHERE DOES IT GET THE STRENGTH?
IT LIES WITHIN THE SEED ... CAN I ALSO BE INSIDE THAT SEED?

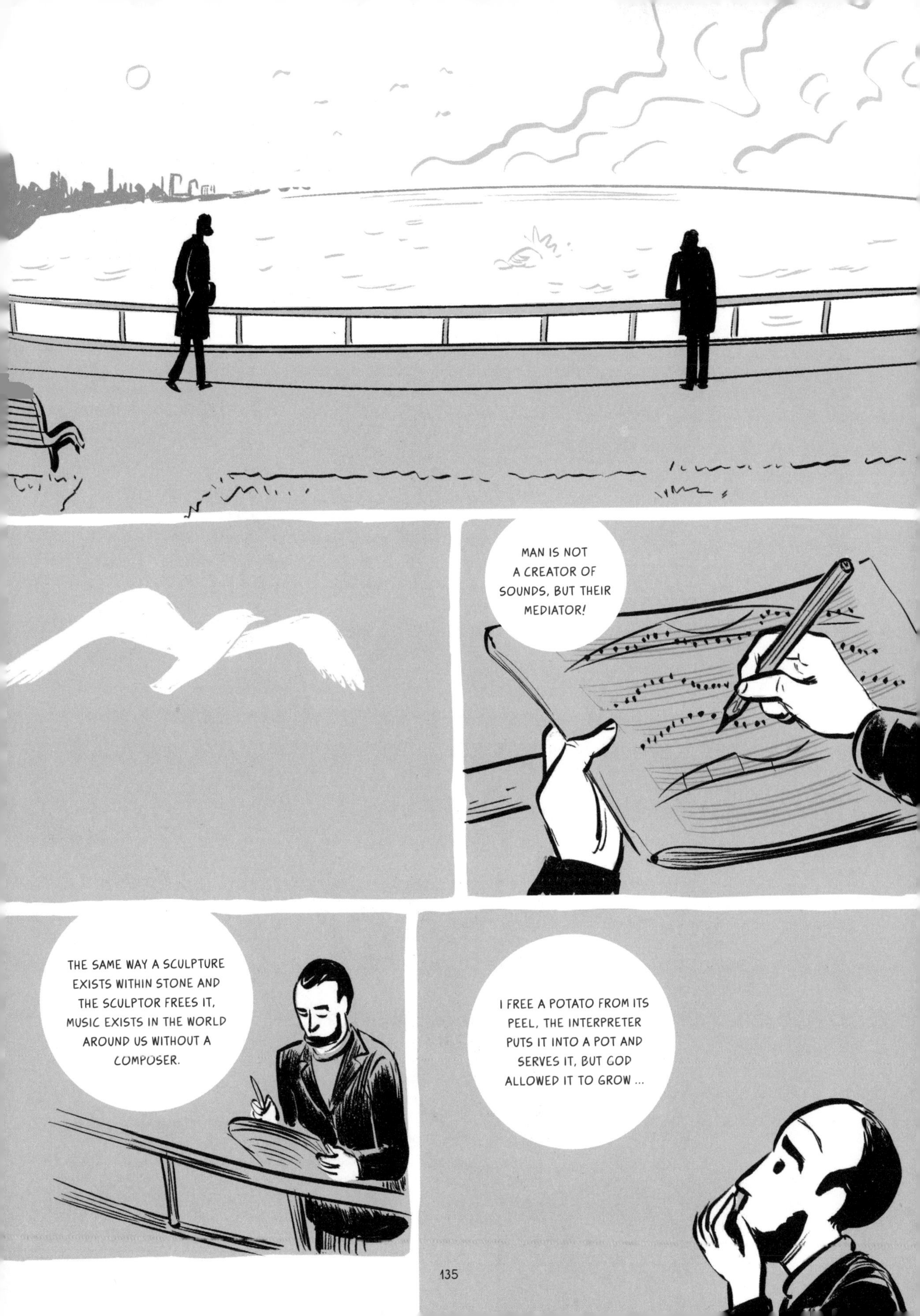
MAN IS NOT A CREATOR OF SOUNDS, BUT THEIR MEDIATOR!
THE SAME WAY A SCULPTURE EXISTS WITHIN STONE AND THE SCULPTOR FREES IT, MUSIC EXISTS IN THE WORLD AROUND US WITHOUT A COMPOSER.
I FREE A POTATO FROM ITS PEEL, THE INTERPRETER PUTS IT INTO A POT AND SERVES IT, BUT GOD ALLOWED IT TO GROW ...

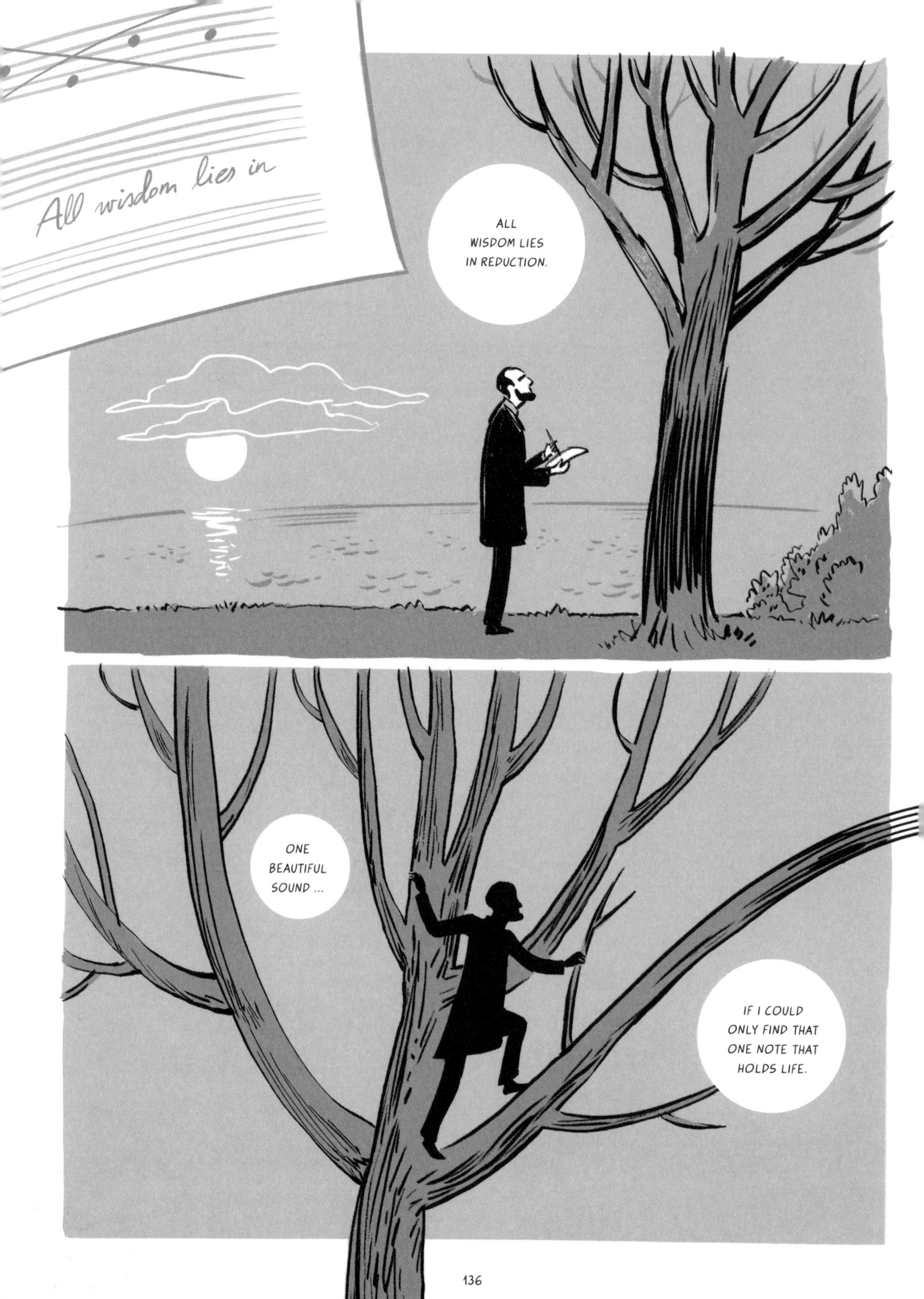
All wisdom lies in
ALL WISDOM LIES IN REDUCTION.
ONE BEAUTIFUL SOUND ...
IF I COULD ONLY FIND THAT ONE NOTE THAT HOLDS LIFE.

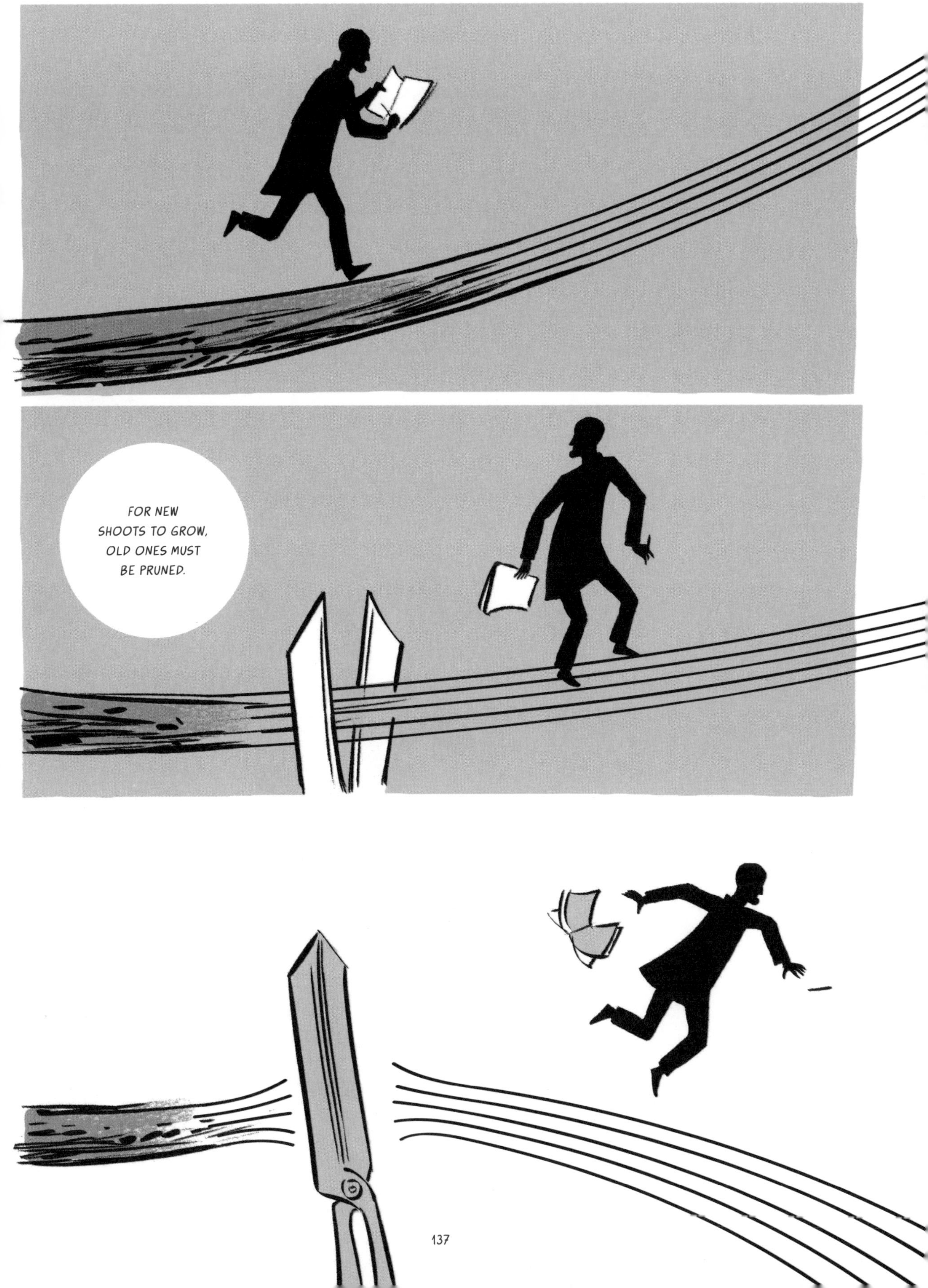
FOR NEW SHOOTS TO GROW, OLD ONES MUST BE PRUNED.

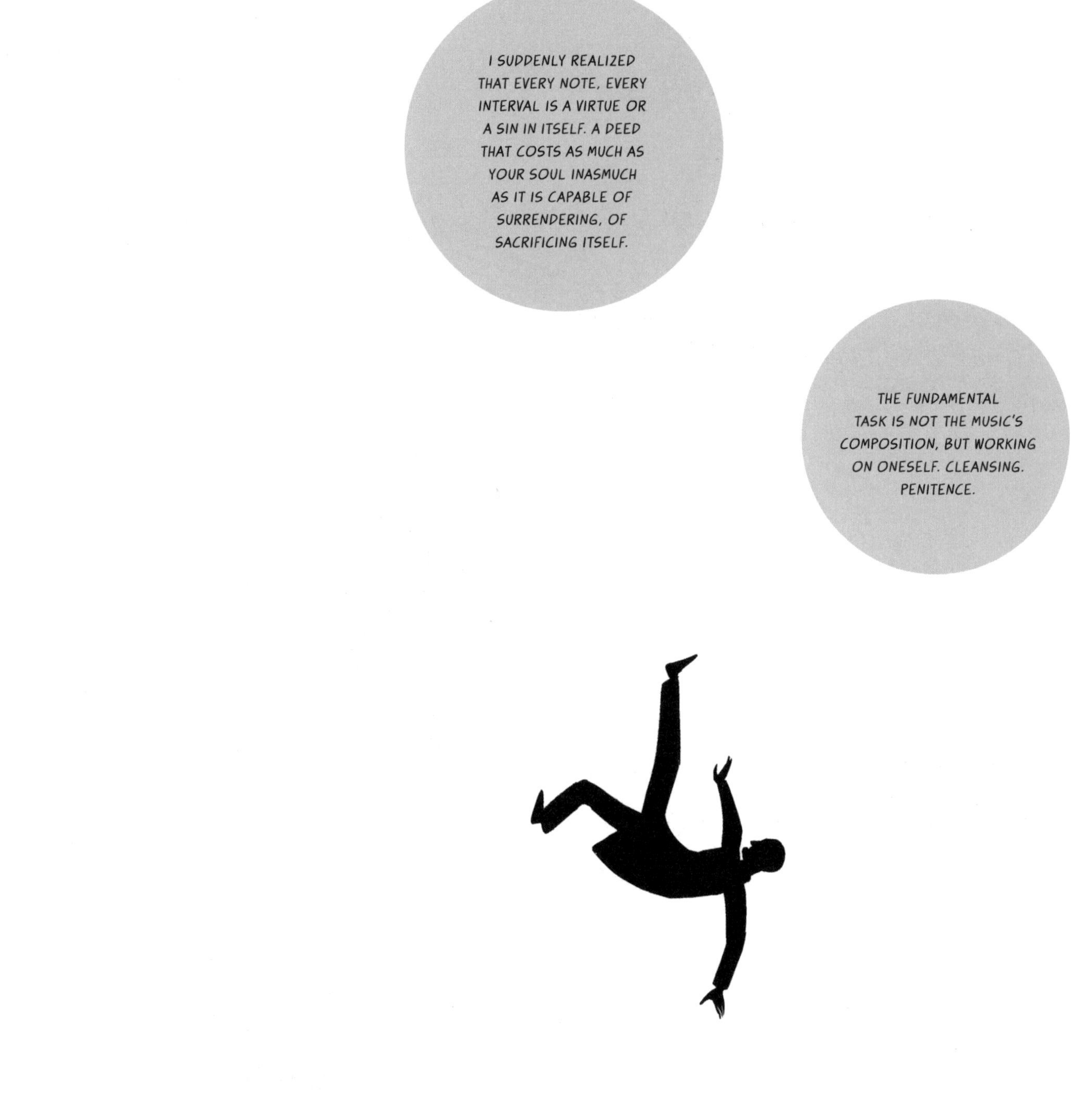
I SUDDENLY REALIZED THAT EVERY NOTE, EVERY INTERVAL IS A VIRTUE OR A SIN IN ITSELF. A DEED THAT COSTS AS MUCH AS YOUR SOUL INASMUCH AS IT IS CAPABLE OF SURRENDERING, OF SACRIFICING ITSELF.
THE FUNDAMENTAL TASK IS NOT THE MUSIC'S COMPOSITION, BUT WORKING ON ONESELF. CLEANSING. PENITENCE.

ALMOST NOTHING IN
OUR CREATIVE WORK
IS MADE BETTER IF WE
OURSELVES DO NOT
BECOME PURER.

MY WHOLE
BEING MUST
BE IN ORDER.
EVERY PART
OF IT.

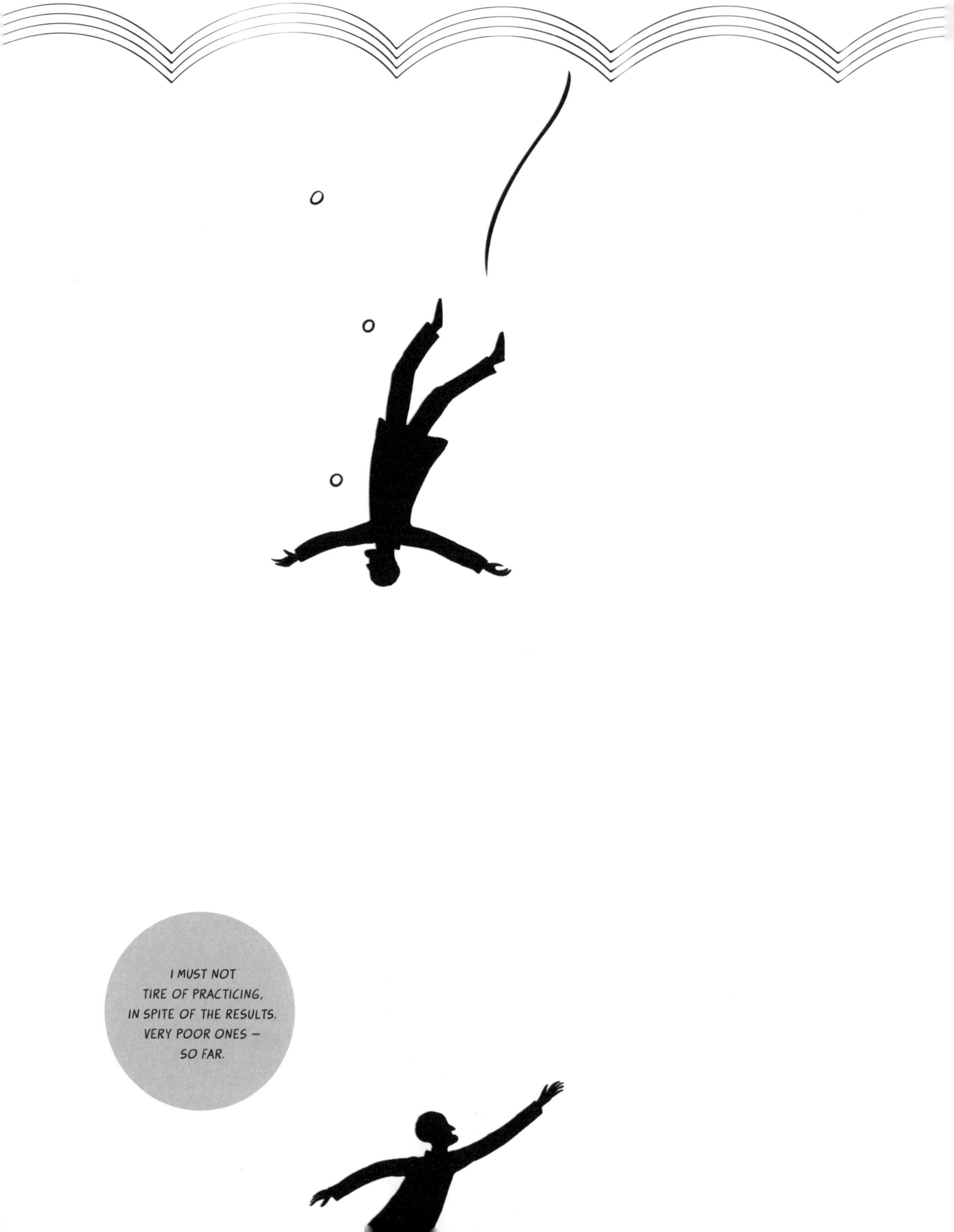
I MUST NOT TIRE OF PRACTICING, IN SPITE OF THE RESULTS. VERY POOR ONES — SO FAR.

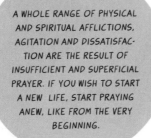

A WHOLE RANGE OF PHYSICAL
AND SPIRITUAL AFFLICTIONS,
AGITATION AND DISSATISFAC-
TION ARE THE RESULT OF
INSUFFICIENT AND SUPERFICIAL
PRAYER. IF YOU WISH TO START
A NEW LIFE, START PRAYING
ANEW, LIKE FROM THE VERY
BEGINNING.

PRAYER IS
BUILDING BLOCKS;
PRAYER IS
CREATION.

AT EVERY MOMENT,
MAKE YOUR RELATIONSHIP
TO GOD ABSOLUTELY
CLEAR.

BELIEVE ME, YOU
WILL NOT REGRET IT.

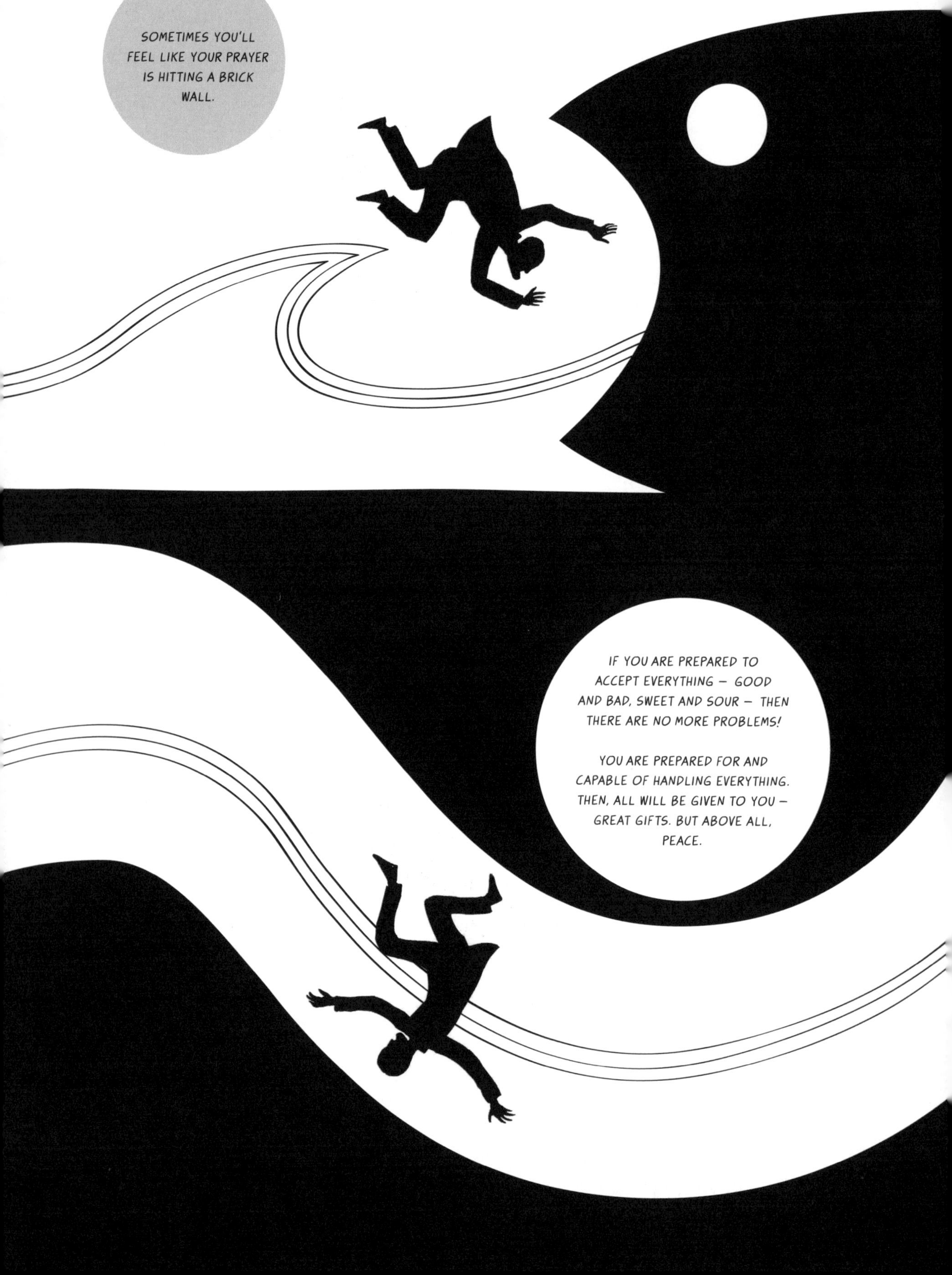
SOMETIMES YOU'LL FEEL LIKE YOUR PRAYER IS HITTING A BRICK WALL.
IF YOU ARE PREPARED TO ACCEPT EVERYTHING – GOOD AND BAD, SWEET AND SOUR – THEN THERE ARE NO MORE PROBLEMS!
YOU ARE PREPARED FOR AND CAPABLE OF HANDLING EVERYTHING. THEN, ALL WILL BE GIVEN TO YOU – GREAT GIFTS. BUT ABOVE ALL, PEACE.

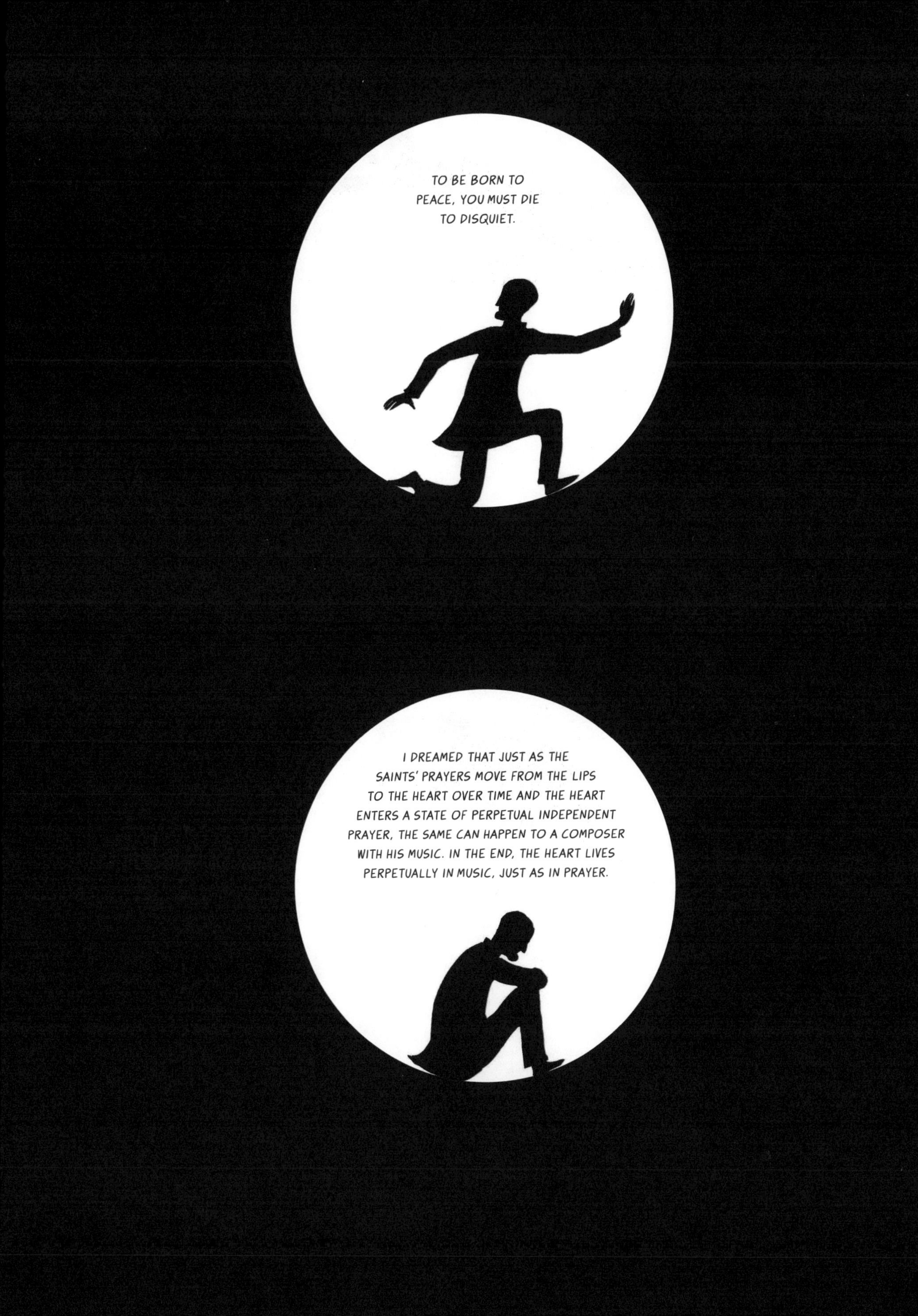
TO BE BORN TO PEACE, YOU MUST DIE TO DISQUIET.
I DREAMED THAT JUST AS THE SAINTS' PRAYERS MOVE FROM THE LIPS TO THE HEART OVER TIME AND THE HEART ENTERS A STATE OF PERPETUAL INDEPENDENT PRAYER, THE SAME CAN HAPPEN TO A COMPOSER WITH HIS MUSIC. IN THE END, THE HEART LIVES PERPETUALLY IN MUSIC, JUST AS IN PRAYER.

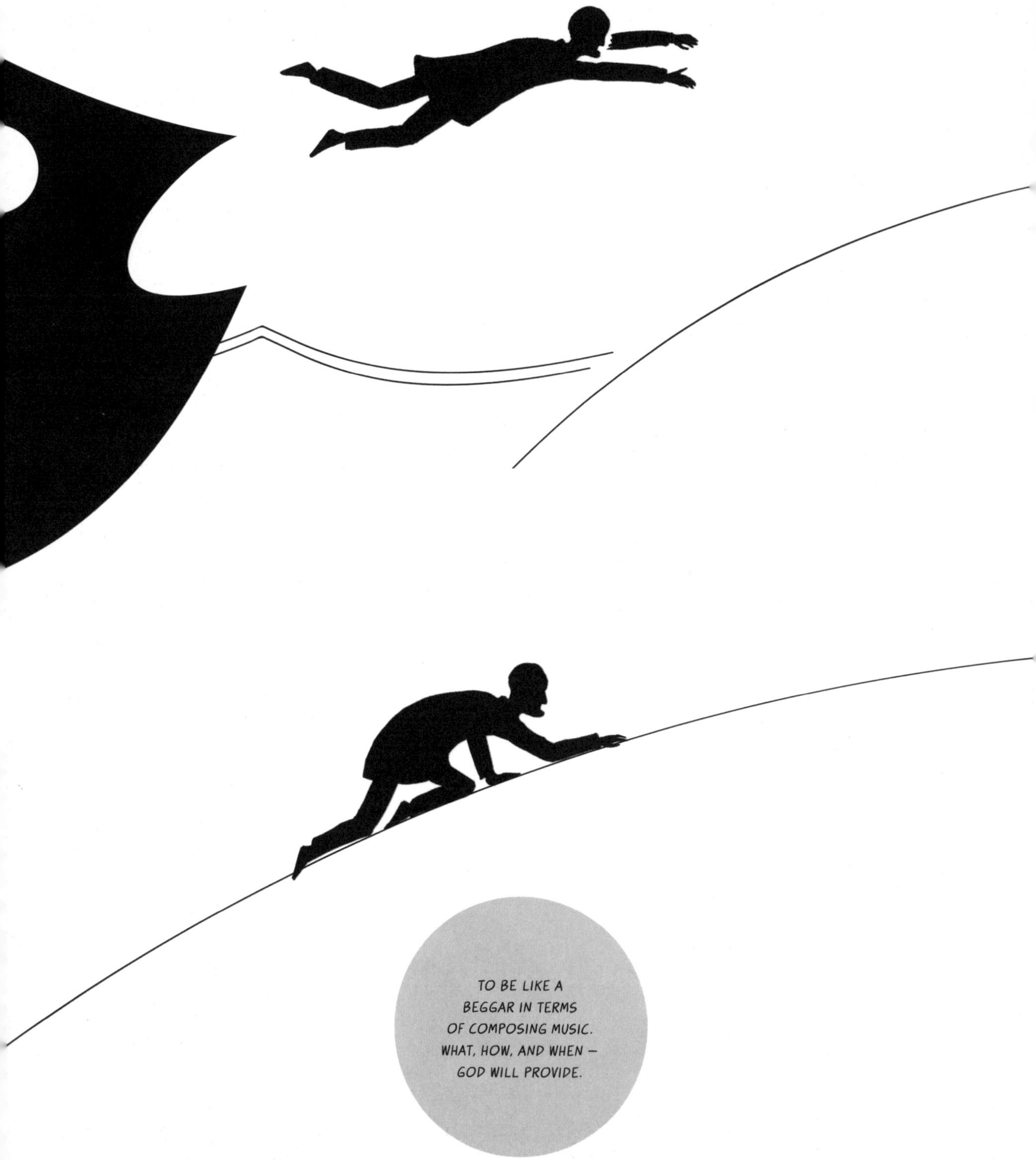
TO BE LIKE A
BEGGAR IN TERMS
OF COMPOSING MUSIC.
WHAT, HOW, AND WHEN —
GOD WILL PROVIDE.

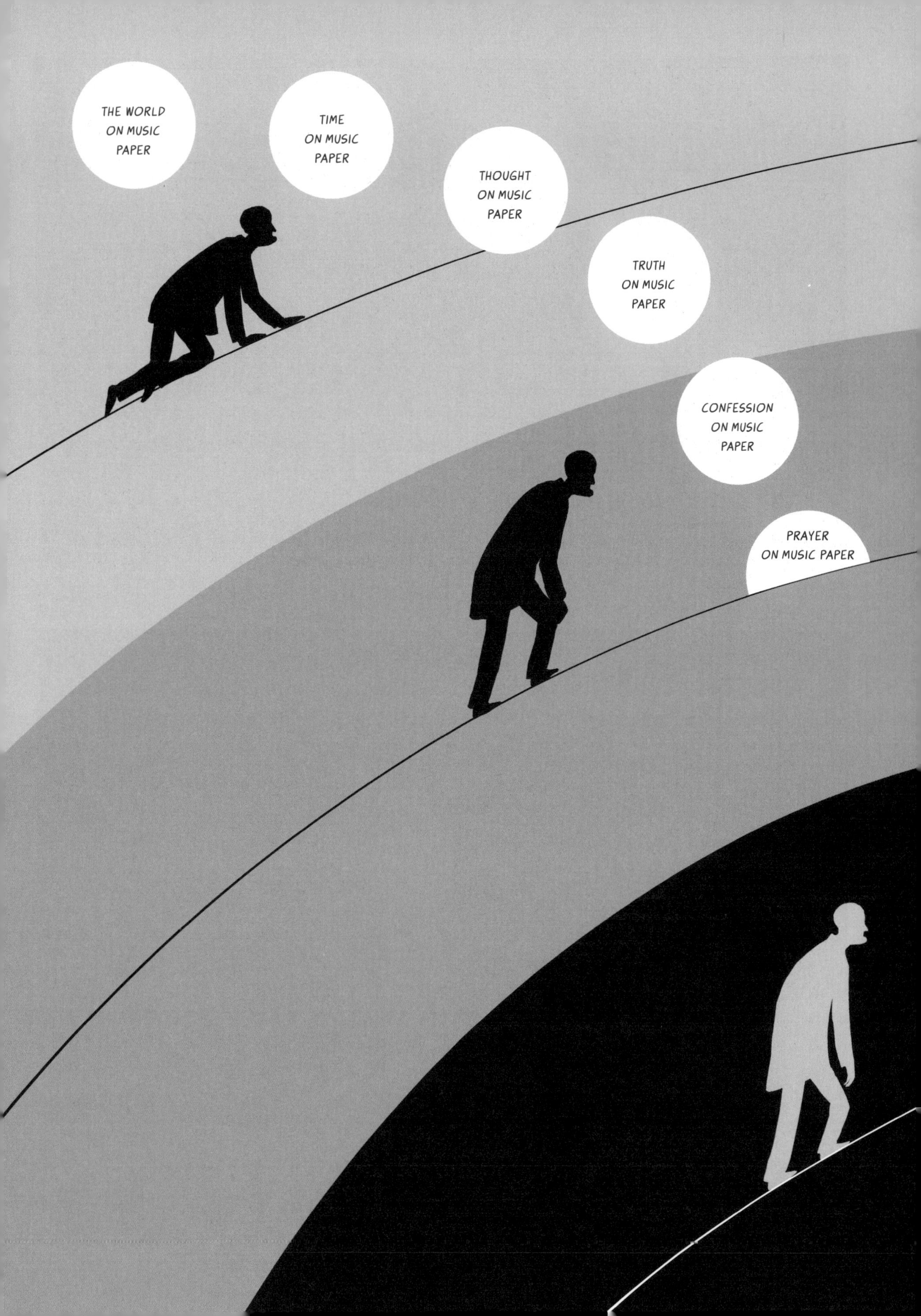
THE WORLD ON MUSIC PAPER
TIME ON MUSIC PAPER
THOUGHT ON MUSIC PAPER
TRUTH ON MUSIC PAPER
CONFESSION ON MUSIC PAPER
PRAYER ON MUSIC PAPER

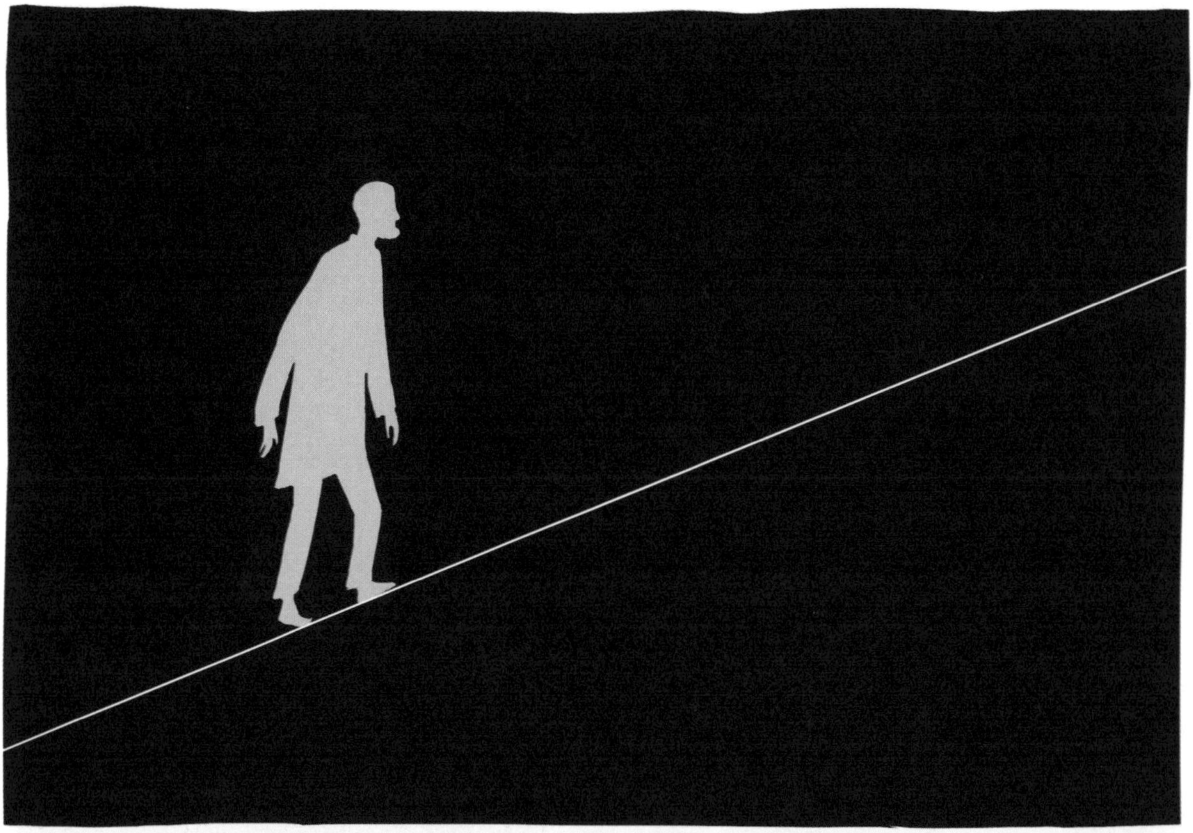

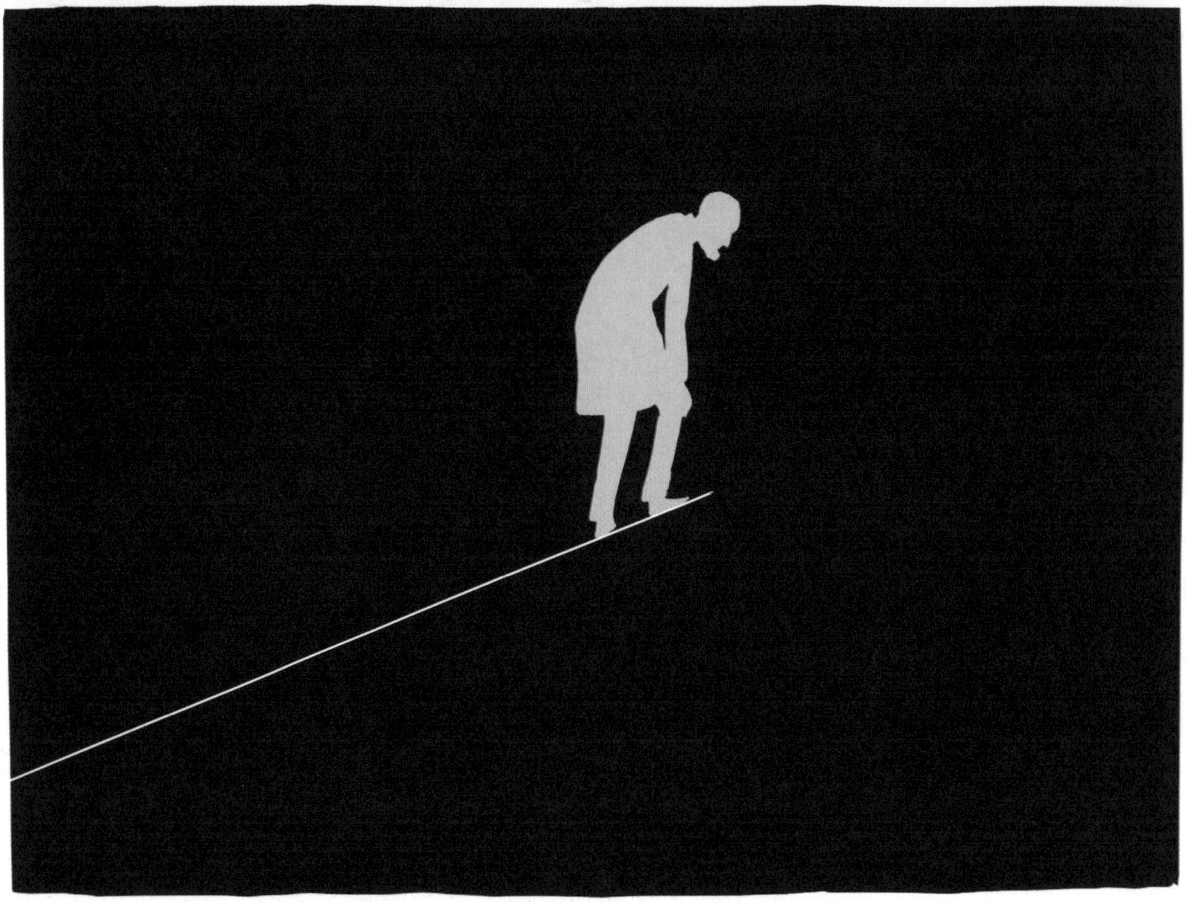

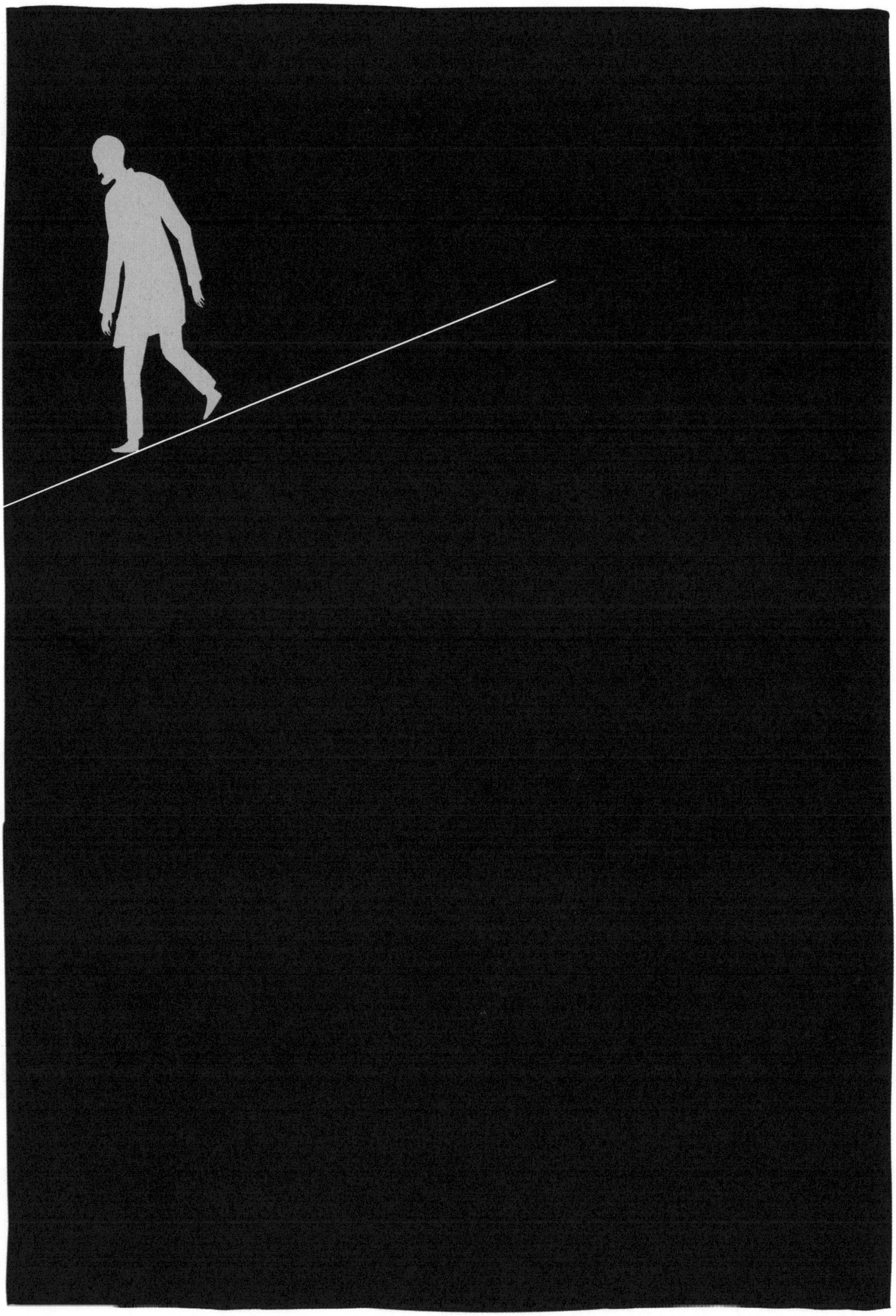

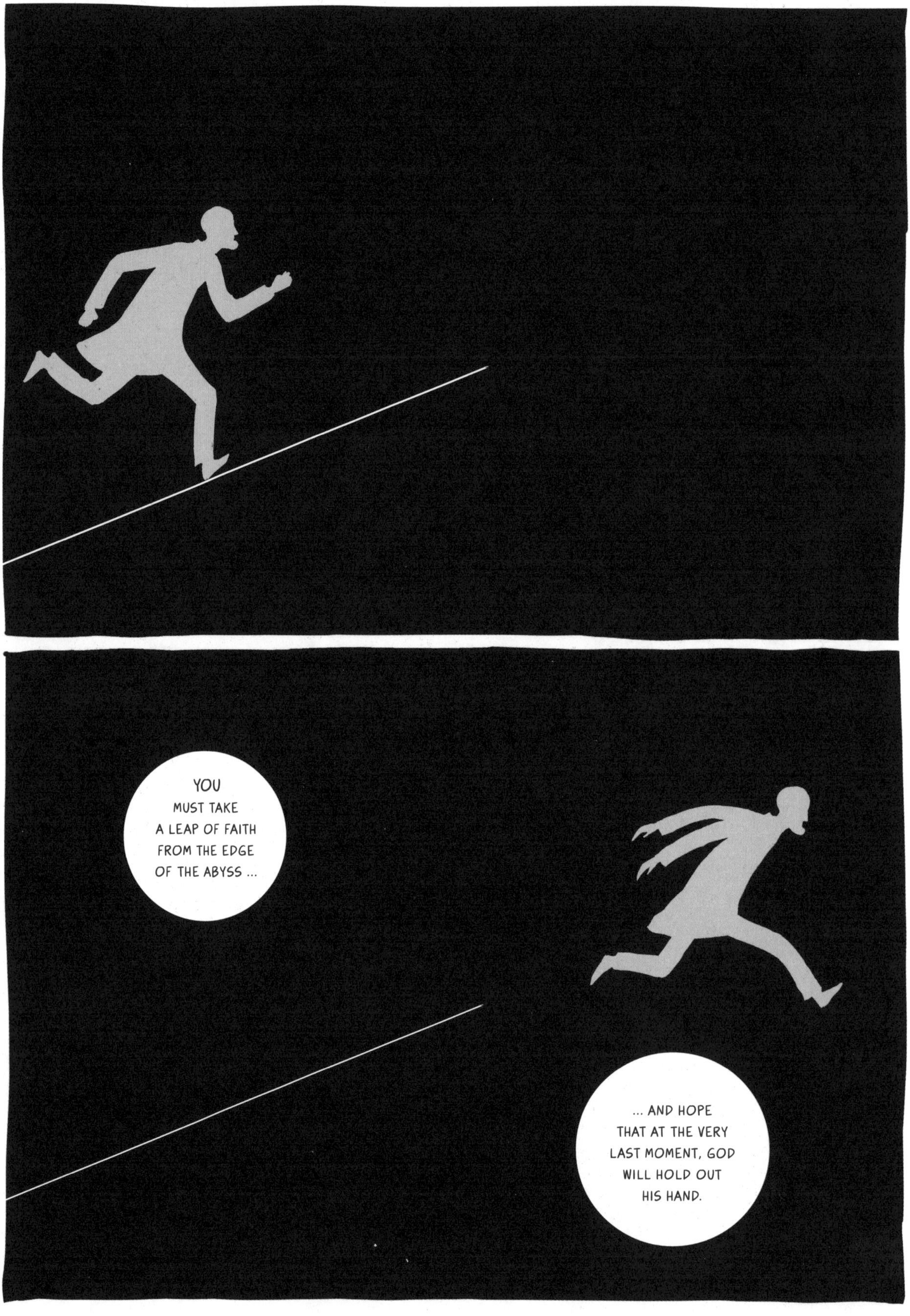
YOU MUST TAKE A LEAP OF FAITH FROM THE EDGE OF THE ABYSS ...
... AND HOPE THAT AT THE VERY LAST MOMENT, GOD WILL HOLD OUT HIS HAND.

III

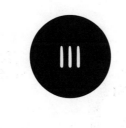

TABULA RASA

ARVO HAS BEGUN COMPOSING SINGLE MELODIC LINES FOR EACH AND EVERY PSALM.

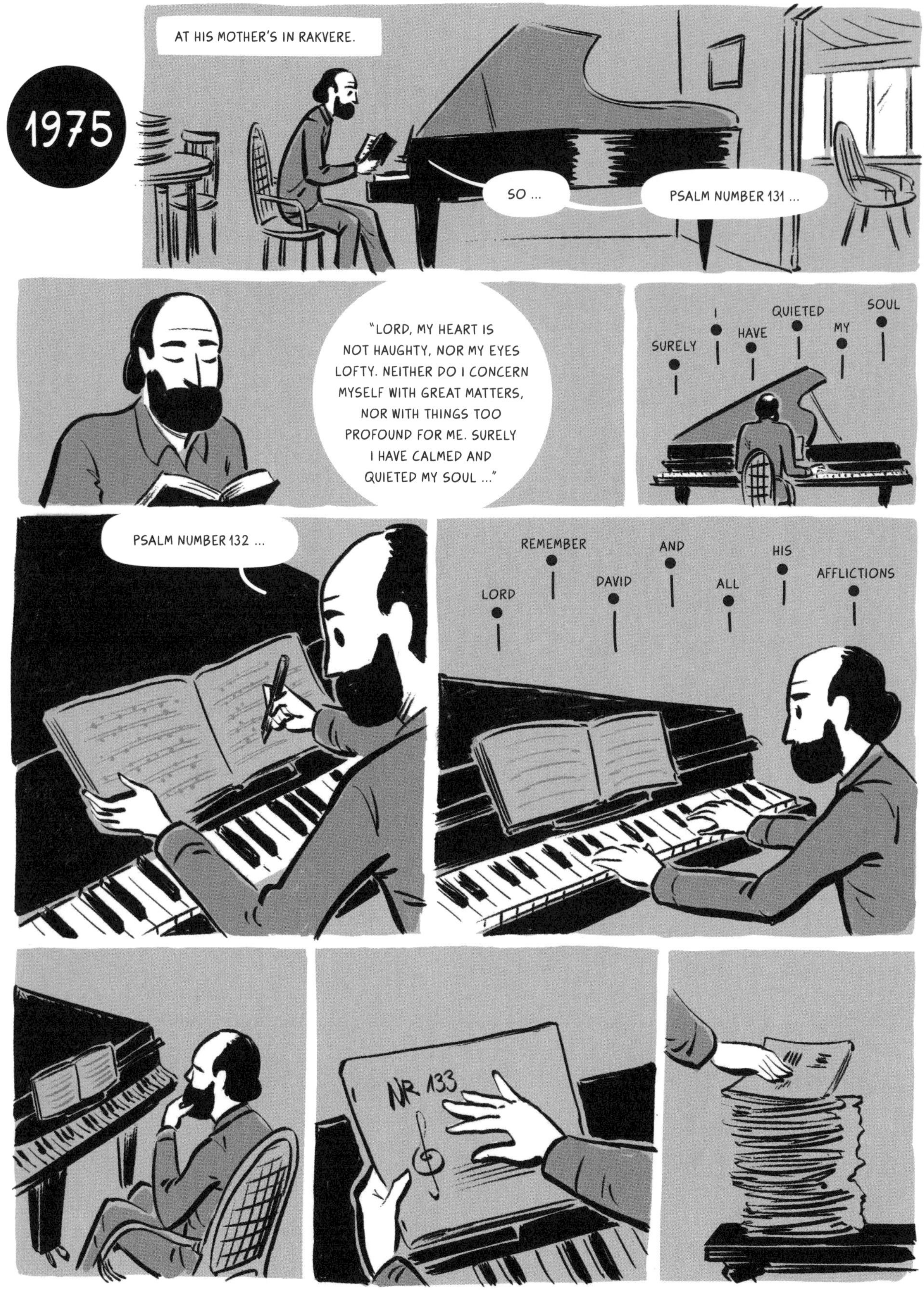
1975
AT HIS MOTHER'S IN RAKVERE.
SO ...
PSALM NUMBER 131 ...
"LORD, MY HEART IS NOT HAUGHTY, NOR MY EYES LOFTY. NEITHER DO I CONCERN MYSELF WITH GREAT MATTERS, NOR WITH THINGS TOO PROFOUND FOR ME. SURELY I HAVE CALMED AND QUIETED MY SOUL ..."
SURELY
I
HAVE
QUIETED
MY
SOUL
PSALM NUMBER 132 ...
LORD
REMEMBER
DAVID
AND
ALL
HIS
AFFLICTIONS
NR 133

AT THEIR MUSTAMÄE APARTMENT, NORA AND ARVO HAVE CREATED A UNIQUE ENVIRONMENT THAT SUPPORTS THEIR SEARCHING.

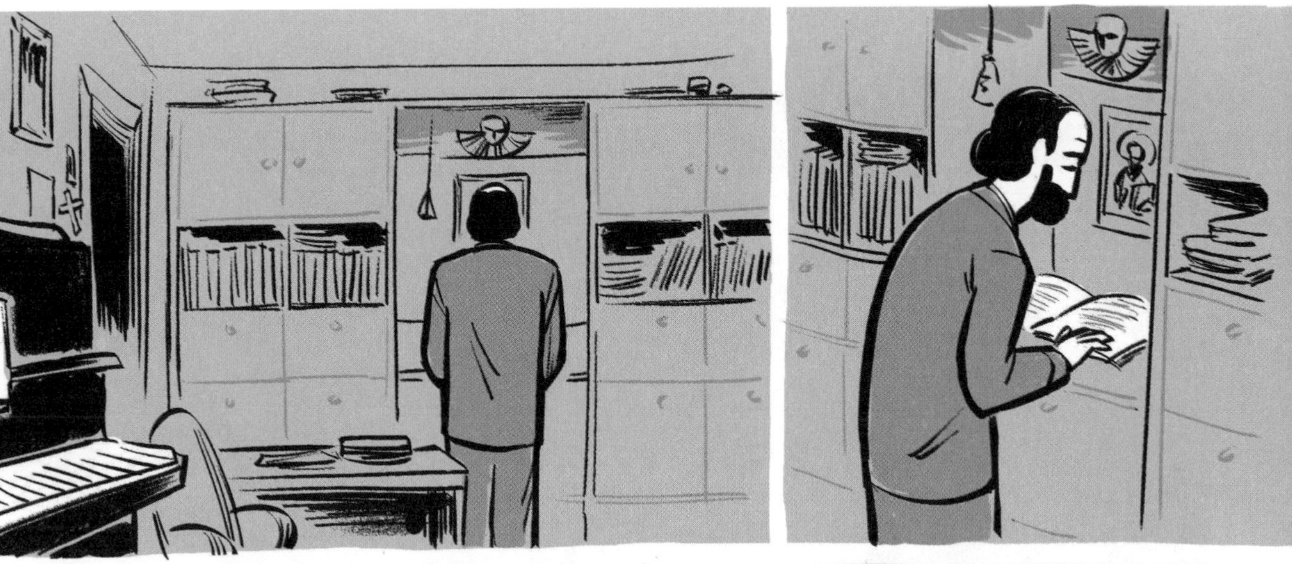

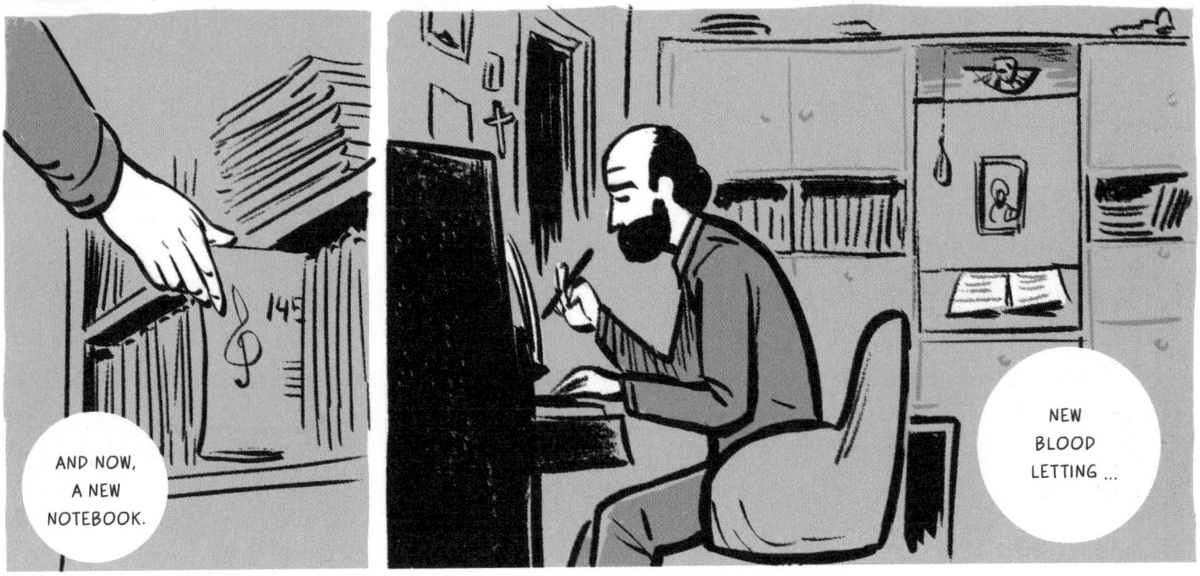
145
AND NOW, A NEW NOTEBOOK.
NEW BLOOD LETTING ...

HE ALSO COMPOSES HUNDREDS OF MELODIES FOR THE JESUS PRAYER.

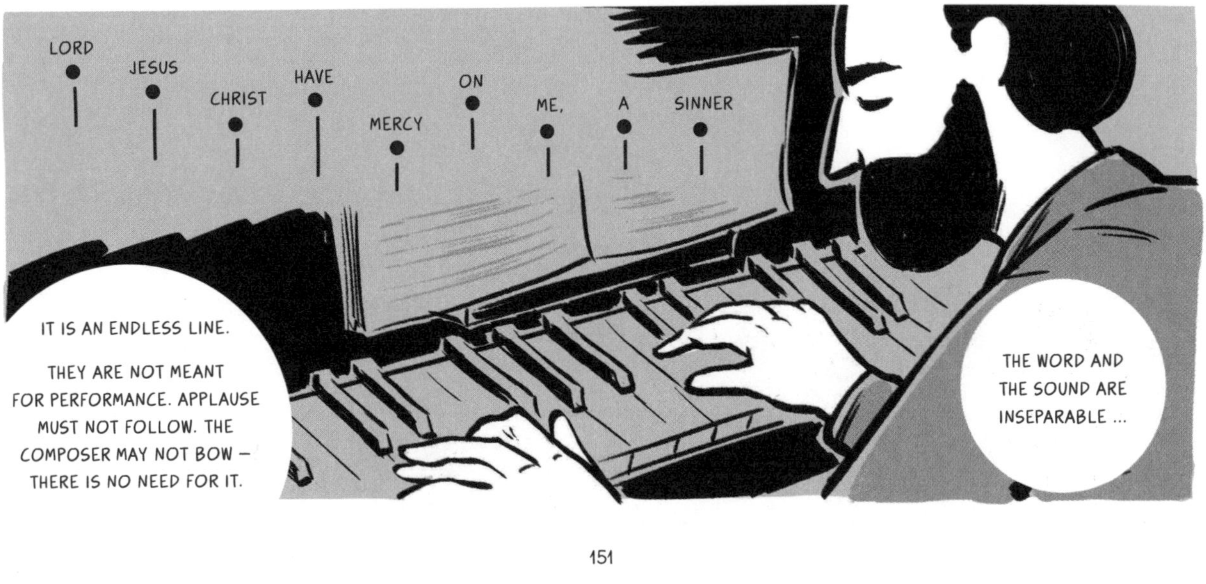
LORD
JESUS
CHRIST
HAVE
MERCY
ON
ME,
A
SINNER
IT IS AN ENDLESS LINE.
THEY ARE NOT MEANT FOR PERFORMANCE. APPLAUSE MUST NOT FOLLOW. THE COMPOSER MAY NOT BOW – THERE IS NO NEED FOR IT.
THE WORD AND THE SOUND ARE INSEPARABLE ...

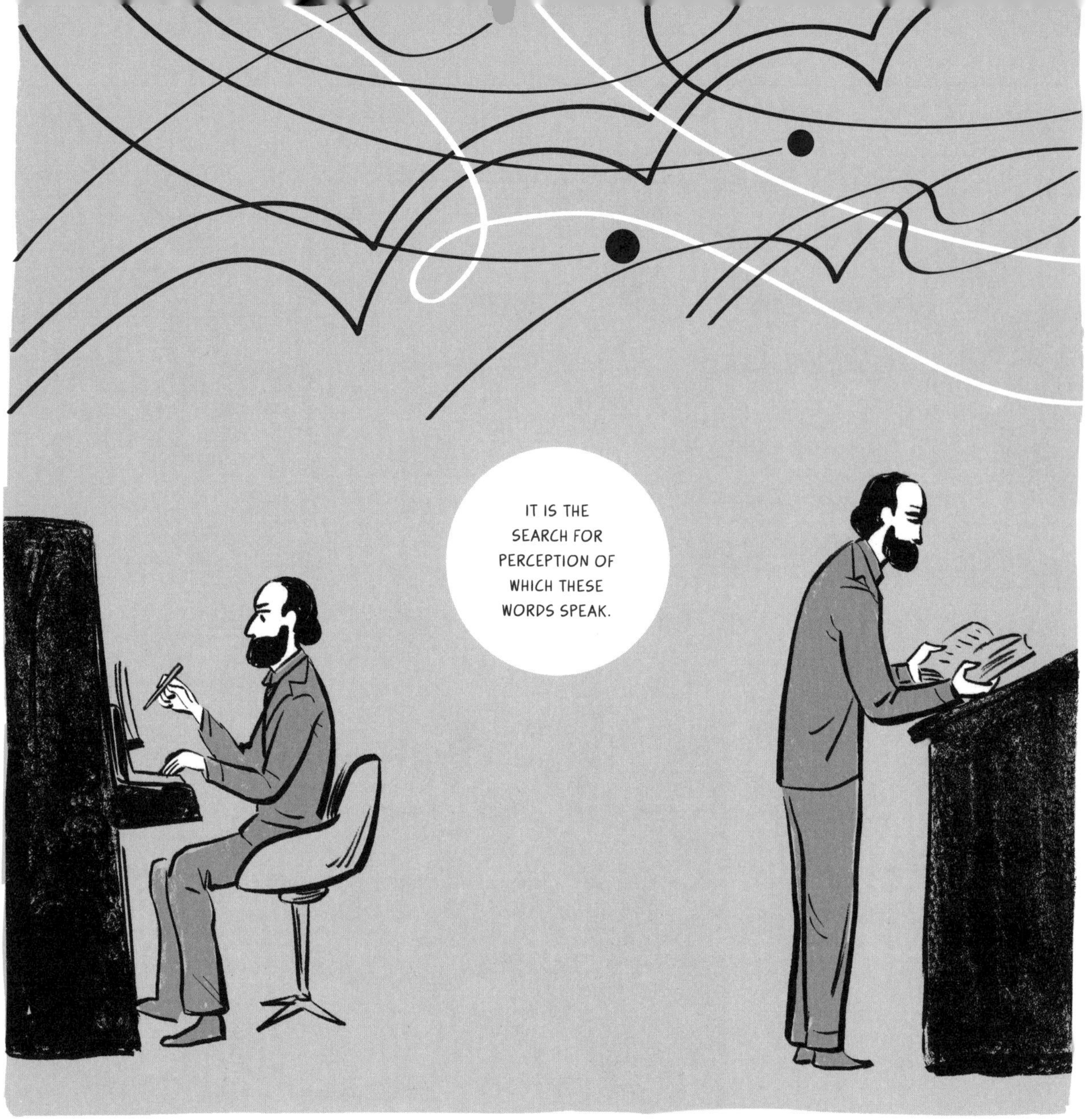
IT IS THE SEARCH FOR PERCEPTION OF WHICH THESE WORDS SPEAK.

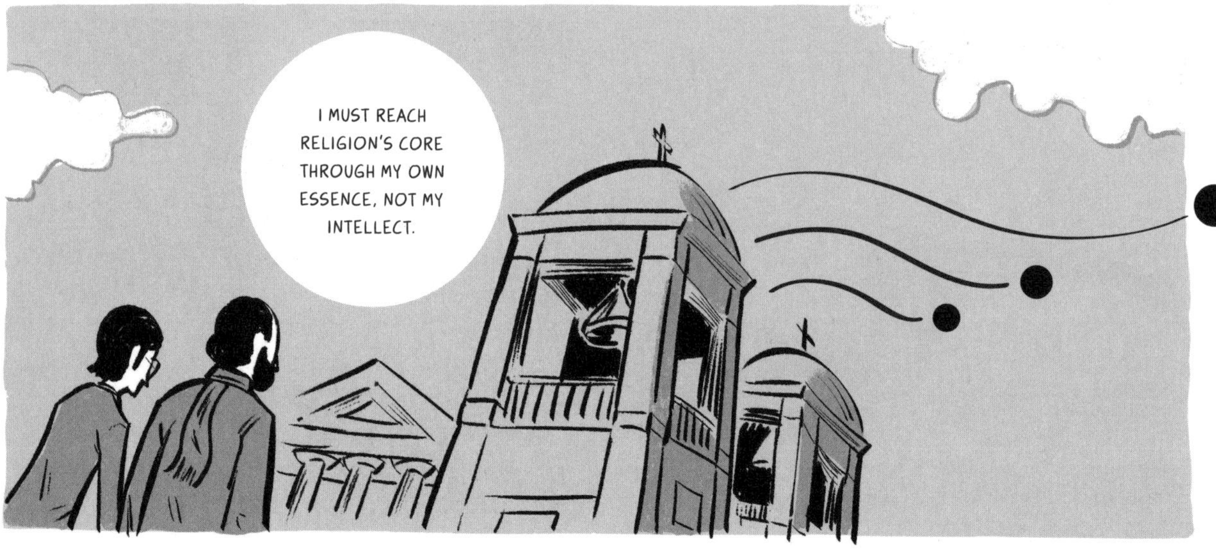
I MUST REACH RELIGION'S CORE THROUGH MY OWN ESSENCE, NOT MY INTELLECT.

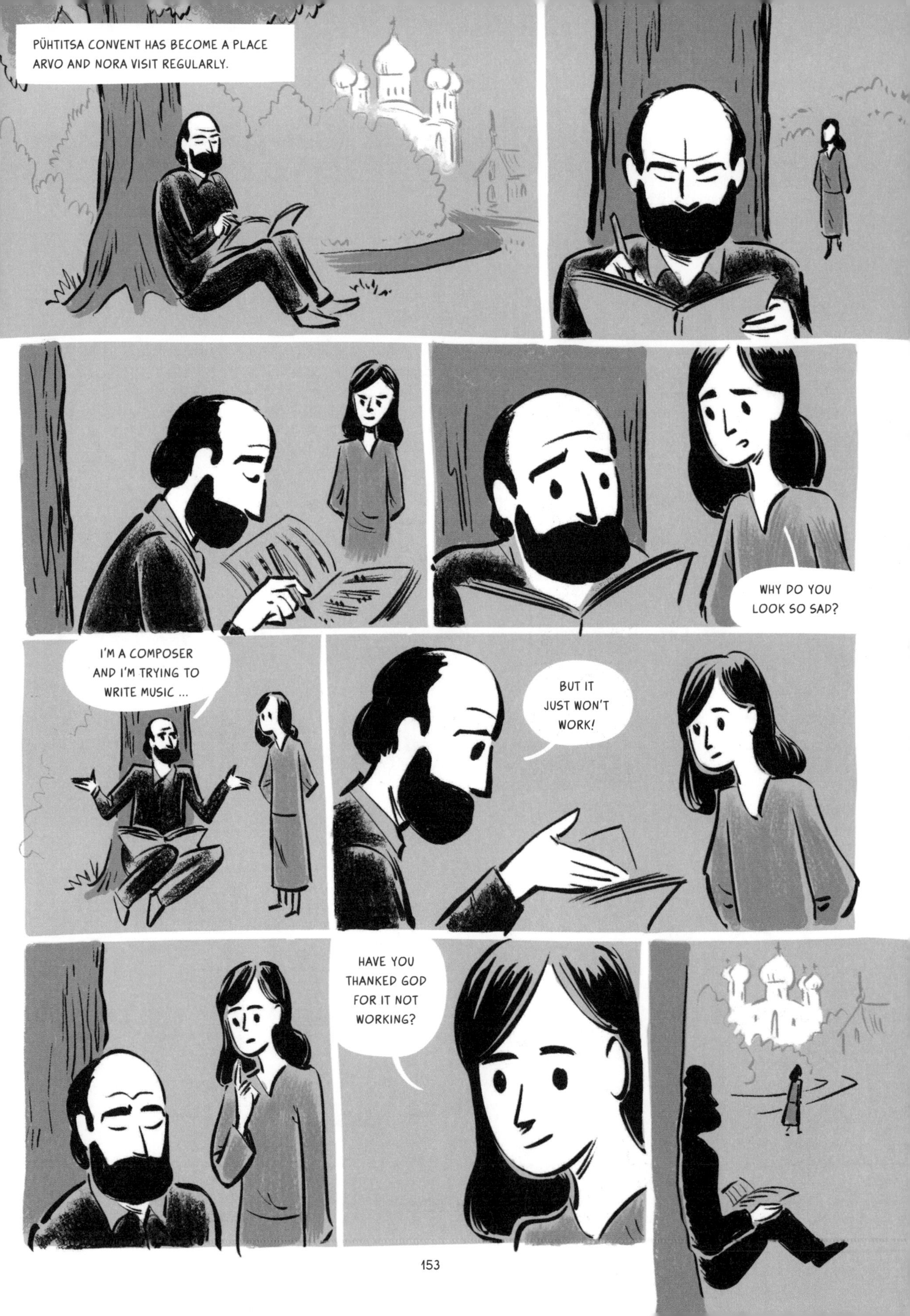
PÜHTITSA CONVENT HAS BECOME A PLACE ARVO AND NORA VISIT REGULARLY.
WHY DO YOU LOOK SO SAD?
I'M A COMPOSER AND I'M TRYING TO WRITE MUSIC ...
BUT IT JUST WON'T WORK!
HAVE YOU THANKED GOD FOR IT NOT WORKING?

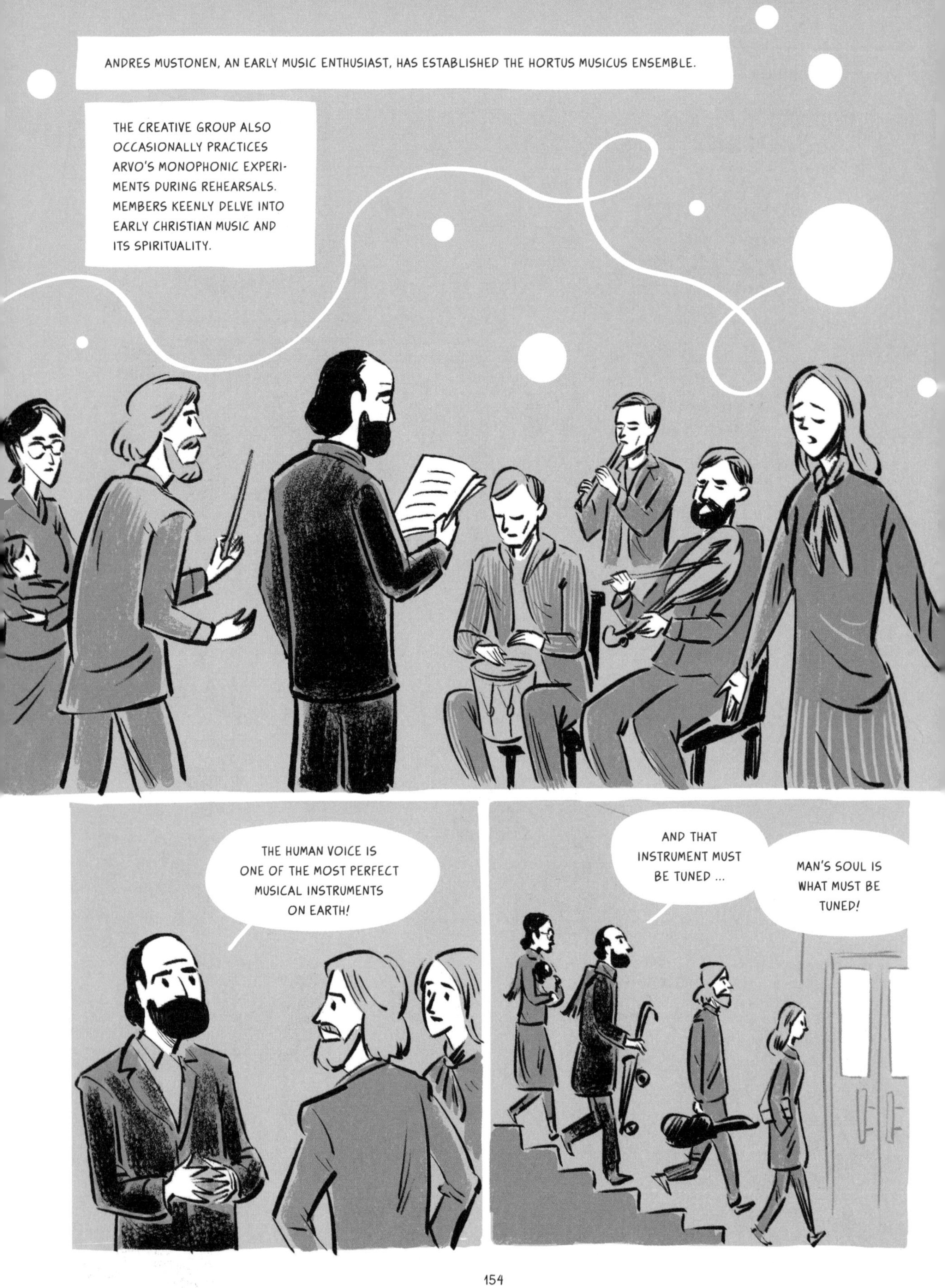
ANDRES MUSTONEN, AN EARLY MUSIC ENTHUSIAST, HAS ESTABLISHED THE HORTUS MUSICUS ENSEMBLE.
THE CREATIVE GROUP ALSO OCCASIONALLY PRACTICES ARVO'S MONOPHONIC EXPERIMENTS DURING REHEARSALS. MEMBERS KEENLY DELVE INTO EARLY CHRISTIAN MUSIC AND ITS SPIRITUALITY.
THE HUMAN VOICE IS ONE OF THE MOST PERFECT MUSICAL INSTRUMENTS ON EARTH!
AND THAT INSTRUMENT MUST BE TUNED ...
MAN'S SOUL IS WHAT MUST BE TUNED!

ANDRES MUSTONEN AND HIS WIFE, HELLE, A SINGER, HAVE FORMED A CLOSE BOND WITH THE PÄRT FAMILY.

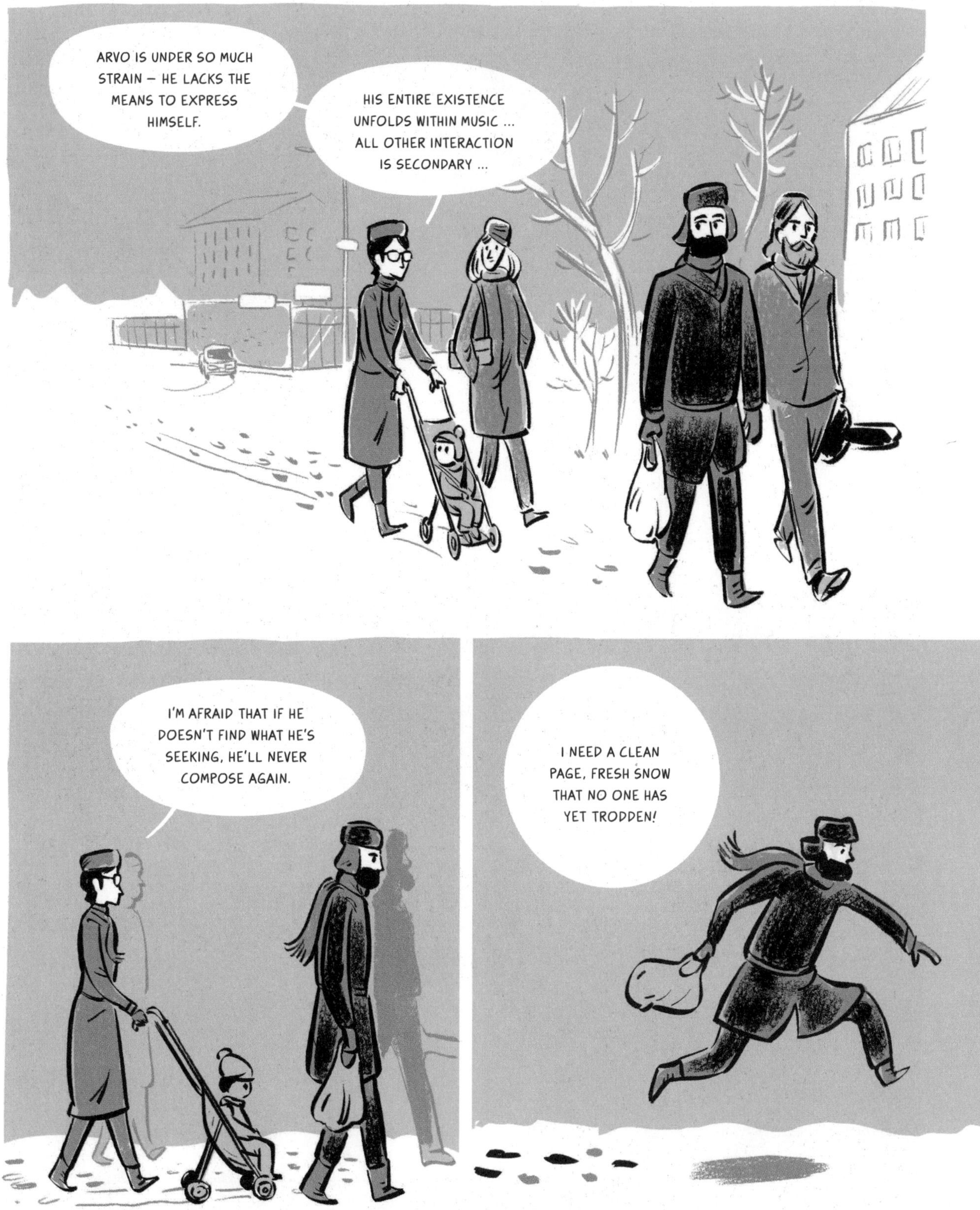
ARVO IS UNDER SO MUCH STRAIN – HE LACKS THE MEANS TO EXPRESS HIMSELF.
HIS ENTIRE EXISTENCE UNFOLDS WITHIN MUSIC ... ALL OTHER INTERACTION IS SECONDARY ...
I'M AFRAID THAT IF HE DOESN'T FIND WHAT HE'S SEEKING, HE'LL NEVER COMPOSE AGAIN.
I NEED A CLEAN PAGE, FRESH SNOW THAT NO ONE HAS YET TRODDEN!

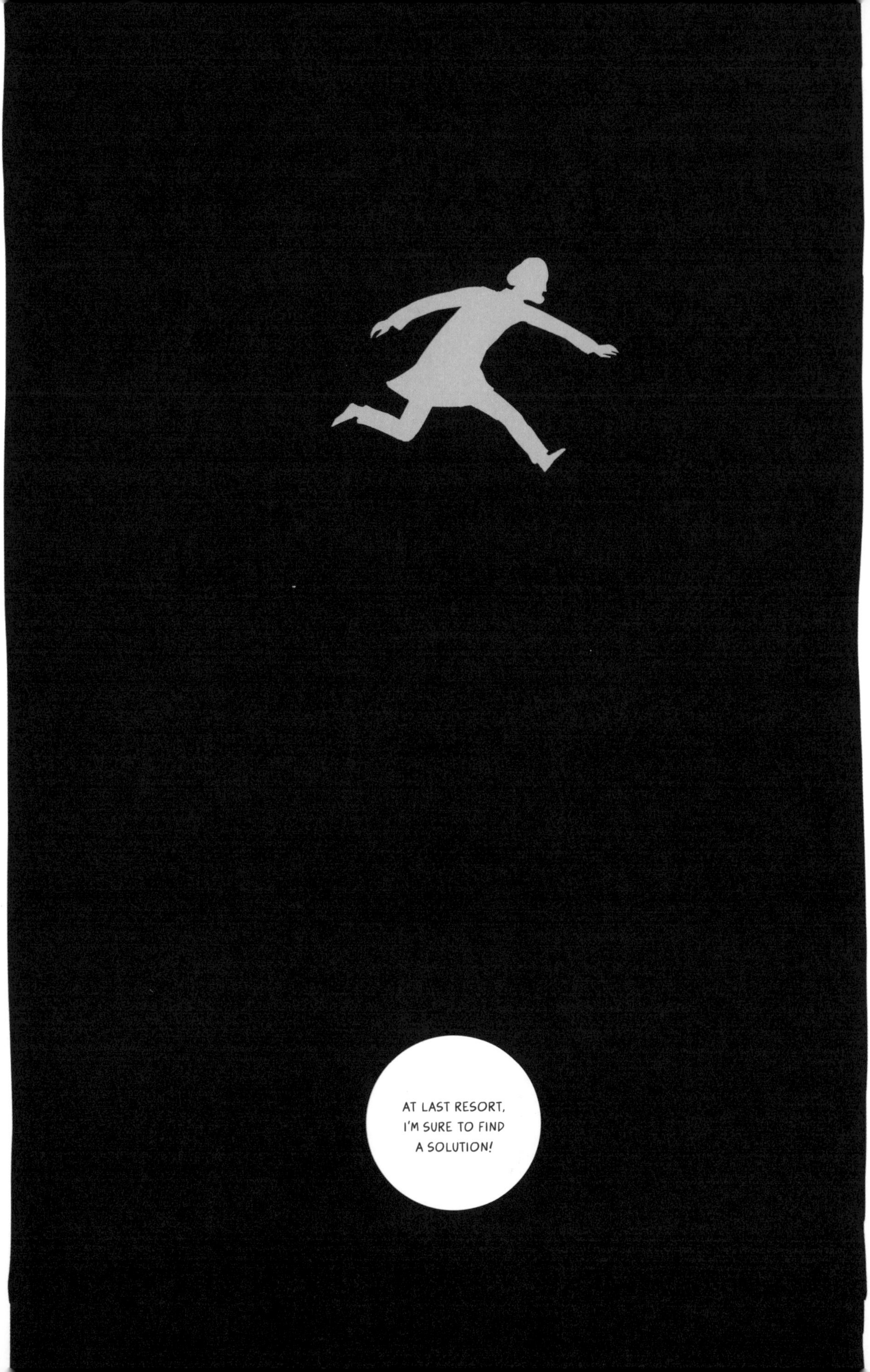
AT LAST RESORT, I'M SURE TO FIND A SOLUTION!

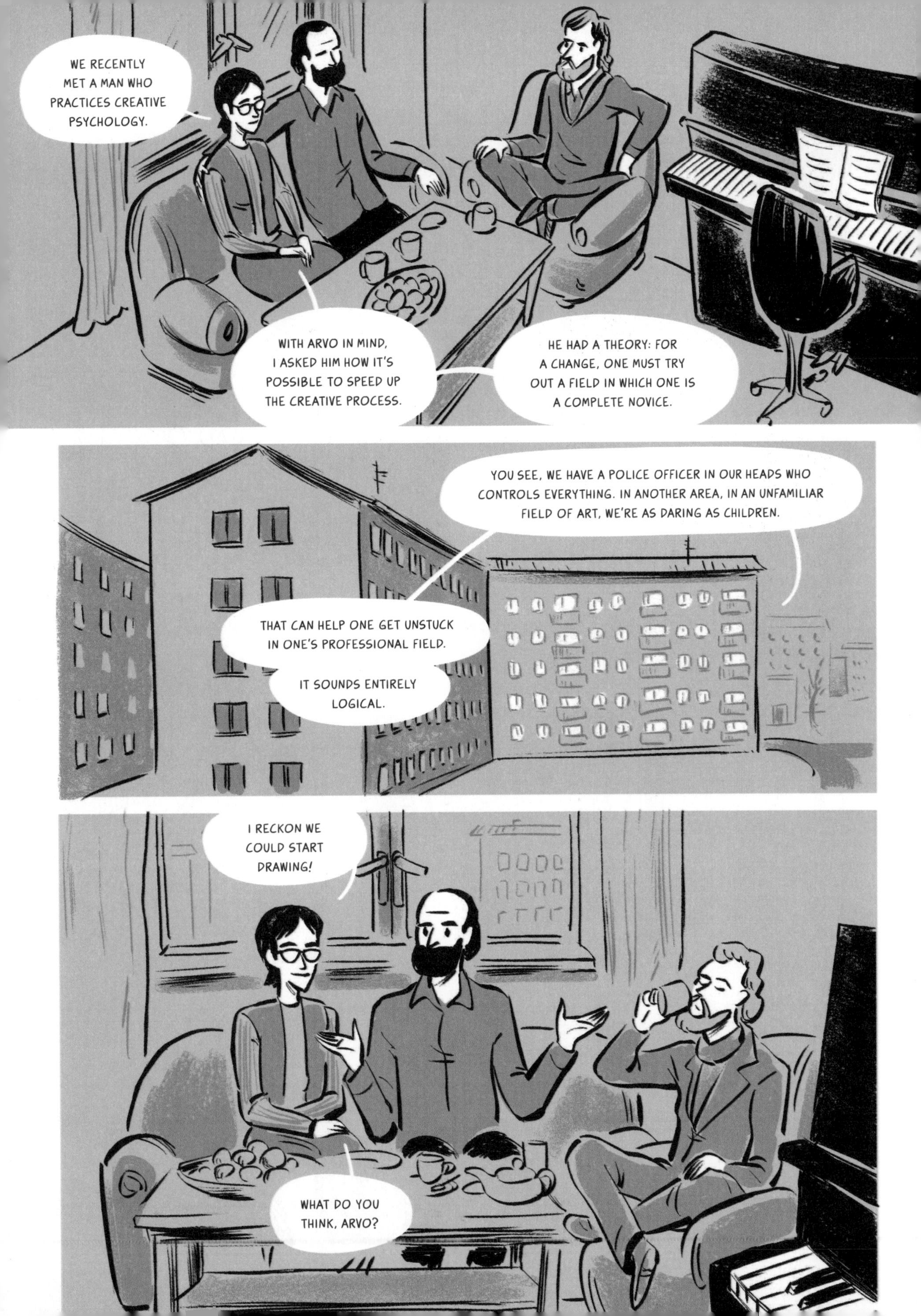
WE RECENTLY MET A MAN WHO PRACTICES CREATIVE PSYCHOLOGY.
WITH ARVO IN MIND, I ASKED HIM HOW IT'S POSSIBLE TO SPEED UP THE CREATIVE PROCESS.
HE HAD A THEORY: FOR A CHANGE, ONE MUST TRY OUT A FIELD IN WHICH ONE IS A COMPLETE NOVICE.
YOU SEE, WE HAVE A POLICE OFFICER IN OUR HEADS WHO CONTROLS EVERYTHING. IN ANOTHER AREA, IN AN UNFAMILIAR FIELD OF ART, WE'RE AS DARING AS CHILDREN.
THAT CAN HELP ONE GET UNSTUCK IN ONE'S PROFESSIONAL FIELD.
IT SOUNDS ENTIRELY LOGICAL.
I RECKON WE COULD START DRAWING!
WHAT DO YOU THINK, ARVO?

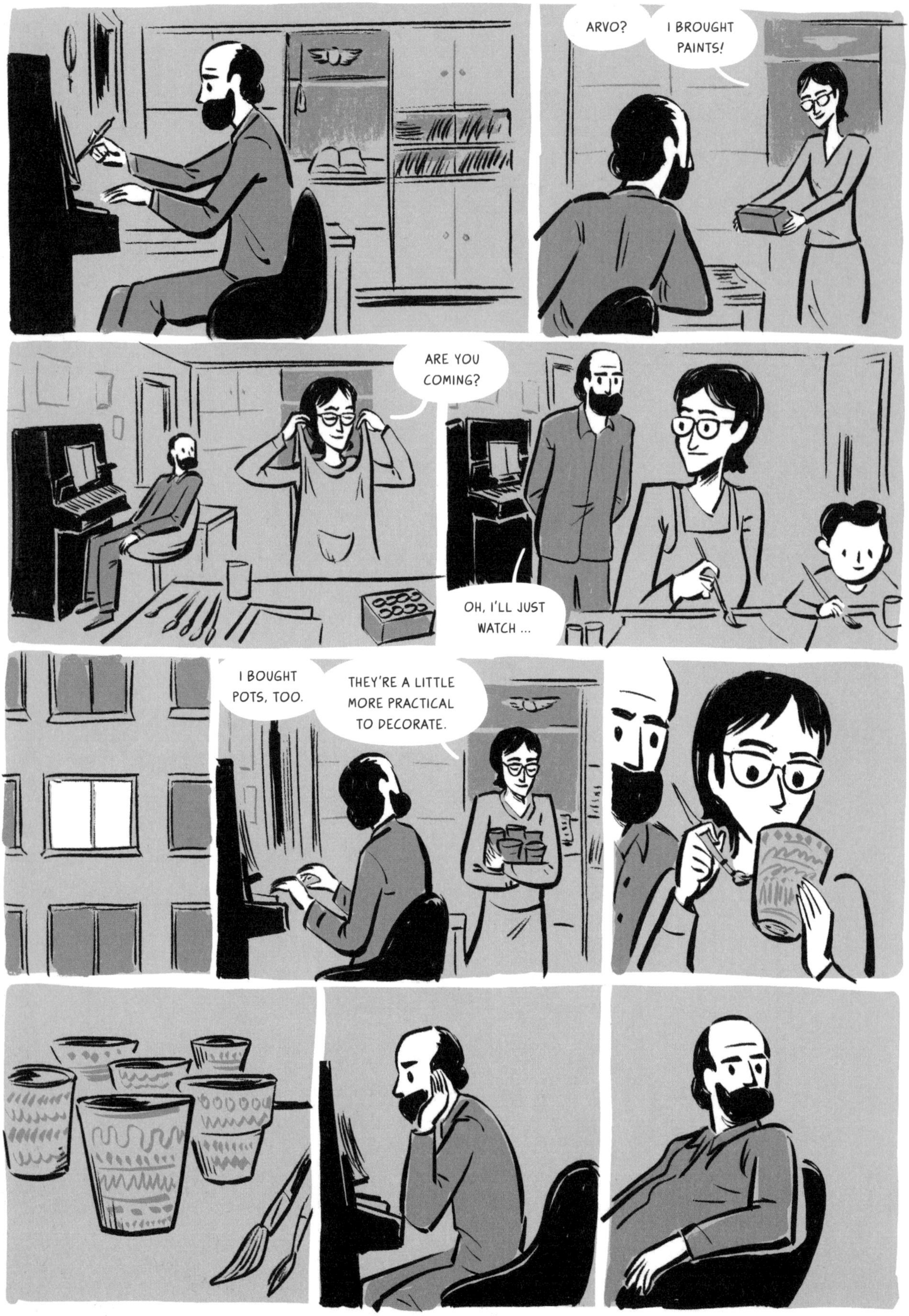
ARVO?
I BROUGHT PAINTS!
ARE YOU COMING?
OH, I'LL JUST WATCH ...
I BOUGHT POTS, TOO.
THEY'RE A LITTLE MORE PRACTICAL TO DECORATE.

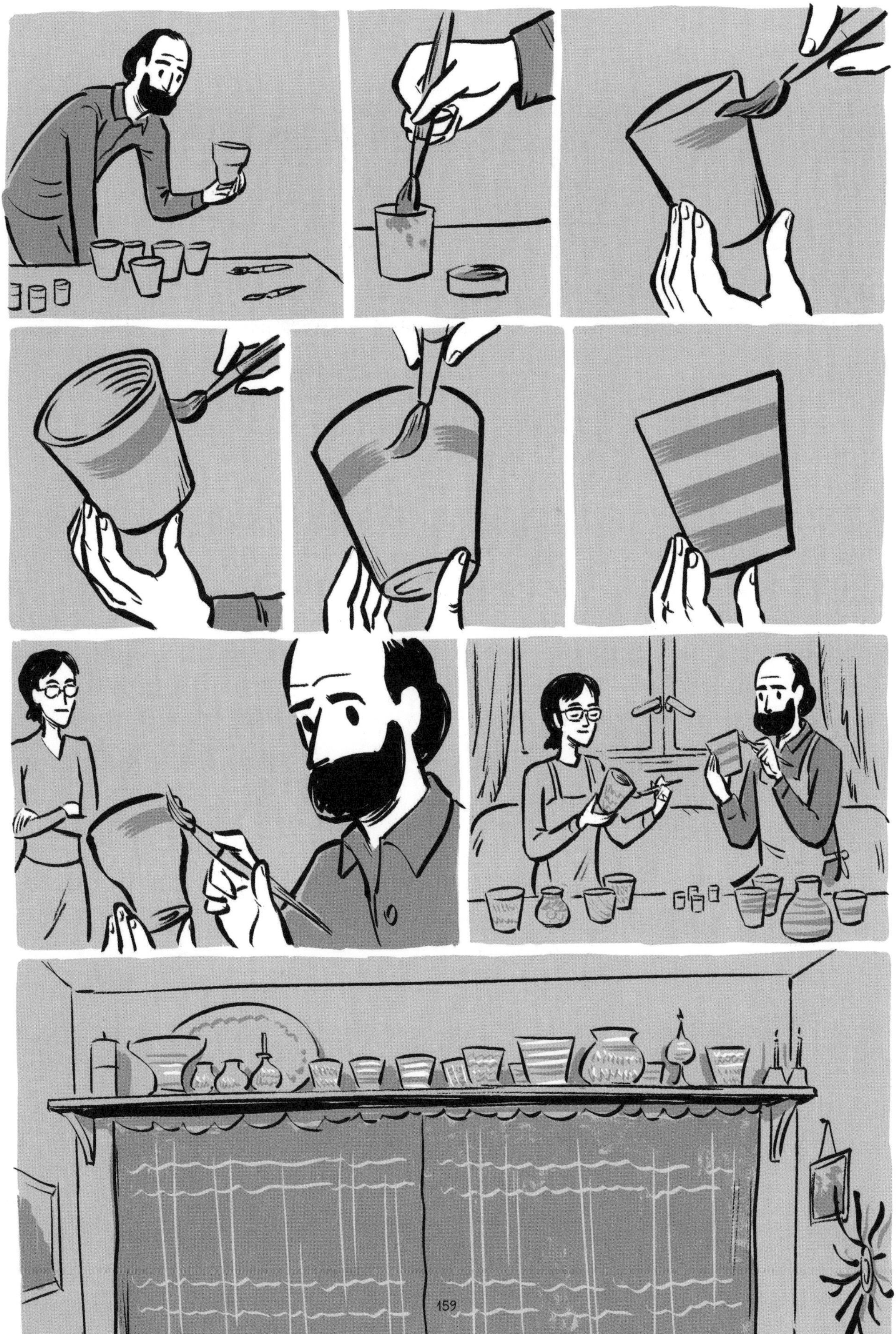

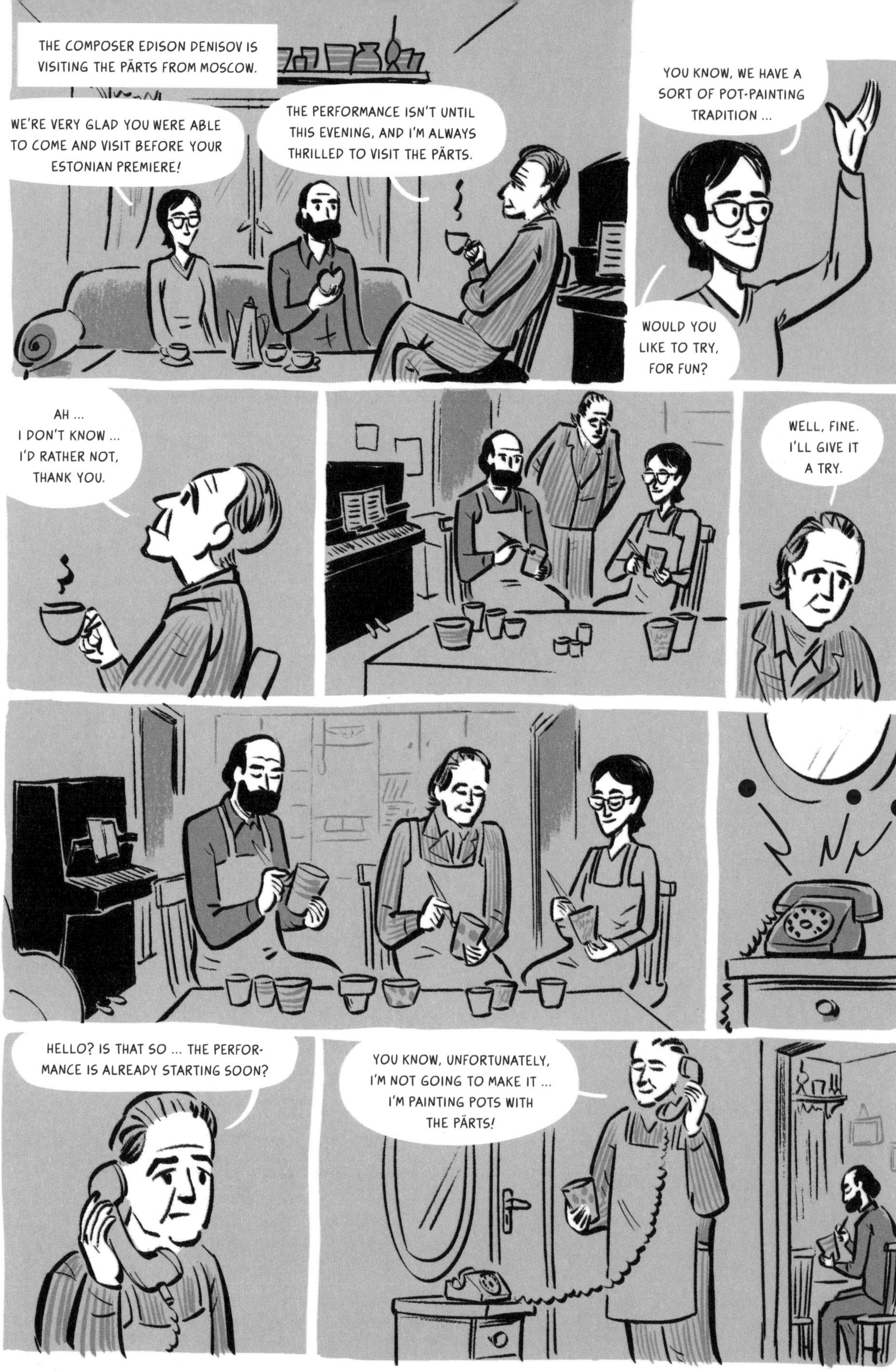
THE COMPOSER EDISON DENISOV IS VISITING THE PÄRTS FROM MOSCOW.
WE'RE VERY GLAD YOU WERE ABLE TO COME AND VISIT BEFORE YOUR ESTONIAN PREMIERE!
THE PERFORMANCE ISN'T UNTIL THIS EVENING, AND I'M ALWAYS THRILLED TO VISIT THE PÄRTS.
YOU KNOW, WE HAVE A SORT OF POT-PAINTING TRADITION ...
WOULD YOU LIKE TO TRY, FOR FUN?
AH ... I DON'T KNOW ... I'D RATHER NOT, THANK YOU.
WELL, FINE. I'LL GIVE IT A TRY.
HELLO? IS THAT SO ... THE PERFORMANCE IS ALREADY STARTING SOON?
YOU KNOW, UNFORTUNATELY, I'M NOT GOING TO MAKE IT ... I'M PAINTING POTS WITH THE PÄRTS!

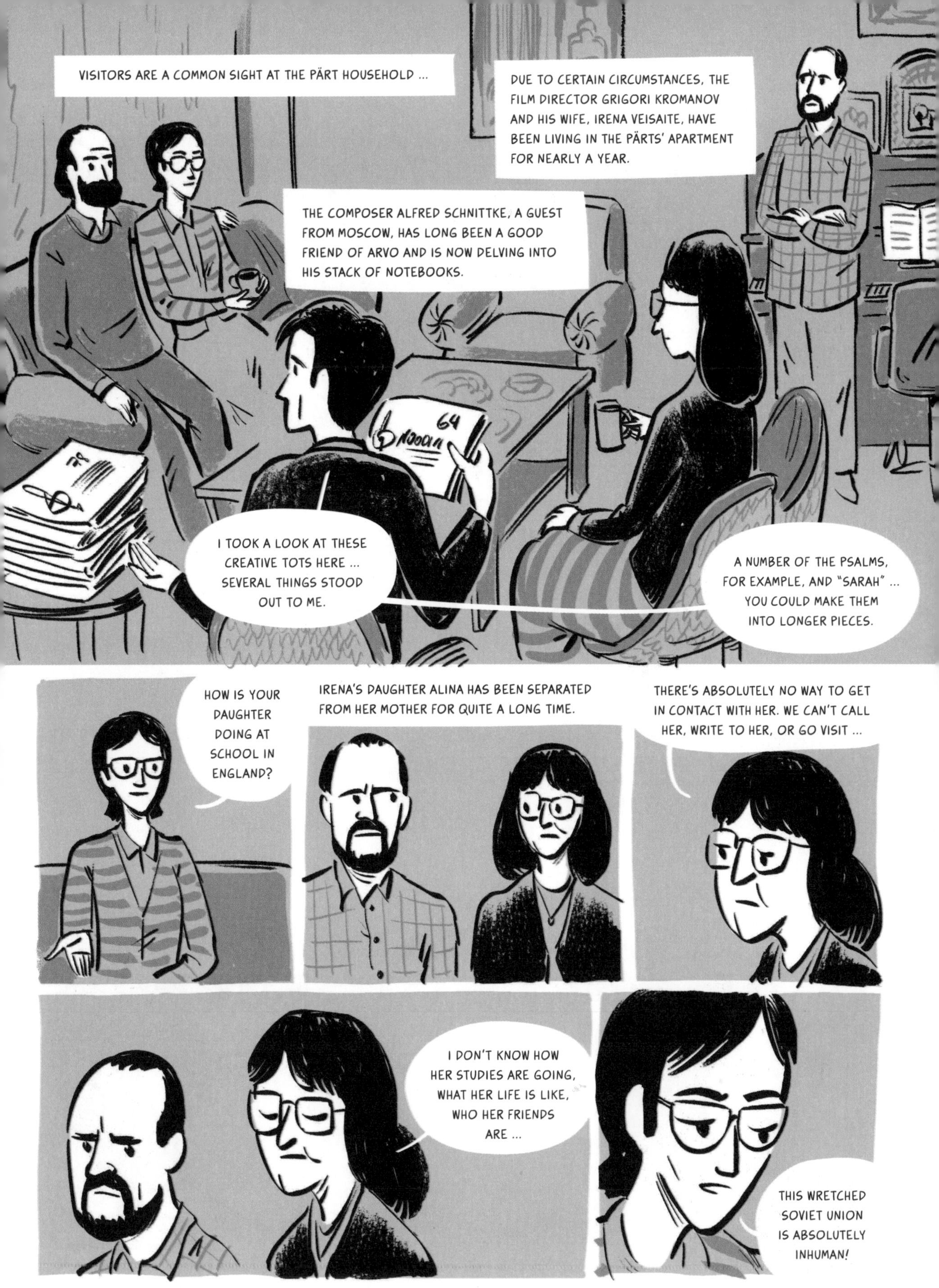
VISITORS ARE A COMMON SIGHT AT THE PÄRT HOUSEHOLD ...
DUE TO CERTAIN CIRCUMSTANCES, THE FILM DIRECTOR GRIGORI KROMANOV AND HIS WIFE, IRENA VEISAITE, HAVE BEEN LIVING IN THE PÄRTS' APARTMENT FOR NEARLY A YEAR.
THE COMPOSER ALFRED SCHNITTKE, A GUEST FROM MOSCOW, HAS LONG BEEN A GOOD FRIEND OF ARVO AND IS NOW DELVING INTO HIS STACK OF NOTEBOOKS.
I TOOK A LOOK AT THESE CREATIVE TOTS HERE ... SEVERAL THINGS STOOD OUT TO ME.
A NUMBER OF THE PSALMS, FOR EXAMPLE, AND "SARAH" ... YOU COULD MAKE THEM INTO LONGER PIECES.
HOW IS YOUR DAUGHTER DOING AT SCHOOL IN ENGLAND?
IRENA'S DAUGHTER ALINA HAS BEEN SEPARATED FROM HER MOTHER FOR QUITE A LONG TIME.
THERE'S ABSOLUTELY NO WAY TO GET IN CONTACT WITH HER. WE CAN'T CALL HER, WRITE TO HER, OR GO VISIT ...
I DON'T KNOW HOW HER STUDIES ARE GOING, WHAT HER LIFE IS LIKE, WHO HER FRIENDS ARE ...
THIS WRETCHED SOVIET UNION IS ABSOLUTELY INHUMAN!

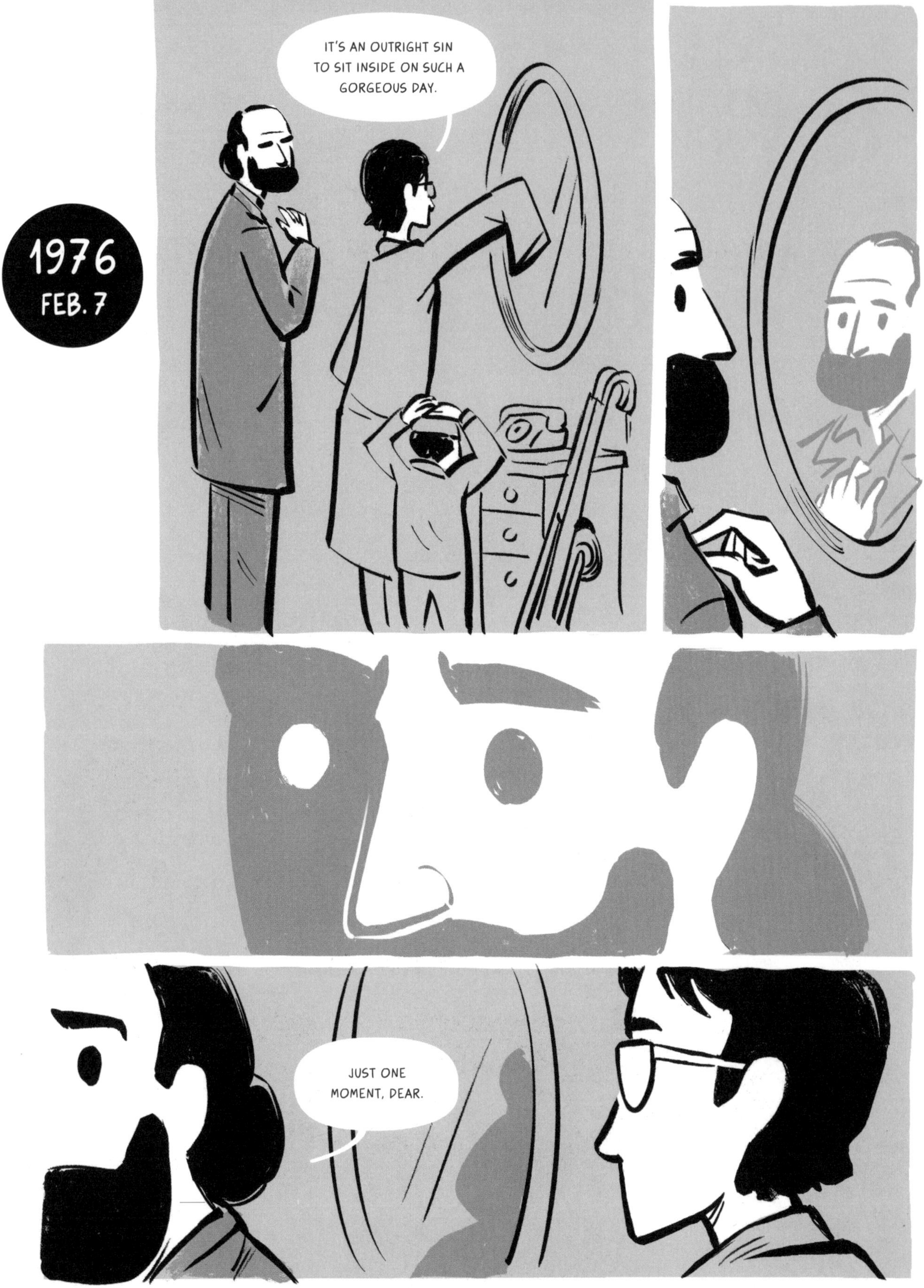
1976
FEB. 7
IT'S AN OUTRIGHT SIN TO SIT INSIDE ON SUCH A GORGEOUS DAY.
JUST ONE MOMENT, DEAR.

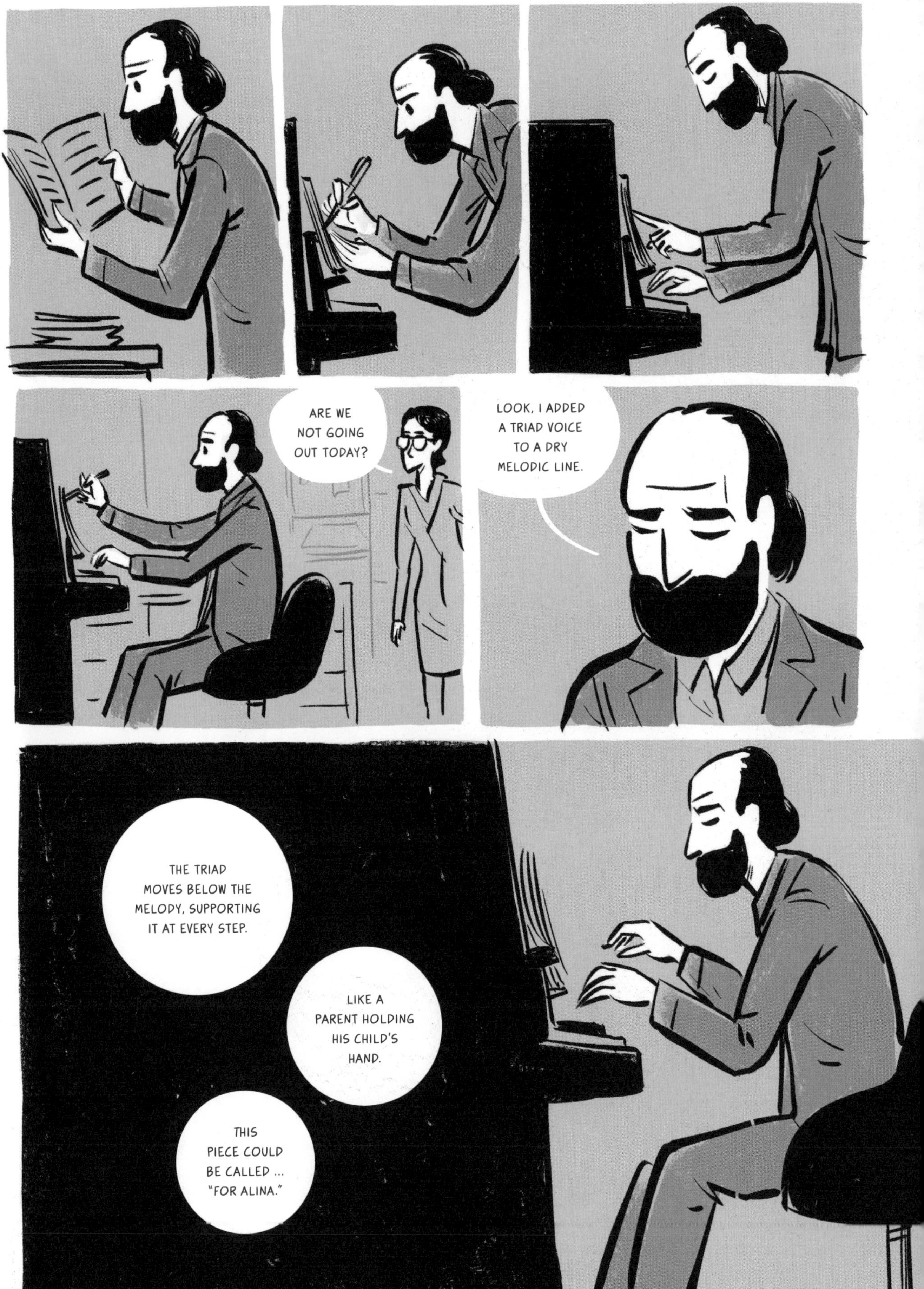
ARE WE NOT GOING OUT TODAY?
LOOK, I ADDED A TRIAD VOICE TO A DRY MELODIC LINE.
THE TRIAD MOVES BELOW THE MELODY, SUPPORTING IT AT EVERY STEP.
LIKE A PARENT HOLDING HIS CHILD'S HAND.
THIS PIECE COULD BE CALLED ... "FOR ALINA."

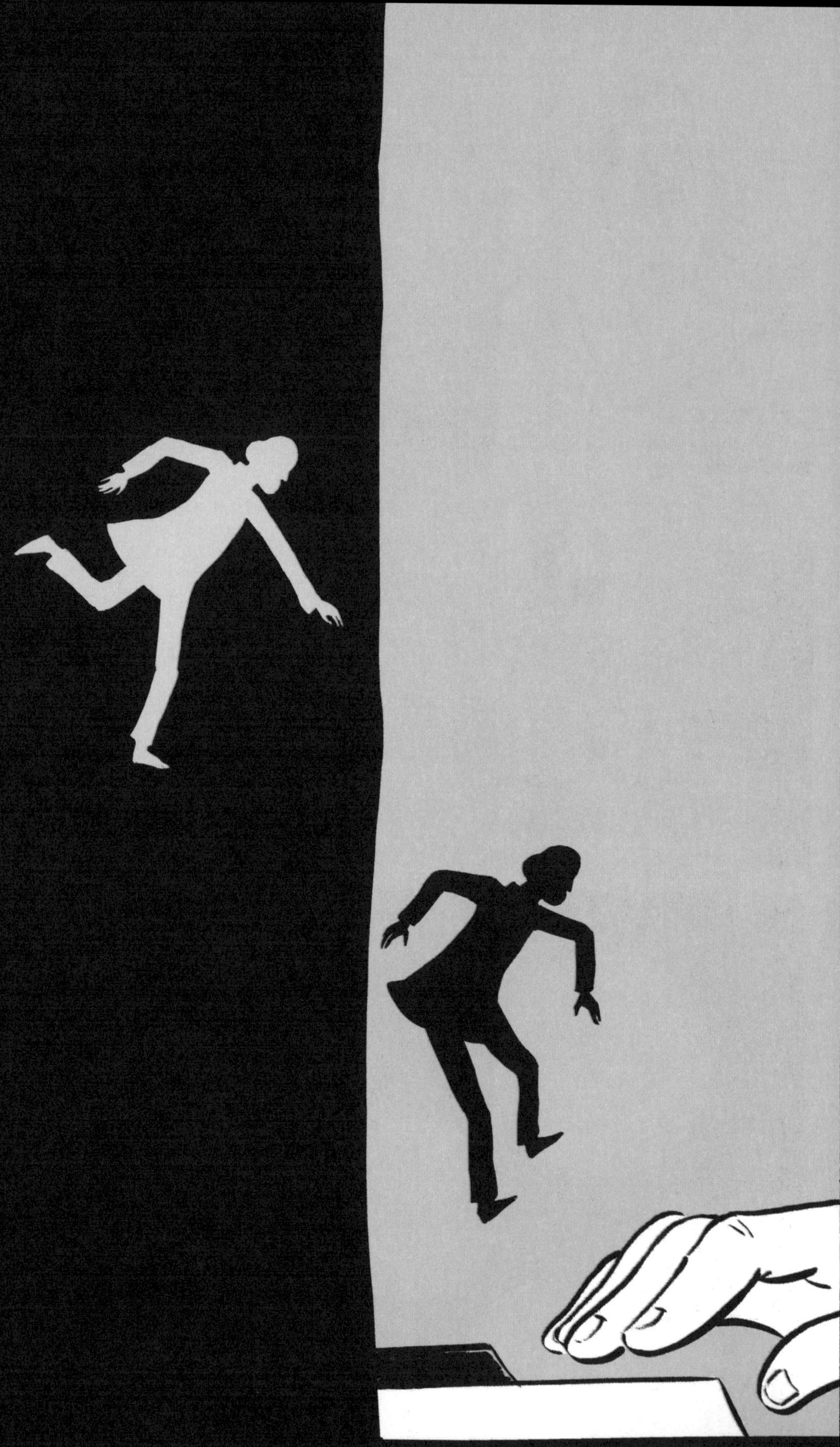

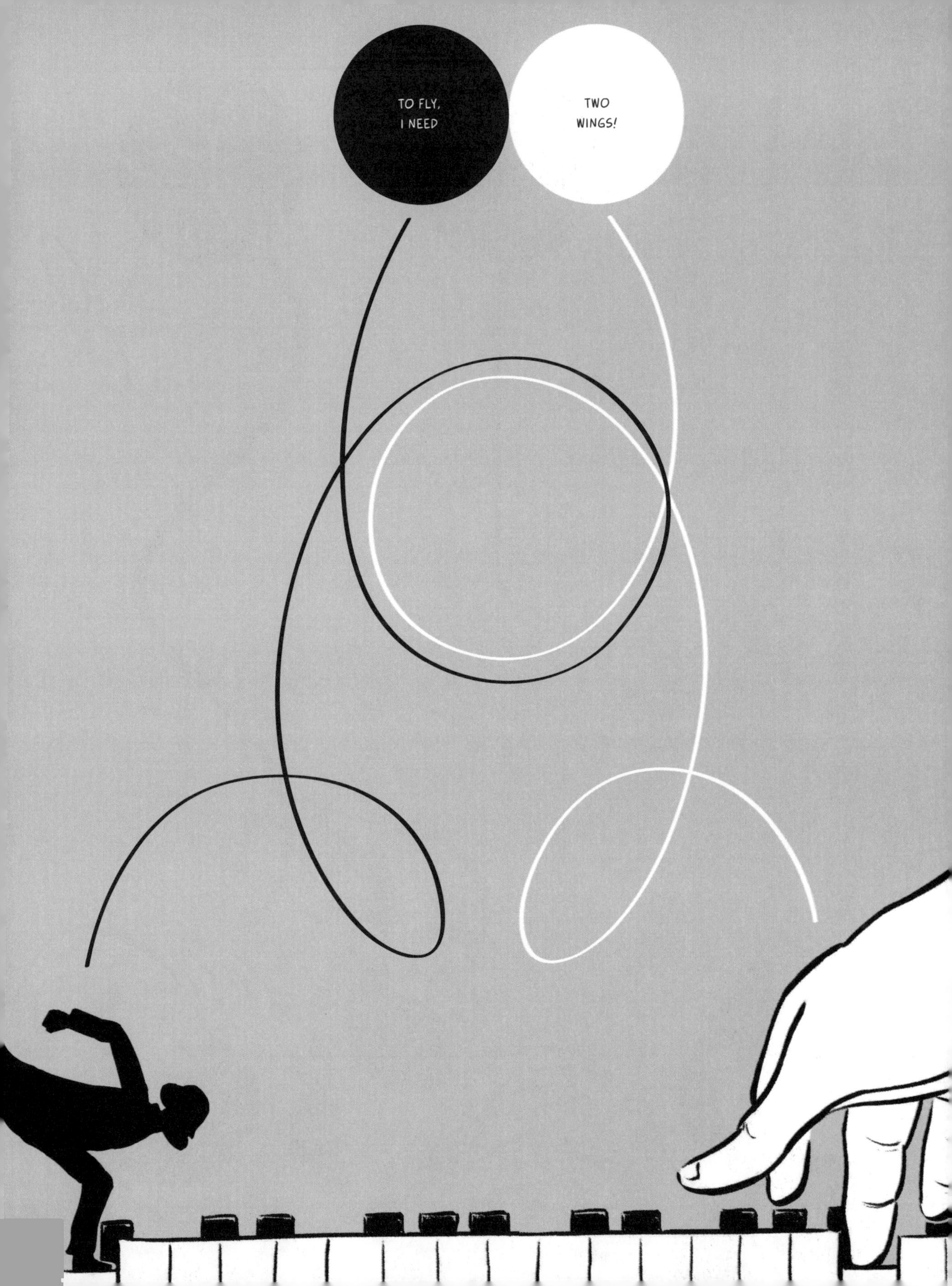
TO FLY,
I NEED
TWO
WINGS!

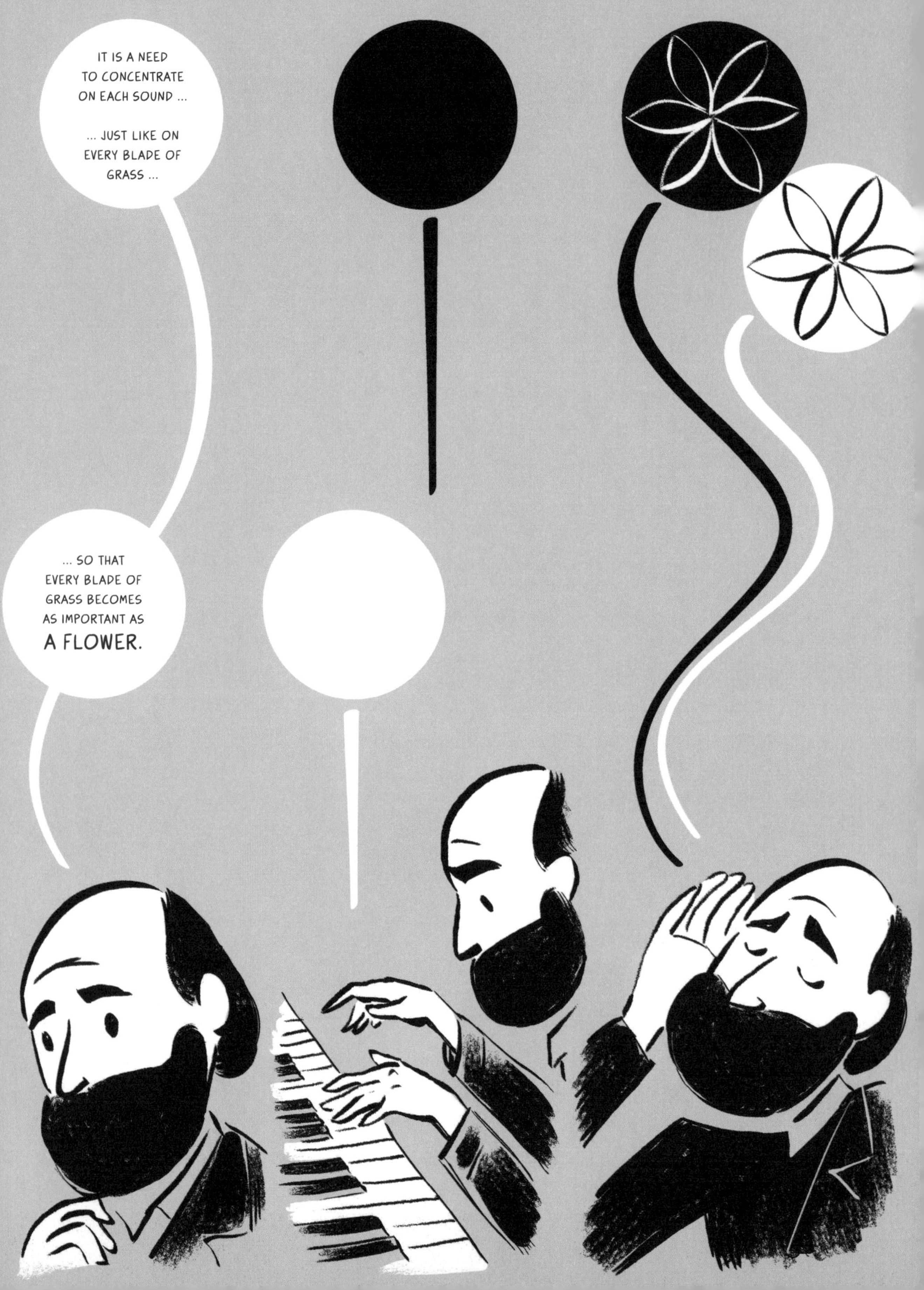
IT IS A NEED TO CONCENTRATE ON EACH SOUND ...
... JUST LIKE ON EVERY BLADE OF GRASS ...
... SO THAT EVERY BLADE OF GRASS BECOMES AS IMPORTANT AS A FLOWER.

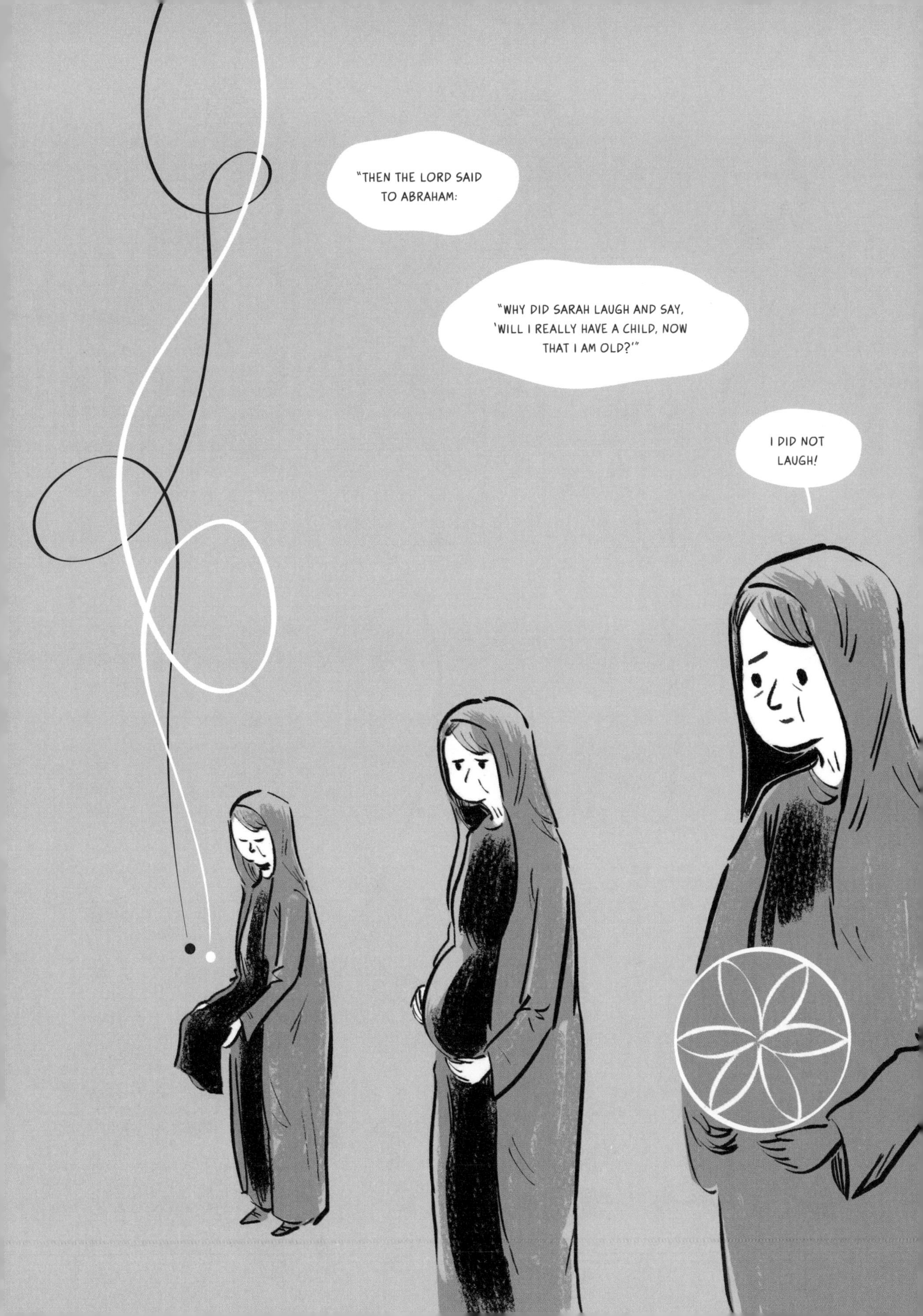
"THEN THE LORD SAID TO ABRAHAM:
"WHY DID SARAH LAUGH AND SAY, 'WILL I REALLY HAVE A CHILD, NOW THAT I AM OLD?'"
I DID NOT LAUGH!

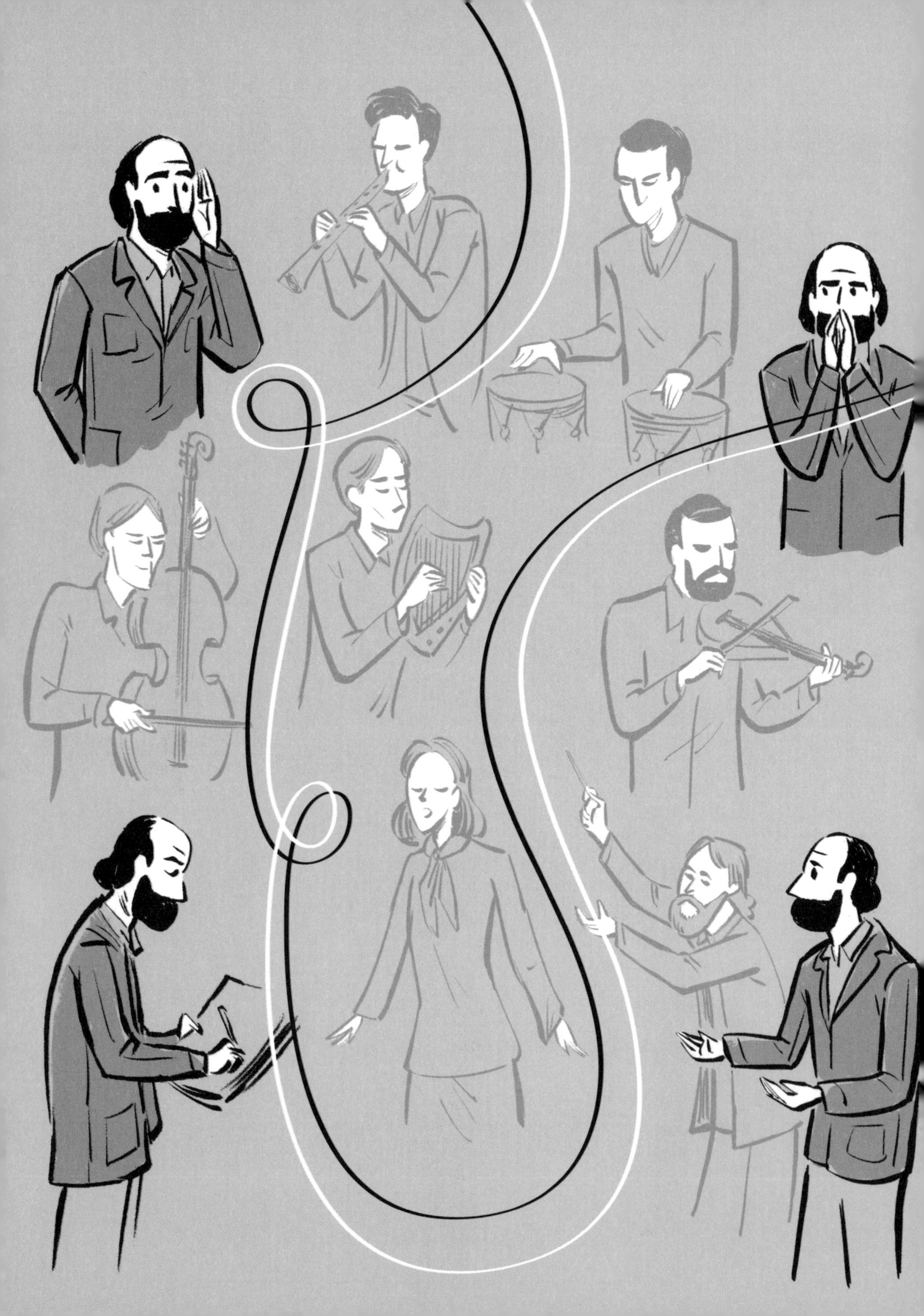

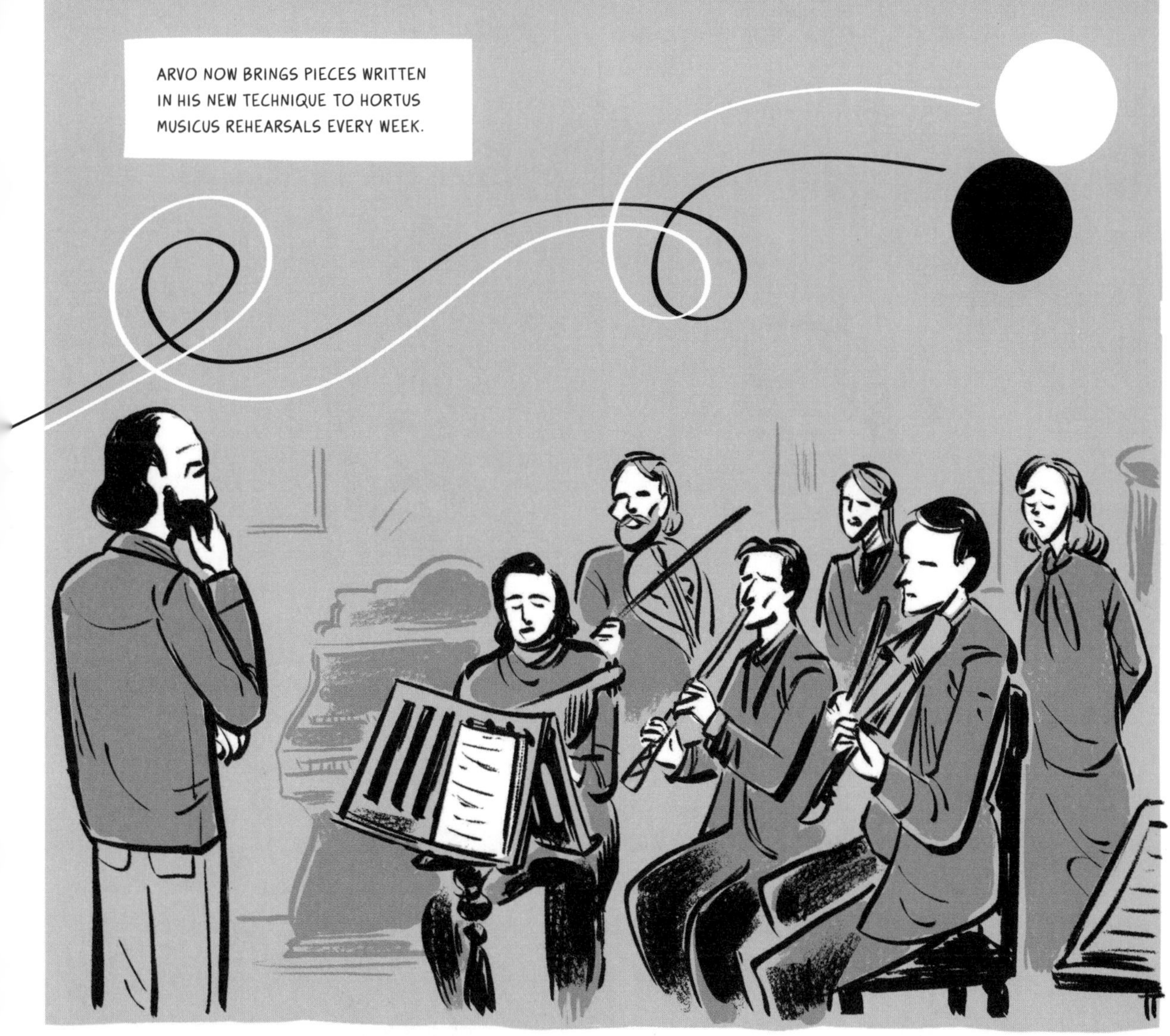
ARVO NOW BRINGS PIECES WRITTEN IN HIS NEW TECHNIQUE TO HORTUS MUSICUS REHEARSALS EVERY WEEK.

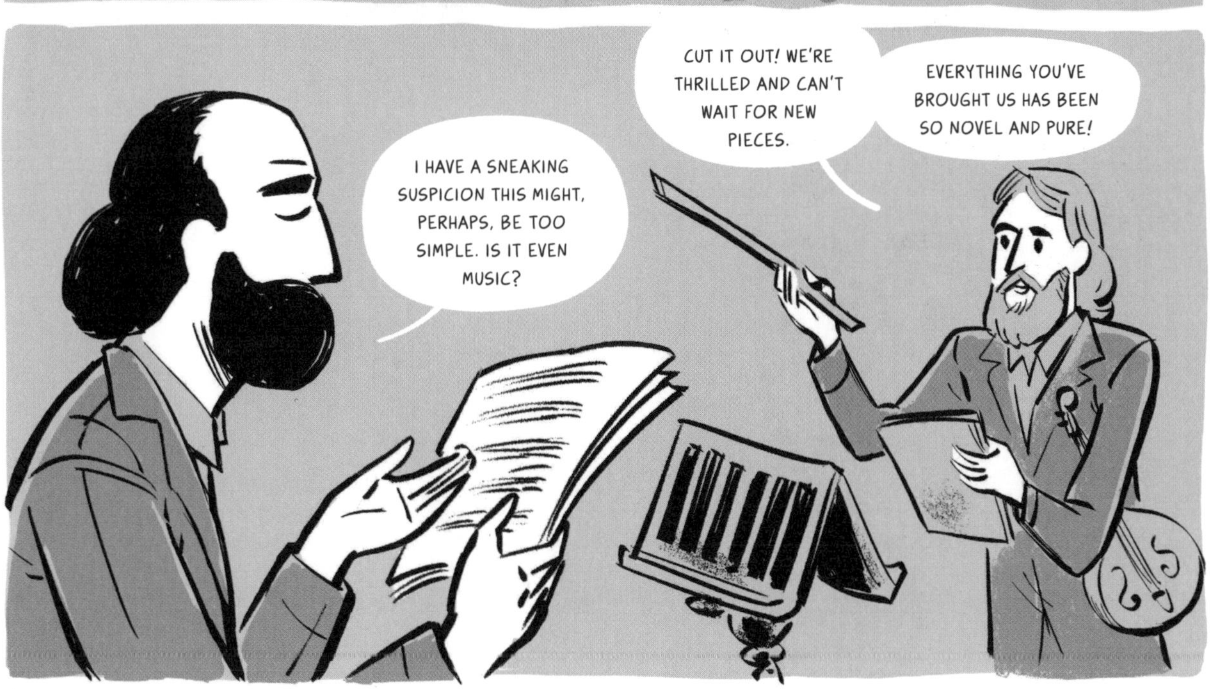
I HAVE A SNEAKING SUSPICION THIS MIGHT, PERHAPS, BE TOO SIMPLE. IS IT EVEN MUSIC?
CUT IT OUT! WE'RE THRILLED AND CAN'T WAIT FOR NEW PIECES.
EVERYTHING YOU'VE BROUGHT US HAS BEEN SO NOVEL AND PURE!

1977

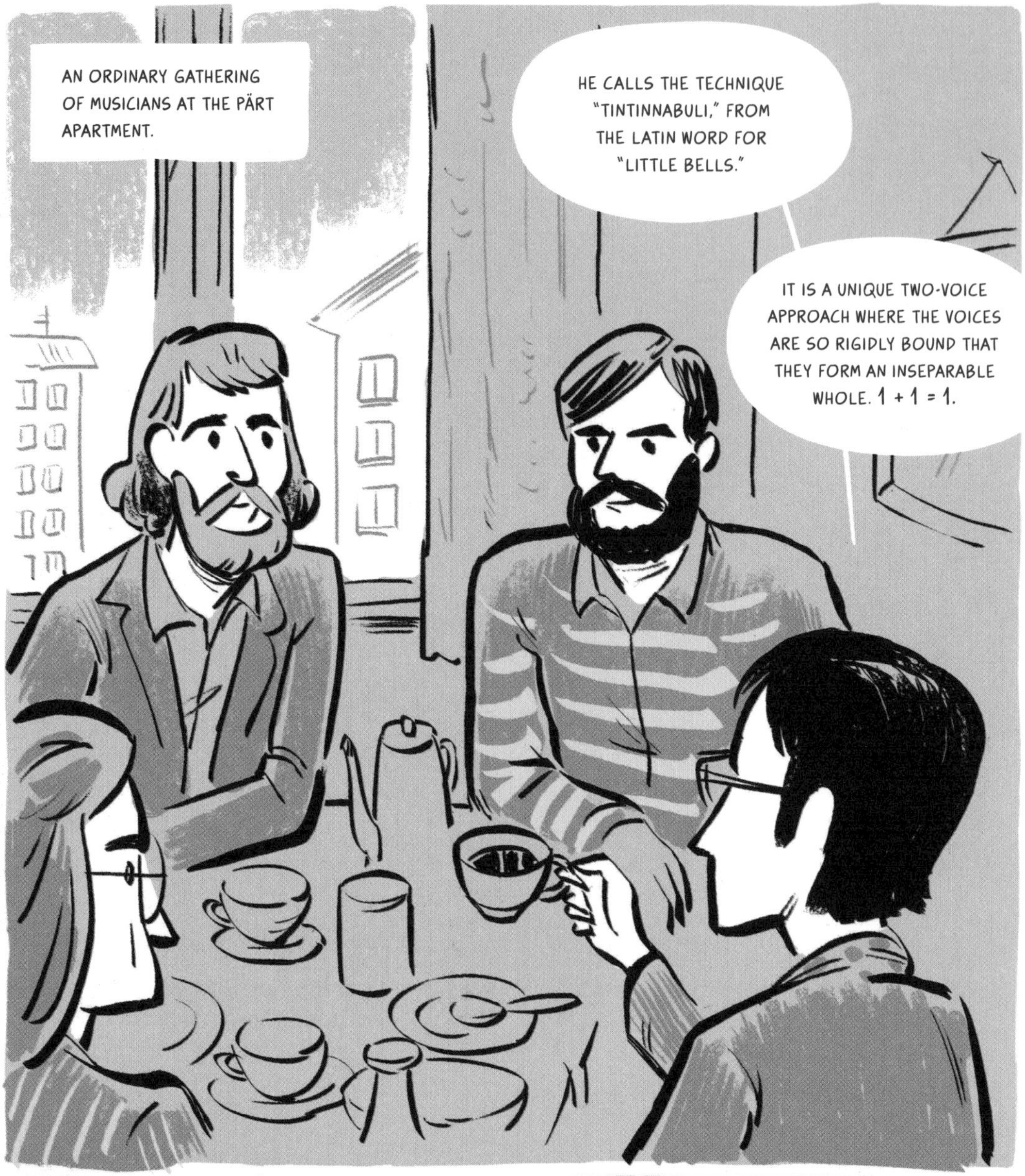
AN ORDINARY GATHERING OF MUSICIANS AT THE PÄRT APARTMENT.
HE CALLS THE TECHNIQUE "TINTINNABULI," FROM THE LATIN WORD FOR "LITTLE BELLS."
IT IS A UNIQUE TWO-VOICE APPROACH WHERE THE VOICES ARE SO RIGIDLY BOUND THAT THEY FORM AN INSEPARABLE WHOLE. 1 + 1 = 1.

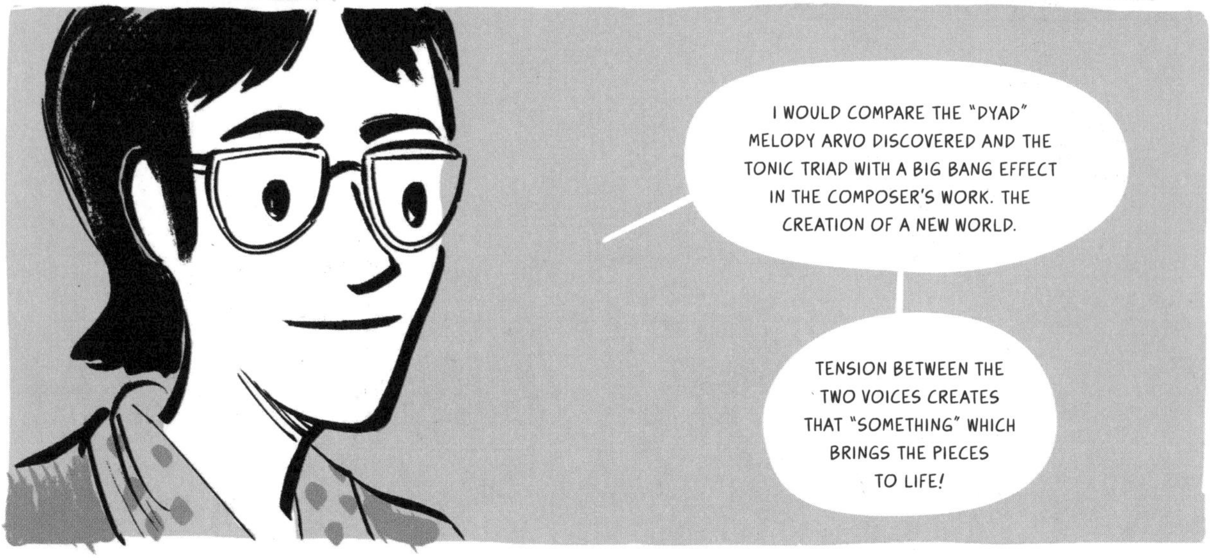
I WOULD COMPARE THE "DYAD" MELODY ARVO DISCOVERED AND THE TONIC TRIAD WITH A BIG BANG EFFECT IN THE COMPOSER'S WORK. THE CREATION OF A NEW WORLD.
TENSION BETWEEN THE TWO VOICES CREATES THAT "SOMETHING" WHICH BRINGS THE PIECES TO LIFE!

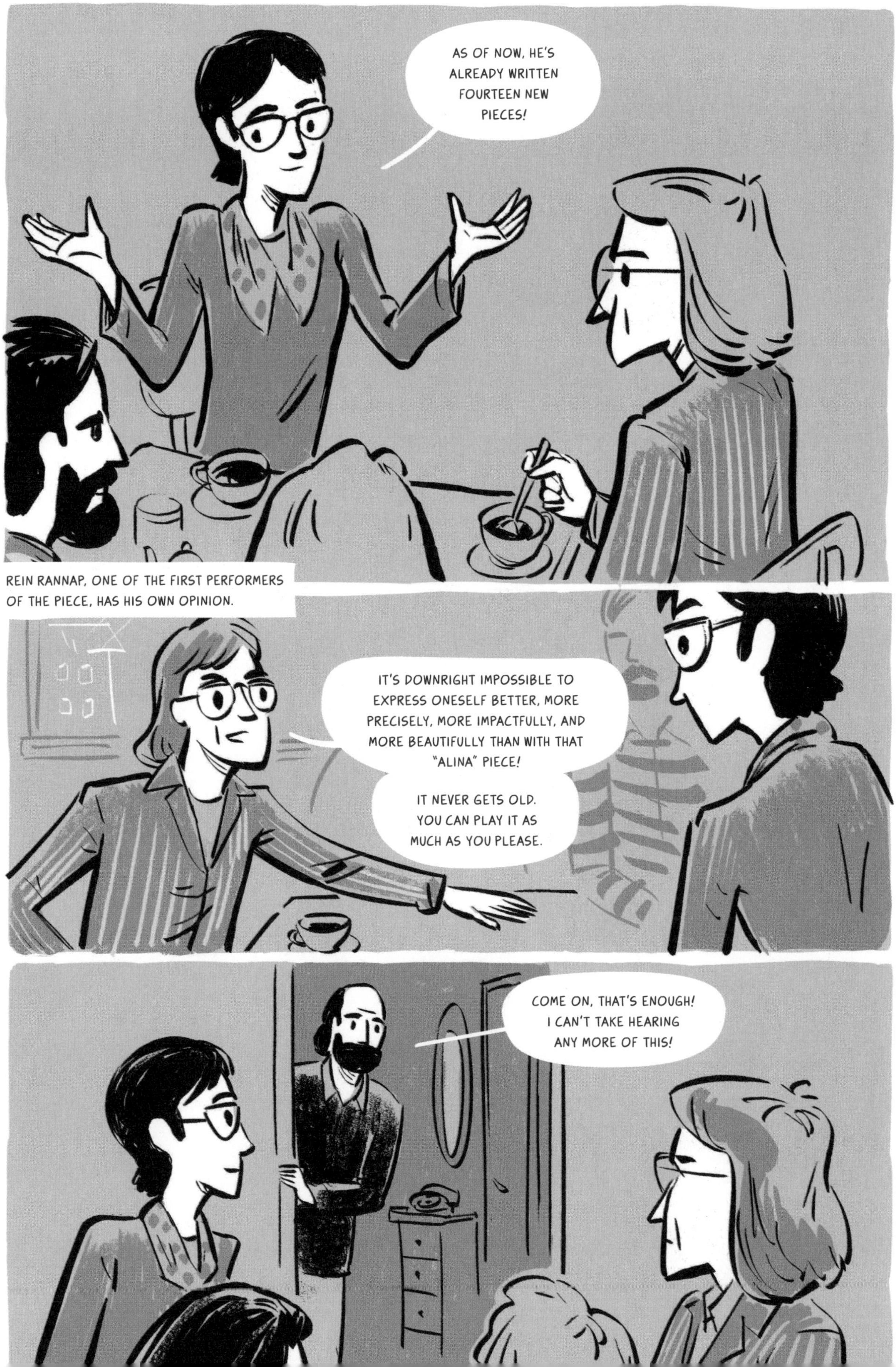
AS OF NOW, HE'S ALREADY WRITTEN FOURTEEN NEW PIECES!
REIN RANNAP, ONE OF THE FIRST PERFORMERS OF THE PIECE, HAS HIS OWN OPINION.
IT'S DOWNRIGHT IMPOSSIBLE TO EXPRESS ONESELF BETTER, MORE PRECISELY, MORE IMPACTFULLY, AND MORE BEAUTIFULLY THAN WITH THAT "ALINA" PIECE!
IT NEVER GETS OLD. YOU CAN PLAY IT AS MUCH AS YOU PLEASE.
COME ON, THAT'S ENOUGH! I CAN'T TAKE HEARING ANY MORE OF THIS!

A WORKING MEETING OF THE COMPOSERS' UNION. JAAN RÄÄTS HAS RISEN TO THE SEAT OF CHAIRMAN.

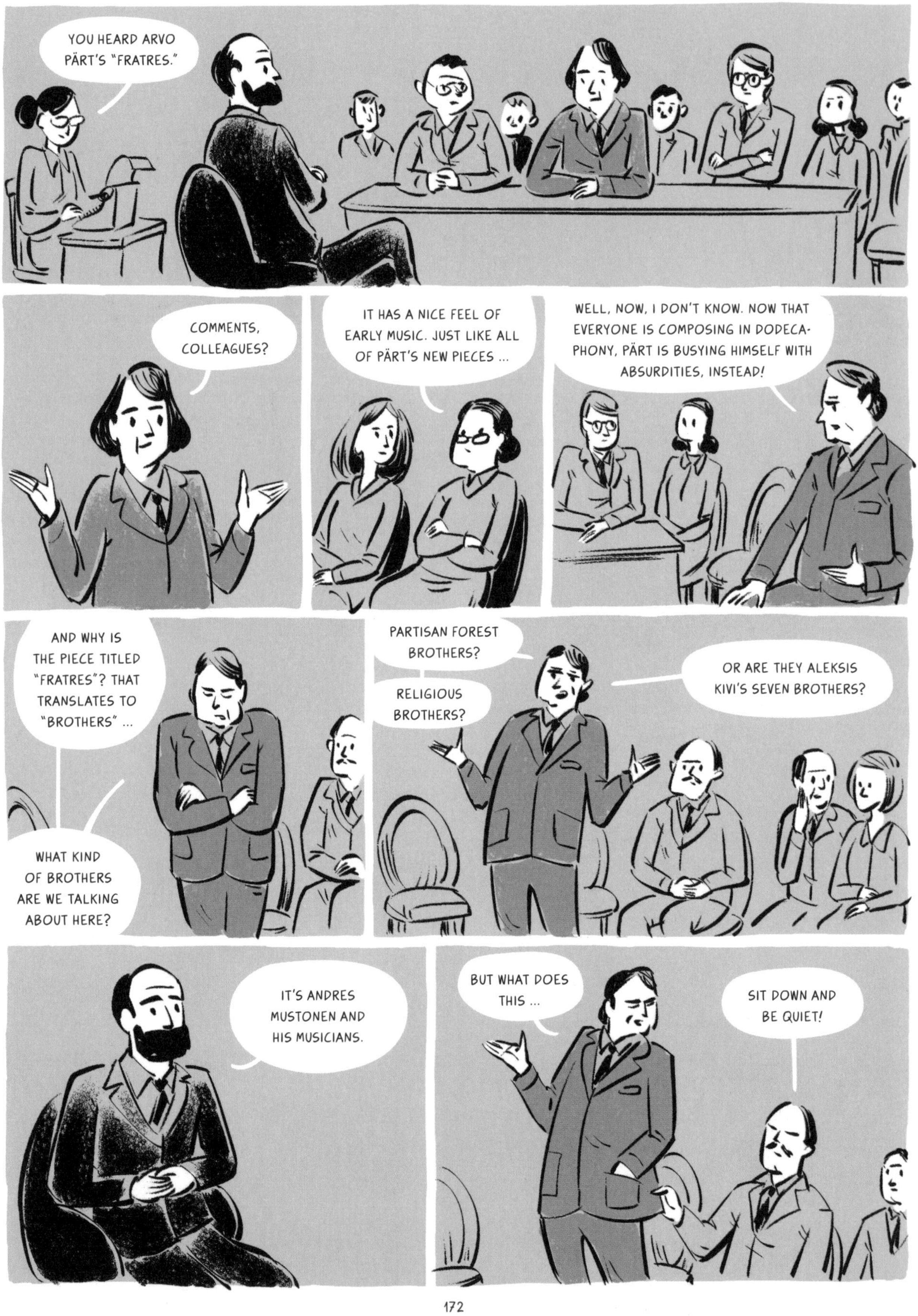
YOU HEARD ARVO PÄRT'S "FRATRES."
COMMENTS, COLLEAGUES?
IT HAS A NICE FEEL OF EARLY MUSIC. JUST LIKE ALL OF PÄRT'S NEW PIECES ...
WELL, NOW, I DON'T KNOW. NOW THAT EVERYONE IS COMPOSING IN DODECAPHONY, PÄRT IS BUSYING HIMSELF WITH ABSURDITIES, INSTEAD!
AND WHY IS THE PIECE TITLED "FRATRES"? THAT TRANSLATES TO "BROTHERS" ...
WHAT KIND OF BROTHERS ARE WE TALKING ABOUT HERE?
PARTISAN FOREST BROTHERS?
RELIGIOUS BROTHERS?
OR ARE THEY ALEKSIS KIVI'S SEVEN BROTHERS?
IT'S ANDRES MUSTONEN AND HIS MUSICIANS.
BUT WHAT DOES THIS ...
SIT DOWN AND BE QUIET!

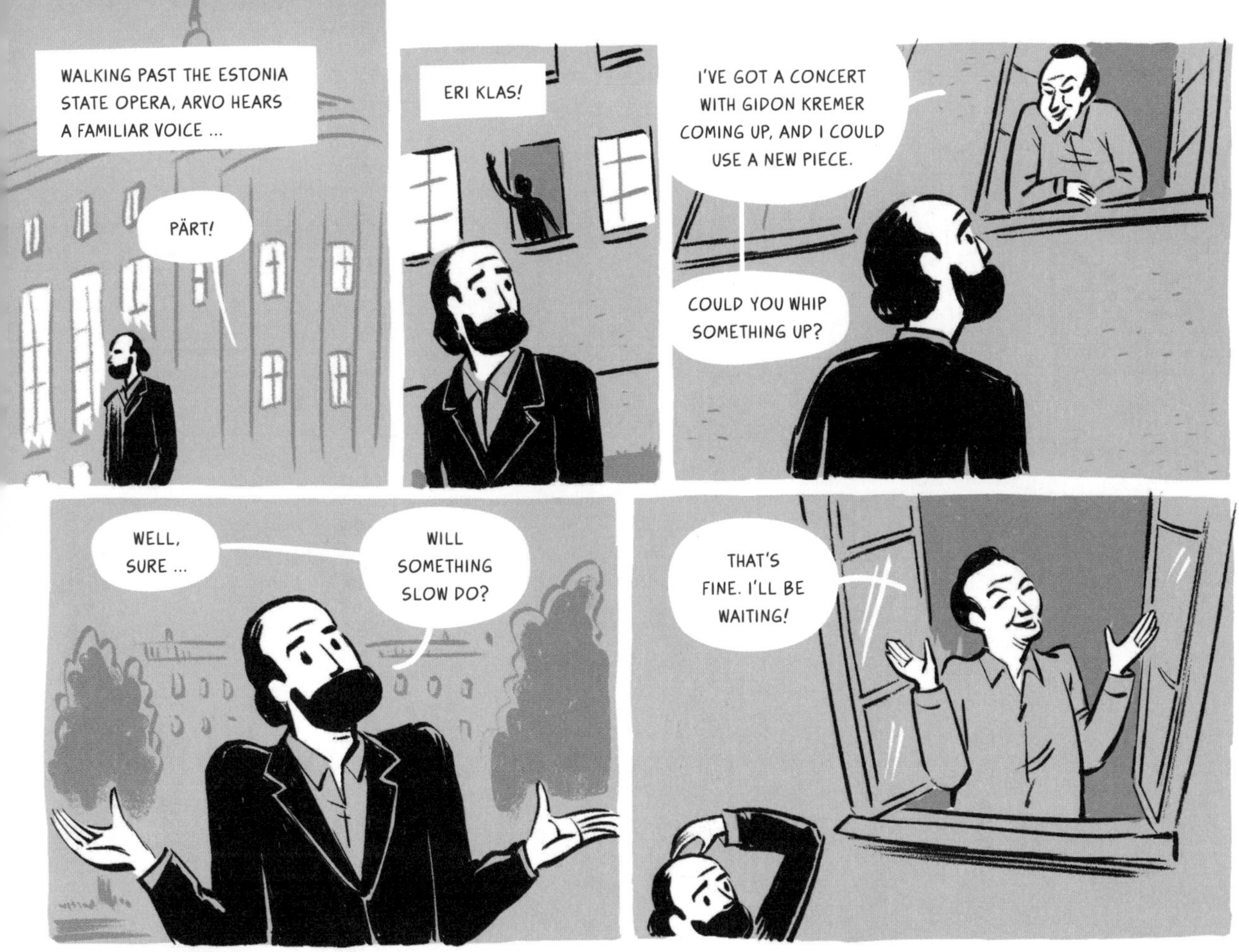
WALKING PAST THE ESTONIA STATE OPERA, ARVO HEARS A FAMILIAR VOICE ...
PÄRT!
ERI KLAS!
I'VE GOT A CONCERT WITH GIDON KREMER COMING UP, AND I COULD USE A NEW PIECE.
COULD YOU WHIP SOMETHING UP?
WELL, SURE ...
WILL SOMETHING SLOW DO?
THAT'S FINE. I'LL BE WAITING!

AT THE COMPOSERS' RESIDENCE IN SUKHUMI, GEORGIA. PÄRT IS COMPOSING A PIECE TITLED "TABULA RASA."

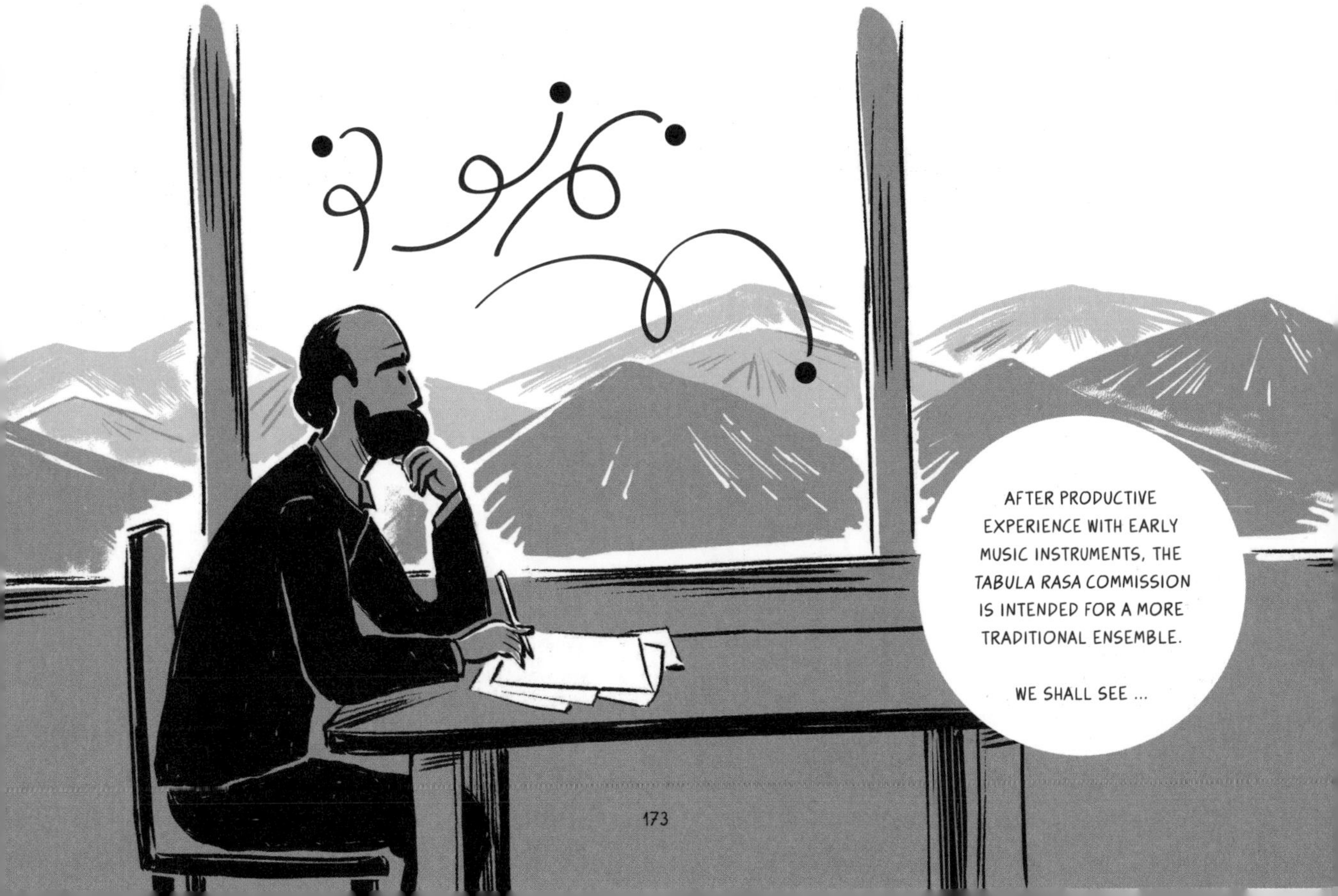
AFTER PRODUCTIVE EXPERIENCE WITH EARLY MUSIC INSTRUMENTS, THE *TABULA RASA* COMMISSION IS INTENDED FOR A MORE TRADITIONAL ENSEMBLE.
WE SHALL SEE ...

REHEARSAL FOR THE PREMIERE OF "TABULA RASA" WITH GIDON KREMER, TATIANA GRINDENKO, ALFRED SCHNITTKE, AND ERI KLAS IN THE TALLINN POLYTECHNIC INSTITUTE'S AUDITORIUM.

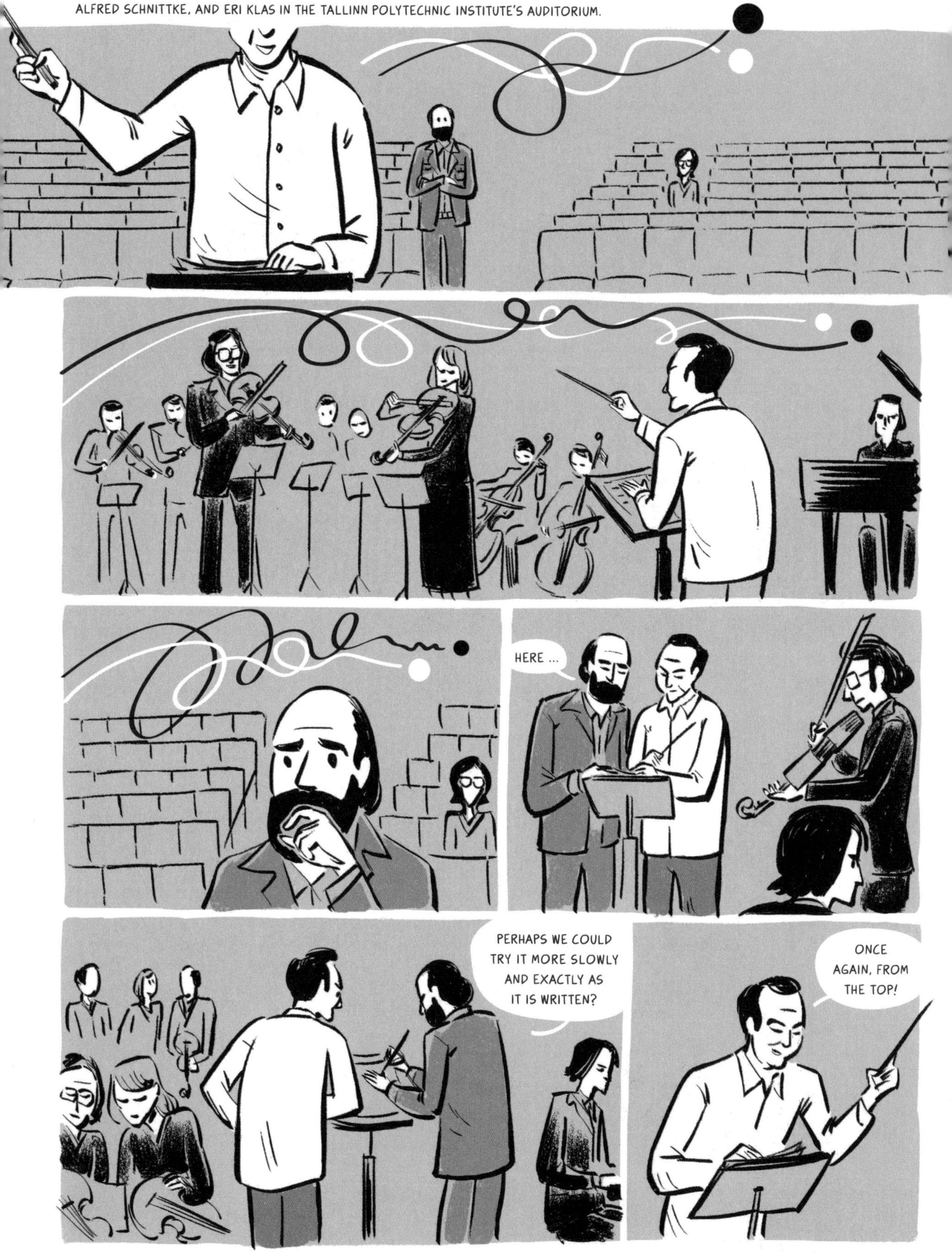
HERE ...
PERHAPS WE COULD TRY IT MORE SLOWLY AND EXACTLY AS IT IS WRITTEN?
ONCE AGAIN, FROM THE TOP!

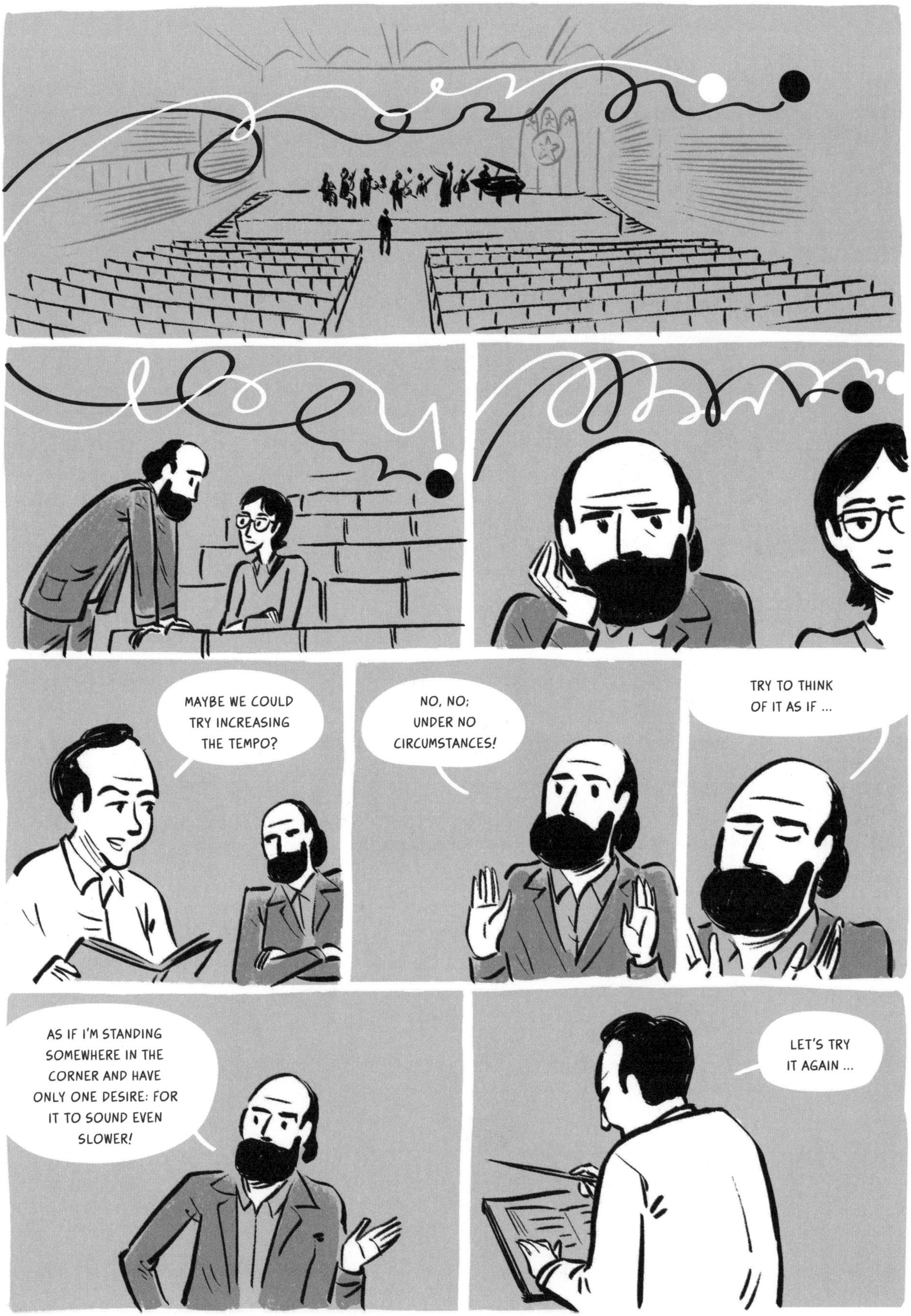
MAYBE WE COULD TRY INCREASING THE TEMPO?
NO, NO; UNDER NO CIRCUMSTANCES!
TRY TO THINK OF IT AS IF ...
AS IF I'M STANDING SOMEWHERE IN THE CORNER AND HAVE ONLY ONE DESIRE: FOR IT TO SOUND EVEN SLOWER!
LET'S TRY IT AGAIN ...

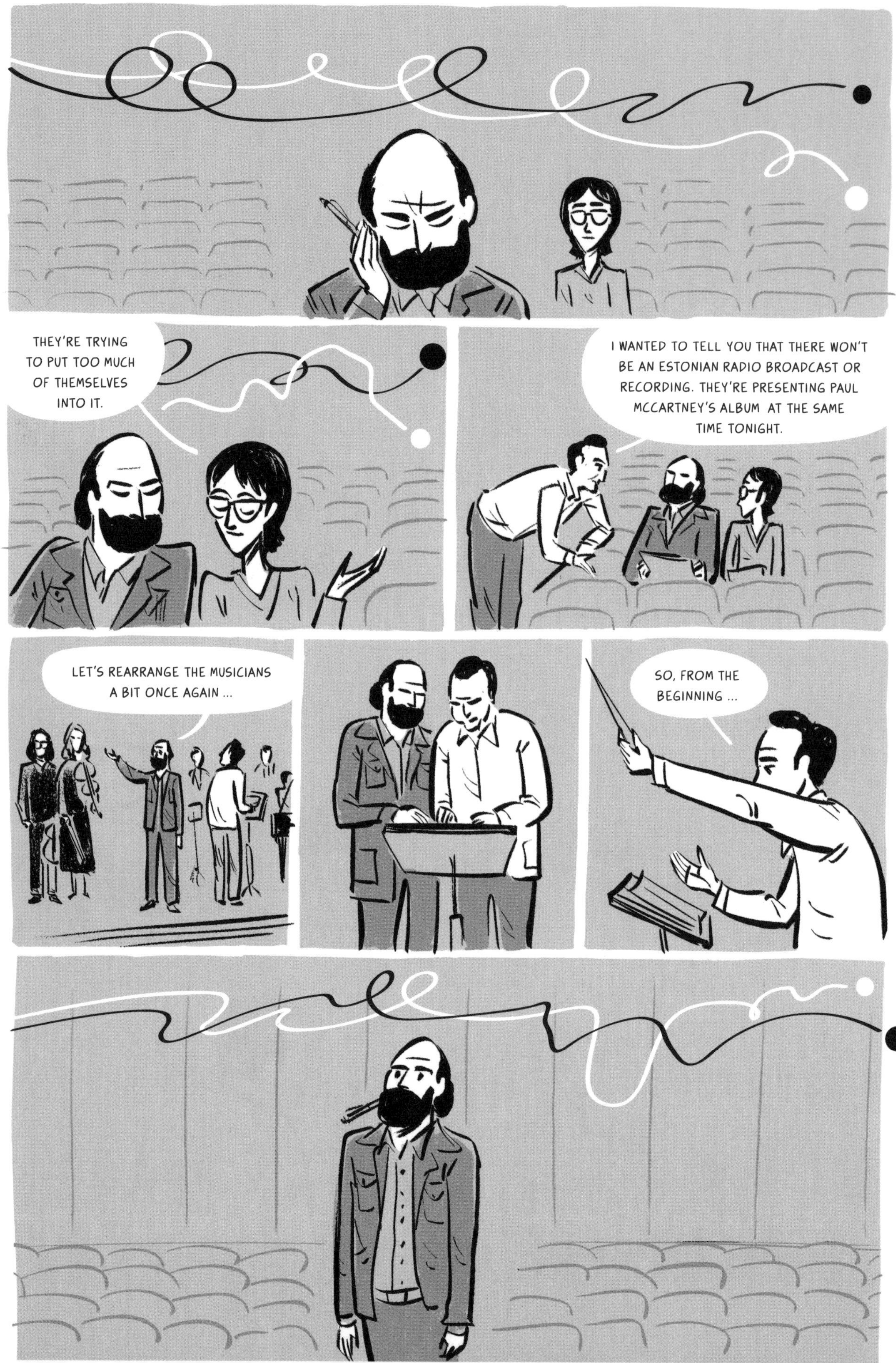
THEY'RE TRYING TO PUT TOO MUCH OF THEMSELVES INTO IT.
I WANTED TO TELL YOU THAT THERE WON'T BE AN ESTONIAN RADIO BROADCAST OR RECORDING. THEY'RE PRESENTING PAUL MCCARTNEY'S ALBUM AT THE SAME TIME TONIGHT.
LET'S REARRANGE THE MUSICIANS A BIT ONCE AGAIN ...
SO, FROM THE BEGINNING ...

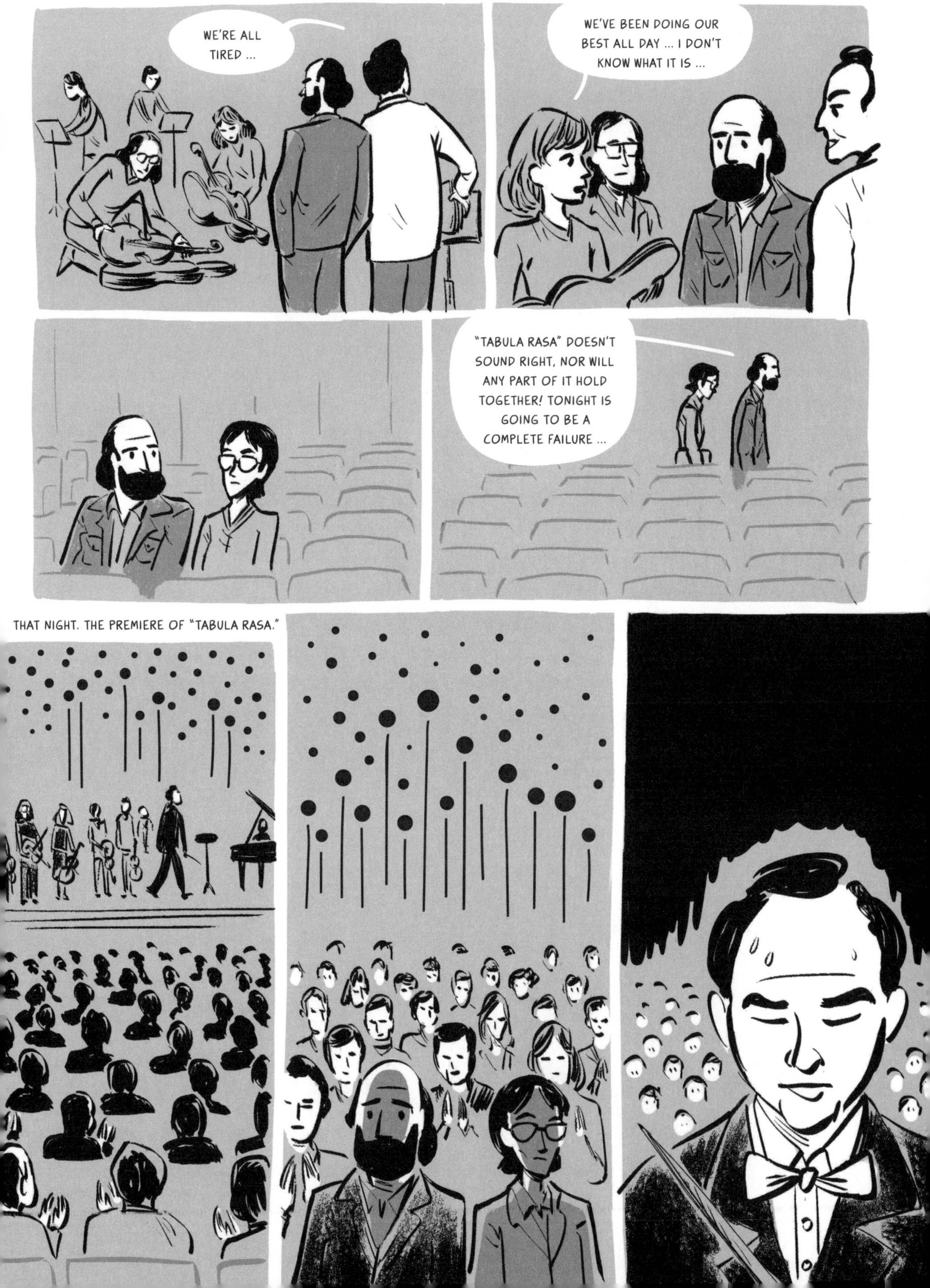
WE'RE ALL TIRED ...
WE'VE BEEN DOING OUR BEST ALL DAY ... I DON'T KNOW WHAT IT IS ...
"TABULA RASA" DOESN'T SOUND RIGHT, NOR WILL ANY PART OF IT HOLD TOGETHER! TONIGHT IS GOING TO BE A COMPLETE FAILURE ...
THAT NIGHT. THE PREMIERE OF "TABULA RASA."

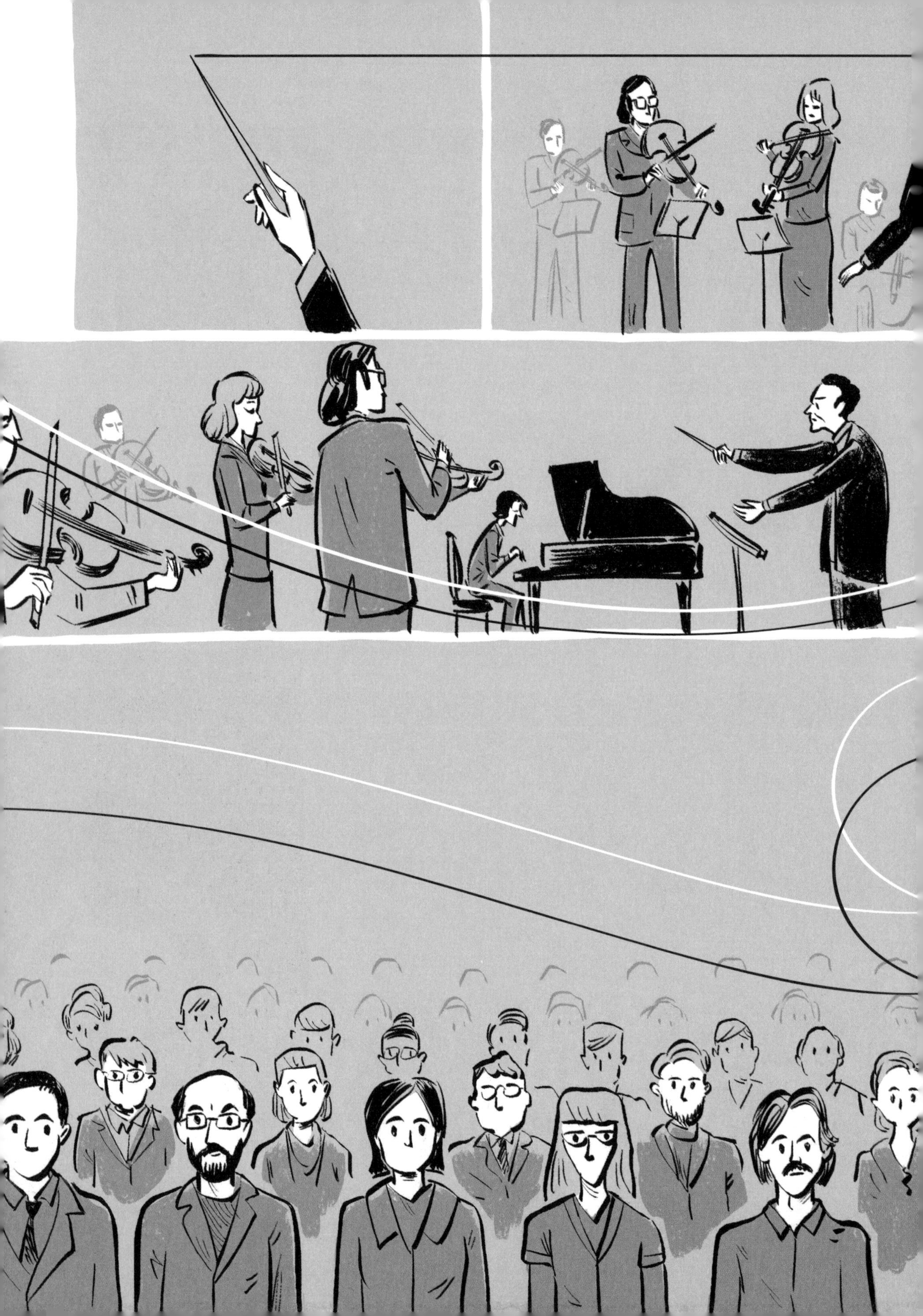

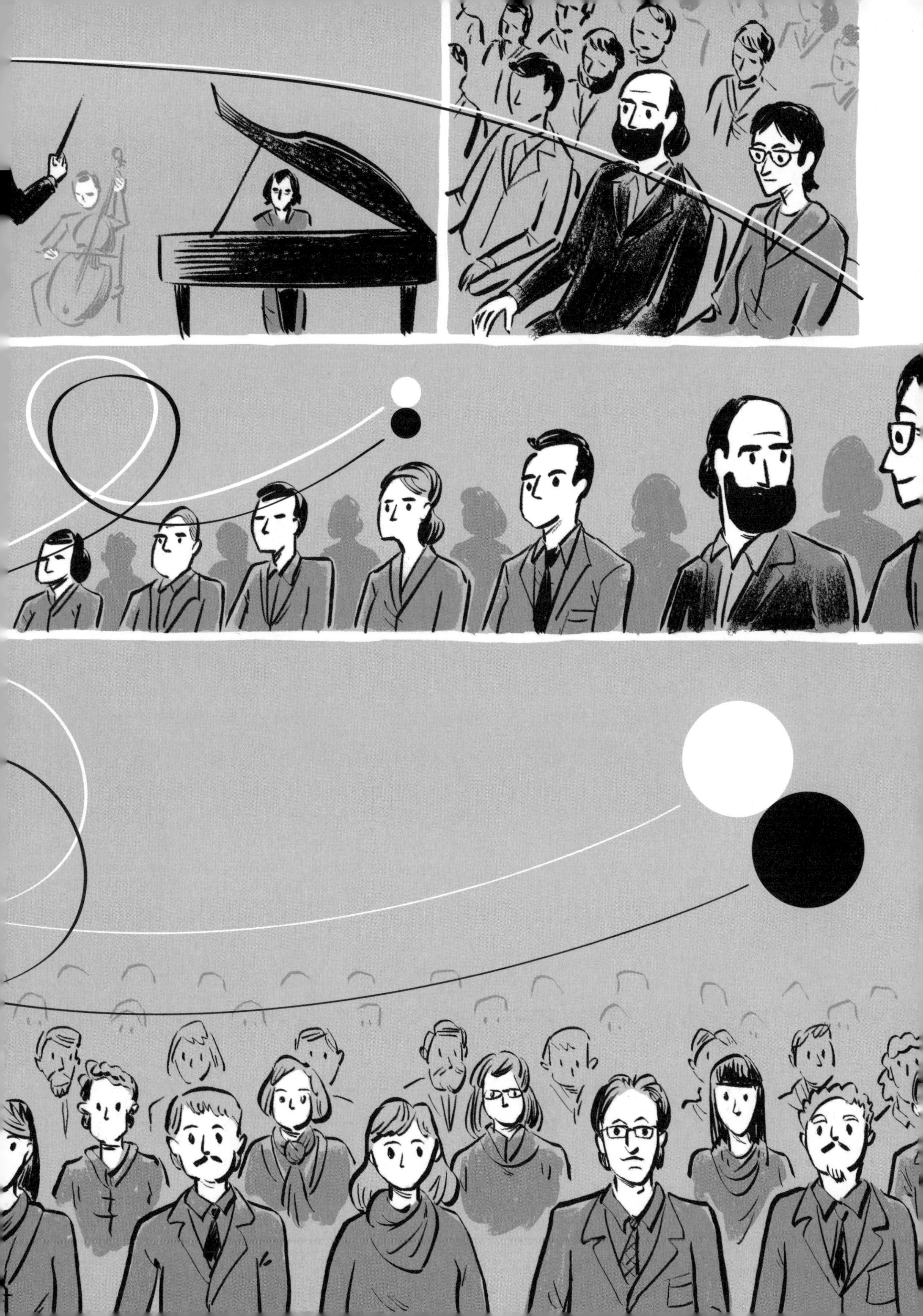

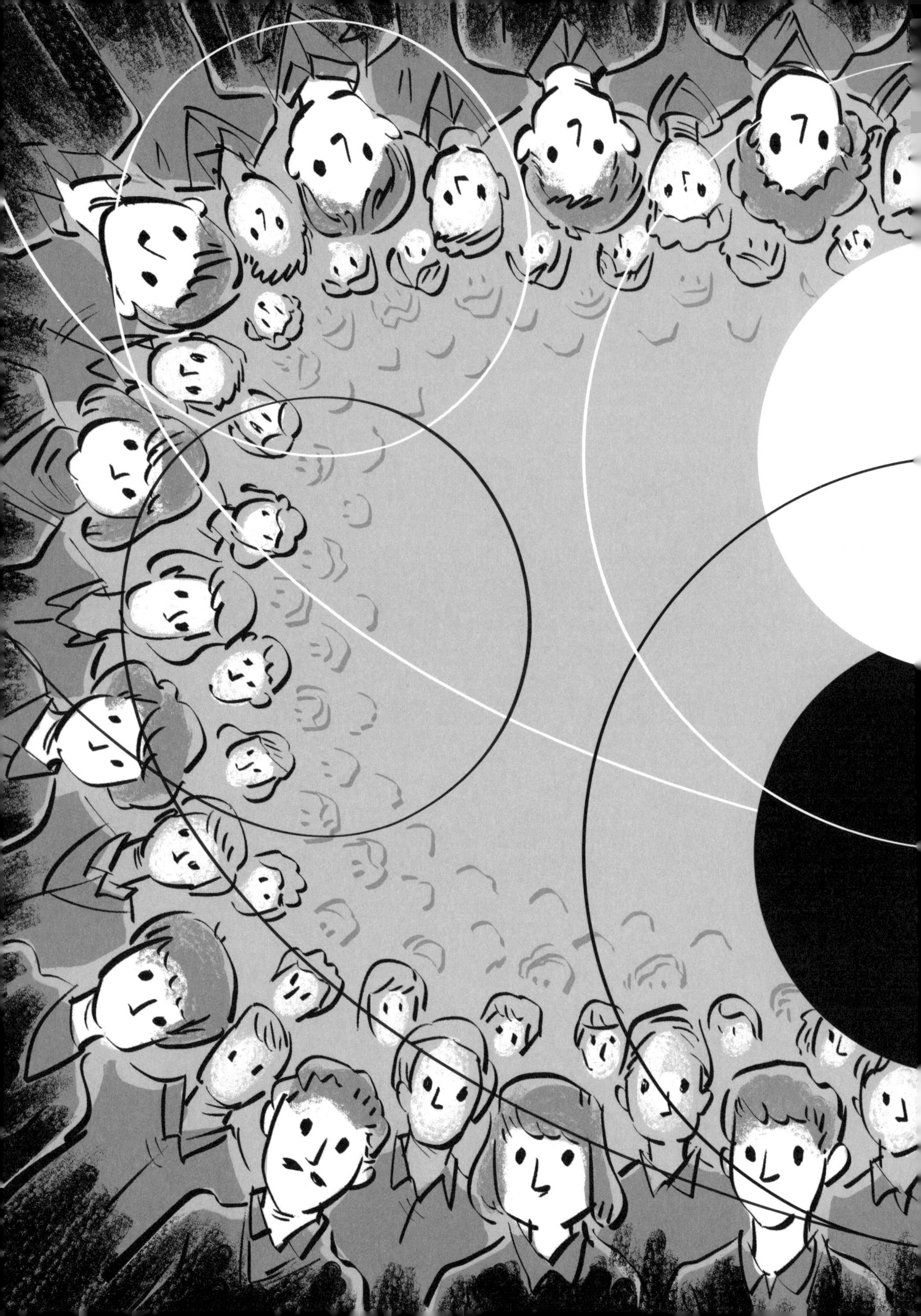

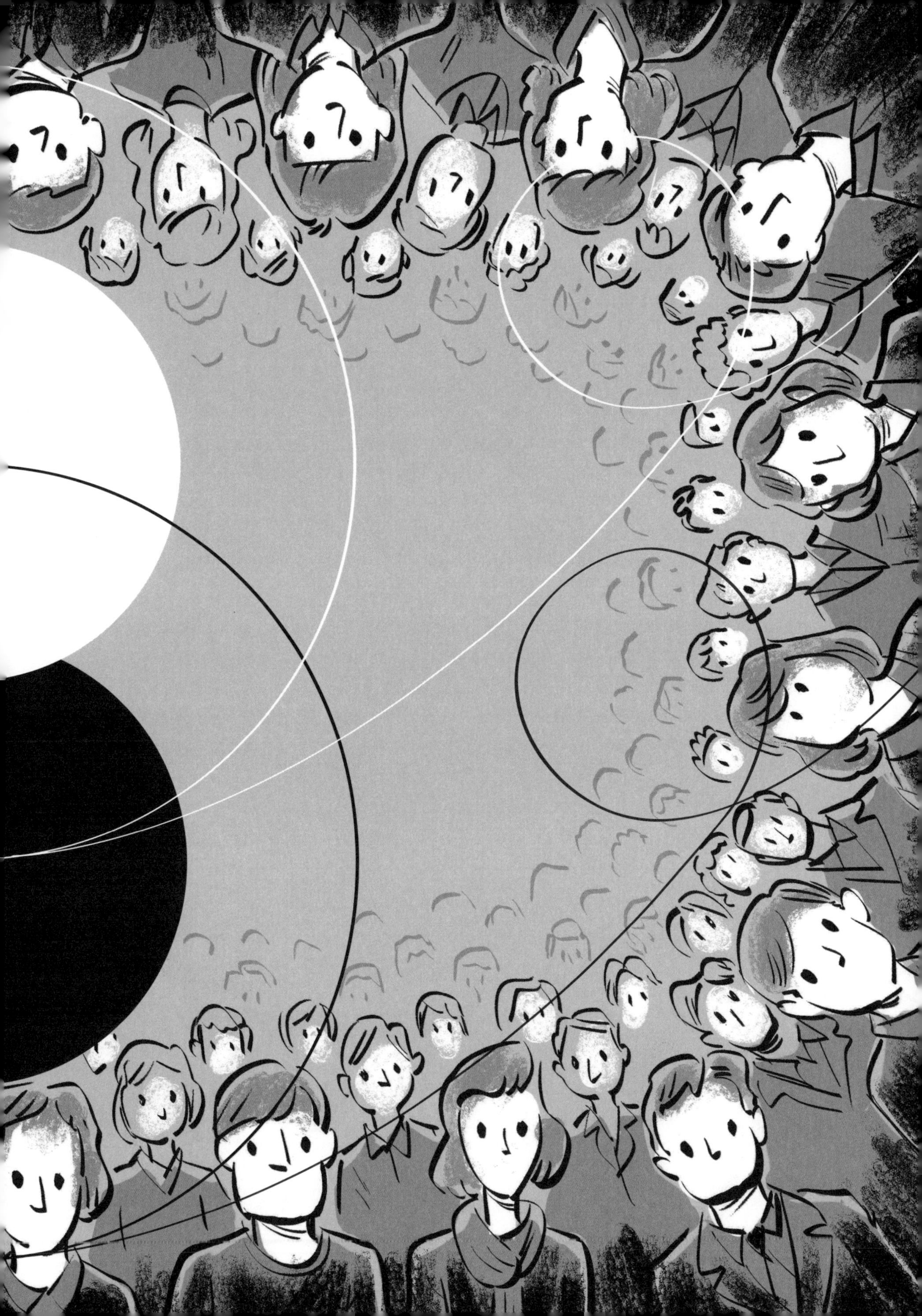

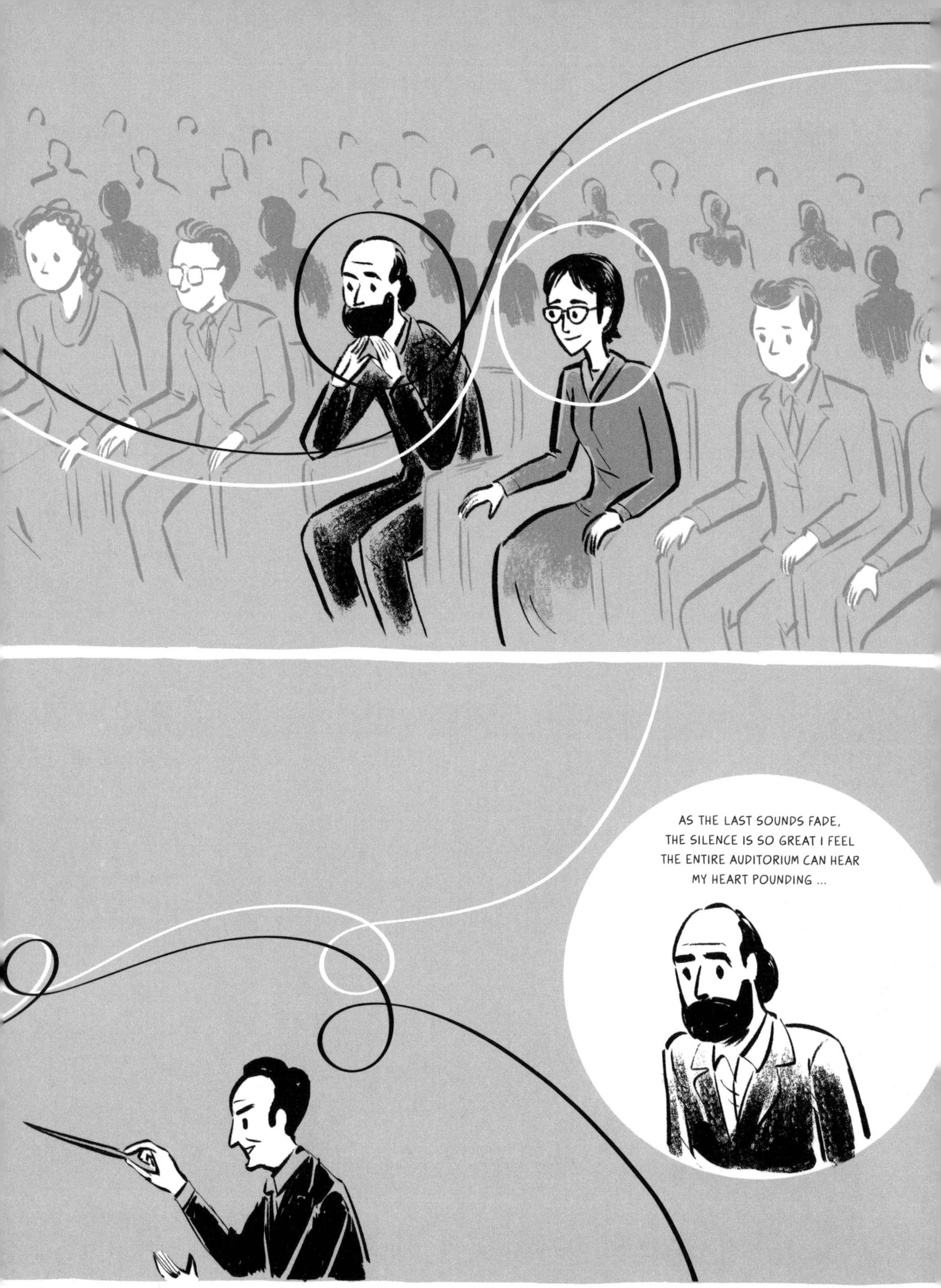
AS THE LAST SOUNDS FADE, THE SILENCE IS SO GREAT I FEEL THE ENTIRE AUDITORIUM CAN HEAR MY HEART POUNDING ...

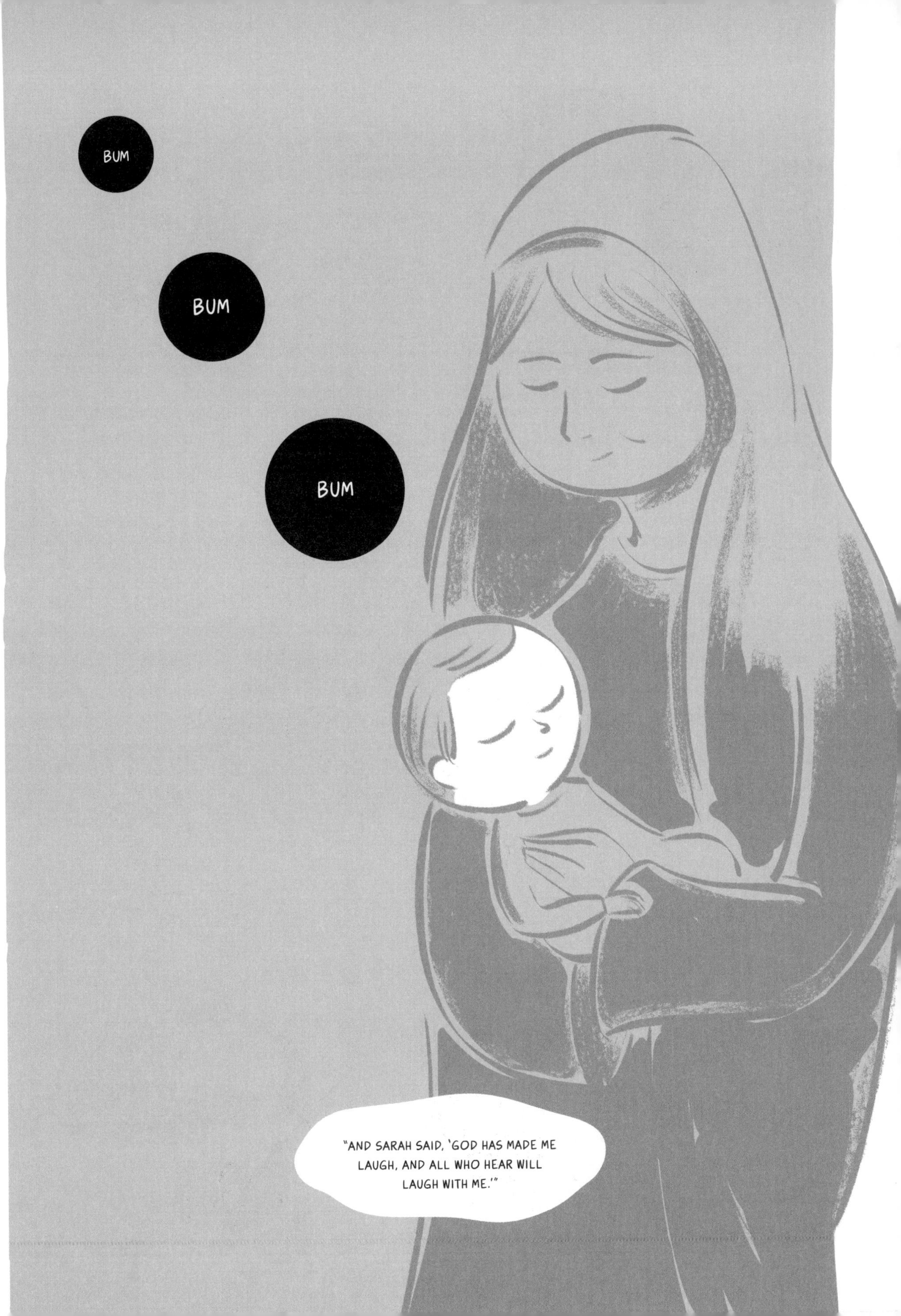
BUM
BUM
BUM
"AND SARAH SAID, 'GOD HAS MADE ME LAUGH, AND ALL WHO HEAR WILL LAUGH WITH ME.'"

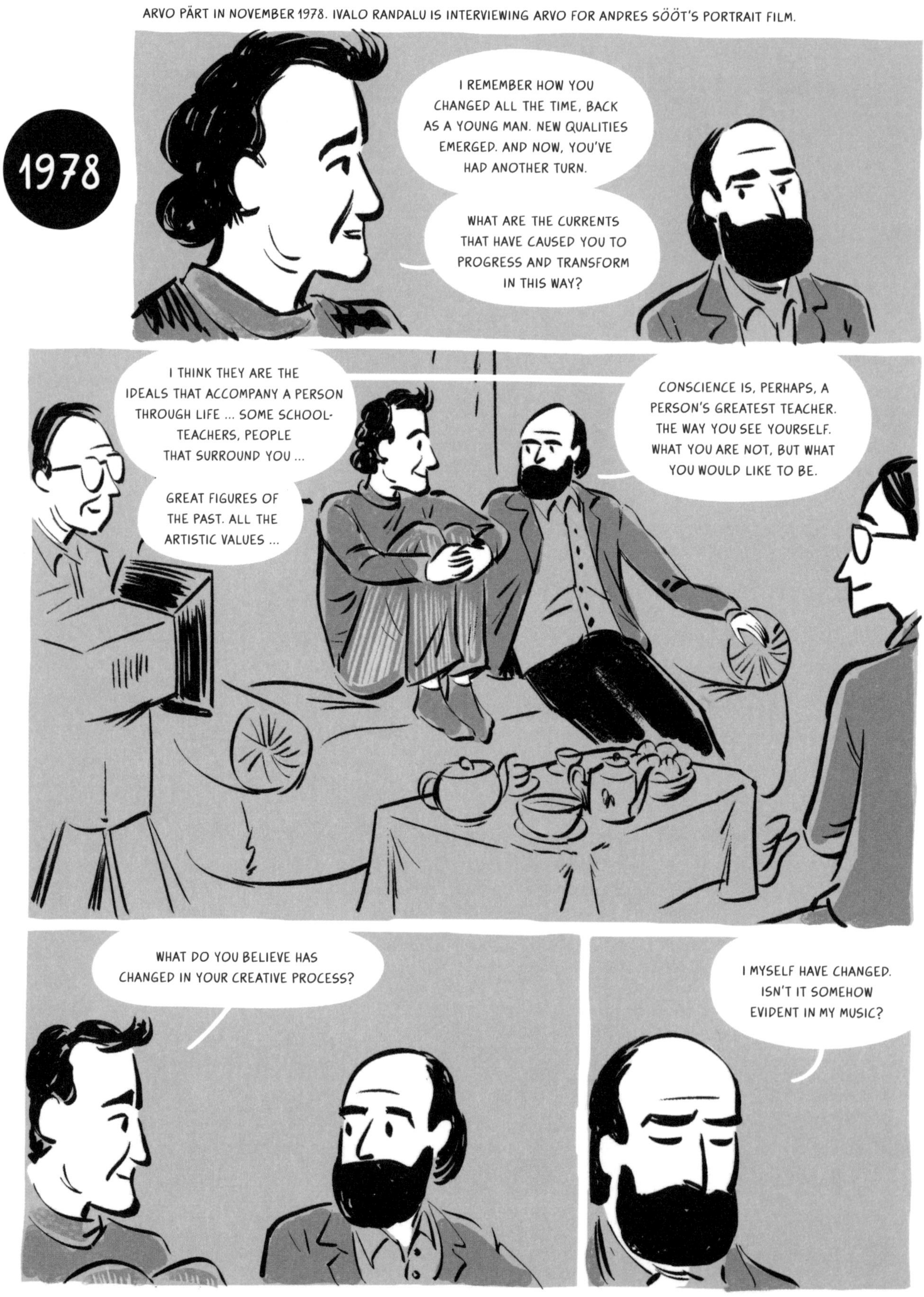
ARVO PÄRT IN NOVEMBER 1978. IVALO RANDALU IS INTERVIEWING ARVO FOR ANDRES SÖÖT'S PORTRAIT FILM.
1978
I REMEMBER HOW YOU CHANGED ALL THE TIME, BACK AS A YOUNG MAN. NEW QUALITIES EMERGED. AND NOW, YOU'VE HAD ANOTHER TURN.
WHAT ARE THE CURRENTS THAT HAVE CAUSED YOU TO PROGRESS AND TRANSFORM IN THIS WAY?
I THINK THEY ARE THE IDEALS THAT ACCOMPANY A PERSON THROUGH LIFE ... SOME SCHOOL-TEACHERS, PEOPLE THAT SURROUND YOU ...
GREAT FIGURES OF THE PAST. ALL THE ARTISTIC VALUES ...
CONSCIENCE IS, PERHAPS, A PERSON'S GREATEST TEACHER. THE WAY YOU SEE YOURSELF. WHAT YOU ARE NOT, BUT WHAT YOU WOULD LIKE TO BE.
WHAT DO YOU BELIEVE HAS CHANGED IN YOUR CREATIVE PROCESS?
I MYSELF HAVE CHANGED. ISN'T IT SOMEHOW EVIDENT IN MY MUSIC?

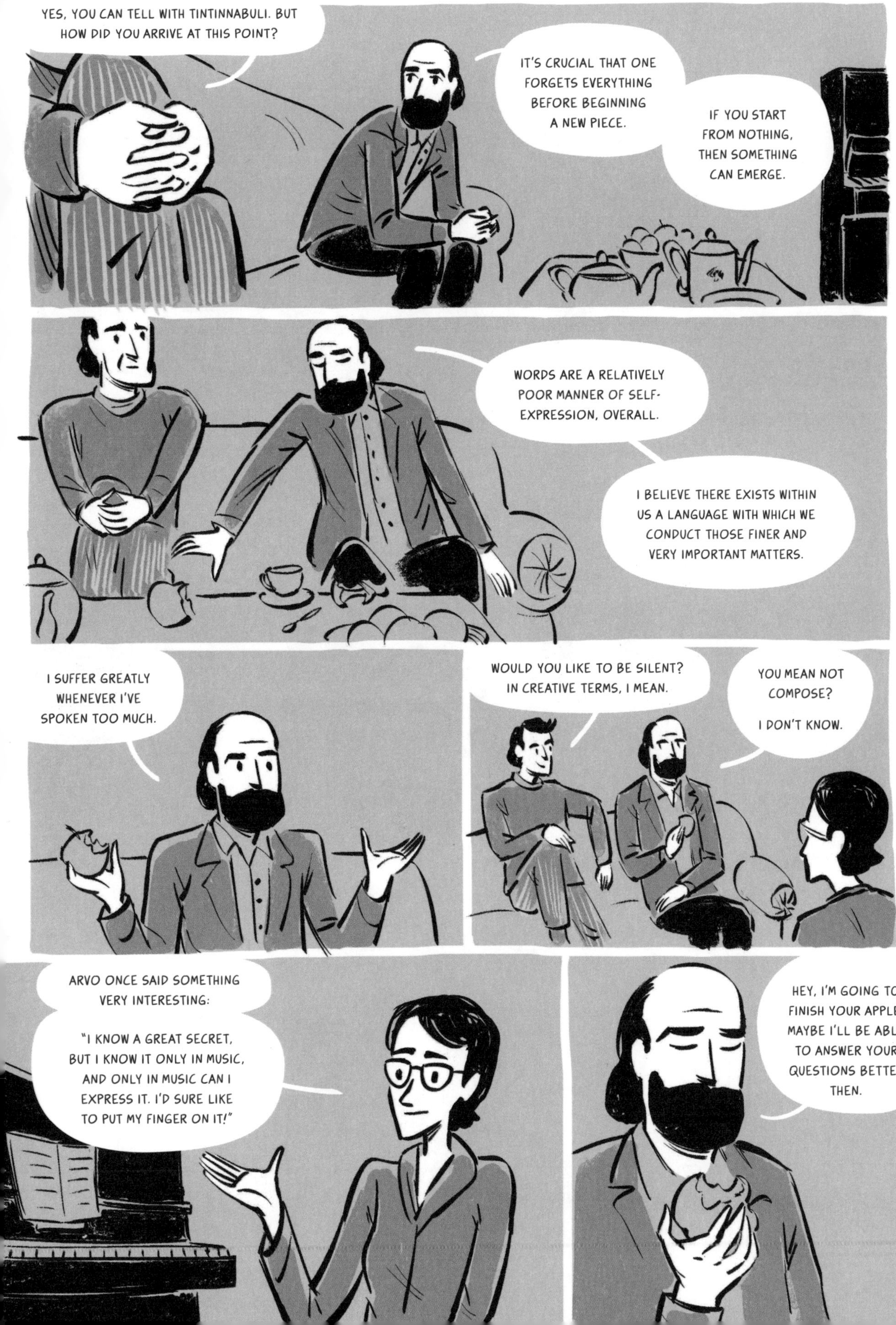
YES, YOU CAN TELL WITH TINTINNABULI. BUT HOW DID YOU ARRIVE AT THIS POINT?
IT'S CRUCIAL THAT ONE FORGETS EVERYTHING BEFORE BEGINNING A NEW PIECE.
IF YOU START FROM NOTHING, THEN SOMETHING CAN EMERGE.
WORDS ARE A RELATIVELY POOR MANNER OF SELF-EXPRESSION, OVERALL.
I BELIEVE THERE EXISTS WITHIN US A LANGUAGE WITH WHICH WE CONDUCT THOSE FINER AND VERY IMPORTANT MATTERS.
I SUFFER GREATLY WHENEVER I'VE SPOKEN TOO MUCH.
WOULD YOU LIKE TO BE SILENT? IN CREATIVE TERMS, I MEAN.
YOU MEAN NOT COMPOSE?
I DON'T KNOW.
ARVO ONCE SAID SOMETHING VERY INTERESTING:
"I KNOW A GREAT SECRET, BUT I KNOW IT ONLY IN MUSIC, AND ONLY IN MUSIC CAN I EXPRESS IT. I'D SURE LIKE TO PUT MY FINGER ON IT!"
HEY, I'M GOING TO FINISH YOUR APPLE. MAYBE I'LL BE ABLE TO ANSWER YOUR QUESTIONS BETTER THEN.

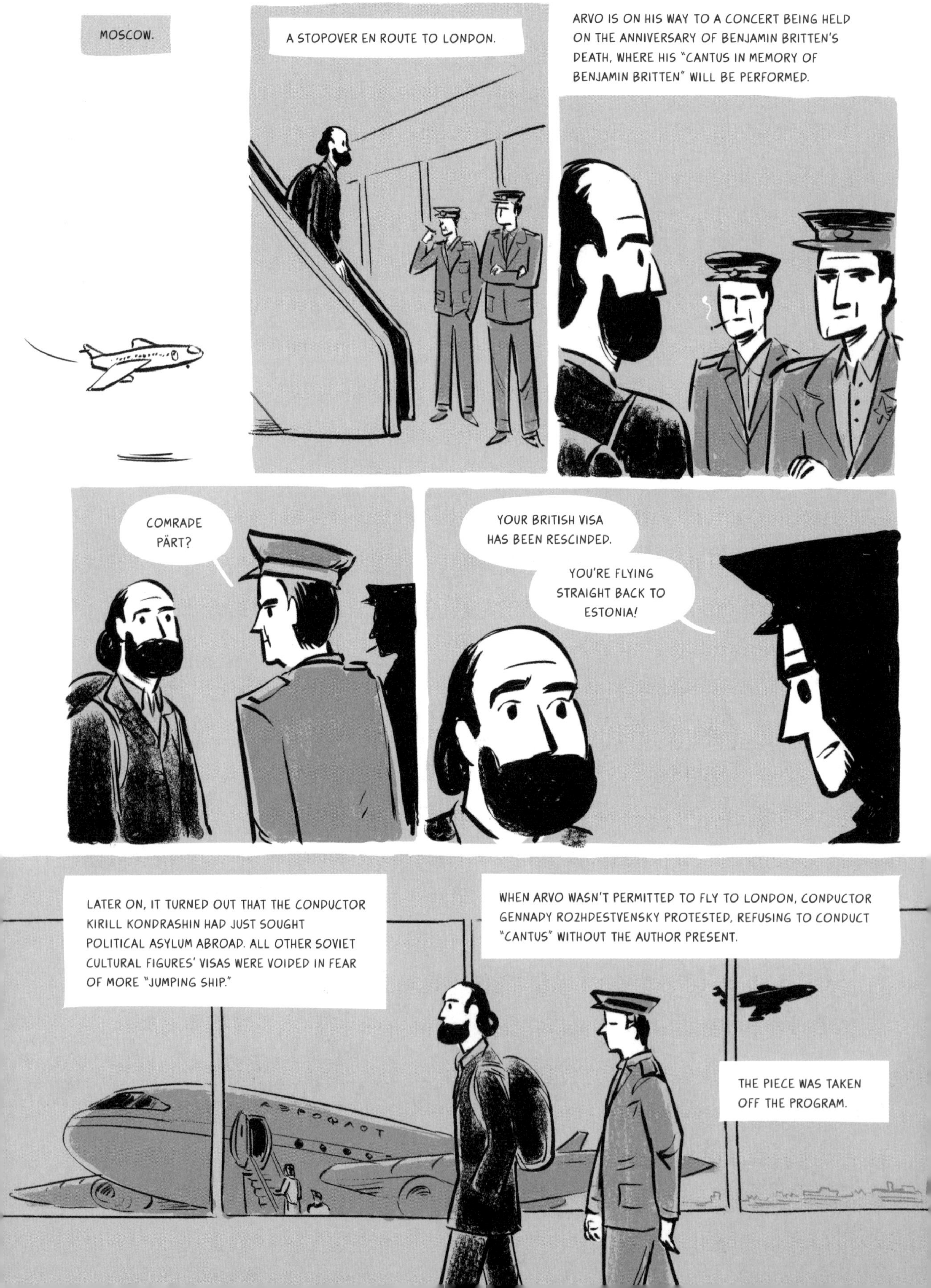
MOSCOW.
A STOPOVER EN ROUTE TO LONDON.
ARVO IS ON HIS WAY TO A CONCERT BEING HELD ON THE ANNIVERSARY OF BENJAMIN BRITTEN'S DEATH, WHERE HIS "CANTUS IN MEMORY OF BENJAMIN BRITTEN" WILL BE PERFORMED.
COMRADE PÄRT?
YOUR BRITISH VISA HAS BEEN RESCINDED.
YOU'RE FLYING STRAIGHT BACK TO ESTONIA!
LATER ON, IT TURNED OUT THAT THE CONDUCTOR KIRILL KONDRASHIN HAD JUST SOUGHT POLITICAL ASYLUM ABROAD. ALL OTHER SOVIET CULTURAL FIGURES' VISAS WERE VOIDED IN FEAR OF MORE "JUMPING SHIP."
WHEN ARVO WASN'T PERMITTED TO FLY TO LONDON, CONDUCTOR GENNADY ROZHDESTVENSKY PROTESTED, REFUSING TO CONDUCT "CANTUS" WITHOUT THE AUTHOR PRESENT.
THE PIECE WAS TAKEN OFF THE PROGRAM.

SUPREME SOVIET OF THE ESTONIAN SSR ASSEMBLY HALL. THE ANNUAL COMPOSERS' UNION CONGRESS IS UNDERWAY.

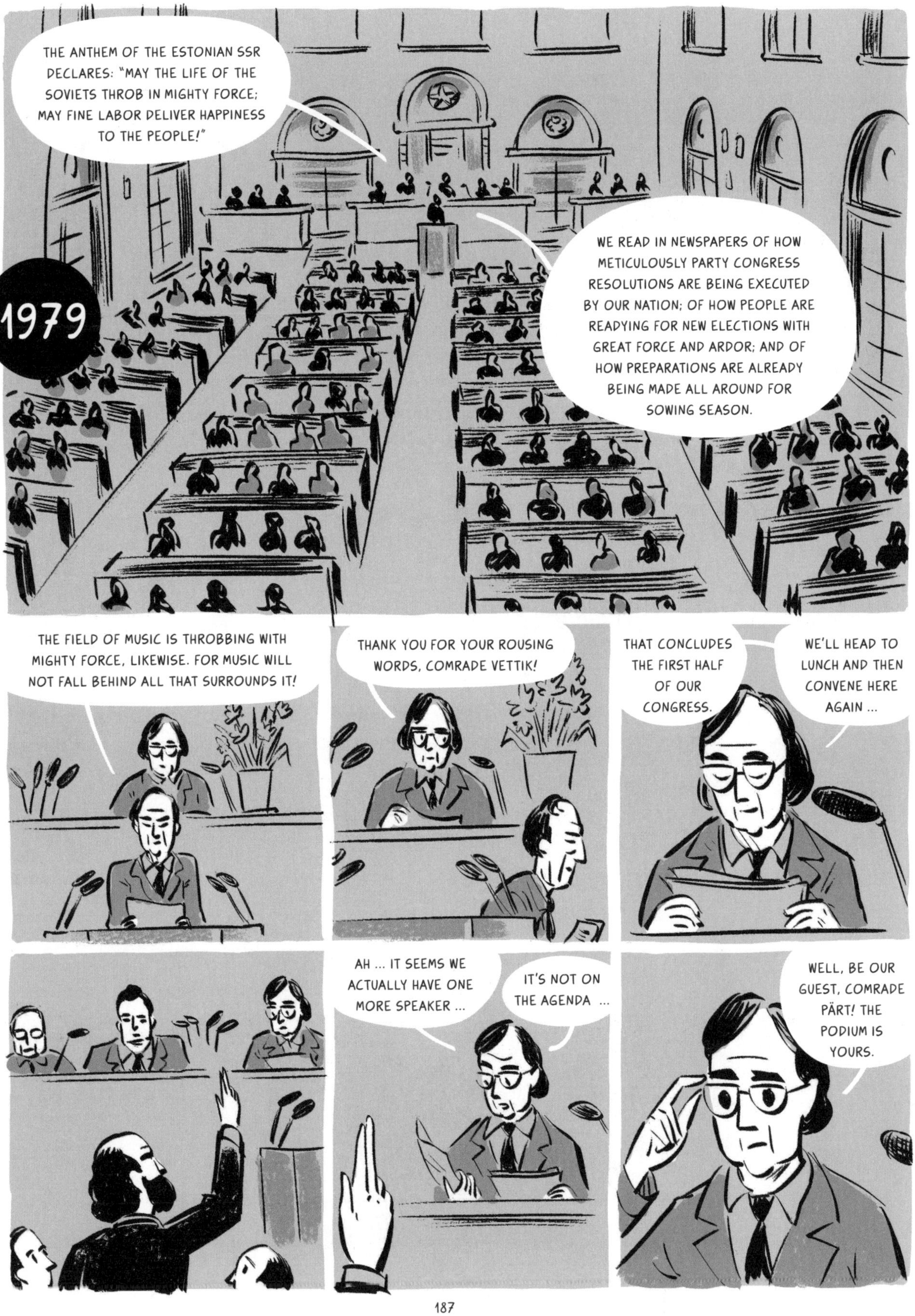
1979
THE ANTHEM OF THE ESTONIAN SSR DECLARES: "MAY THE LIFE OF THE SOVIETS THROB IN MIGHTY FORCE; MAY FINE LABOR DELIVER HAPPINESS TO THE PEOPLE!"
WE READ IN NEWSPAPERS OF HOW METICULOUSLY PARTY CONGRESS RESOLUTIONS ARE BEING EXECUTED BY OUR NATION; OF HOW PEOPLE ARE READYING FOR NEW ELECTIONS WITH GREAT FORCE AND ARDOR; AND OF HOW PREPARATIONS ARE ALREADY BEING MADE ALL AROUND FOR SOWING SEASON.
THE FIELD OF MUSIC IS THROBBING WITH MIGHTY FORCE, LIKEWISE. FOR MUSIC WILL NOT FALL BEHIND ALL THAT SURROUNDS IT!
THANK YOU FOR YOUR ROUSING WORDS, COMRADE VETTIK!
THAT CONCLUDES THE FIRST HALF OF OUR CONGRESS.
WE'LL HEAD TO LUNCH AND THEN CONVENE HERE AGAIN ...
AH ... IT SEEMS WE ACTUALLY HAVE ONE MORE SPEAKER ...
IT'S NOT ON THE AGENDA ...
WELL, BE OUR GUEST, COMRADE PÄRT! THE PODIUM IS YOURS.

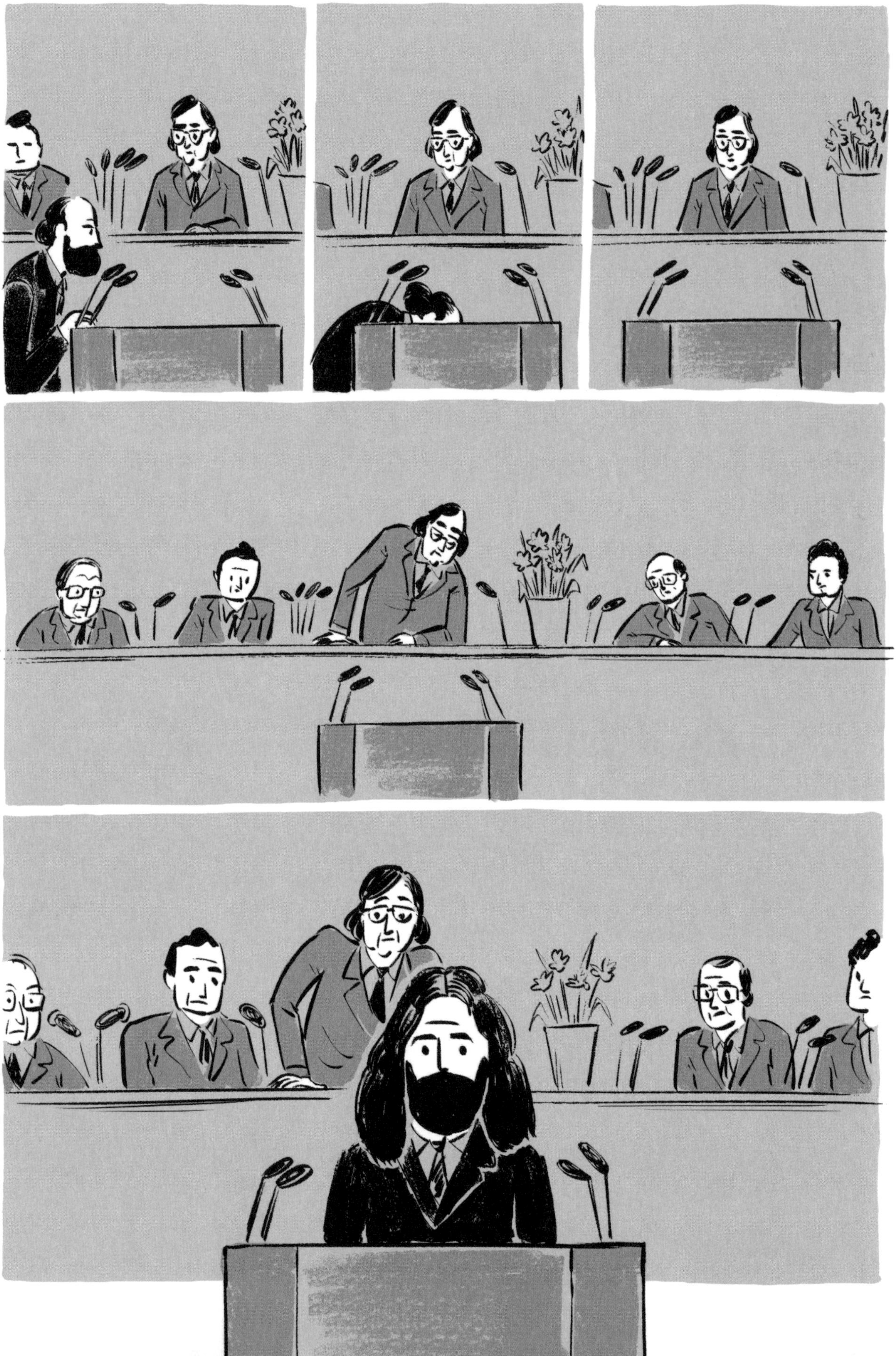

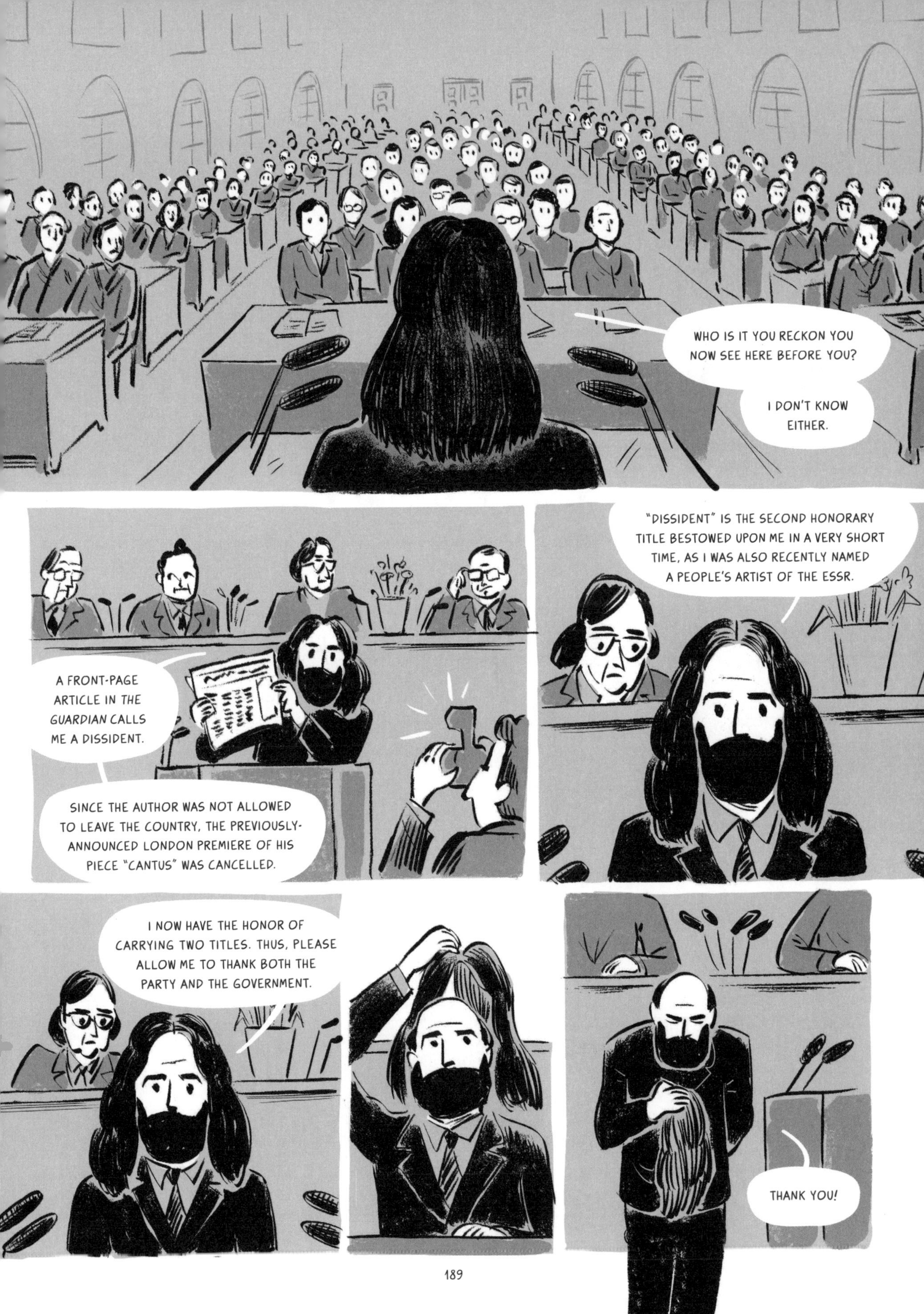
WHO IS IT YOU RECKON YOU NOW SEE HERE BEFORE YOU?
I DON'T KNOW EITHER.
A FRONT-PAGE ARTICLE IN THE GUARDIAN CALLS ME A DISSIDENT.
SINCE THE AUTHOR WAS NOT ALLOWED TO LEAVE THE COUNTRY, THE PREVIOUSLY-ANNOUNCED LONDON PREMIERE OF HIS PIECE "CANTUS" WAS CANCELLED.
"DISSIDENT" IS THE SECOND HONORARY TITLE BESTOWED UPON ME IN A VERY SHORT TIME, AS I WAS ALSO RECENTLY NAMED A PEOPLE'S ARTIST OF THE ESSR.
I NOW HAVE THE HONOR OF CARRYING TWO TITLES. THUS, PLEASE ALLOW ME TO THANK BOTH THE PARTY AND THE GOVERNMENT.
THANK YOU!

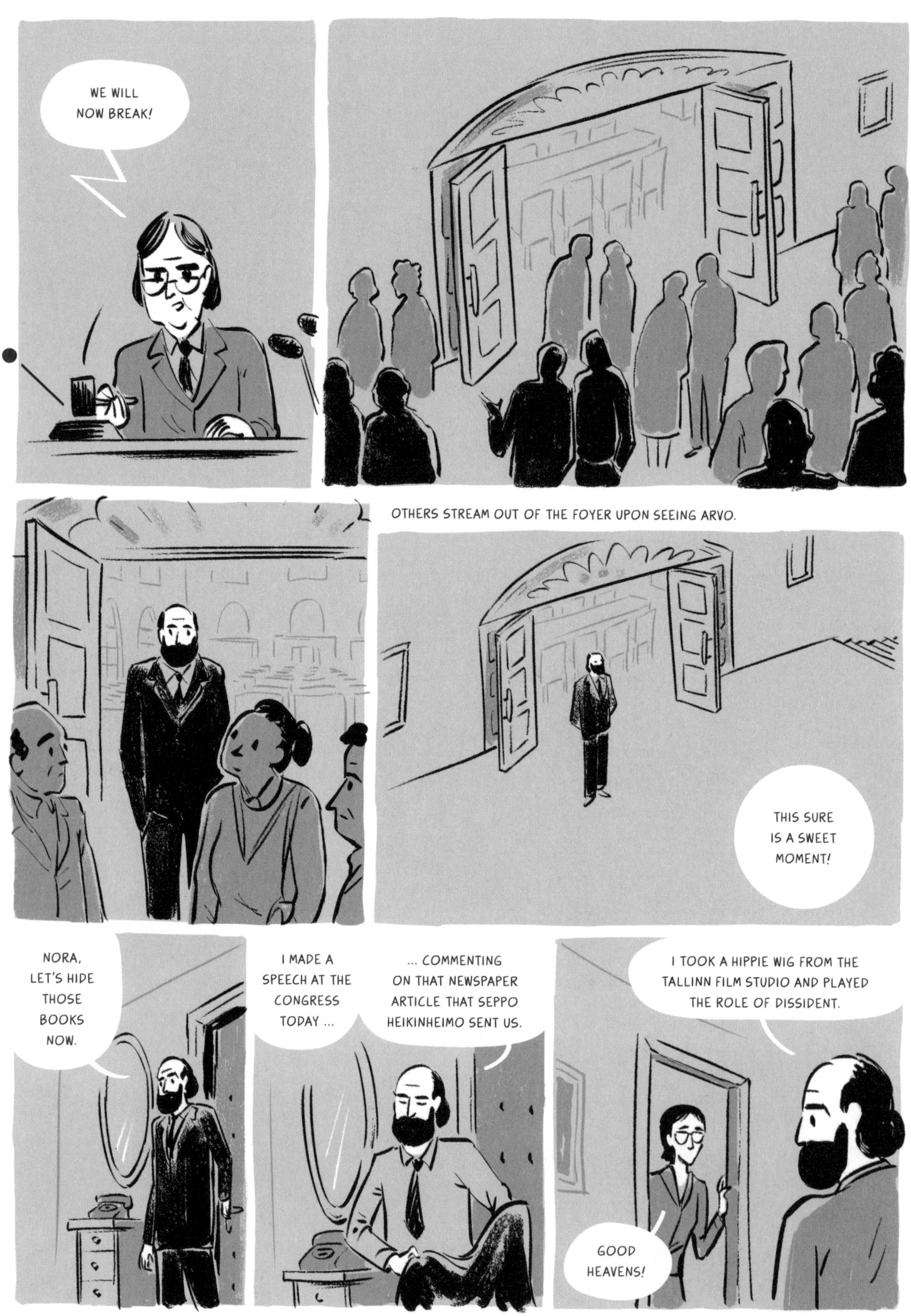
WE WILL NOW BREAK!
OTHERS STREAM OUT OF THE FOYER UPON SEEING ARVO.
THIS SURE IS A SWEET MOMENT!
NORA, LET'S HIDE THOSE BOOKS NOW.
I MADE A SPEECH AT THE CONGRESS TODAY ...
... COMMENTING ON THAT NEWSPAPER ARTICLE THAT SEPPO HEIKINHEIMO SENT US.
I TOOK A HIPPIE WIG FROM THE TALLINN FILM STUDIO AND PLAYED THE ROLE OF DISSIDENT.
GOOD HEAVENS!

AT PÜHTITSA CONVENT, THE PÄRTS MEET MISHA, AN ITINERANT MONK FROM RUSSIA. HE'S KNOWN AROUND THE CONVENT AS A "HOLY FOOL."

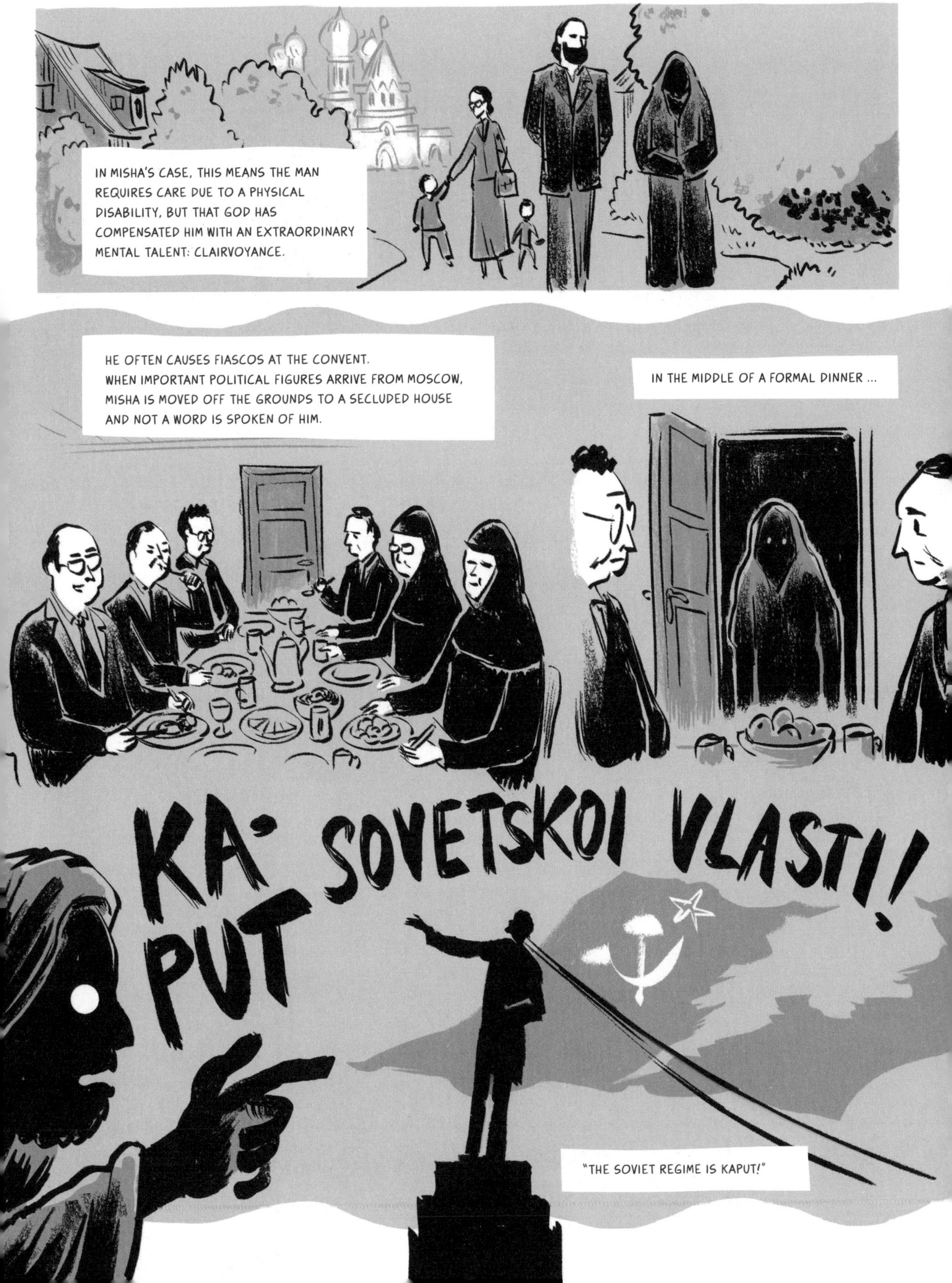
IN MISHA'S CASE, THIS MEANS THE MAN REQUIRES CARE DUE TO A PHYSICAL DISABILITY, BUT THAT GOD HAS COMPENSATED HIM WITH AN EXTRAORDINARY MENTAL TALENT: CLAIRVOYANCE.
HE OFTEN CAUSES FIASCOS AT THE CONVENT. WHEN IMPORTANT POLITICAL FIGURES ARRIVE FROM MOSCOW, MISHA IS MOVED OFF THE GROUNDS TO A SECLUDED HOUSE AND NOT A WORD IS SPOKEN OF HIM.
IN THE MIDDLE OF A FORMAL DINNER ...
KA' PUT SOVETSKOI VLASTI!
"THE SOVIET REGIME IS KAPUT!"

MISHA ALSO STAYS WITH THE PÄRTS IN TALLINN FOR A SHORT WHILE. IT ISN'T EASY, AS IT'S LIKE LIVING WITH A SMALL CHILD.

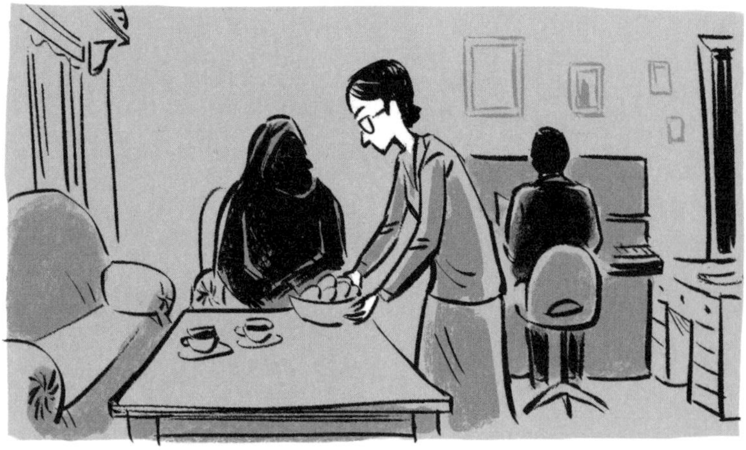

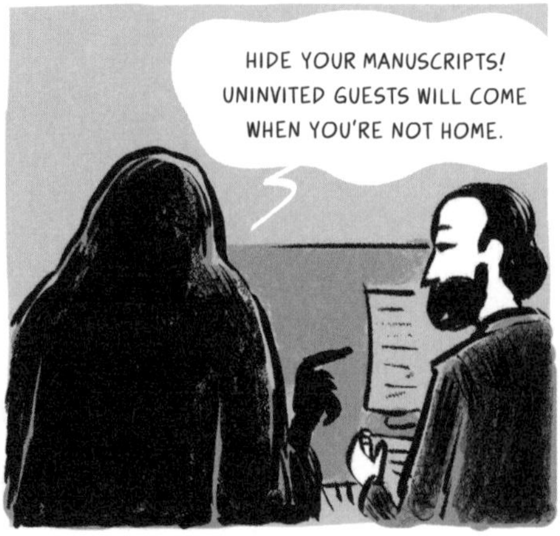
HIDE YOUR MANUSCRIPTS! UNINVITED GUESTS WILL COME WHEN YOU'RE NOT HOME.

ARVO HELPS MISHA RETURN TO RUSSIA, TRAVELING A LONG DISTANCE WITH THE MONK.

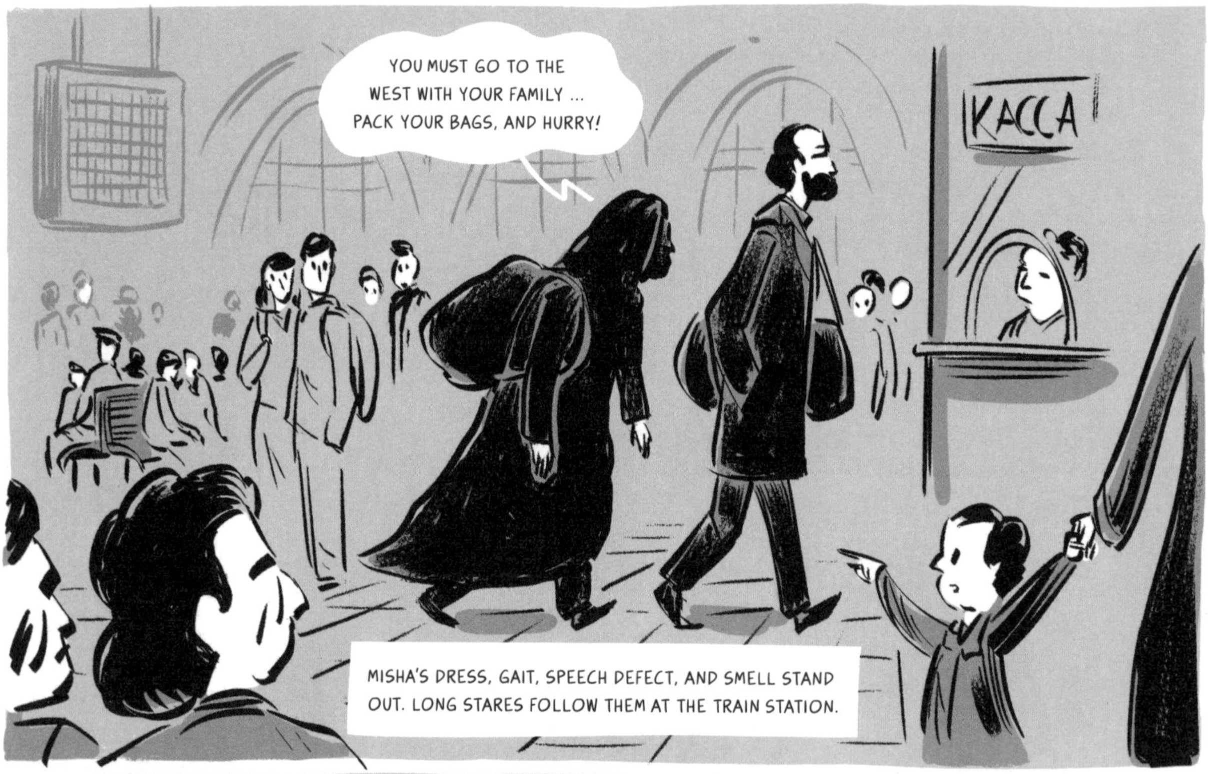
YOU MUST GO TO THE WEST WITH YOUR FAMILY ... PACK YOUR BAGS, AND HURRY!
KACCA
MISHA'S DRESS, GAIT, SPEECH DEFECT, AND SMELL STAND OUT. LONG STARES FOLLOW THEM AT THE TRAIN STATION.

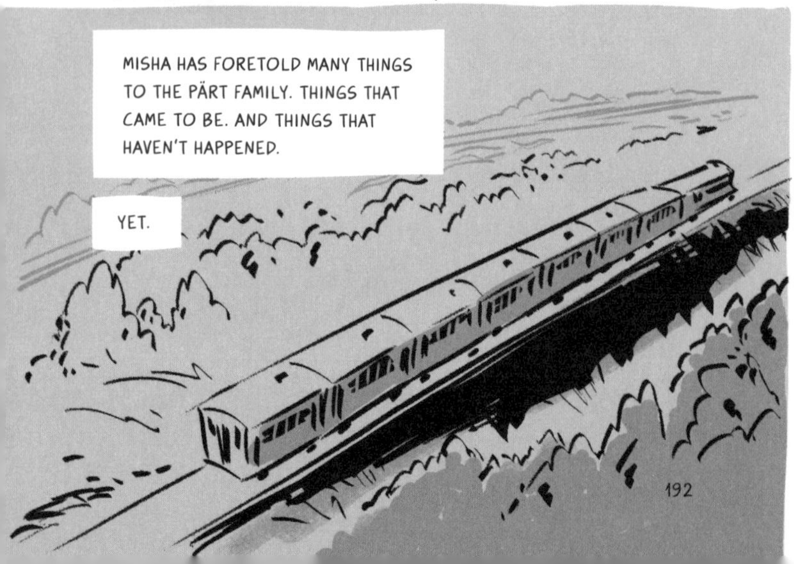
MISHA HAS FORETOLD MANY THINGS TO THE PÄRT FAMILY. THINGS THAT CAME TO BE. AND THINGS THAT HAVEN'T HAPPENED.
YET.

MISHA'S ATTITUDE HAS MADE ARVO THINK THAT IF GOD TRULY SEES AND KNOWS ALL, WHY TRY TO HIDE ANYTHING FROM HIM?

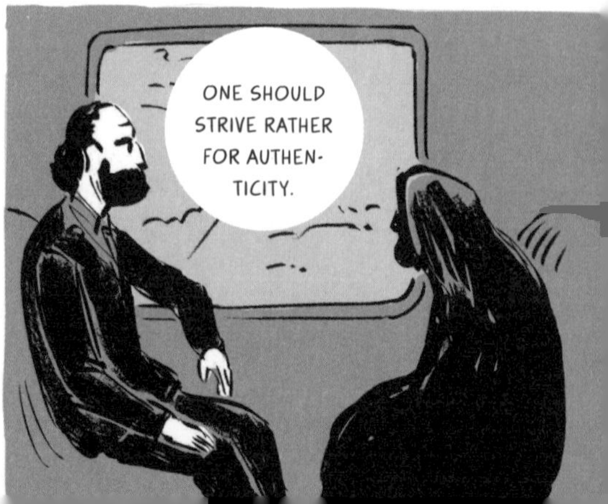
ONE SHOULD STRIVE RATHER FOR AUTHEN-TICITY.

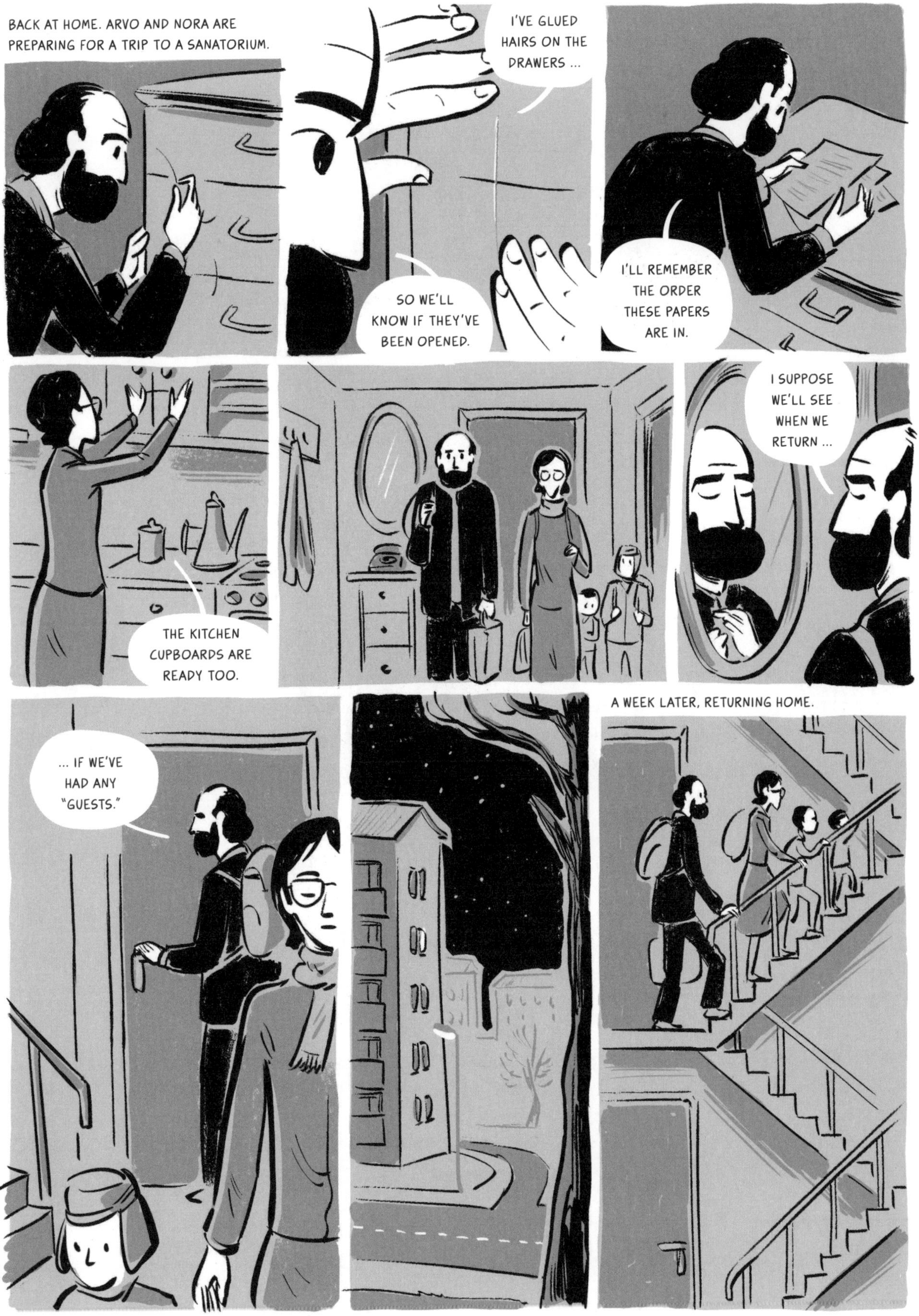
BACK AT HOME. ARVO AND NORA ARE PREPARING FOR A TRIP TO A SANATORIUM.
I'VE GLUED HAIRS ON THE DRAWERS ...
SO WE'LL KNOW IF THEY'VE BEEN OPENED.
I'LL REMEMBER THE ORDER THESE PAPERS ARE IN.
THE KITCHEN CUPBOARDS ARE READY TOO.
I SUPPOSE WE'LL SEE WHEN WE RETURN ...
... IF WE'VE HAD ANY "GUESTS."
A WEEK LATER, RETURNING HOME.

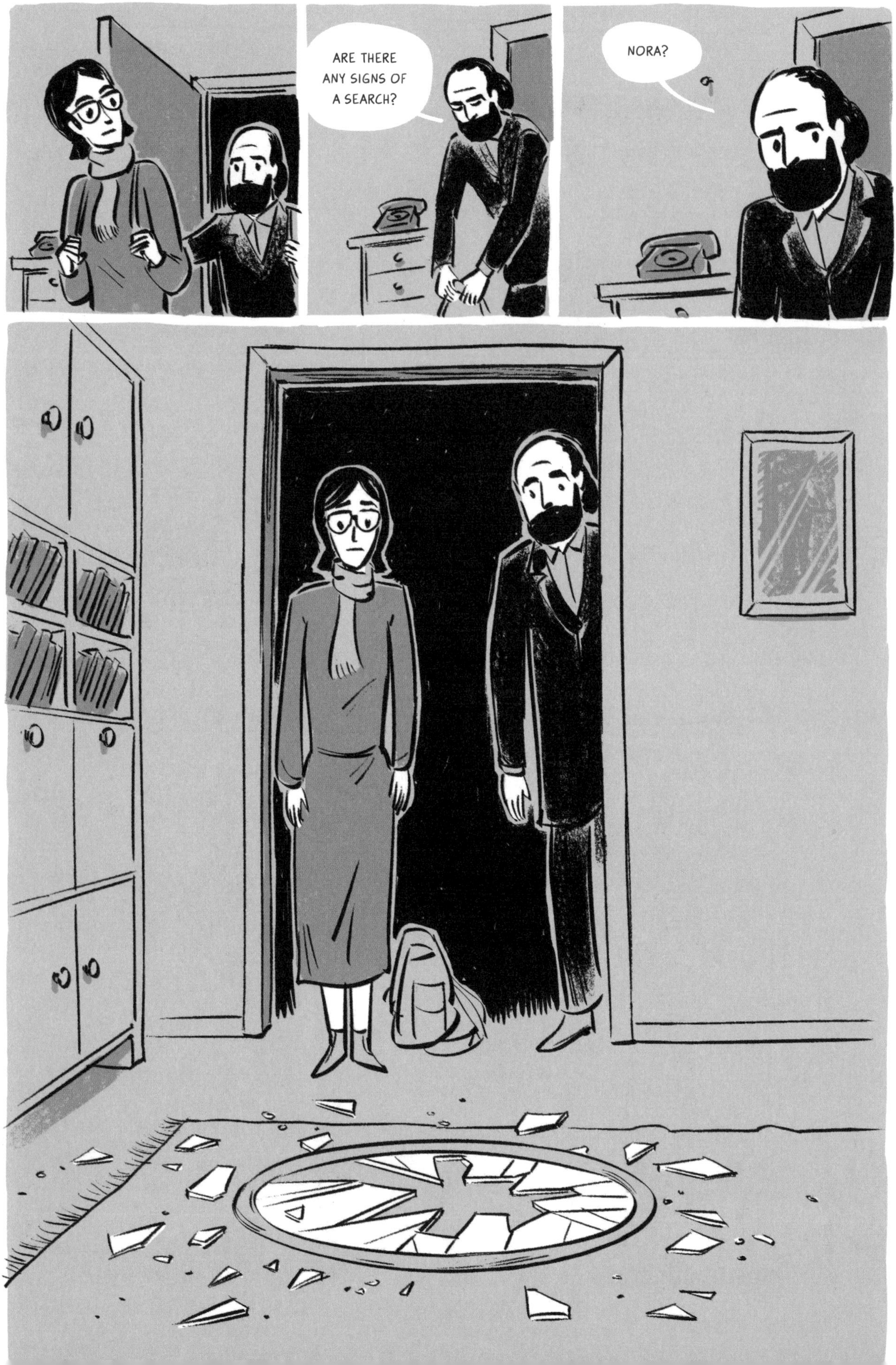
ARE THERE ANY SIGNS OF A SEARCH?
NORA?

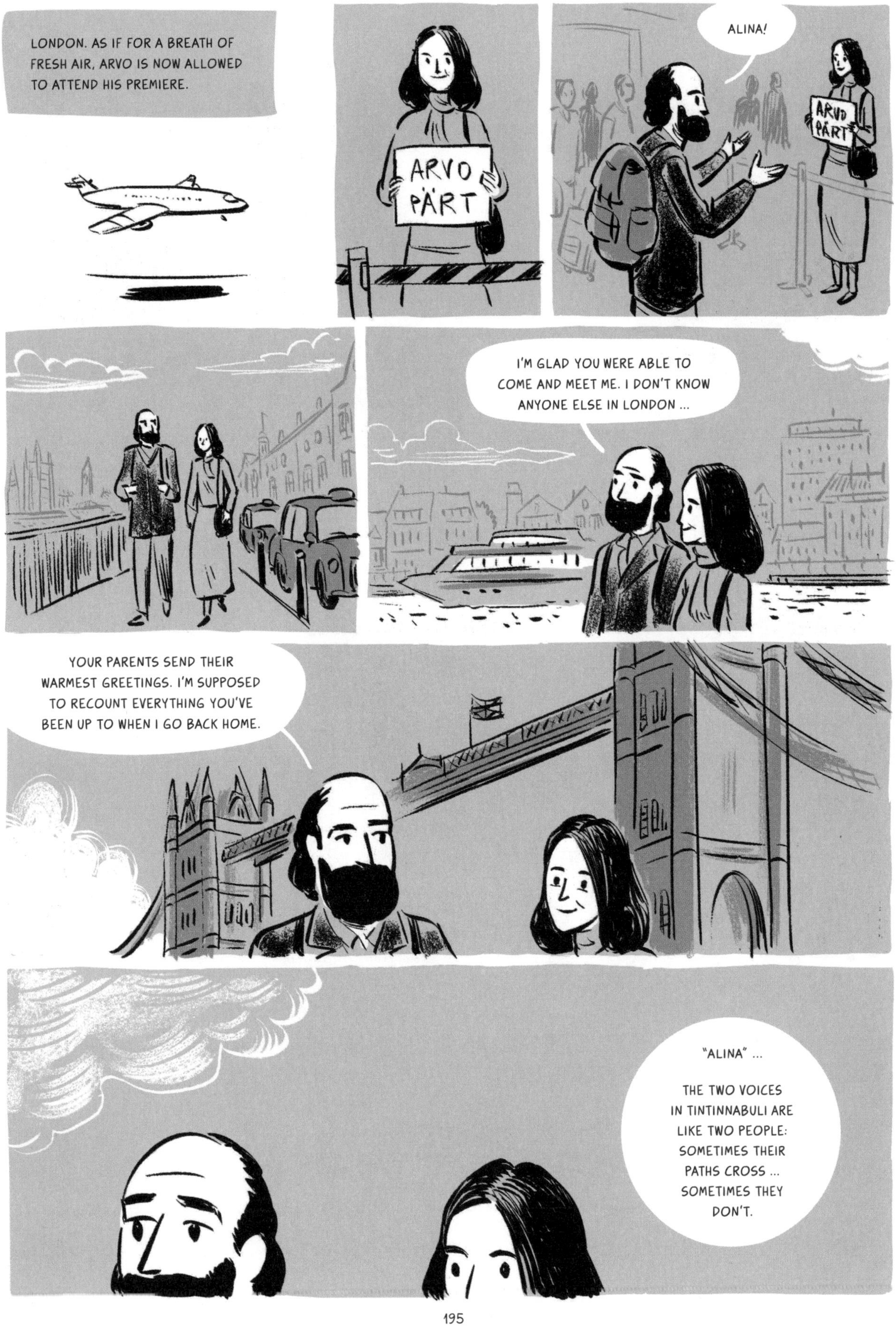
LONDON. AS IF FOR A BREATH OF FRESH AIR, ARVO IS NOW ALLOWED TO ATTEND HIS PREMIERE.
ARVO PÄRT
ALINA!
ARVO PÄRT
I'M GLAD YOU WERE ABLE TO COME AND MEET ME. I DON'T KNOW ANYONE ELSE IN LONDON ...
YOUR PARENTS SEND THEIR WARMEST GREETINGS. I'M SUPPOSED TO RECOUNT EVERYTHING YOU'VE BEEN UP TO WHEN I GO BACK HOME.
"ALINA" ...
THE TWO VOICES IN TINTINNABULI ARE LIKE TWO PEOPLE: SOMETIMES THEIR PATHS CROSS ... SOMETIMES THEY DON'T.

A FEW MONTHS BEFORE NEW YEAR'S, OLAF UTT FROM THE COMMUNIST PARTY CENTRAL COMMITTEE VISITS THE PÄRTS.

FRIENDS!

YOU HAVE TWO CHILDREN. A FAMILY REQUIRES CARE AND CONSIDERATION.

ELEONORA, YOUR PARENTS LIVE IN ISRAEL.

YOU AND YOUR FAMILY MAY EMIGRATE TO BE WITH THEM, AND THEY CAN OFFER YOU SUPPORT.

WE'LL MEET YOU HALFWAY AND WILL HELP WITH THE NECESSARY PAPERWORK.

GOOD LUCK!

THE OFFER IS THE ONLY LEGAL WAY FOR THE PÄRTS TO LEAVE THE SOVIET UNION.

AS USUAL, THAT WHICH IS DECIDED IN THE CORRIDORS OF POWER HAPPENS ON A "VOLUNTARY BASIS."

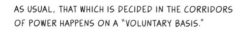

WHAT'S CLEAR IS THAT THE PÄRTS ARE BEING THROWN OUT OF THE COUNTRY. AND ONE CAN ONLY LEAVE THE USSR FOR GOOD.

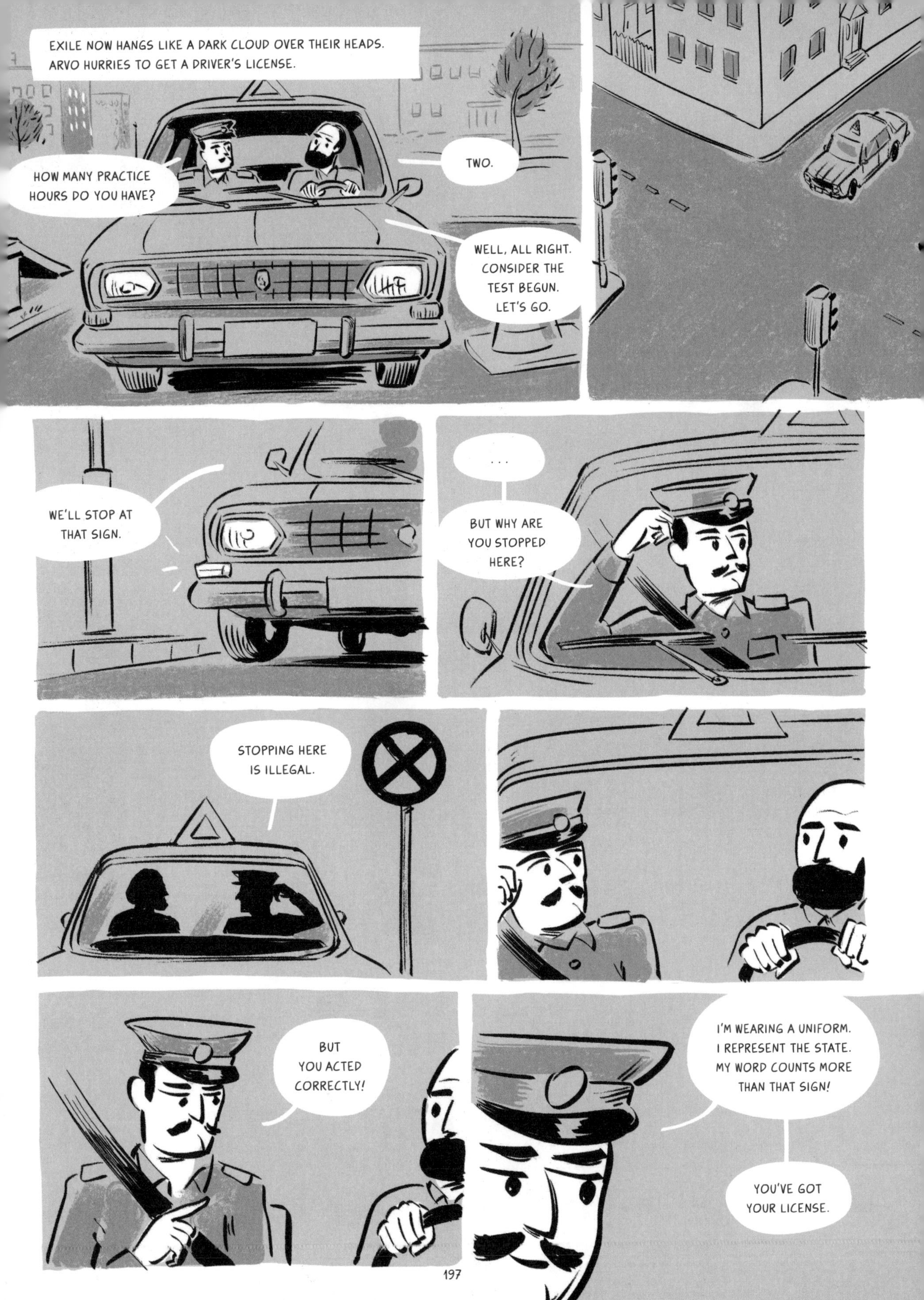
EXILE NOW HANGS LIKE A DARK CLOUD OVER THEIR HEADS. ARVO HURRIES TO GET A DRIVER'S LICENSE.
HOW MANY PRACTICE HOURS DO YOU HAVE?
TWO.
WELL, ALL RIGHT. CONSIDER THE TEST BEGUN. LET'S GO.
WE'LL STOP AT THAT SIGN.
. . .
BUT WHY ARE YOU STOPPED HERE?
STOPPING HERE IS ILLEGAL.
BUT YOU ACTED CORRECTLY!
I'M WEARING A UNIFORM. I REPRESENT THE STATE. MY WORD COUNTS MORE THAN THAT SIGN!
YOU'VE GOT YOUR LICENSE.

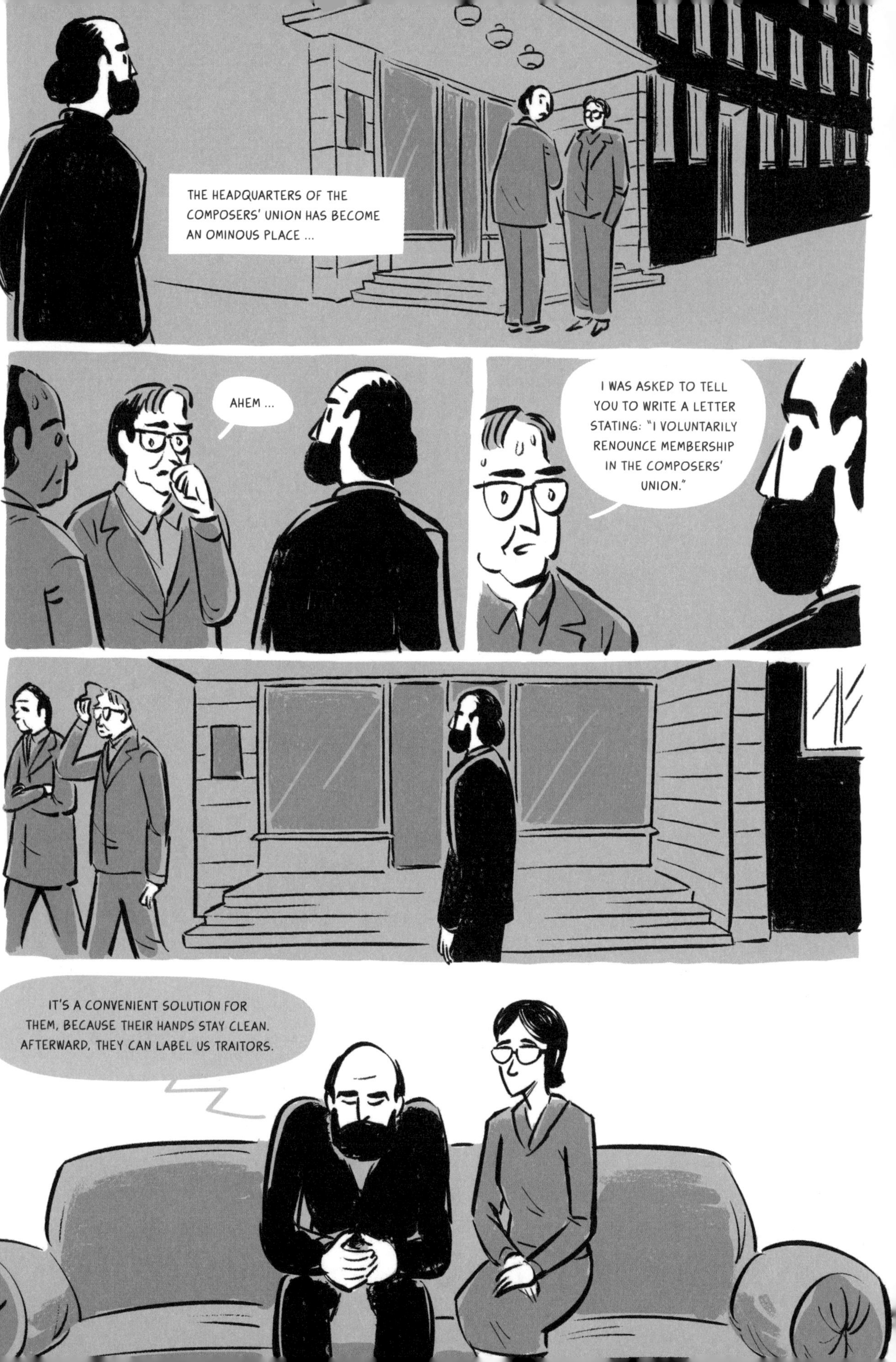
THE HEADQUARTERS OF THE COMPOSERS' UNION HAS BECOME AN OMINOUS PLACE ...
AHEM ...
I WAS ASKED TO TELL YOU TO WRITE A LETTER STATING: "I VOLUNTARILY RENOUNCE MEMBERSHIP IN THE COMPOSERS' UNION."
IT'S A CONVENIENT SOLUTION FOR THEM, BECAUSE THEIR HANDS STAY CLEAN. AFTERWARD, THEY CAN LABEL US TRAITORS.

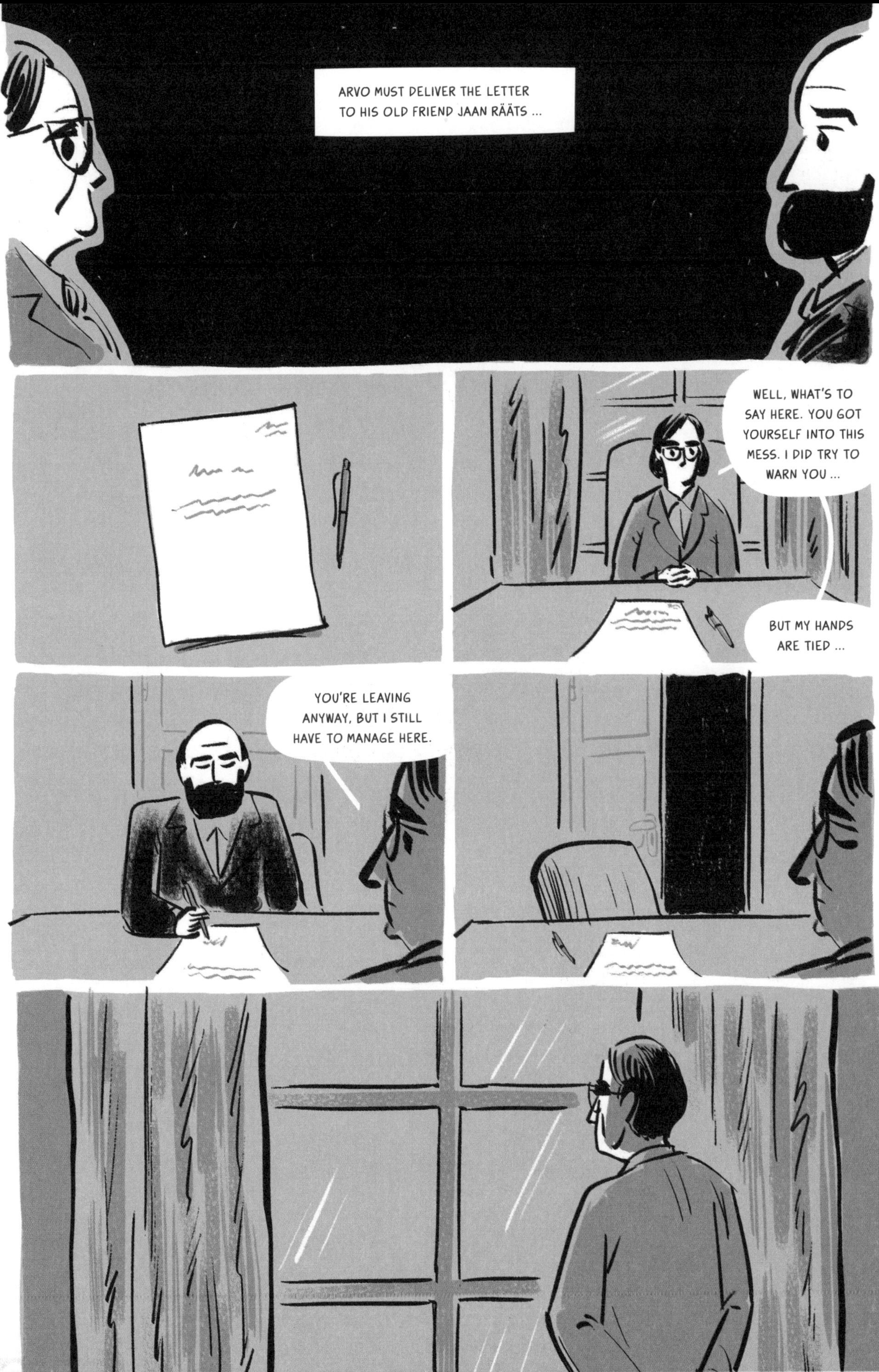
ARVO MUST DELIVER THE LETTER TO HIS OLD FRIEND JAAN RÄÄTS ...
WELL, WHAT'S TO SAY HERE. YOU GOT YOURSELF INTO THIS MESS. I DID TRY TO WARN YOU ...
BUT MY HANDS ARE TIED ...
YOU'RE LEAVING ANYWAY, BUT I STILL HAVE TO MANAGE HERE.

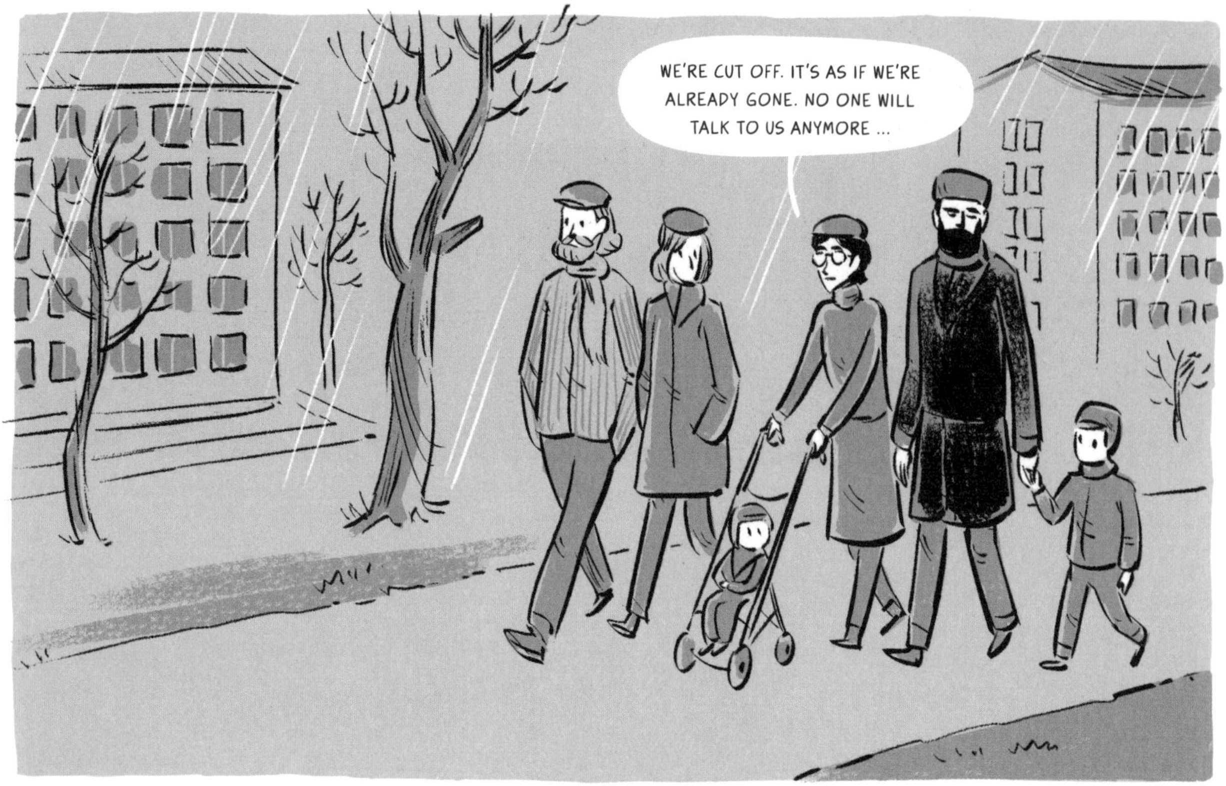
WE'RE CUT OFF. IT'S AS IF WE'RE ALREADY GONE. NO ONE WILL TALK TO US ANYMORE ...

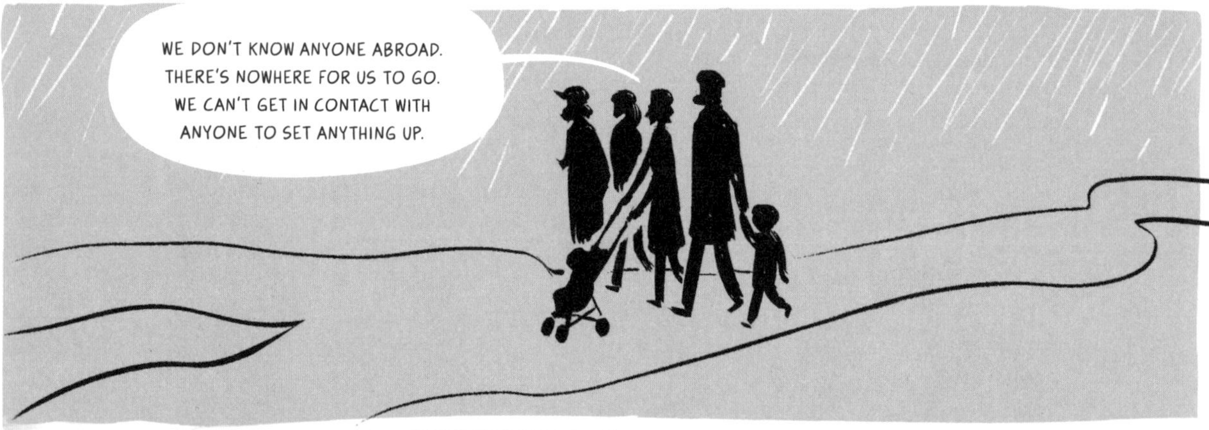
WE DON'T KNOW ANYONE ABROAD. THERE'S NOWHERE FOR US TO GO. WE CAN'T GET IN CONTACT WITH ANYONE TO SET ANYTHING UP.

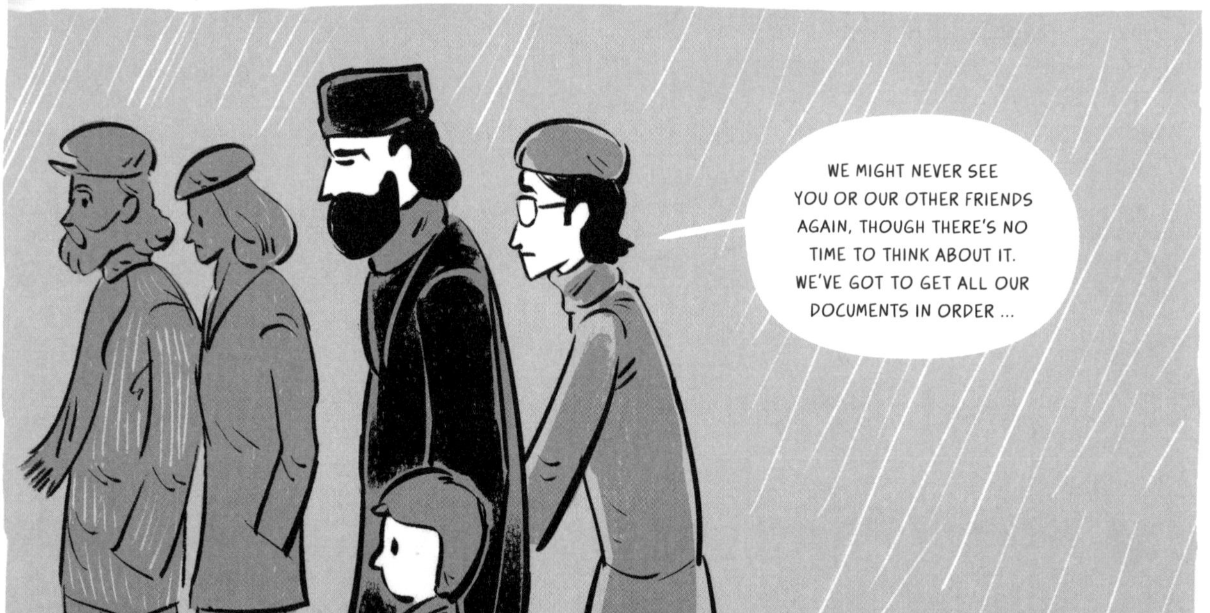
WE MIGHT NEVER SEE YOU OR OUR OTHER FRIENDS AGAIN, THOUGH THERE'S NO TIME TO THINK ABOUT IT. WE'VE GOT TO GET ALL OUR DOCUMENTS IN ORDER ...

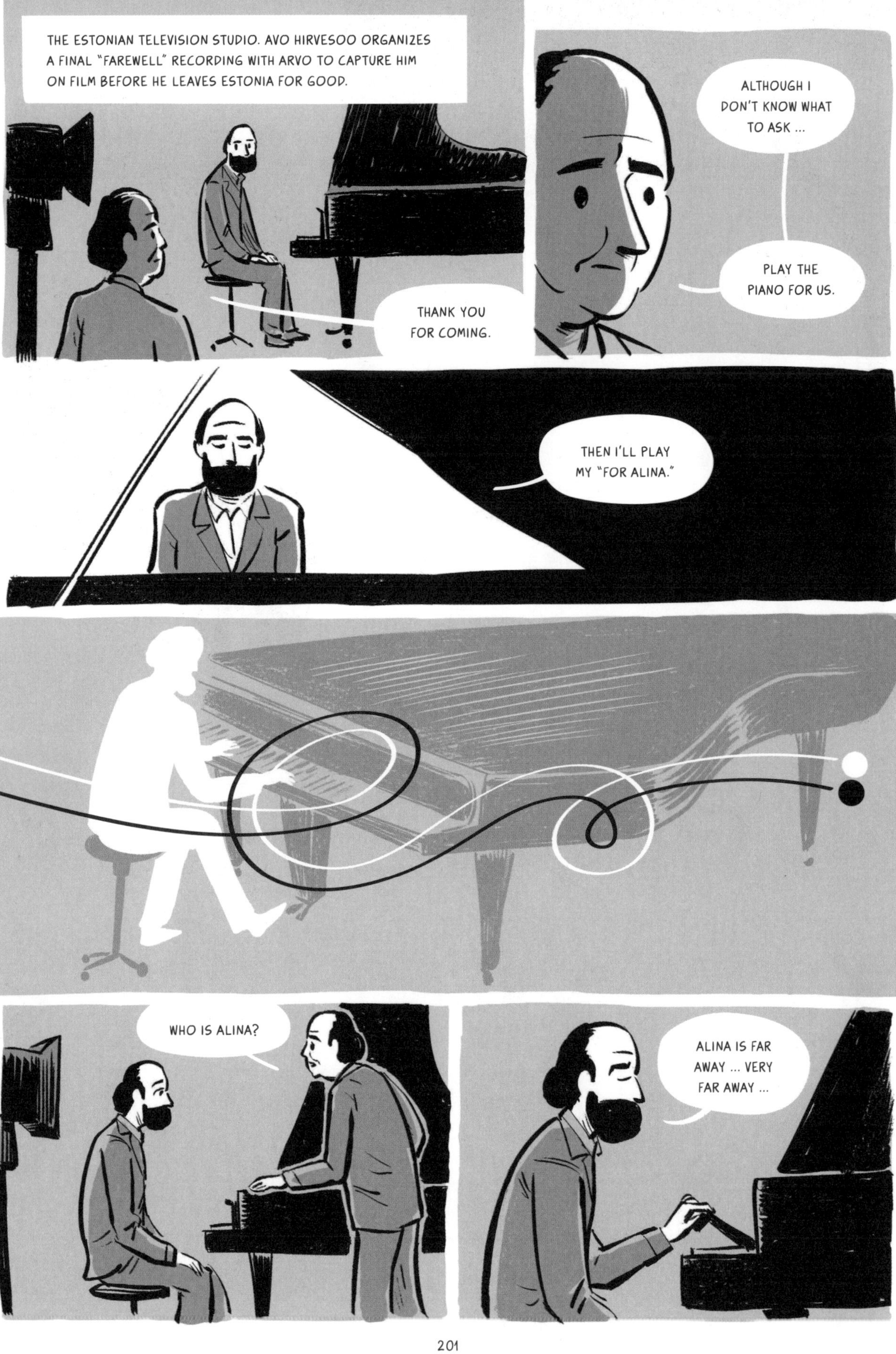
THE ESTONIAN TELEVISION STUDIO. AVO HIRVESOO ORGANIZES A FINAL "FAREWELL" RECORDING WITH ARVO TO CAPTURE HIM ON FILM BEFORE HE LEAVES ESTONIA FOR GOOD.
THANK YOU FOR COMING.
ALTHOUGH I DON'T KNOW WHAT TO ASK ...
PLAY THE PIANO FOR US.
THEN I'LL PLAY MY "FOR ALINA."
WHO IS ALINA?
ALINA IS FAR AWAY ... VERY FAR AWAY ...

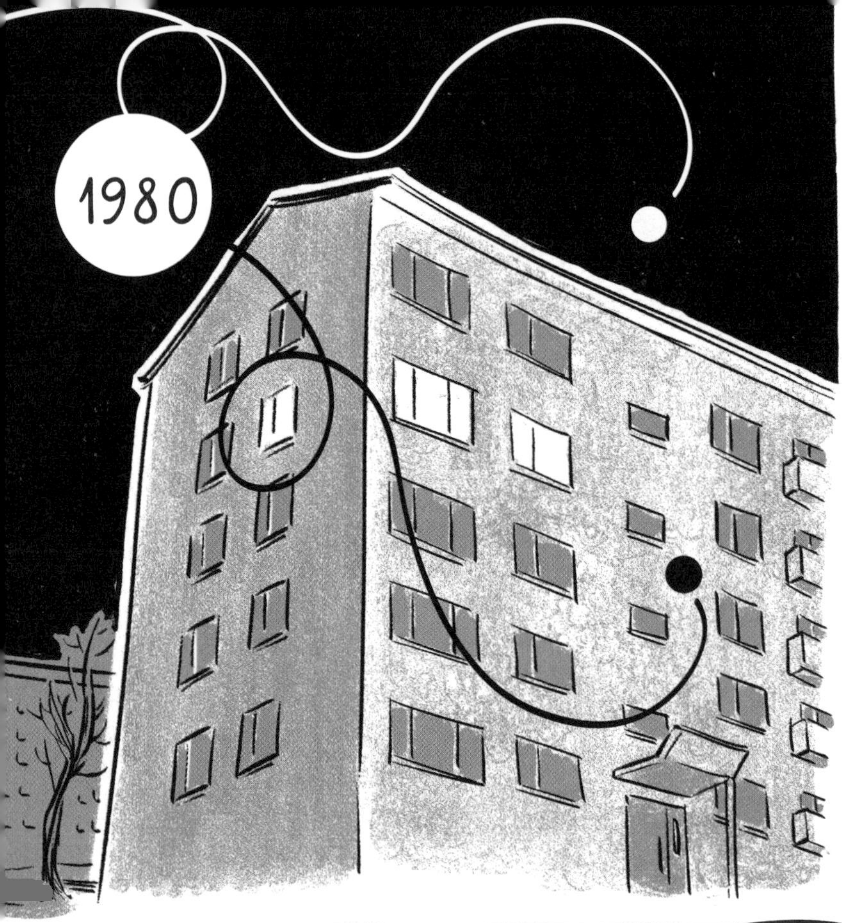
1980

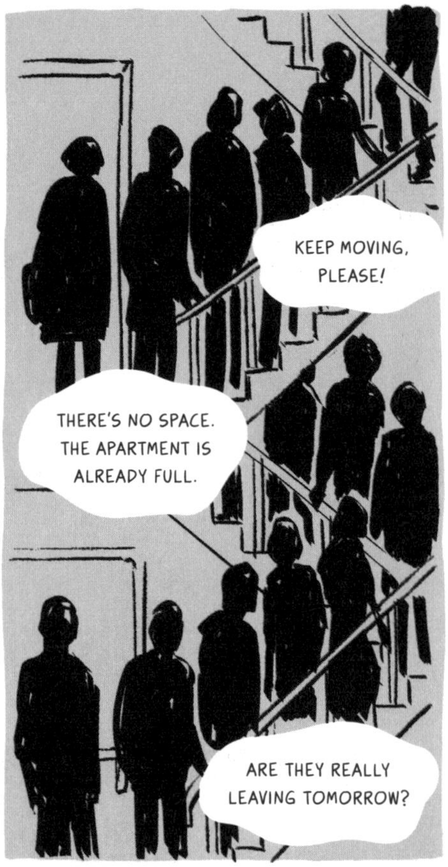
KEEP MOVING, PLEASE!
THERE'S NO SPACE. THE APARTMENT IS ALREADY FULL.
ARE THEY REALLY LEAVING TOMORROW?

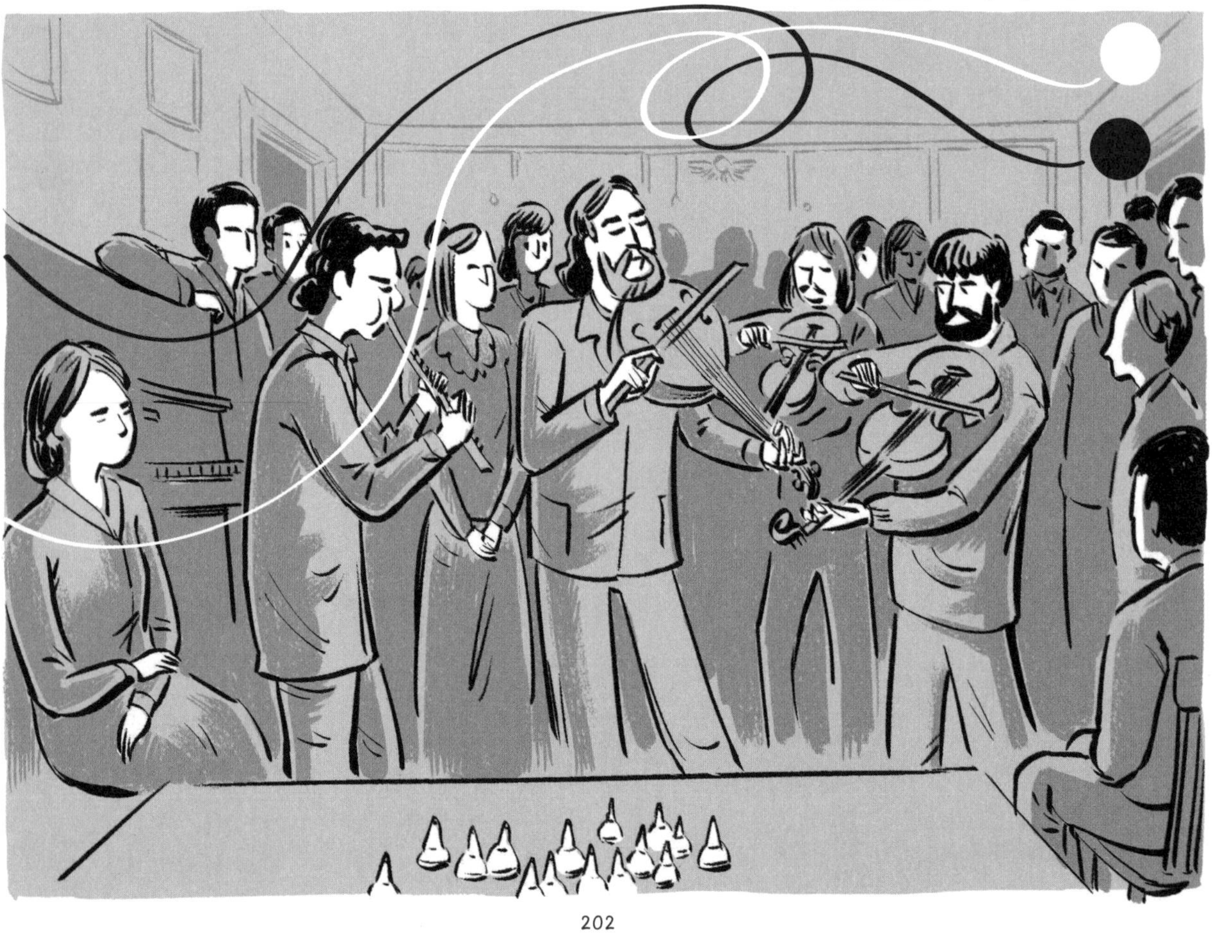

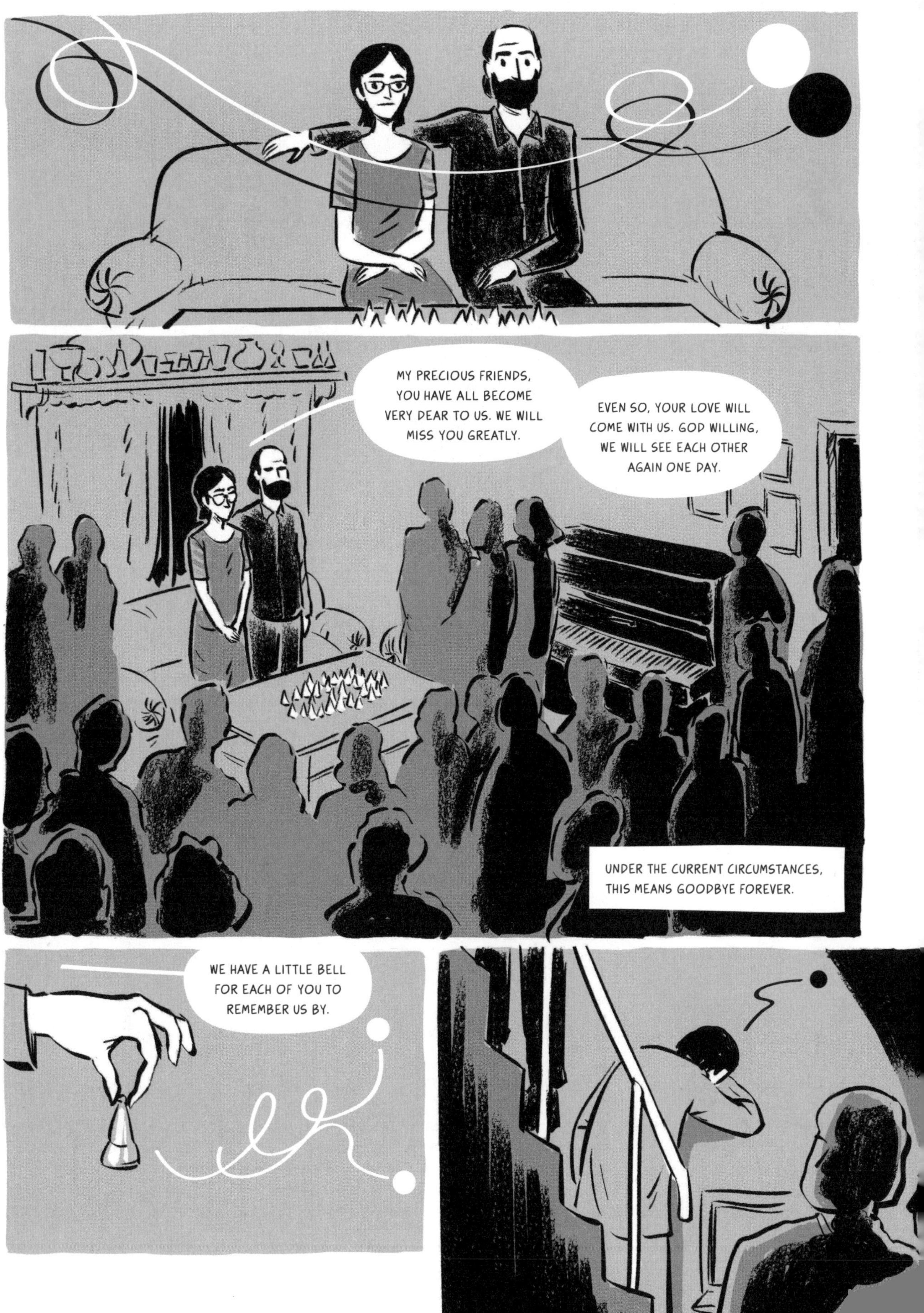
MY PRECIOUS FRIENDS, YOU HAVE ALL BECOME VERY DEAR TO US. WE WILL MISS YOU GREATLY.
EVEN SO, YOUR LOVE WILL COME WITH US. GOD WILLING, WE WILL SEE EACH OTHER AGAIN ONE DAY.
UNDER THE CURRENT CIRCUMSTANCES, THIS MEANS GOODBYE FOREVER.
WE HAVE A LITTLE BELL FOR EACH OF YOU TO REMEMBER US BY.

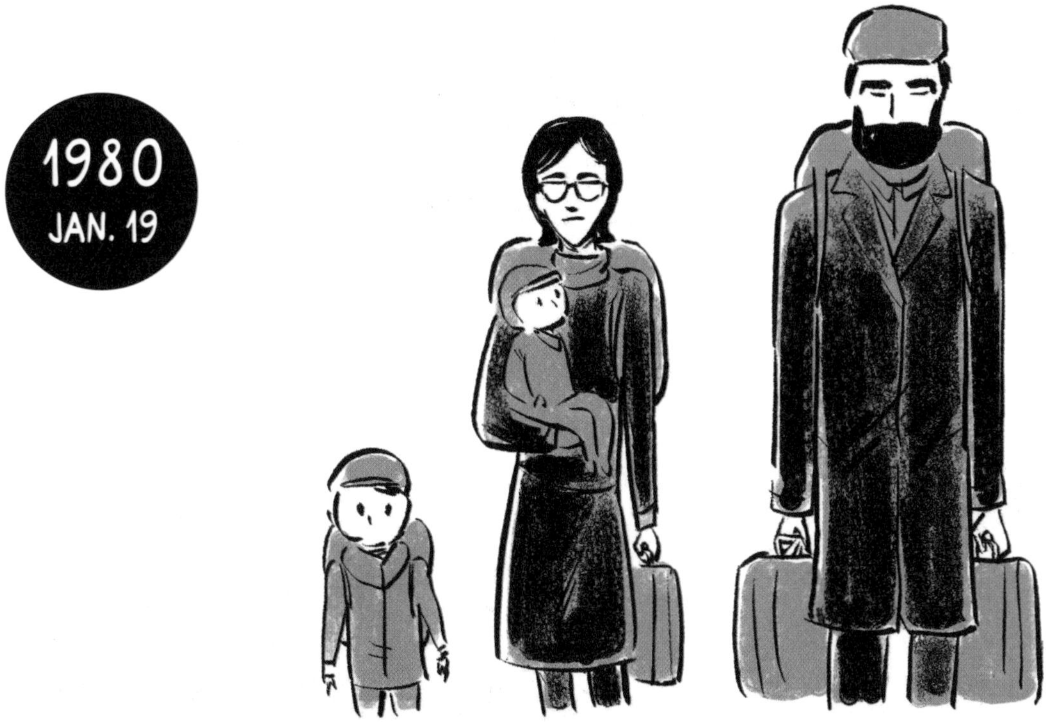
1980
JAN. 19

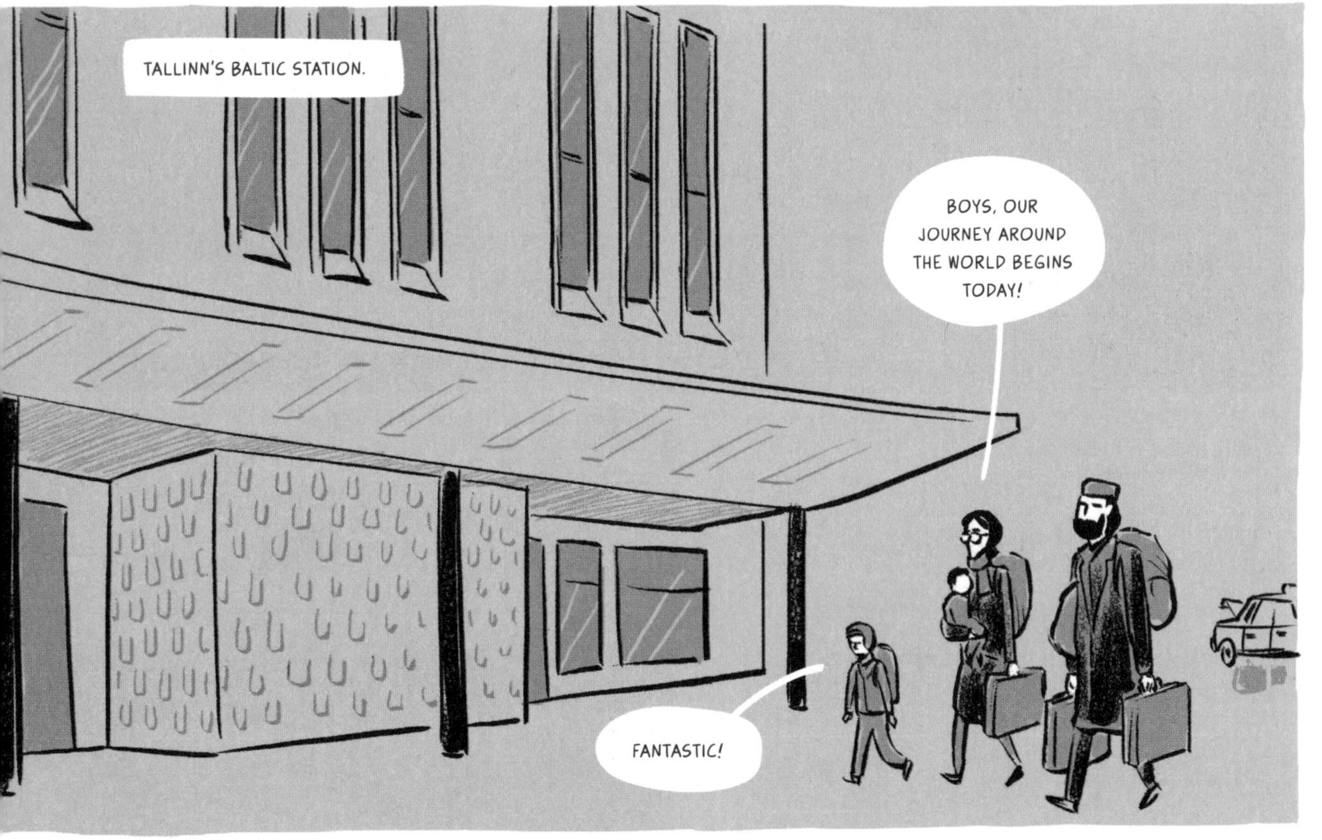
TALLINN'S BALTIC STATION.
BOYS, OUR JOURNEY AROUND THE WORLD BEGINS TODAY!
FANTASTIC!

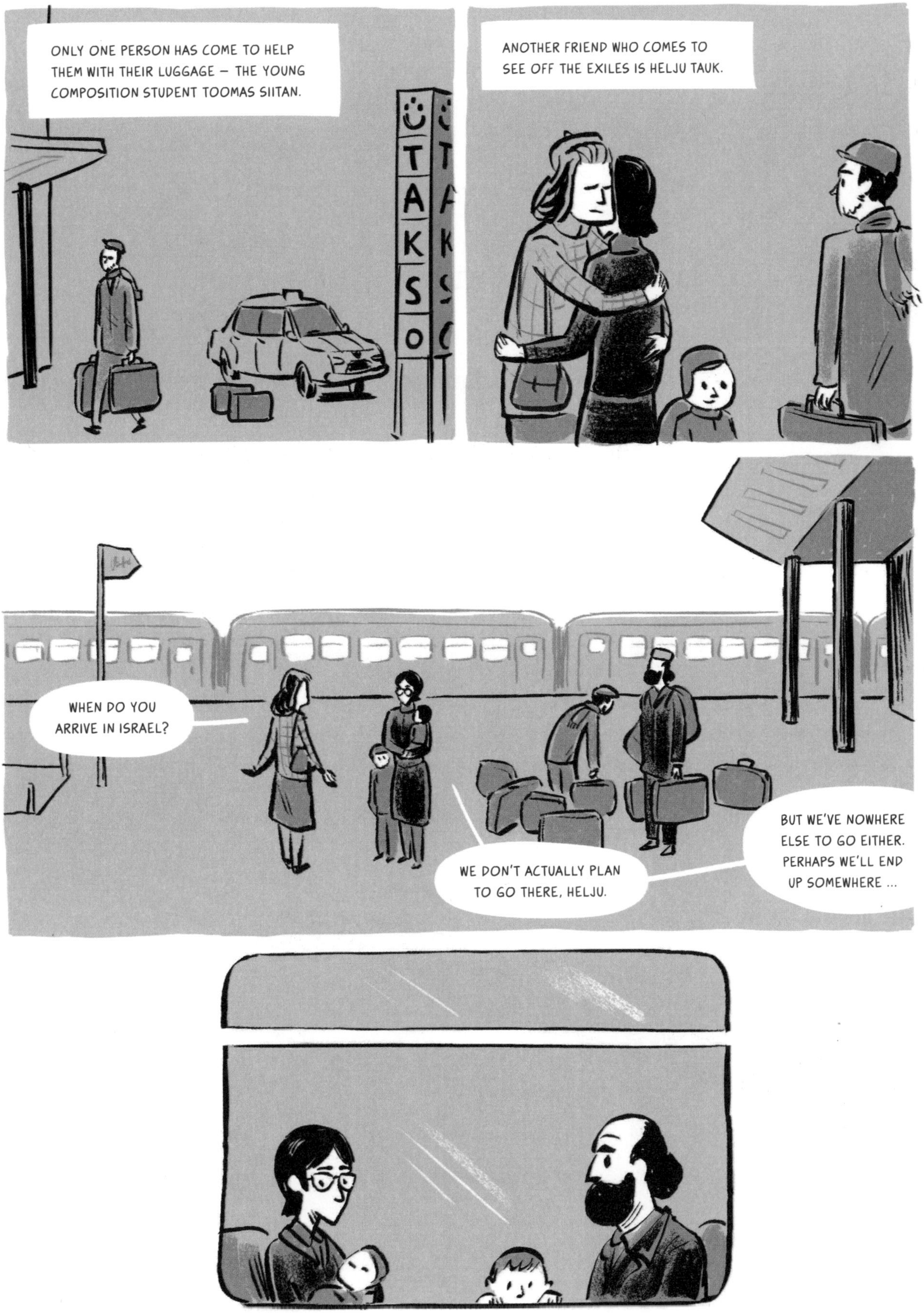
ONLY ONE PERSON HAS COME TO HELP THEM WITH THEIR LUGGAGE – THE YOUNG COMPOSITION STUDENT TOOMAS SIITAN.
TAKSO
ANOTHER FRIEND WHO COMES TO SEE OFF THE EXILES IS HELJU TAUK.
WHEN DO YOU ARRIVE IN ISRAEL?
WE DON'T ACTUALLY PLAN TO GO THERE, HELJU.
BUT WE'VE NOWHERE ELSE TO GO EITHER. PERHAPS WE'LL END UP SOMEWHERE ...

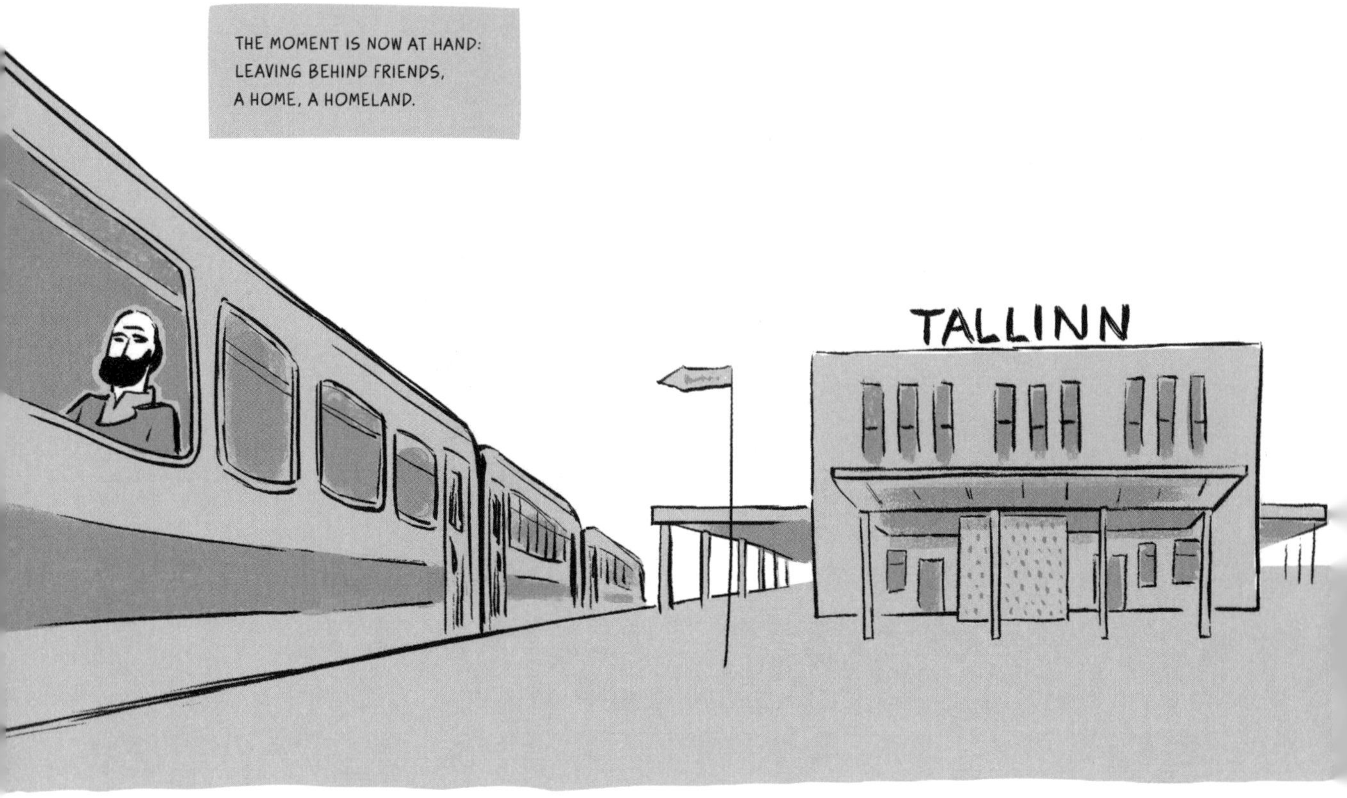
THE MOMENT IS NOW AT HAND: LEAVING BEHIND FRIENDS, A HOME, A HOMELAND.
TALLINN

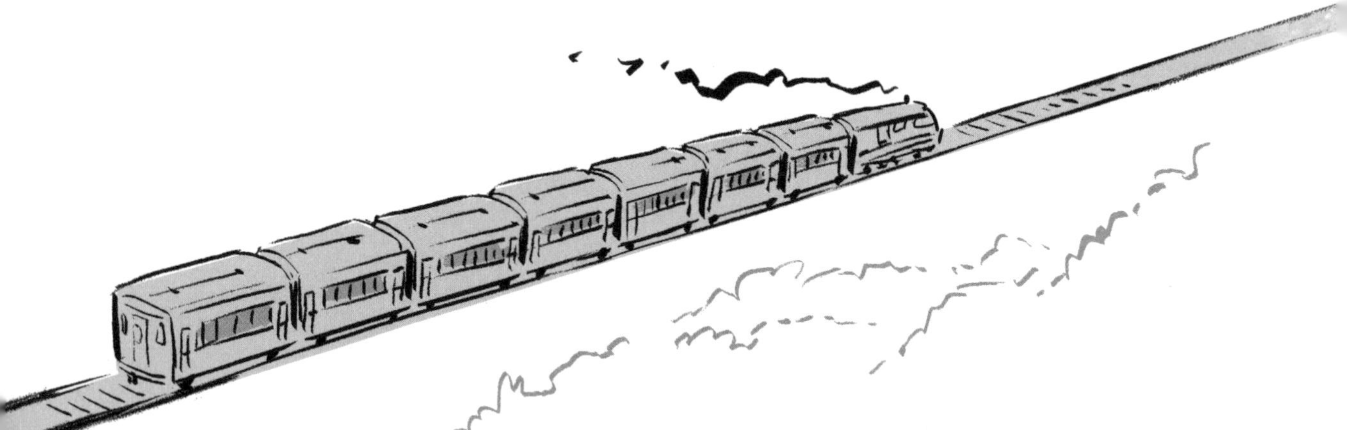

TOOMAS SIITAN HAS DECIDED TO TRAVEL WITH THEM TO THE SOVIET BORDER, EVEN THOUGH ASSOCIATING WITH THE NOW "UNDESIRABLE PERSONS" COULD LEAVE A PAINFUL STAMP ON HIS FUTURE.

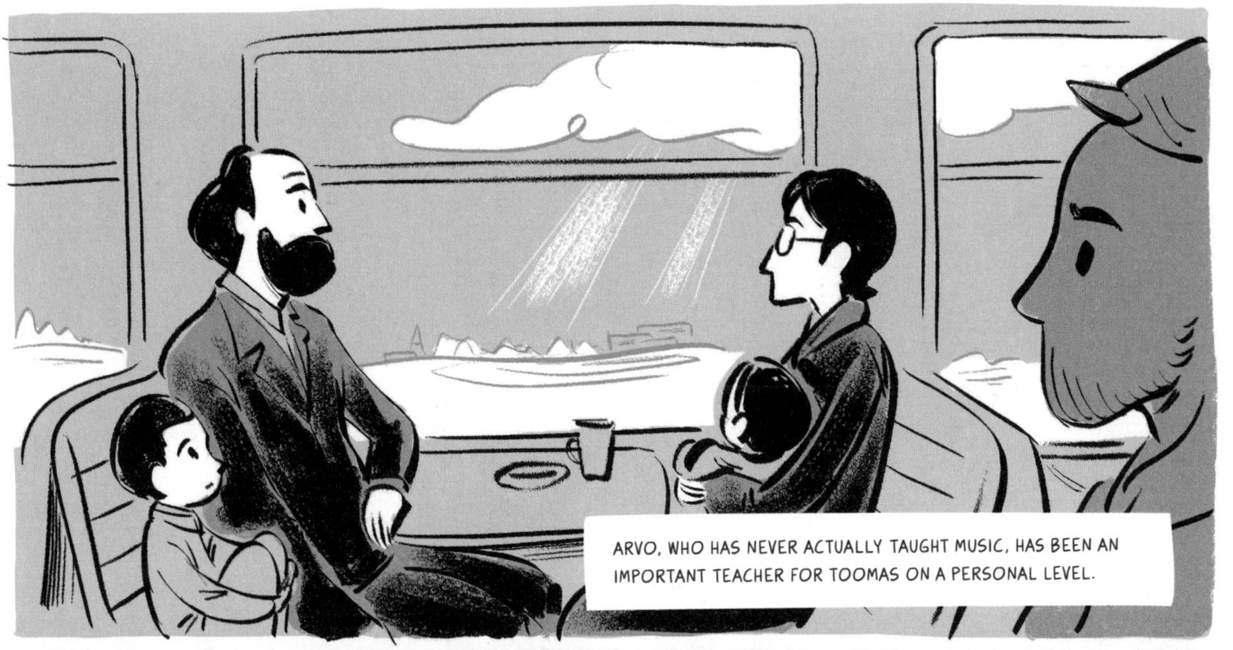
ARVO, WHO HAS NEVER ACTUALLY TAUGHT MUSIC, HAS BEEN AN IMPORTANT TEACHER FOR TOOMAS ON A PERSONAL LEVEL.

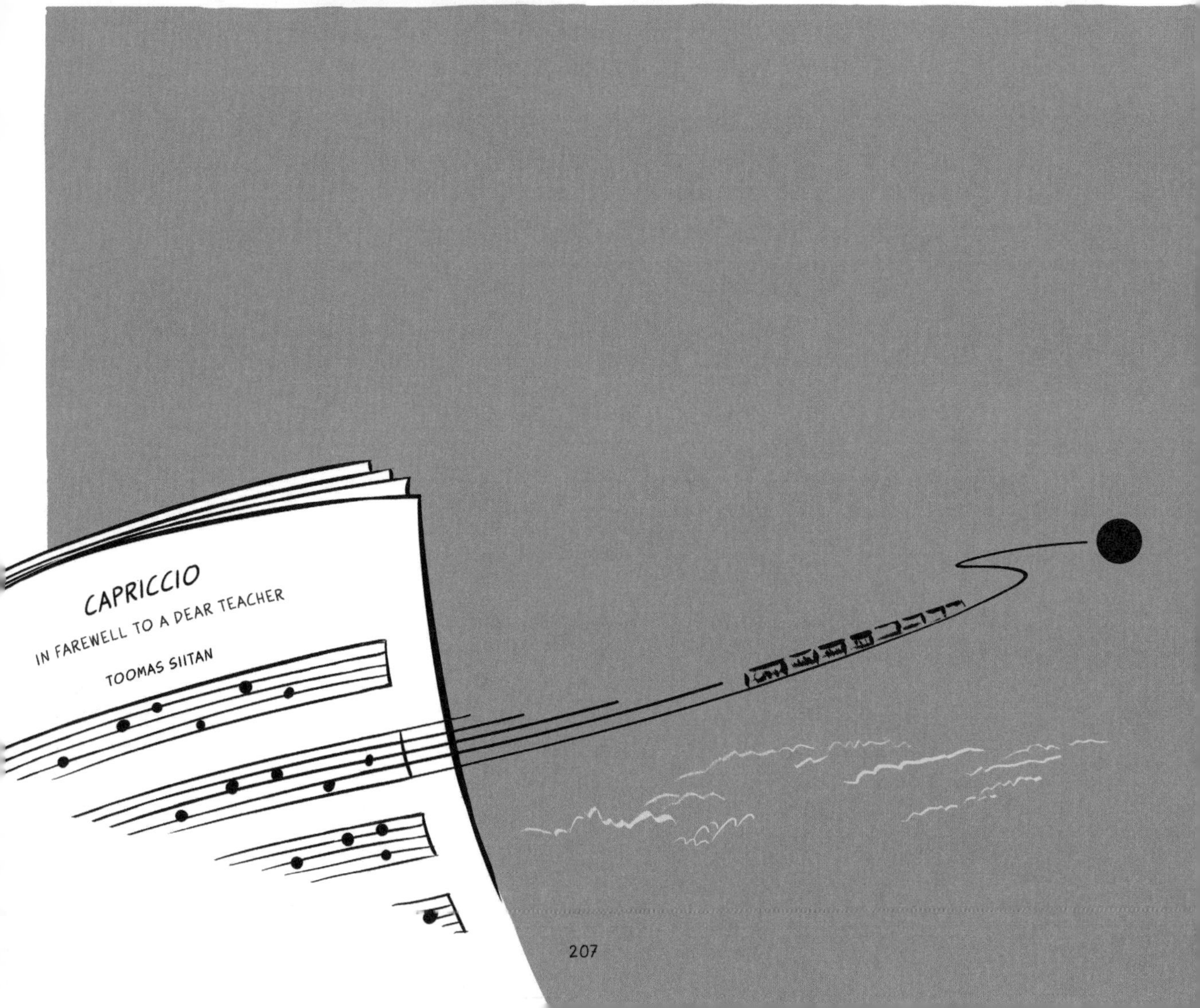
CAPRICCIO
IN FAREWELL TO A DEAR TEACHER
TOOMAS SIITAN

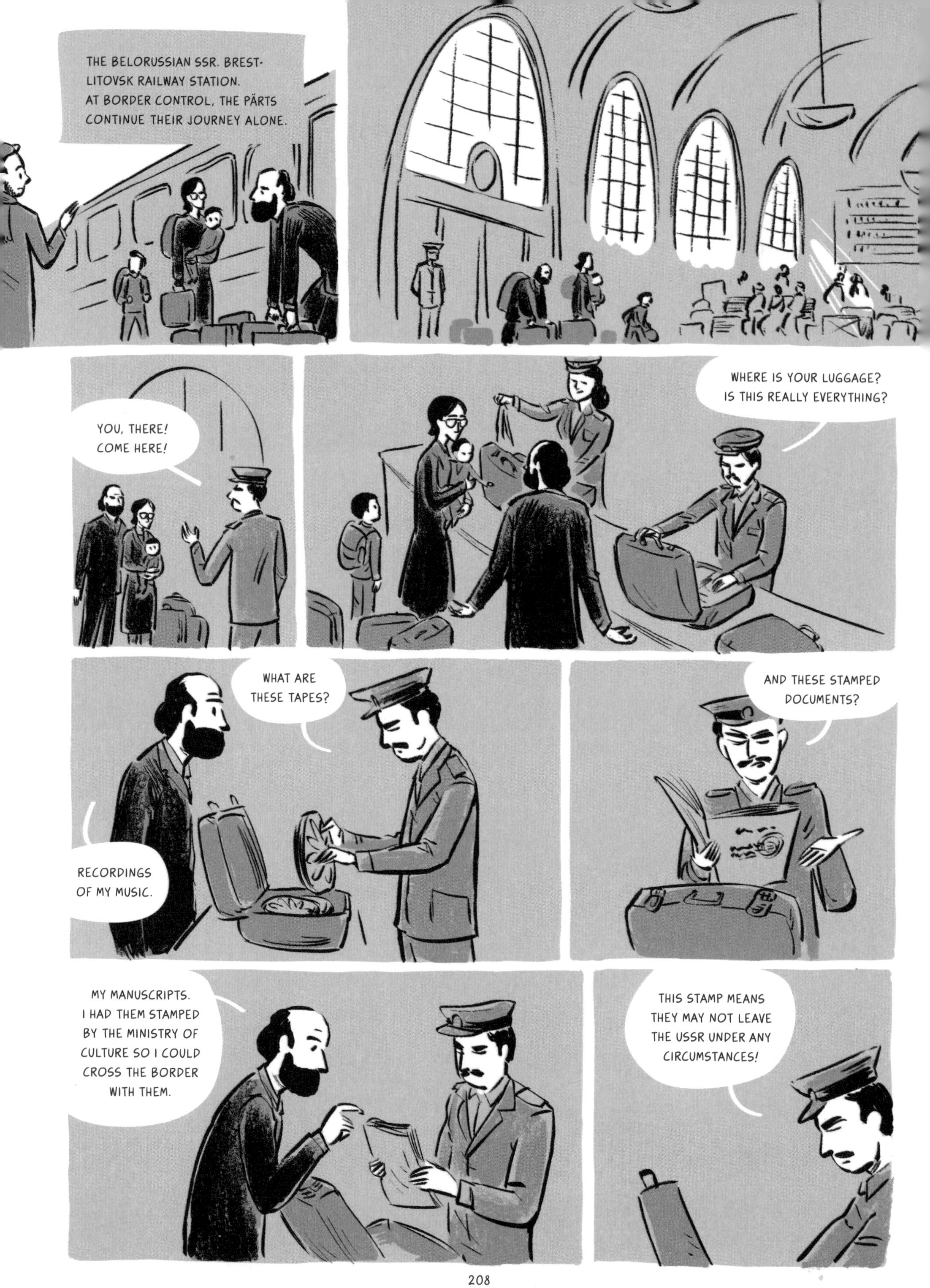
THE BELORUSSIAN SSR. BREST-LITOVSK RAILWAY STATION. AT BORDER CONTROL, THE PÄRTS CONTINUE THEIR JOURNEY ALONE.
YOU, THERE! COME HERE!
WHERE IS YOUR LUGGAGE? IS THIS REALLY EVERYTHING?
WHAT ARE THESE TAPES?
RECORDINGS OF MY MUSIC.
AND THESE STAMPED DOCUMENTS?
MY MANUSCRIPTS. I HAD THEM STAMPED BY THE MINISTRY OF CULTURE SO I COULD CROSS THE BORDER WITH THEM.
THIS STAMP MEANS THEY MAY NOT LEAVE THE USSR UNDER ANY CIRCUMSTANCES!

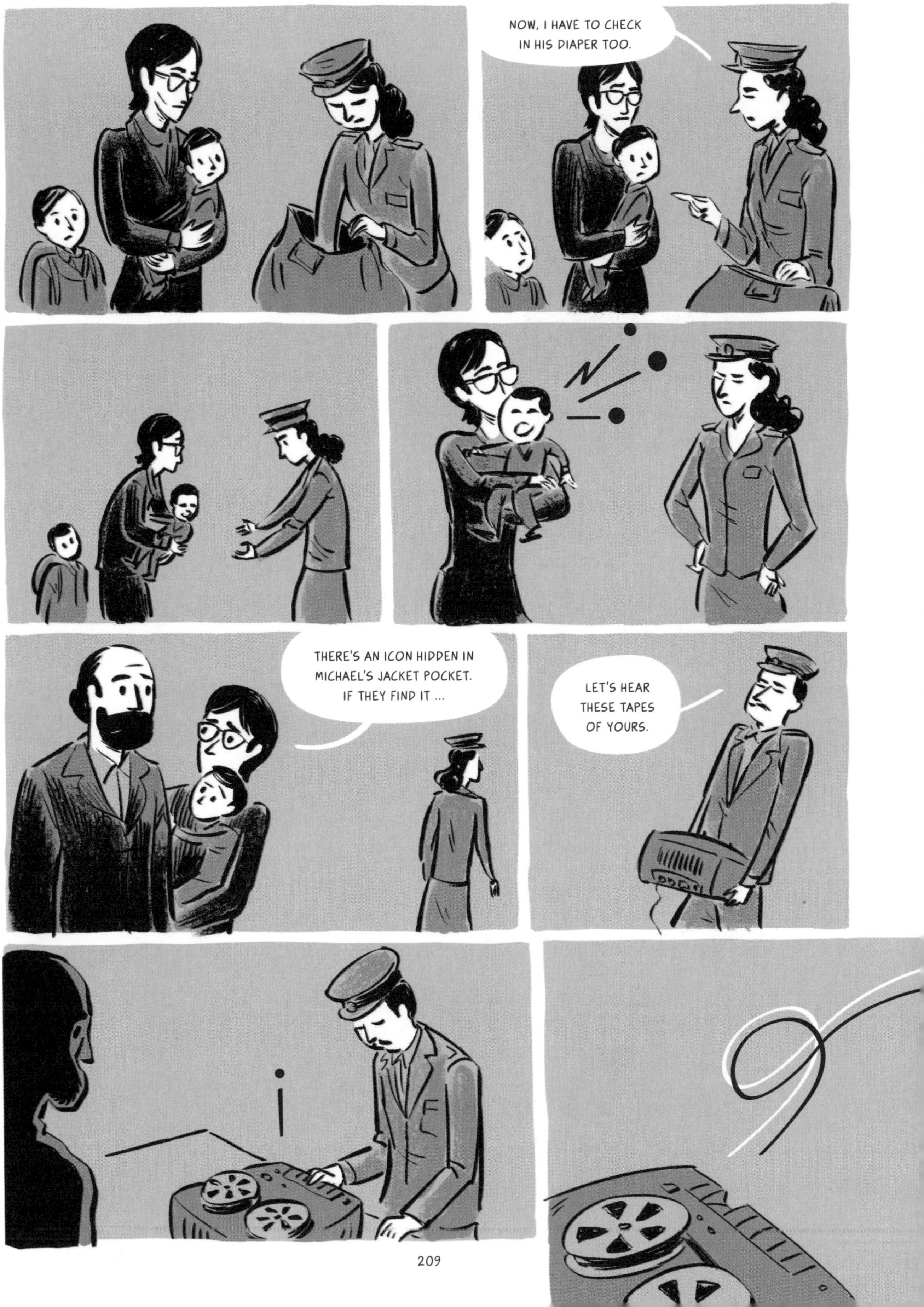
NOW, I HAVE TO CHECK IN HIS DIAPER TOO.
THERE'S AN ICON HIDDEN IN MICHAEL'S JACKET POCKET. IF THEY FIND IT ...
LET'S HEAR THESE TAPES OF YOURS.

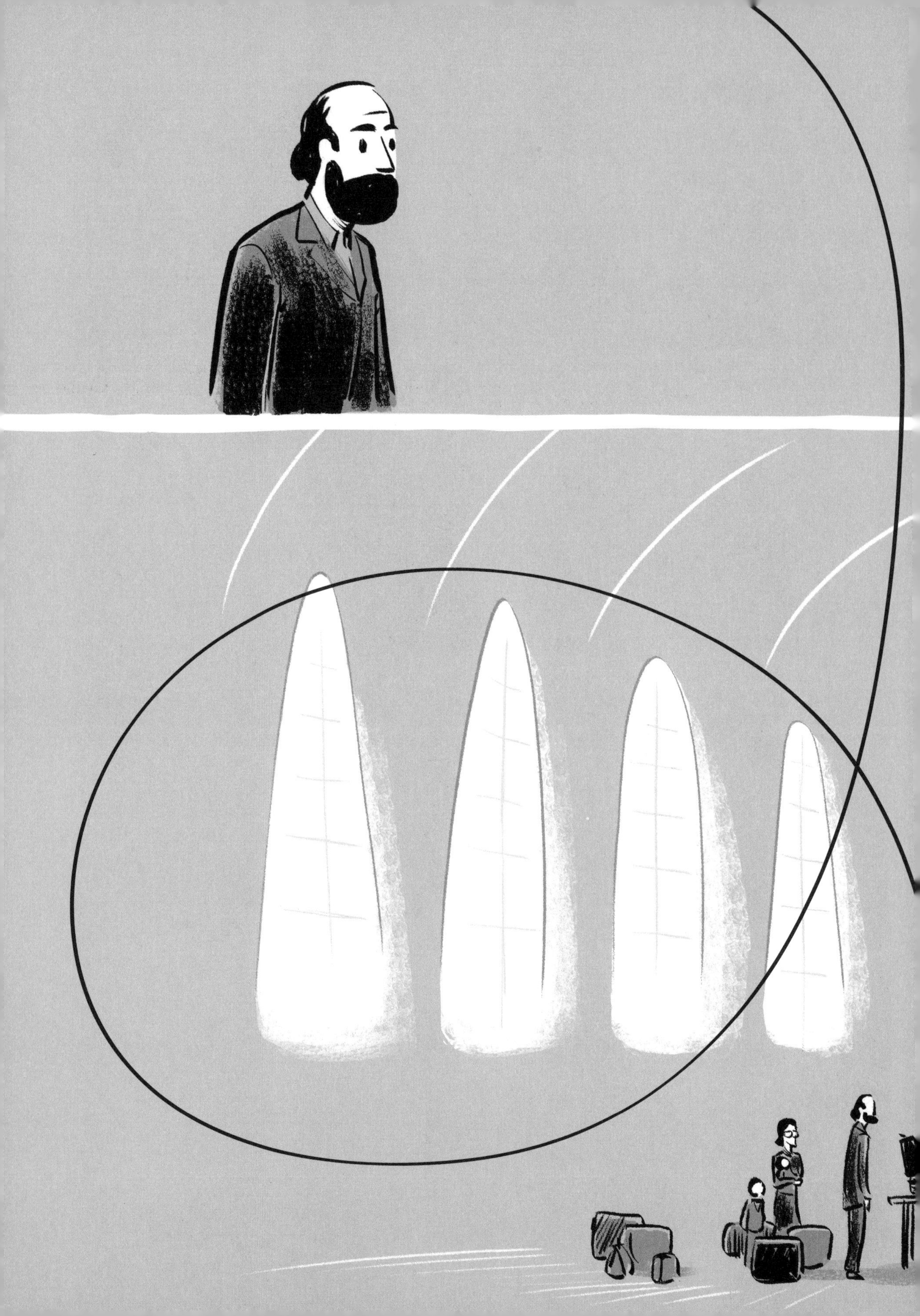

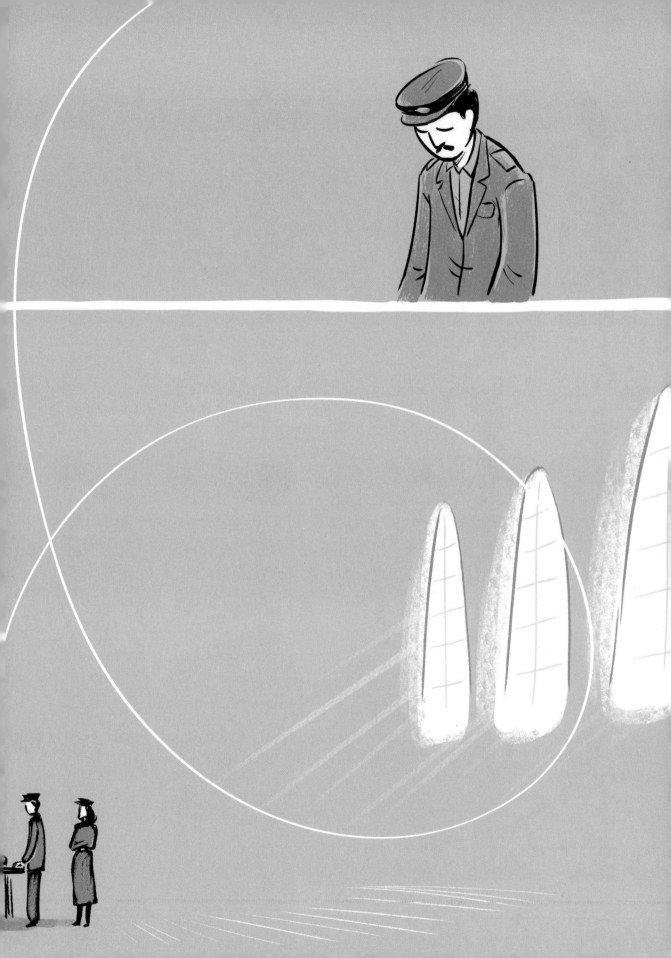

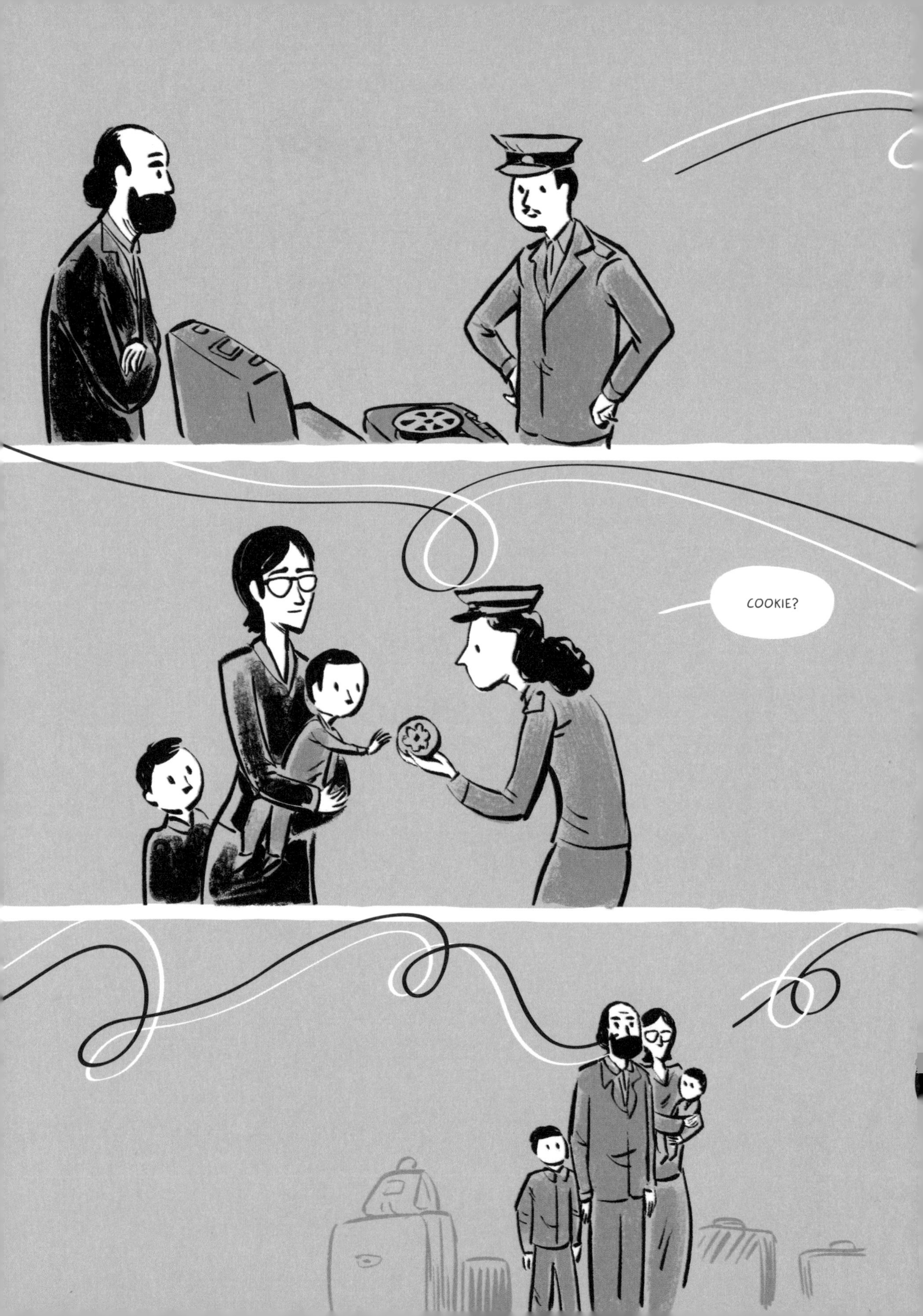
COOKIE?

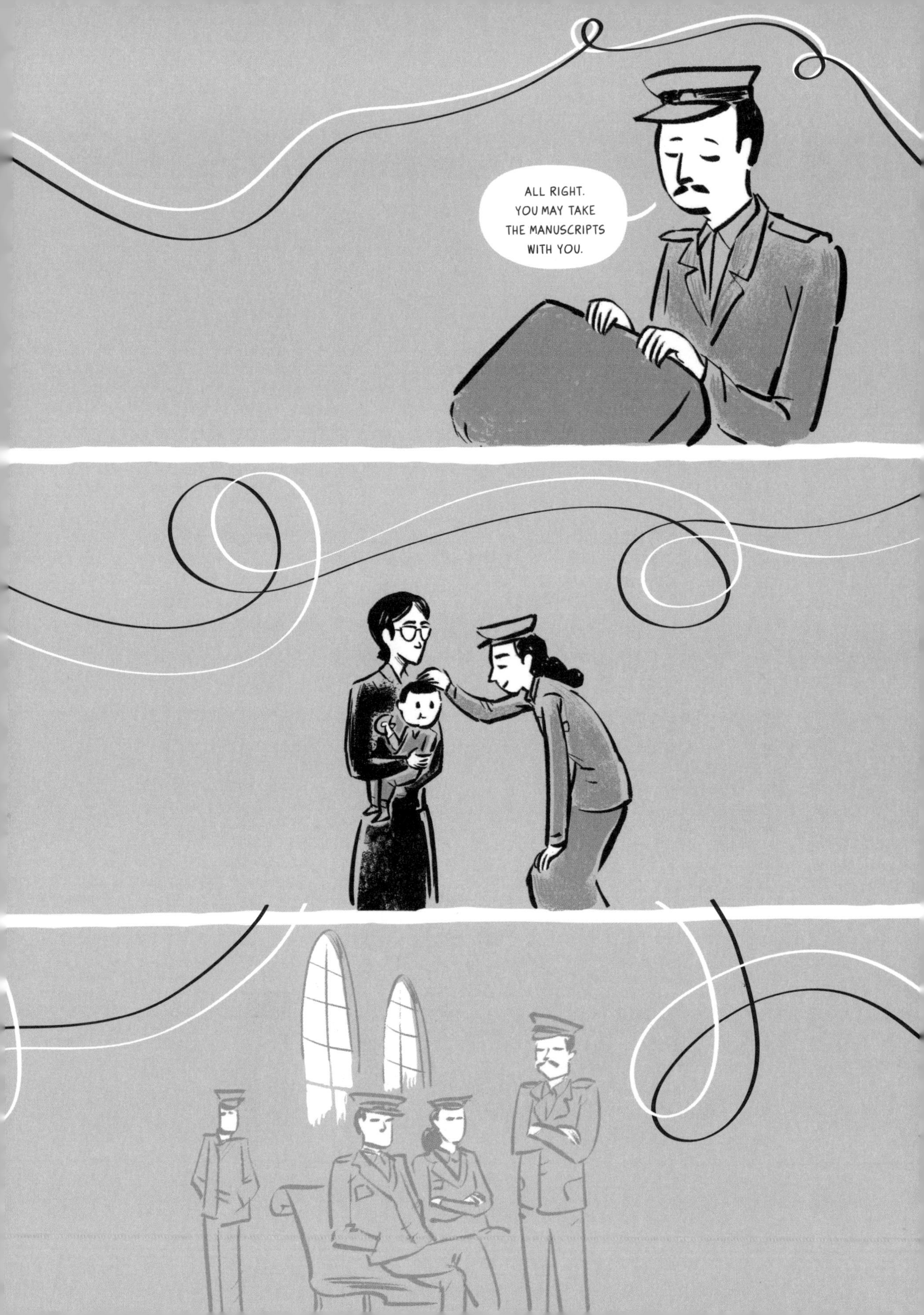
ALL RIGHT. YOU MAY TAKE THE MANUSCRIPTS WITH YOU.

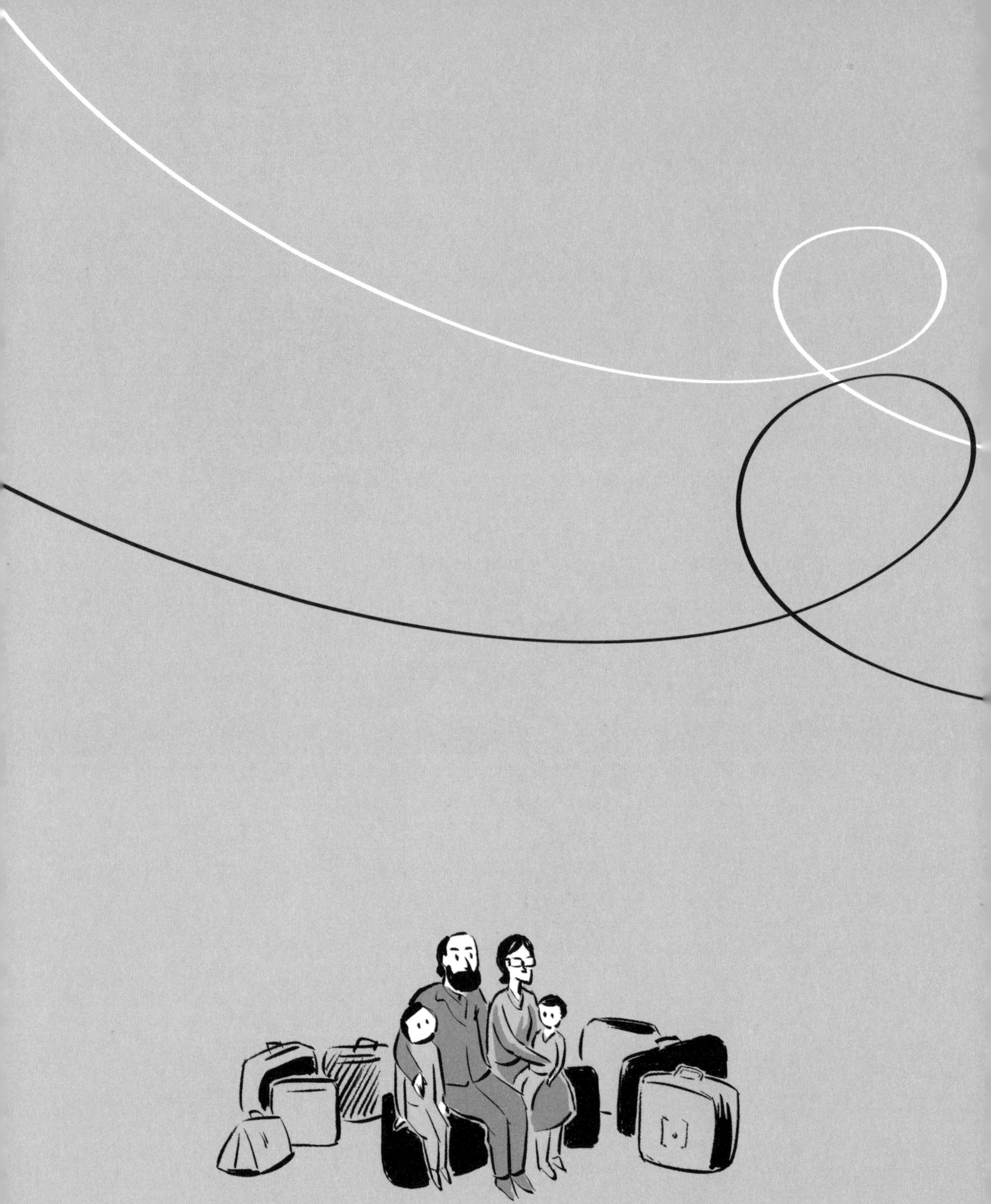

AT SEVEN O'CLOCK ON SUNDAY MORNING, WHEN THE PÄRTS ARE AT THE VIENNA TRAIN STATION WAITING TO BE SENT TO AN IMMIGRATION CAMP, A REPRESENTATIVE OF UNIVERSAL EDITION CALLS THEM OUT OF THE CROWD OF IMMIGRANTS AND OFFERS THEM AUSTRIAN CITIZENSHIP ALONG WITH A PUBLISHING CONTRACT. THE PÄRTS AGREE. TO THIS DAY, UNIVERSAL EDITION IS THE PUBLISHER OF ARVO PÄRT'S WORKS. TWO DAYS AFTER THEIR DEPARTURE, THE BORDERS OF THE SOVIET UNION ARE CLOSED FOR A LENGTHY TIME DUE TO THE SOVIET-AFGHAN WAR.

THE PÄRTS LIVE IN VIENNA FOR A YEAR AND A HALF, AFTER WHICH THE FAMILY MOVES TO BERLIN, WHERE THEY REMAIN FOR MANY YEARS. PÄRT'S ALBUM *TABULA RASA*, RECORDED BY ECM, IS RELEASED IN 1984 AND SETS THE FOUNDATIONS FOR A COOPERATIVE PARTNERSHIP THAT CONTINUES TO THIS DAY.

IN 1981, NORA AND ARVO PÄRT MEET ARCHIMANDRITE SOPHRONY, FOUNDER OF THE MONASTERY OF ST. JOHN THE BAPTIST IN ESSEX, ENGLAND, AND DEVELOP A FRIENDSHIP THAT LASTS UNTIL HIS DEATH IN 1993. THEIR RELATIONSHIP WITH FATHER SOPHRONY, WHICH WILL DEEPLY IMPACT THEIR LATER LIFE, ALSO OPENS UP FOR THEM THE WORLD OF HIS OWN TEACHER'S WRITINGS: THOSE OF SAINT SILOUAN, WHICH LATER BECAME OF NOTEWORTHY IMPORTANCE IN ARVO PÄRT'S WORKS.

THE INDEPENDENT REPUBLIC OF ESTONIA IS FORMALLY RESTORED IN 1991. ON JANUARY 19, 2010 — COINCIDENTALLY THIRTY YEARS AFTER THEIR EXILE, TO THE DAY — THE PÄRTS MOVE BACK TO THE COUNTRY.

IN 2018, AS PART OF EVENTS MARKING THE CENTENARY OF ESTONIAN INDEPENDENCE, THE ARVO PÄRT CENTRE OPENS ITS DOORS TO VISITORS IN LAULASMAA, ESTONIA.

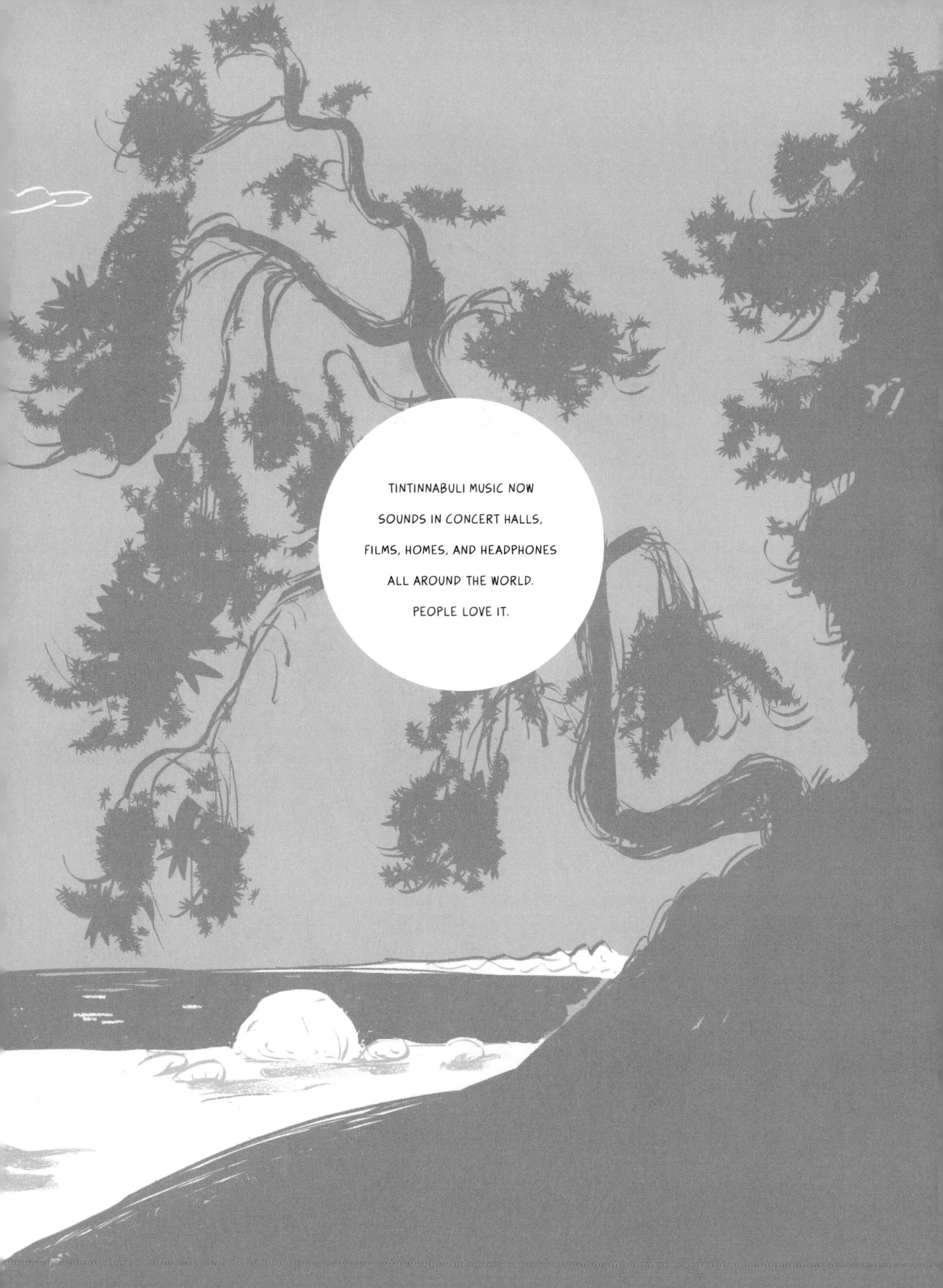
TINTINNABULI MUSIC NOW SOUNDS IN CONCERT HALLS, FILMS, HOMES, AND HEADPHONES ALL AROUND THE WORLD. PEOPLE LOVE IT.

THE CAST

ARVO PÄRT

LINDA PÄRT

MAXIMILIAN KUHLBERG

ILLE MARTIN

IVALO RANDALU

HEIMAR ILVES

HEINO ELLER

LYDIA AUSTER

JAAN RÄÄTS

HILLE PÄRT (AASMÄE)

ERI KLAS

EUGEN KAPP

VALTER OJAKÄÄR

HEINO PARS

HELJU TAUK

KULDAR SINK

TOOMAS VELMET

AVO HIRVESOO

NEEME JÄRVI

OLAF UTT

ELBERT TUGANOV

ELEONORA PÄRT

VALERI POVEDSKI

ANDRES MUSTONEN

HELLE MUSTONEN

ALFRED SCHNITTKE

ALINA

TATJANA GRINDENKO

GIDON KREMER

TOOMAS SIITAN

THE SETTING

1918 – 1940 – REPUBLIC OF ESTONIA
1940 – 1941 – FIRST SOVIET OCCUPATION
1941 – 1944 – GERMAN OCCUPATION
1944 – 1991 – SECOND SOVIET OCCUPATION
1991 – REPUBLIC OF ESTONIA

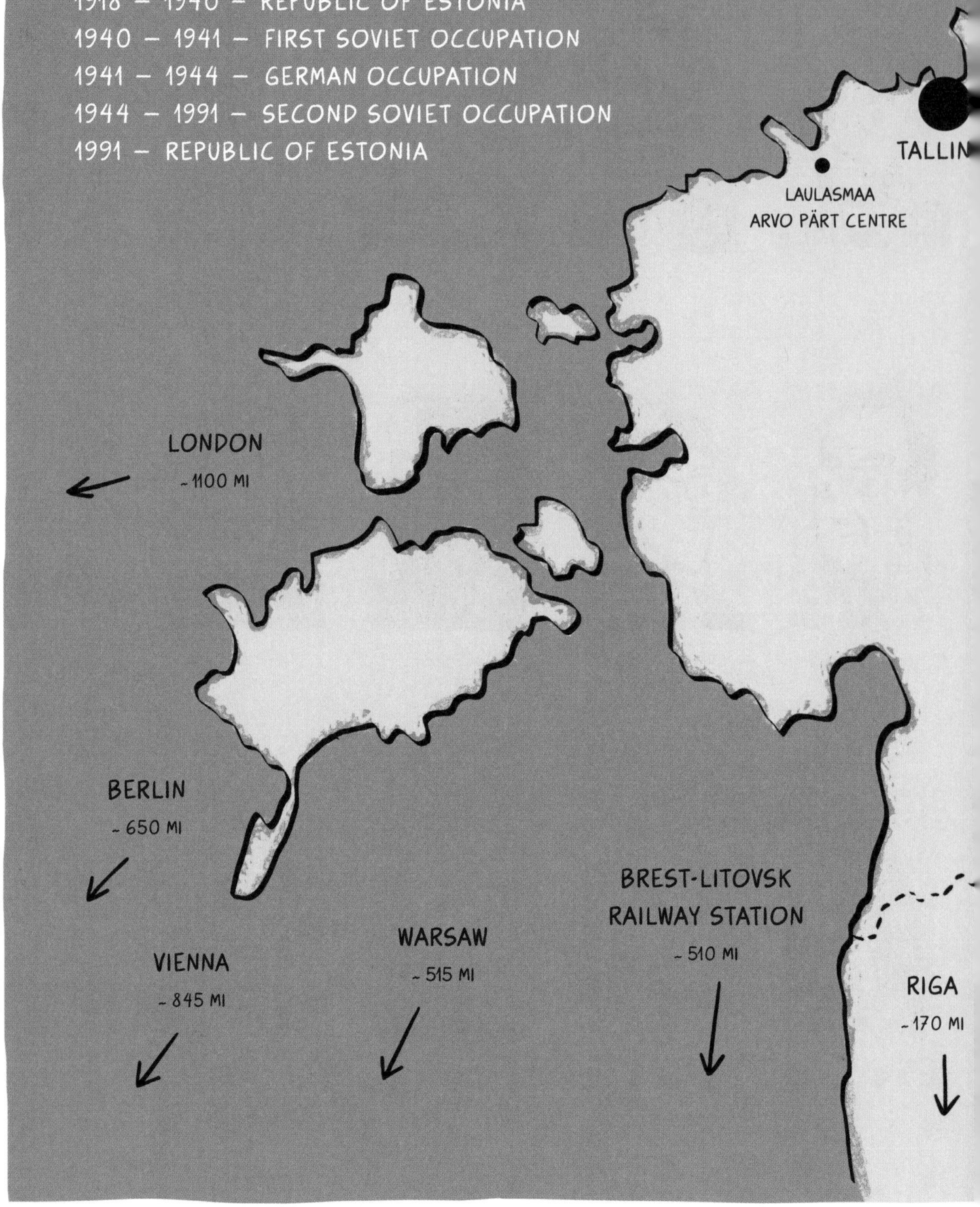
TALLIN
LAULASMAA
ARVO PÄRT CENTRE
LONDON
~1100 MI
BERLIN
~650 MI
VIENNA
~845 MI
WARSAW
~515 MI
BREST-LITOVSK
RAILWAY STATION
~510 MI
RIGA
~170 MI

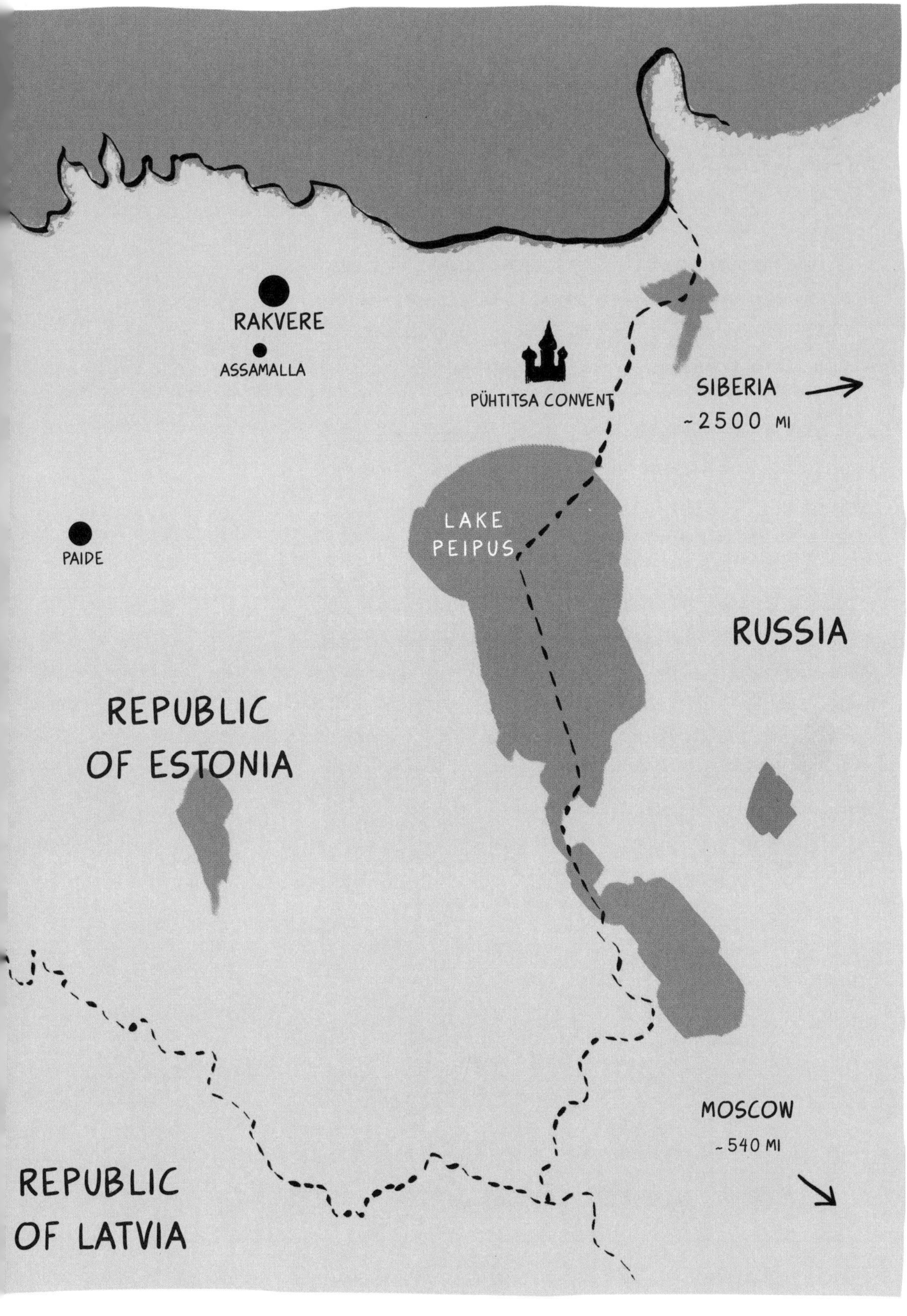
RAKVERE
ASSAMALLA
PÜHTITSA CONVENT
SIBERIA
~2500 MI
LAKE
PEIPUS
PAIDE
RUSSIA
REPUBLIC
OF ESTONIA
MOSCOW
~540 MI
REPUBLIC
OF LATVIA

AFTERWORD

WHILE GATHERING MATERIALS FOR THIS STORY, READING AND LISTENING TO PEOPLE'S RECOLLECTIONS, AND PIECING TOGETHER INFORMATION SHARD BY SHARD, I REALIZED THAT HISTORY IS ALWAYS SUBJECTIVE. EACH PERSON HAS HIS OR HER OWN PATH; A PERSONAL TIMELINE. THE TIME GIVEN TO THEM IS A VERY PERSONAL GIFT.

AT THE SAME TIME, OBJECTIVITY LOOKS UPON US WITHOUT DISAPPROVAL, WITH LOVE. IF WE PAY IT HEED, THERE IS HOPE THAT OUR ABILITY AND WILL TO OBSERVE OTHERS MORE OBJECTIVELY WILL INCREASE BY SEEKING IT ON OUR OWN PATH. IN DOING SO, STEP BY STEP, WE GROW EVER CLOSER TO LOVE.

THIS STORY IS AN INTERPRETATION OF SEVERAL PEOPLE'S RESPECTIVE JOURNEYS. IT IS A SUBJECTIVE GLANCE, ONE REPRESENTATION OF MANY POSSIBLE REPRESENTATIONS; IDIOSYNCRATIC, BUT FAR FROM THE SOLE POSSIBLE ONE. I HOPE IT OPENS MANY A DOOR TO FURTHER QUESTS.

JOONAS SILDRE
TALLINN, 2018

THANKS

TO NORA AND ARVO PÄRT, WHO SUPPORTED ME GREATLY, SACRIFICING THEIR VALUABLE TIME AND ENERGY.

TO IMMO MIHKELSON, WHOSE RADIO DOCUMENTARY SERIES ON ARVO PÄRT INSPIRED ME TO MAKE THIS WORK.

TO ELINA SILDRE AND OUR CHILDREN, WHO WERE PATIENT AND OFFERED ME LOVE AND SUPPORT.

TO THE ARVO PÄRT CENTRE AND ALL OTHERS WHO HELPED IN THIS BOOK'S COMPLETION.